THE POETRY-FILM NEXUS IN LATIN AMERICA
EXPLORING INTERMEDIALITY ON PAGE AND SCREEN

LEGENDA

LEGENDA is the Modern Humanities Research Association's book imprint for new research in the Humanities. Founded in 1995 by Malcolm Bowie and others within the University of Oxford, Legenda has always been a collaborative publishing enterprise, directly governed by scholars. The Modern Humanities Research Association (MHRA) joined this collaboration in 1998, became half-owner in 2004, in partnership with Maney Publishing and then Routledge, and has since 2016 been sole owner. Titles range from medieval texts to contemporary cinema and form a widely comparative view of the modern humanities, including works on Arabic, Catalan, English, French, German, Greek, Italian, Portuguese, Russian, Spanish, and Yiddish literature. Editorial boards and committees of more than 60 leading academic specialists work in collaboration with bodies such as the Society for French Studies, the British Comparative Literature Association and the Association of Hispanists of Great Britain & Ireland.

The MHRA encourages and promotes advanced study and research in the field of the modern humanities, especially modern European languages and literature, including English, and also cinema. It aims to break down the barriers between scholars working in different disciplines and to maintain the unity of humanistic scholarship. The Association fulfils this purpose through the publication of journals, bibliographies, monographs, critical editions, and the MHRA Style Guide, and by making grants in support of research. Membership is open to all who work in the Humanities, whether independent or in a University post, and the participation of younger colleagues entering the field is especially welcomed.

ALSO PUBLISHED BY THE ASSOCIATION

Critical Texts
Tudor and Stuart Translations • *New Translations* • *European Translations*
MHRA Library of Medieval Welsh Literature

MHRA Bibliographies
Publications of the Modern Humanities Research Association

The Annual Bibliography of English Language & Literature
Austrian Studies
Modern Language Review
Portuguese Studies
The Slavonic and East European Review
Working Papers in the Humanities
The Yearbook of English Studies

www.mhra.org.uk
www.legendabooks.com

MOVING IMAGE

Legenda/Moving Image publishes cutting-edge work on any aspect of film or screen media from Europe and Latin America. Studies of European-language cinemas from other continents, and diasporic and intercultural cinemas (with some relation to Europe or its languages), are also encompassed. The series seeks to reflect a diversity of theoretical, historical, and interdisciplinary approaches to the moving image, and includes projects comparing screen media with other art forms. Research monographs and collected volumes will be considered, but not studies of a single film. As innovation is a priority for the series, volumes should predominantly consist of previously unpublished material.

Proposals should be sent with one or two sample chapters to the Editor, Professor Emma Wilson, Corpus Christi College, Cambridge CB2 1RH, UK.

Managing Editor
Dr Graham Nelson, 41 Wellington Square, Oxford OX1 2JF, UK

www.legendabooks.com

The Poetry-Film Nexus in Latin America

Exploring Intermediality on Page and Screen

❖

EDITED BY
BEN BOLLIG AND DAVID M. J. WOOD

l

LEGENDA

Moving Image 11
Modern Humanities Research Association
2022

Published by Legenda
an imprint of the Modern Humanities Research Association
Salisbury House, Station Road, Cambridge CB1 2LA

ISBN 978-1-78188-915-2 (HB)
ISBN 978-1-78188-916-9 (PB)

First published 2022

Copy-Editor: Richard Correll

CONTENTS

❖

ACKNOWLEDGEMENTS

❖

The editors would like to thank a number of people and organizations who were instrumental in various ways to the completion of this book.

We would like to thank the Moving Image series editor, Emma Wilson, for her enthusiasm and support for this project, and the Managing Editor at Legenda, Graham Nelson, for his hard work and commitment in seeing the book through to completion.

We are grateful to Raúl Perrone for allowing us to use the image from his film *CINICOS* on the cover.

We are very grateful to Sonia García López for her insightful critical comments on the Introduction; to Gabriela Torres Vigil for her excellent copy-editing work on the entire manuscript; and to Annabel Rowntree for compiling the index.

We are also grateful to our external peer reviewers, who must remain anonymous — they know who they are, and we offer our thanks.

We'd like to thank our colleagues at *Journal of Latin American Cultural Studies* for their intellectual companionship over the years.

Ben Bollig would like to thank his colleges at Oxford, St Catherine's and St John's, and the Faculty of Medieval and Modern Languages, for granting him leave in 2020, and Carlos Fonseca Grigsby, who took care of his teaching and admin duties with dedication and intelligence.

David Wood would like to thank the UNAM's Programa de Superación del Personal Académico and Conacyt's Apoyos para Estancias Sabáticas programme for granting him sabbatical funding in 2017–18, as well as his hosts at the Centre of Latin American Studies and Fitzwilliam College, Cambridge in 2017–19, when we conceived and carried out the initial phase of this book.

*   *   *   *   *

Just as we were correcting the proofs of this volume, news reached us that one of the contributors, Erica Segre, had tragically passed away. A brilliant teacher, scholar and analyst of Latin American visual culture, and a hugely enthusiastic contributor to this book even during her prolonged illness, Erica was a passionate advocate for our field. She will be sorely missed.

Oxford/Mexico City, 2021

NOTES ON THE CONTRIBUTORS

❖

Carlos Adriano is a film artist and independent scholar, with a PhD in Film (USP — University of São Paulo; Fapesp's Fellowship [São Paulo Research Foundation]; 2008) and two Post-Doctorals, in Arts (PUC-SP — Pontifical Catholic University São Paulo; Fapesp's Fellowship; 2014) and in Film (USP; Capes's Fellowship [Coordination for the Improvement of Higher Education Personnel]; 2017). His work is the subject of a chapter in the book *The Sublimity of Document: Cinema as Diorama (Avant-doc 2)* by Scott MacDonald (Oxford University Press, 2019). His retrospectives include: Festival do Rio (2002); 56th Festival of Locarno (2003); Instituto Tomie Ohtake (films installed in projections, displays, loops; 2019). His films have been exhibited in the Museum of Modern Art (MoMA, New York) and in the Tate Modern (London), and shown at festivals in Bilbao, Bologna, Denver, Havana, Locarno, Madrid, Osnabrück, Paris, Philadelphia, Pordenone, Rotterdam, and Toronto. His *sem título # 5: A Rotina terá seu Enquanto* (2019) was awarded Best Short (24th It's All True; São Paulo); his *sem título # 1 : Dance of Leitfossil* (2014) was awarded Best Film (Golden Reel International Underground Film Festival; Ulaanbaatar); his *A Voz e o Vazio: a Vez de Vassourinha* (1998) was awarded Best Documentary Short (36th Chicago Film Festival). He was born in São Paulo, Brazil, in 1966.

Ben Bollig is Professor of Spanish American Literature at the University of Oxford and Director of Studies for Modern Languages at St Catherine's College, Oxford. He holds a PhD from King's College, London and he has previously taught there and at Westminster University and the University of Leeds. His books include *Politics and Public Space in Contemporary Argentine Poetry: The Lyric and the State* (2016); *Modern Argentine Poetry. Displacement, Exile, Migration* (2011); and *Néstor Perlongher. The Poetic Search for an Argentine Marginal Voice* (2008). His translations include *The Foreign Passion/La pasión extranjera* by Cristian Aliaga (2016) and, with Alejandra Crosta, a bilingual anthology of British and Irish poetry in Spanish translation, *Antropófagos en las islas* (2016). He has recently completed a further book of translations of travel prose-poems by Cristian Aliaga and a monograph on the film-poetry nexus in Argentina. He is an editor of *Journal of Latin American Cultural Studies*; Hispanic Editor of the MHRA Critical Texts series; and a member of the *Comité científico* of the Argentine journal *El taco en la brea*.

Adam Feinstein is a British author, poet, translator, Hispanist, journalist, film critic and autism researcher. His biography, *Pablo Neruda: A Passion for Life,* was first published by Bloomsbury in 2004 and reissued in an updated edition in 2013 (Harold Pinter called it 'a masterpiece'). His book of translations from Neruda's

Canto General, with colour illustrations by the celebrated Brazilian artist, Ana Maria Pacheco, was published by Pratt Contemporary in 2013. He also wrote the introduction to the Folio Edition of Jorge Luis Borges' *Labyrinths*, which appeared in 2007. Arc published his new book of translations, *The Unknown Neruda,* in 2019 and a new collection of his rhyming translations of the great Nicaraguan poet, Rubén Darío, came out in two separate editions in 2020 (published first by the Instituto Nicaragüense de Cultura in Managua and then by Shearsman in London). His book, *A History of Autism: Conversations with the Pioneers* (Wiley-Blackwell, 2010), received widespread acclaim, as did his *Autism Works: A Guide to Employment Across the Entire Spectrum* (Routledge, 2018). Feinstein has given numerous lectures on Neruda and autism around the world. His presentations in the UK include talks at Cambridge and Oxford Universities and at the Royal Society in London. He broadcasts regularly for the BBC and writes for the *Guardian,* the *Observer,* the *Financial Times* and the *Times Literary Supplement.* His own poems and his translations (of Neruda, Federico García Lorca, Mario Benedetti and others) have appeared in numerous magazines, including *Agenda, Acumen, PN Review, Poem* and *Modern Poetry in Translation.* He is currently working on two novels and a book on Argentinian cinema. He has been a Royal Literary Fund Fellow.

Irina Garbatzky holds a PhD in Humanities and Arts (Universidad Nacional de Rosario). She is Associate Researcher at IECH-CONICET (Institute of Critical Studies in Humanities — National Scientific and Technical Research Council), Argentina and Head of Practical Assignments in the Subject of Ibero-American Literature I (UNR). Her books include: *Los ochenta recienvivos. Poesía y performance en el Río de la Plata* (author, Beatriz Viterbo, 2013), and *Expansiones. Literatura en el campo expandido del arte* (editor, Yo soy Gilda, 2013). She is a member of the research teams at the Centro de Estudios en Literatura Argentina, Centro de Estudios en Teoría y Crítica Literaria (both in UNR) and Caribbean Studies Group (UBA). In 2018, she obtained a DAAD Research Stays scholarship for University Academics and Scientists to stay as a visiting researcher at the Ibero-Amerikanisches Institut (Berlin). She has published articles on the archive of the avant-garde, conceptualisms and performance in Latin America, new readings of the Cuban Special Period, and trajectories of the Neo-Baroque. With Ana Porrúa she is co-editor of the journal *El jardín de los poetas. Revista de teoría y crítica de poesía latinoamericana.*

Camila Gatica Mizala is a postdoctoral research fellow at the Instituto de Historia, Pontificia Universidad Católica de Chile. She teaches modules on Contemporary History of the Americas, as well as Cinema and Latin American History at the same institution. She is also an Associate Fellow at the Institute of Latin American Studies, University of London. Her research interests include the cultural history of twentieth-century Latin America, cinema reception, and cultural diplomacy.

Eduardo Paredes Ocampo is a DPhil student in Medieval and Modern Languages (Spanish) at the University of Oxford. His academic work is focused on performance studies — mainly on theatre and film. He is currently finishing a thesis on the contemporary adaptations of Calderón de la Barca's *La vida es sueño* in Spain. He also writes poetry, is an editor, and has directed theatre.

Erica Segre was Senior Lecturer in Hispanic and Latin American Studies (and a translator of fiction and non-fiction). Her research and teaching interests related to nineteenth-century Latin-American literature and thought, and twentieth-century and contemporary visual culture (art, photography, illustration and film). She taught in the Spanish and Portuguese Department and the Centre of Latin American Studies, University of Cambridge and was a Senior Fellow and Director of Studies at Trinity College. Her works include *Intersected Identities: Strategies of Visualization in Nineteenth- and Twentieth-Century Mexican Culture* (2007); contributing editor to *Ghosts of the Revolution in Mexican Literature and Visual Culture: Revisitations in Modern and Contemporary Creative Media* (2013) and to *México Noir: Rethinking the Dark in Contemporary Writing and Visual Culture (art, film, photography)* (2019).

Nicolás Suárez holds a PhD in Literature from the Universidad de Buenos Aires. He teaches Literary Theory at the Universidad Nacional de las Artes and has taught Argentine Literature at the Universidad de Buenos Aires. He has received research grants from the CONICET and the DAAD. In 2017, his book *The Work and Life of Sarmiento in Cinema* was awarded in the National and Federal Contest of Studies on Argentine Cinema, held by the Argentine National Institute of Cinema and Audiovisual Arts. He received the Best Essay Award by a Graduate Student in 2017–2018, from the Film Section of the Latin American Studies Association. In 2019, he was awarded the First Prize in the Domingo Di Núbila Essay Contest, held by the Argentine Association of Audiovisual and Film Studies. He also studied Filmmaking at ENERC, and at Elías Querejeta Zine Eskola in San Sebastián. He directed the short film *Centauro* (2017) and co-directed the feature film *Hijos Nuestros* (2015), which were screened at festivals in Berlin, Biarritz, Mar del Plata, Málaga, and Guadalajara.

Jessica Wax-Edwards is an independent scholar and currently an Honorary Research Fellow at Royal Holloway University of London, where she received her PhD in 2018. Her research interests include memory, violence and politics in twentieth century and contemporary Mexican visual culture. She has published articles on Latin American fiction and documentary cinema, graphic art and photography and is currently working on her monograph *Violence, Victims and the Ethics of Representation: the Visual Legacy of Felipe Calderón (2006–2012)*.

David M. J. Wood is Researcher at the Institute of Aesthetic Research, National Autonomous University of Mexico. He is the author of *El espectador pensante: el cine de Jorge Sanjinés y el Grupo Ukamau* (UNAM/La Carreta, 2017) and coeditor of *Latin American Cultural Studies: A Reader* (Routledge, 2017) and *Cine mudo latinoamericano: inicios, nación, vanguardias y transición* (UNAM, 2015), as well as special journal issues on film and poetry in Latin America and on documentary and institutional cinema in Mexico. He is currently writing a book on film archiving and archive-films in Mexico. He is an editor of the *Journal of Latin American Cultural Studies*, and a member of the advisory boards of *Studies in Spanish & Latin American Cinemas* and *Anales del Instituto de Investigaciones Estéticas*.

Chrystian Zegarra holds a PhD in Hispanic Literature from the University of

California, Los Angeles. He works as Associate Professor of Spanish at Colgate University in Hamilton, New York, where he teaches courses on Latin American literature and film. He has published the monograph *El celuloide mecanografiado*, which analyzes the relationship between Peruvian author Emilio Adolfo Westphalen's avant-garde poetry and the experimental cinema of the 1920s and 1930s. His articles dealing with formal and thematic connections between Latin American literature and film have appeared in journals such as *Bulletin of Hispanic Studies*, *Hispamérica*, *Inti*, *Hispanic Poetry Review*, *Revista de Crítica Literaria Latinoamericana*, *Mester*, and *Hispanic Journal*. He currently serves as contributing editor to the *Handbook of Latin American Studies* (Library of Congress and University of Texas Press).

INTRODUCTION

❖

The Poetry–Film Nexus in Latin America

Ben Bollig and David M. J. Wood

In a special journal issue published in 2014, we set out to explore 'the diverse modes of formal, aesthetic and ideological exchange between the poetic and the cinematic' registers in Latin American cultural production from the early twentieth century onwards (Bollig and Wood, eds, 2014: 115). As we laid out in our introduction, we wished to stimulate research on the 'cross-fertilization and increasing convergence between [these] two artistic media' (123). To do so, we took as our starting point the concept of adaptation, which has been a choice topic for film theorists since the very emergence of the discipline, from André Bazin's early reflections on 'mixed', or 'impure' (to follow the French original) cinema to recent volumes by Speranza (2002), Stam (2005), MacCabe et al. (2011), and others. Whereas adaptation studies have tended to focus on narrative literature (prose fiction, theatre) as source material for the screen, our aim was to 'examine the aesthetic and political effects of film's adaptation of poetry, and the mutual and productive relationship between the two forms' (Bollig and Wood, eds, 2014: 116).[1] As a scholar primarily specializing in poetry (Bollig) and another working predominantly on film (Wood), we wanted to explore the many ways in which our two areas of expertise overlapped and interacted both in theoretical terms and in concrete examples of cultural production from across Latin America.

The current volume aims to develop and continue this line of research with a broader theoretical and methodological focus that goes beyond the purview of adaptation by presenting a series of thematically linked chapters that explore the broader aspects of the poetry–film nexus in Latin America, considering diverse modes of intermedial exchange between both forms. As well as the adaptation of poems to film, these include the characterization of poets on screen; the role of poets as filmmakers and/or screenwriters and vice versa; the concept of the 'poetic film'; approaches to the 'cinema of poetry' (drawing on writings by Pier Paolo Pasolini, in particular); poetic documentaries; poetry's responses to film form and aesthetics; and the appropriation of poetry in avant-garde film. Contributions range in focus from early silent cinema to contemporary works, and from Mexico and Cuba through Brazil to the Southern Cone. Approaches include close readings of films, culturally informed analyses, and more theoretical considerations of film poetics.

The links between film and poetry can be intense and productive. In a fictional interview with the invented poet Jillian Kwon in the Argentine poet and translator Ezequiel Zaidenwerg's recent collection of heteronymous poetry, we read, as part of a response to the question of how the (invented) poet started to read poetry: 'Y, por supuesto, no podemos olvidarnos de la cita de "Funeral Blues" de la película *Cuatro bodas y un funeral*. Un clásico de la comedia romántica' [And, of course, we can't forget the use of 'Funeral Blues' in the film *Four Weddings and a Funeral*. A classic of romantic comedy] (Zaidenwerg 2018: 235). Auden's 'Funeral Blues' started life as a parody of bombastic odes to deceased dictators but morphed into a moving song of loss; in *Four Weddings* it is the means by which Matthew (John Hannah) reveals, in an emotive reading, delivered almost straight to camera, his relationship with and love for the recently deceased Gareth (Simon Callow). The poem is, to paraphrase Speranza, an 'asset' for the film; but the film transformed the status of the poem, and Auden's work more generally, as well as revealing to the general public a tacit homoeroticism not explicit in the piece. And it also, in Zaidenwerg's interpretation, can inspire viewers to become poets. It is such surprising — but intense, and influential — connections that this volume intends to explore.

Any attempt to define poetry would vastly exceed the scope and purpose of this Introduction, needing to summarize a debate that perhaps starts with Plato and Aristotle and would take in the aesthetics of Kant, Hegel, and in the twentieth century Heidegger, Badiou, and many others — without even beginning to stray from the path of the Western canon. For Kant poetry holds 'the first rank among all arts' (2008: 155); while for Heidegger it is a form of 'projective saying' that summoned up the truth of the nation, from Ancient Greece to Nazi Germany (2001: 71). Such has been the importance of poetry over the centuries.

Put more simple, poetry is 'an instance of verbal art', 'bound speech', and 'a heightened mode of discourse' (Preminger and Brogan 1993: 938). Poetry's exceptionality with regard to ordinary language is stressed by many theorists, from the Russian Formalists through to M. H. Abrams and his notion of 'poetic diction', of poetry as a 'different language' (1993: 163). The roots of the term are found in the Greek *poiesis* (ποίησις), or making, and this very general sense stays with us in the use of the term 'poetics', for many an alternative to 'aesthetics' when thinking about film.

For a number of commentators, particularly those with an inheritance from the Romantics or the surrealists, poetry exceeds actual poems as linguistic utterances. For Cocteau — as discussed below — poetry is not a medium, but rather the very essence of art, that cinema and other media could access. Tarkovsky (2017), similarly, while including his father's poems in his films, separates literature and cinema, seeing poetry as a substrate that can be accessed via carefully crafted filmmaking. For Octavio Paz (1967), poetry is a form of knowledge, a powerful means of revealing and potentially transforming the world. In a volume on contemporary Latin American poetry, William Rowe writes of poetry as 'a means of active discovery, and not simply a fulfilment, however well expressed, of what has been theorized already' (Rowe 2000: 5).

The majority of the contributors to this volume stick quite closely to the definition of poetry as verbal art; but the notion of poetics, as shorthand for the technical decisions made by directors and their aesthetic effects in film, is present too. As editors, we have been ecumenical in our approach. This respects a sense found in many of these pieces, and the theories they mobilize, that poetry has an import that goes beyond the words on the page, as a fundamental basis of other arts, or a potentially revolutionary verbal, cultural act.

Beyond Adaptation: From Medium Specificity to Intermediality

Ideas around adaptation have been central to the practice and analysis of film since the earliest days of cinema. At the same time, the *specificity* of film as a form in its own right has been stressed by many of its theorists: a notion that film theory in the medium's initial decades itself adopted and adapted from earlier criticism on aesthetics and the fine-arts. As early as 1766, Lessing offered a critique of those commentators who judged painting by the standards of poetry and vice versa. The German philosopher offered instead an argument for specificity in art (1930: 4), what he called 'the peculiar nature of Art and its necessary limits and requirements' (16). Lessing outlined a series of reasons for which classical sculpture differs from contemporary or near contemporary poetry (9). Poetry, he argued, has the advantage of relying on imagination more than painting or sculpture (13): 'the material limits of [plastic] art confine her imitative effort to one single moment' (14); painting can be realized 'only from one point of view' (14), an opinion of course that predates the efforts of cubist and other experimental and avant-garde artists to include multiple perspectives within a single work. Poetry, meanwhile, has more than 'a single line' (17) with which to work or play.

Lessing argued that not 'every feature which the descriptive poet uses can be used with like effect on the canvas or in the marble' (30). And he continued:

> When one says that the artist imitates the poet, or that the poet imitates the artist, this is capable of two interpretations. Either the one makes the work of the other the actual subject of his imitation, or they have both the same subject and the one borrows from the other the style and fashion of the imitation. [...] When, however, poet and artist, as not seldom happens, view the subjects that they have in common from an identical standpoint, it can hardly fail that there should be agreement in many particulars without implying the slightest degree of imitation or common aim between them. (33)

In a striking sentence, Lessing seems to anticipate cinematic montage: 'to the poet alone belongs the art of depicting with negative traits, and by mixing them with positive to bring two images into one' (39). The implication, then, is that cinema — inexistent in his day — might escape some of the limitations placed on painting and sculpture: 'what the material painting drawn from [Homer] exhibits the poet leads us up to through a whole gallery of pictures' (51). The effect described is similar to what the successive nature of the images in film can achieve. Cinema's advantage, then, is time: 'if painting [...] must wholly renounce time, then continuous actions as such cannot be reckoned amongst her subjects [...] Poetry on the other hand ...'[2] (55); and we might add, this all changes with film and montage. Lessing added, tellingly from the point of view of students of the poetry–film nexus, 'charm is beauty in motion' (80). A century and a half later, Eisenstein would connect montage with the Japanese poetic form of haiku, as we discuss below. For the Soviet filmmaker, however, rather than overcoming painting's incapacity to convey time, cinema — and specifically montage — energized an expressive potential already present in painting. In his essay on El Greco, Eisenstein suggested that the sixteenth-century Spanish-Greek painter had already reflected time by placing elements contiguously, rather than continuously as cinema does. If El Greco managed to 'bring together in a single space a series of elements that in fact are dispersed, scattered, too extensive to behold in a single look', cinematic montage 'is a way of "bringing together" in a single space — on the screen — diverse elements (fragments) of a phenomenon that are filmed on different scales from distinct points of view and from various places' (Eisenstein 2014: 13).[3]

In cinema's first decades, critics and theorists such as Vachel Lindsay, Hugo Munsterberg, Jean Epstein and Rudolf Arnheim drew on the tradition of medium-specificity initiated by Lessing in their various efforts to justify the new technological medium's status as art, both establishing links between the motion-picture and more established forms, and identifying the cinema's essential characteristics that differentiated it from its forebears (Stam 2000: 33–37). In his foundational 1911 essay 'The Birth of the Sixth Art', the Italian futurist art critic Ricciotto Canudo celebrated the cinematograph as a wholly original form that brought together what he called the 'Rhythms of Space (the Plastic Arts) and the Rhythms of Time (Music and Poetry)', so creating the 'astonishing apotheosis' of a *Plastic Art in Motion* that was capable of rendering '"real" life [...] *stylized in speed*'[4] (Canudo 2014: 595–96; 598). Jean Epstein built upon the essay by Canudo — whom he called 'the missionary of poetry in the cinema' — in developing Louis Delluc's concept of *photogénie*, a term that referred to 'the purest expression of cinema'. For Epstein, 'every art builds its forbidden city, its own exclusive domain, autonomous, specific, and hostile to anything that does not belong' (2012: 293). Just as painting should free itself of representational and narrative concerns and literature should turn its back on facile 'twists and turns of plot' that are more proper to 'a charade [or] a game of cards' (293), cinema should dedicate itself to what he called 'photogenic mobility' (294): a four-dimensional mode of spatio-temporal expression by which the film camera lens was capable of 'revealing the inner nature of things'. Thanks to *photogénie*, Epstein claimed that cinema had become 'poetry's most powerful medium' (296). Just as Eisenstein saw cinema as one more medium through which the already-existing temporality of montage could be conveyed, Epstein's comments suggest that, rather than cinema and poetry existing as distinct media, poetry can be conceived as an underlying mode or a 'language' that can be expressed through different media, whether literary, plastic, or cinematic.

Cinema's early theorists thought of cinema's poetic potential, then, as being both specific to cinema itself and a result of the medium's ability to harness and to advance the properties of existing art forms. As David Rodowick has rightly pointed out, while medium-specificity criticism is 'an injunction against hybrid forms', cinema's specificity is precisely 'how it functions as a hybrid medium'; the fact that 'it is comprised of multiple components irreducible, one would think, to a single essence, and thus remains open to a plethora of diverse and even incompatible styles and formal approaches' (2007: 36). This medial hybridity — or 'intermediality' — is now a central part of the zeitgeist of film and screen scholarship: firstly with the onset of video in the 1980s, as in Raymond Bellour's concept of the 'between-images' (Bellour 2018); and subsequently and more intensely with the rise of the digital technologies that have become so central to the production, dissemination and consumption of moving-images. But the term 'intermedia' itself has a longer history than one might think. As Dick Higgins notes, 'the word "intermedia" appears in the writings of Samuel Taylor Coleridge in 1812 in exactly its con-temporary sense — to define works which fall conceptually between media that are already known' (Higgins 1984: 23). Strictly, the term used was 'intermedium', in the singular, in an essay on Spenser and allegory (Coleridge et al. 1836).

In the twentieth century, the term 'intermedia' (re-)emerges on the US exp-erimental art scene — although, as RosaLee Goldberg (2011) has noted, the multifaceted practices of US artists can be traced at least back to the avant-gardes, including Dada and Futurism. As Higgins, again, defines it, 'intermedia [is] the fusion of two or more discrete media', including performance, Fluxus, and experimental art. For Higgins, 'the happening developed as an intermedium, an uncharted land that lies between collage, music and the theater' (1984: 22). To give an example, 'in intermedia [...] the visual element (painting) is fused conceptually with the words' (24). At the same time, 'the term [intermedia] is not prescriptive' (25): it does not set out a particular recipe or manifesto for how these combinations and encounters should be conducted. The term also emerges in the Buenos Aires art scene at the turn of the 1970s, for example in the 1970 exhibition curated by Jorge Glusberg, *Argentina Inter-Medios* (Kozak 2018: 563).

The term reappears in the 2000s in literary and art scholarship, although now altered slightly, as 'intermediality'. In his study of the term, Julio Prieto observes,

> the appearance of the concept of intermediality in critical discourse is linked to the technomediatic global culture of late capitalism, and in particular the exponential growth of media software linked to new information technologies that have been in continuous development since the appearance of the Internet. (2017: 9)

He argues that, 'intermediality is not a substitute for intertextuality' (2017: 9). Prieto distinguishes between what he calls 'conservative' forms of intermediality (such as certain radio adaptations of literature, or commercial cinema versions of nineteenth-century novels, to use Prieto's examples) and *transformative* uses', for example: 'the appeal to poetry, political theory and popular *cordel* literature in Glauber Rocha's *cinema novo*'[5] (2017: 13). Furthermore, 'one of the most productive areas in intermedial studies develops in dialogue with visual culture studies and what we could loosely term "philosophies of the image" in the second half of the twentieth century' (Prieto 2017: 14). One particular effect of intermediality that he notes is 'intermedial estrangement as an opening towards an*other* vision' (2017: 15). For Walter Bruno Berg, meanwhile, the 'inter-medial' refers to 'the *concomitant* effects of the totality of the media involved'[6] (2002: 128); he stresses the role of both media *and* texts in intermediality (2002: 129). In both Prieto's and Berg's assessments, the notion of *medium* itself is a question that requires further attention. Would poetry and political theory both be media in the same way that *cordel* literature is, for example, the latter referring to a very specific form of printing and circulating popular poetry in north-eastern Brazil? The status of cinema, too, as medium — potentially at the expense of its hard-won status as art in its own right — is also controversial. Such questions are at the forefront of our contributors' analyses.

One important area of constant intermedial experimentation in the twentieth century has been in what many critics refer to as 'expanded cinema'. Walley calls this the 'liberation of cinema from the confines of the standard uses of celluloid film' (2011: 24). These might include 'cinema as performance, as object, as concept, as any alternative material that could serve as projector, filmstrip, screen, etc.' (2011: 47). With reference to Annette Michelson, Walley writes that 'the erasure of boundaries between the arts and the ethic of intermedia at the heart of expanded cinema threatened to derail radical filmmaking's quest for autonomy and drain cinema of its potential power' (25). Related to this is an ongoing debate about the longevity of film itself — as 'a viable alternative to digital that needs to be protected from extinction' (50). In terms of contemporary cinema, we might note for example Mariano Llinás's use of a *camera obscura* for the last part of his 2018 epic *La flor*. This wholly antiquated piece of technology, disassembled in front of the camera in the final reel, is used to create a grainy, sepia look for the final section, a tale of women captured by an indigenous tribe. At the same time, Llinás's film quotes liberally from José Hernández's *gaucho* epic poem of the 1870s, *Martín Fierro*, and in particular Part 1, known as the *Ida*, or journey out. Thus plot, literary intertext, and technique, meet in striking fashion.

Theories of intermediality have been particularly popular amongst German- and Dutch-based scholars in the early years of the twenty-first century. As Kirsten von Hagen puts it, 'research into intermediality seeks to underline the study of reciprocal relationships, intermedial spaces, passages and differences that occur in intermedial dialogue' (2006: 242). Chiel Kattenbelt (2008) offers a useful taxonomy of terms for referring to forms of cultural production that cross or blur medial boundaries:

> 'multimediality' refers to the occurrence where there are many media in one and the same object; 'transmediality' refers to transfer from one medium to another medium (media change); and 'intermediality' refers to the co-relation of media in the sense of mutual influences between media. (2008: 20–21)

Under 'transmediality', she observes that 'most feature films that are based on a novel are transpositions of stories, which do not take into account the specific literary features of the original narration' (2008: 23); we might add that this is all the more the case for poetry.

Intermediality, then, consists of 'co-relations between different media that result in a redefinition of the media that are influencing each other, which in turn leads to a refreshed perception' (Kattenbelt 2008: 25). She sees this as similar to Eisenstein's 'montage of attractions': 'the different elements of the performance should, so to say, crash with each other, with the result that a new energy is released' (Kattenbelt 2008: 26).

As Rajewsky points out, 'much of what is generally treated under the heading of intermediality is in no way a novelty' (2005: 44). She highlights the risks of narrow approaches to intermediality 'when one individual approach [...] lays claim to having grasped' the concept (2005: 45). It is, then,

> foremost a generic term for all those phenomena that [...] in some way take place *between* media. [...] those configurations which have to do with a crossing of borders between media, and which thereby can be differentiated from *intra*medial phenomena as well as from *trans*medial phenomena (i.e. the appearance of a certain motif, aesthetic, or discourse across a variety of different media. (2005: 46)

There exists a debate over whether intermediality is 'a fundamental condition or category' or a 'critical category for the concrete analysis of specific individual media products or configurations' (Rajewsky 2005: 47). Use of the term runs the risk of becoming vague and even meaningless: 'the intermedial quality of a film adaptation, for example, is hardly comparable — or is comparable only in the broadest sense — to the intermediality of so-called filmic writing' (50).

A similarly taxonomic approach can be found in the work of Ginette Verstraete (2010): 'the study of intermediality takes as its starting point the specificity of the medium/media involved — a specificity not unrelated to the autonomy of art — even when this specificity is being radically questioned through the larger media environment within which it is situated' (2010: 8). For Verstraete,

> every medium is always already intermedial [...] intermediality as the interaction between, and within, media, is made to critically re-evaluate the function of communication, entertainment, representation, mediation, meaning, expression... by the (singular) medium. This is, of course, where art — marking the usual unusual — comes in. (2010: 9)

In conclusion, she argues, 'intermediality asks difficult questions not only about art and media — and their interrelations — but also about the institutional boundaries we draw around them' (11).

In his study *What Pictures Want*, the critic W. J. T. Mitchell looks at the central role of 'poetry' — in the broadest sense — to what he calls 'picturing': 'Poetry (as "making," or *poeisis*) is fundamental to picturing. Pictures are themselves products of poetry, and a poetics of pictures addresses itself to them, as Aristotle proposed' (Mitchell 2005: xv). This forms part of a strong thesis around the impurity of media: '*All media are mixed media*. There are no "pure" media [...], though the search for the essence of a medium [...] is a utopia that seems inseparable from the artistic deployment of any medium'[7] (Mitchell 2005: 215). We thus need to 'put into question the received idea that a medium has something called "specificity"' (Mitchell 2005: 198).

The assault on specificity is not without its detractors. In their introduction to a collection of essays on 'Impure Cinema', Lúcia Nagib and Anne Jerslev assess this term, drawn from Bazin, and originally translated into English and popularized as 'mixed cinema'. It is, they argue, a 'method', not an object (2014: xxi). The 'ultimate boundary' of intermediality is the 'division between art and life' (xxiv). In her contribution to the same volume, Nagib highlights the special status for Bazin of screen adaptations of theatre and literature for the cinema (2014: 24). She goes on to argue that 'the obstinate champions of hybridization, in particular those coming from cultural studies, must confront the fact that this has already been achieved by an overwhelming and irresistible globalization' (2014: 21). Here then is the bind: the attraction of the non-specific, the hybrid, and the impure; alongside the need to acknowledge what is specific in cinema. Nagib continues, proposing 'the intermedial phenomenon not as an accomplished project or an end in itself, but as a problem, that is to say, the site of a crisis, or default of means, that requires other, metaphorical procedures in order to fill in a gap which is at the very core of artistic creation' (21). Her conclusion is a Rancierean, dissensus-based reading of the politics of intermediality.

In his chapter in the same volume, Philip Rosen analyses André Bazin's original theorizing around specificity in cinema: 'cinema's specificity is to be not specific'. For Bazin, literary adaptation played an important role in the cinema: 'a key authentic issue propelling the development of [...] cinema' (Rosen 2014: 12). As Rosen concludes, 'Bazin's polemic against purist theory entails an insistence on the historicity of cinema and the historicity of its specificity' (13).

To sum up, then, while intermediality and hybridity are now widely used concepts to discuss a variety of contemporary media, including film, one must remember that these are not politically or aesthetically unproblematic terms; and at the same time medium specificity is a particularly pertinent issue for cinema, a medium that seems both to thrive in practice on non-specificity while seeking in theory its own specificity as part of a strategy of artistic self-validation, over the years. For this study, specific points of contact between poetry and film — such as links between montage and haiku — are of particular relevance.

Conceptions of Film-Poetry and the Poetic Film in Film Theory and Film Praxis

The debates outlined above are deeply linked to the historical development of ideas about film-poetry and poetic cinema. As we have seen, thinkers such as Canudo, Delluc and Epstein saw cinema's poetic dimension as emanating from the particular configuration of expressive tools that was peculiar to the cinematograph. As we noted in our 2014 work, Sergei Eisenstein (1949: 93) explained his concept of film montage — which for him was the very essence of cinema — as a rendition into moving-images of the Japanese poetic form of the haiku, which he saw as composed of 'montage phrases. Shot lists', in which '[t]he simple combination of two or three details of a material kind yields a perfectly finished representation of another kind — psychological'. Likewise, early notions of film-poetry or the *cine-poem*, also originating in the avant-garde traditions of silent and early sound cinema, drew heavily on theoretical and critical discussions that turned between medium-specificity and ideas of hybridity. The surrealists shared Eisenstein's interest in cinema's potential for throwing up visual associations, as well as his fascination for cinema's potential links with Freud's writings on dreamwork. The surrealists saw in cinema an ideal apparatus for the 'liberation of unconscious energies in the juxtaposition of disparate energies' (Sitney 2015: 128) that is in evidence, for instance, in Luis Buñuel and Salvador Dalí's surrealist masterpiece *Un chien andalou* (1929), or in Man Ray's *Emak-Bakia* (1926).[8] In this latter *cinépoème* (as Ray's film proclaims itself to be in the opening credits), the film camera itself features onscreen as a detonator of jarring perspectives through disorienting framing and apparently impossible camera movements, and unsettling juxtapositions through montage. Jean Cocteau likewise stated that his own cine-poetry emerged from the unexpected links between events and image: the basis of a cinematic aesthetic that sought to elevate spectators to a state of sleep-hypnosis that would, in turn, enable them to see deep inside themselves (Cocteau 2015: 29). In Cocteau's picture *Le Sang d'un poète* [The Blood of a Poet] (1932) — whose opening intertitles playfully announce the piece as a 'realistic documentary of unreal events' — the French cine-poet sought to 'film poetry the way that the Williamson brothers film the bottom of the sea [...]. It meant capturing the poetic state' (1985: 62).[9] For Cocteau, the poetic was out there for the catching, and cinema an ideal 'weapon' (1994: 31) for hunting it.

For Cocteau (as for the surrealists, with whom he had considerable disagreements), cine-poetry occupied an artistic sphere that was quite separate from commercial narrative cinema, which he rejected as drab and sentimental. By contrast the US avant-garde filmmaker Joseph Cornell — whose work is described by P. Adams Sitney as 'a persuasive test case for the viability of a cinema of lyrical poetry' (2015: 113) — used mainstream narrative cinema as the raw material for his own cine-poetic aesthetics, which worked towards a deconstruction of the grammar of the motion-picture. In *Rose Hobart* (1936), widely acknowledged as the foundational work of found-footage filmmaking, Cornell re-appropriated, re-edited, and re-soundtracked footage from the Universal Pictures talkie drama *East of Borneo* (George Melford, 1931), converting and remixing the transitional shots that are the bread-and-butter of Hollywood continuity editing into a poetic choreography of spatial, temporal and narrative discontinuities and non sequiturs. The questions of how cinema could be a vehicle of lyric poetry, and how cinematic lyricism related or might relate to narrative cinema, were central in the American avant-garde cinema of the following decade, not least in the work of Cornell's erstwhile assistant Stan Brakhage.

These questions were addressed by the participants in a 1953 roundtable discussion on 'Poetry and the Film' hosted by the New York film society *Cinema 16* (transcribed in Maas 1963), beginning with a taxonomy laid out by poet and film critic Parker Tyler, which distinguished firstly between 'poetry as an auditory medium' (i.e. verbal or written poetry and music) and 'poetry as a visual medium'. The latter was exemplified with works of 'pure cinema' emphasizing a 'surrealist poetry of the image' and generally dispensing with words altogether: the aforementioned *Le Sang d'un poète* and *Un chien andalou* [An Andalusian Dog], and *Lot in Sodom* (James Sibley Watson, 1933); as well as later avant-garde films by the likes of Maya Deren and Kenneth Anger. Tyler further identified the following subsections of poetry as a visual medium:

- the cine-poem, which unlike our discussion of the term above, comprises 'impressionistic [...] pictorial conceptions of city life, of nature' (presumably referring to city-symphony films such as *Man with a Movie Camera* (Dziga Vertov, 1929) or *A Bronx Morning* (Jay Leyda, 1931)) and which 'stressed abstract patterns';
- the 'poetry of painting in motion — the pure abstract film', such as the work of Norman McLaren and the Whitney brothers;
- the cinema of 'naturalistic poetry' pioneered by Robert Flaherty: that is, the poetic dimension of documentary cinema; and
- the dream and hallucination sequences contained within mainstream narrative cinema.

Tyler then proceeds to categorize the following types of films that illustrate 'poetry as a visual-verbal medium':

- the 'fantasy films of Jean Vigo' (which he acknowledges as principally visual);
- avant-garde films that are 'set to poems or to poetic prose' (naming Sidney Peterson, the roundtable chair Willard Maas, and Ian Hugo as exponents);
- Sergei Eisenstein's 'severe formalism', in which 'montage borders on pure poetry' (although it is unclear what the verbal element is to Eisenstein's films according to Tyler);
- the 'myth films' of Cocteau, such as *La Belle et la Bête* [Beauty and the Beast] (1946);
- 'naturalistic poetry documents' such as *The River* (Pare Lorentz, 1938) and *Le Sang des bêtes* [Blood of the Beasts] (Georges Franju, 1949): a category that stands as the sound-film equivalent of the 'cinema of naturalistic poetry' above; and
- the 'fifty-fifty fusion' (presumably, films that mix visual and verbal poetry in equal measure), such as film adaptations of Shakespeare plays; the BBC TV movie of T. S. Eliot's *Murder in the Cathedral* (1947); and filmed operas.

While Tyler's taxonomy is undoubtedly useful in distinguishing different uses of poetic devices in different cinematic styles, it tends to fragment and isolate his corpus by separating films and tendencies by genre, and it fails to establish precisely what the *poetic* dimension of each of his categories comprises. In her own interventions, Maya Deren more incisively defined 'poetic structure' in cinema as 'a "vertical" investigation of a situation, in that it probes the ramifications of the moment, and is concerned with its qualities and depth, [... and] creates visible or auditory forms for something that is invisible, which is the feeling, or the emotion, of the metaphysical content of the movement' (Maas 1963). By contrast she conceived *narrative* structure as 'the "horizontal" attack of the drama, which is concerned with the development'. Deren acknowledged that, across different cinematic genres, any combination of both structures was conceivable: that is, narrative and poetic registers are not opposed but rather exist on a continuum that ebbs and flows through the texture of cinema.[10]

Deren's expansive vision of cinema's poetic dimension stands in stark contrast with Italian writer and filmmaker Pier Paolo Pasolini's notion of the 'cinema of poetry' that emerged in the following decade, in what was perhaps the most influential theoretical text on cinema and poetry published in the second half of the twentieth century (Pasolini 1976). Pasolini shared with his surrealist and avant-garde forebears an interest in cinema's proximity to dream states and the medium's 'naturally poetic' nature (quoted in Sitney 2015: 21). However, quite unlike the historical avant-garde's self-reflexive, anti-narrative and montage-centric notions of the cine-poem, in which the motion picture apparatus itself figures on occasion as a tool for poetic expression (as in *Emak-Bakia* and *Man with a Movie Camera*, both discussed above), Pasolini's 'cinema of poetry' emphasized immersive narration and the sequence shot. For the Italian, most cinema to date, both commercial and arthouse, had largely adopted what he called a 'language of prose': a narration-based style in which all of cinema's irrational and oneiric properties were 'exploited as an unconscious factor of shock and glamour' in an evasive and spectacular 'hypnotic *monstrum*' (1976: 547). By contrast Pasolini identified a tendency in recent art cinema — particularly in pictures such as *Red Desert* (Michelangelo Antonioni, 1964) and *Before the Revolution* (Bernardo Bertolucci, 1964) — an ability to tap cinema's specifically poetic 'language', which he located in a rendition into cinematic terms of the literary technique of free indirect style: that is, in which 'the author penetrates entirely into the spirit of his character, of whom he thus adopts not only the psychology but also the language' (1976: 549). Since cinema cannot perform this act with a simple linguistic operation as can, say, the novel, the cinema of poetry works on a stylistic level. In *Red Desert*, to take Pasolini's paradigmatic example, Antonioni conveys the neurosis of his protagonist Giuliana (Monica Vitti) directly through elements of film style that blur the distinction between objective and subjective shots. This is obtained, for instance, by framing Giuliana from what appear to be subjective point-of-view long-shots but without revealing any narrative source, or by generating uncertainty as to whether jarring sound effects are extra-diegetic or internal diegetic elements: stylistic tropes that work Giuliana's paranoia into the very substance of the film. Thus, in Pasolini's words, Antonioni '*has substituted, wholly, the world-view of a sick woman for his own vision, which is delirious with estheticism*'[11] (553). Crucially for Pasolini, this ability for film style to enable the bourgeois filmmakers who practise it (Antonioni, Bertolucci, Godard) 'to speak indirectly — through some narrative alibi — in the first person' (557) makes the cinema of poetry a tool of bourgeois class consciousness: a 'recuperation, by bourgeois culture, of the territory it had lost in the battle with Marxism and its possible revolution' (557). The theorization of the cinema of poetry is, then, a specifically political act. In J. D. Rhodes's words, '[t]he style that, in a sense, constitutes the "cinema of poetry," or art cinema, becomes itself a historical protagonist through which one may perhaps grasp, or begin to fumble toward some sense of, the totality of "neocapitalism"' (2010: 154).

Pasolini's work has been influential in a variety of — at times surprising — ways in Latin America. While his interest in the interconnection between poetry and film remains present, his political critique of the practice of certain directors has perhaps been less well remembered. A number of the pieces in this volume strive to restore precisely that acuity of sociopolitical analysis in their studies of the poetry–film nexus. In many cases, the authors — and others, working elsewhere — assess the fusion of poetic and audiovisual languages in varieties of film that come after Pasolini's moment, including video and digital cinema, and various forms of media art that blur the boundaries between film, poetry, and other forms. The next section looks more specifically at some of these connections in Latin America.

Cinema-Poetry Connections in Latin America

The relationship between film and poetry in Latin America is a two-way street. From cinema's early days in the late nineteenth and early twentieth centuries, *modernista* poets such as the Nicaraguan Rubén Darío and the Mexicans Luis G. Urbina and Amado Nervo showed a keen interest in the cinematograph, chronicling the ways in which the emerging form was reshaping everyday experience. In the following years avant-garde writers sought to revolutionize poetic form by suffusing it with cinematic elements, from the Peruvian Carlos Oquendo de Amat's *5 metros de poemas* (1927) to his compatriot César Vallejo's 'poesía nueva' [new poetry], which drew upon the expressive potential of filmic properties such as montage, as studied by Maria Chiara d'Argenio (2015) and Michelle Clayton (2012: 170), among others. Meanwhile, national filmmaking traditions have looked to epic poetry for aesthetic inspiration, cultural validation, or sources of ideological critique, as in the case of the Mexican indigenist romance *Tabaré* (Luis Lezama, 1917, of which there is no known extant print), adapted from a nineteenth-century Uruguayan epic poem; or the gaucho genre in Argentina, from the silent epics *Nobleza gaucha* (Humberto Cairo, 1915) and *El último centauro* (Enrique Queirolo, 1924), to the left-wing Peronist *Los hijos de Fierro* (1975) and the children's animation *Martín Fierro: La película* (Norman Ruiz and Liliana Romero, 2007), which variously dramatize or allegorize national history drawing on José Hernández's foundational poem *El gaucho Martín Fierro/La vuelta de Martín Fierro* (1872/1879). To varying degrees, such films seek to integrate epic style into their cinematic renditions of national history through techniques such as panoramic shots, monumental characterization, spatial construction, and narrative voices using epic rhythm and rhyme structures (Bollig 2012), (Suárez 2018).

The original and copy model often found in journalistic or popular assessments of such reworkings of national epics was intrinsic to the ideas of medium-specificity that, as we suggested in the previous section, were behind some of the historical avant-garde's thinking about poetic cinema. Júlia González de Canales Carcereny offers a panorama of links between film and poetry, from Epstein's notion of *photogénie*, which we discussed above, to the different waves of poetic film in the 1920s, 1960s, and today. González de Canales rightly points out that, for

Epstein, 'literature and cinema have modes of artistic composition that, although autonomous, are intrinsically linked, with poetry being particularly related to cinema in its desire to suggest rather than to tell' (2017: 119). Here and elsewhere, she further points out that for Russian formalist critics such as Boris Eikhenbaum (author of a 1927 book on film theory titled *Poetika kino*), Victor Shklovsky, and Yuri Tynianov, the essence and the stylistic autonomy of poetic cinema lay in montage. For Tynianov, 'Shots in film do not "unfold" in a sequential, gradual order, they are precisely *exchanged*. This is the foundation of montage. They replace each other just as a single verse line, a single metrical unit, replaces another one on a precise boundary. Film makes *a jump* from shot to shot, just as verse makes a jump from line to line' (Tynyanov, quoted in González de Canales 2019: 277). González de Canales contrasts these ideas of poetic cinema with those of Pasolini (as discussed above) and Andrei Tarkovsky in the 1960s, showing how both currents inform a certain tendency towards a poetic register in twenty-first-century Latin American cinema — an issue that we will come to shortly.

What is missing from González de Canales's account is the extent to which both avant-garde notions of cine-poetry and Pasolini's writings on the cinema of poetry were either taken up or developed in parallel in avant-garde cultural production in Latin America, in diverse literary and moving-image movements. In his recent study, Sergio Delgado Moya (2017: 32–33) analyses a variety of examples of intermedial connections traced by poetry in Mexico and Brazil, from the avant-garde period and beyond, including the use of medical and advertising language in the poetry of *estridentismo* founder Manuel Maples Arce or the earlier twentieth-century work of 'Parnassian' poets such as Olavo Bilac. He also studies the engagement of Brazilian concrete poets with both advertising and forms of muralism made popular in post-revolution Mexico (2017: 41). In the case of the Mexican poet Octavio Paz — who entered into a productive dialogue with Haroldo de Campos and other Brazilian *concretistas* — Delgado Moya examines his simultaneous critique and employment of examples of contemporary consumer culture in experimental poems from the 1960s (2017: 42; also Chapter Three); he observes that, 'The replicas of mass culture and advertising Paz built into his most experimental poems emerge as powerful reflections on language in the age of consumer culture' (152). This is closely related to an interest on the part of Paz, inherited from the early twentieth-century avant-gardes, in the possibility of 'convergence between cinema and poetry' (148) which takes place against a backdrop of 'renewed interest in interartistic collaboration' in Mexico in the 1960s. This would feed into Paz's attempts to create a movie from his experimental 'simultanist' poetry book, *Blanco* (1967): 'a cinematographic projection of the book, or, better said, the projection of its reading (silent at times, out loud at other times)' (Paz, cited in Delgado Moya 2017: 150). Delgado Moya continues: 'In the film adaptation of *Blanco*, both the world as sensible image and language as instrument are bracketed out to make way for the act of reading' (151). Paz's plans for the film — which never came to fruition in his lifetime — also set the course for his increasing participation in Mexican television, in particular for the media conglomerate Televisa, later in his career. Ángel Miquel, who has also written on Paz's relationship with cinema, has pointed out the poet's affinity with Luis Buñuel, with whom he shared a hostility towards classical Mexican narrative cinema, and whose films Paz described as 'la primera irrupción deliberada de la poesía en el arte cinematográfico' [poetry's first deliberate incursion into film art] (Paz, quoted in Miquel 2015: 121–22). In a 1953 roundtable discussion, Buñuel set out his own conception of cinema as an 'instrument of poetry', in turn citing Paz's statement that 'Basta que un hombre encadenado cierre sus ojos para que pueda hacer estallar el mundo' [A chained man only needs to close his eyes to make the world explode] (Paz, quoted in Buñuel 1958: 1). Buñuel claimed that cinema, in the hands of a free poetic sprit — that is, freed from the constraints of industry — was 'capaz de arrebatarlo [al hombre] como ninguna otra expresión humana' [capable of captivating [man] like no other human expression] (Buñuel 1958: 2) by 'expresar el mundo de los sueños, de las emociones, del instinto' [express[ing] the world of dreams, of emotions, of instinct] (Buñuel 1958: 2). Closely aligned with his surrealist counterparts such as Man Ray (whom he cited in his talk), as well as Jean Cocteau, Buñuel singled out cinema's capacity for flexible, non-realist spatial and temporal dynamics as central to its ability to express the unconscious. His own films consistently bear this out, constantly upbraiding the spatial and temporal logic of narrative continuity, playfully replacing conventional film syntax with absurd parataxis and merging the temporality of dream into that of waking life.

Buñuel was a key reference point for the multifarious 'New Cinemas' that emerged and developed in Latin America during the 1960s and 1970s, many of which tapped the expressive and subversive potential of the poetry–film nexus in diverse ways. A little-known but brilliantly executed example is the work of the Mexican writer Salvador Elizondo, whose rediscovered 1965 film *Apocalypse 1900* combines shots of still images with music and poetry readings. The images include period representations of Paris, erotic art, images of factories, surgery, as well as human illness and infirmity; the music is taken from Wagner, Chopin, and others; with male and female voice-overs of texts from Baudelaire, Lautréamont, Bataille, Breton and Cocteau. The film creates an at times breathless rhythm by cutting from still to still, with a provocative interplay between image, text and music: a multimedia production in keeping with the dissident surrealist aesthetics that informed Elizondo's best-known novel, from the same year, *Farabeuf o la crónica de un instante*. Importantly, the different materials work together without discernible hierarchy.

More directly political instances of intermedial exchange between cinema and poetry can be found in the work of the Cuban filmmaker Santiago Álvarez, who used what Maria Chiara D'Argenio, in our previous edited work, called 'poetic patterns' to construct a revolutionary filmmaking praxis that combined 'actual poems, [...] poetic devices such as metaphors and [...] genres close to poetry such as songs, the use of still photography and found footage and a "poetic" experimental approach to documentary' (2014: 130). Carolina Larraín (2009) also analyses Santiago Álvarez's use of poetic elements in his 1973 film *El tigre saltó y mató, pero morirá... morirá...* on the 1973 coup in Chile against Salvador Allende, comparing it with analogous strategies in Patricio Guzmán's *Salvador Allende* (2004). Larraín shows how the two filmmakers approach poetry both as a textual medium that is read or performed in their films, and as an expressive structuring device that allows them to confront trauma through metaphor, rhythmic expression, figurative language and semantic ambivalence. Such work demonstrates the extent to which Latin American filmmakers have engaged the relationship between film-poetry and liberation struggles, both in a directly political sense and in terms of the poetic register's ability to train the viewer's eye and ear to think beyond received meanings, to unthink conventional signifying processes, and to resist closure. Similarly Álvaro Vázquez Mantecón (2015), drawing on Walter Benjamin, has shown how, in their avant-garde films of the 1960s and 1970s, Mexican cineastes Rubén Gámez, Gelsen Gas and Alfredo Gurrola used diverse poetic registers in their search for allegorical modes of expression, opposed to conventional modes of cinematic narrative, as part of a wider critique of capitalism, developmentalism, modernization and state violence.

Contemporary experimental cinema and media art has also frequently resorted to this anti-narrative, lyrical avant-garde poetic mode. To cite one example, the Colombian filmmaker Felipe Guerrero drew on the countercultural *nadaísta* movement of the 1950s and 1960s in his 2006 experimental film *Paraíso*, as Wood (2014) examined in our previous edited collection. Although *nadaísmo* centred more on poetry and public happenings than film, Guerrero's work achieves a transtextual approach to the *nadaísta* verse of Jaime Jaramillo Escobar (known as X-504), deploying found footage and visual and aural montage to express the historical density of the audiovisual archive of violence in Colombia. In the same collection, Constanza Ceresa analysed Martín Gambarotta's poetry collection *Punctum* (1996) alongside Martín Rejtman's film *Silvia Prieto* (1999), showing how both artists forged an emancipatory, anti-narrative 'nueva economía del lenguaje' [new economy of language] (Ceresa 2014: 180) capable of criticizing the emerging neoliberal order in 1990s Argentina from within the relations of production of the present, also following Walter Benjamin. The abstract, political, archival media art made by contemporary artists such as Bruno Varela or the Los Ingrávidos collective, both in Mexico, is another case in point. Varela, for instance, generates creative, intentionally duplicitous interplay between text and image in his work, confronting documentary or fake-documentary images with parallel poems written in the form of subtitles that do anything but fulfil their conventional, explicative function. Varela's films often take the form of unsolvable puzzles; the sound and images that populate them frequently bear the marks of analogue, magnetic or digital decay (which itself is sometimes faked): poetic ambiguity and its material substrate.

By contrast contemporary art cinema has, as González de Canales (2017) has noted, looked more towards Pasolini's notion of the cinema of poetry, as well as Tarkovsky's lyrical cinema. Tarkovsky becomes a key figure for both Lisandro Alonso and Carlos Reygadas — and, as Adam Feinstein argues in this volume, also the Chilean cineaste Pablo Larraín. González de Canales offers a theory that Reygadas makes 'filmic haiku' (2017: 117ff). This consists of observation of nature

(128–29), using ambient sound and sparse dialogue, alongside ordering that appears simple but is in fact complex: it explicitly rejects realist or neorealist observation, incorporating elements of haptic cinema (133) and what Gonzalo Aguilar has called a 'poetics of indetermination' (Aguilar, quoted in González de Canales 2017: 130). Laura Martins has also drawn parallels between Tarkovsky and the Argentine documentary filmmaker Gustavo Fontán, who fixes his gaze on 'the materiality of nature' (Martins 2014: 168) through long, contemplative shots that heighten vision so as to render the invisible visible; to create a 'sensorial experience in which the *textual* value of the image unfolds' (171); and, ultimately, to teach us 'to look, to glimpse, to listen' (175). And the influence, at varying levels of directness, of Pier Paolo Pasolini has been felt in both poetry and film throughout the Americas — in the poetry of Sergio Raimondi, or the films of Glauber Rocha, Raúl Perrone or José Celestino Campusano, to give just some examples — as studied in the essays compiled by Kohen and Russo (2017), in their collection *Los condenados*. The authors take a particular interest in Pasolini's active engagement with and championing of the struggles of oppressed groups both at home and in post- and neocolonial contexts, often within a tricontinental frame that linked Latin American artists and activists to, for example, counterparts in Africa or the Middle East. For his part, Adalberto Müller draws extensively on both Pasolini's cinema of poetry and Cocteau's poetic cinema in analysing three different cinematic approaches, from the 1980s to the 2000s, to the mid-century Brazilian poet Manoel de Barros. Müller is particularly interested in Pasolini's casting of the cinema of poetry as an expressive mode that allows reality to be revealed rather than masked. Müller argues that, just as de Barros's ecological poetry adopts new dramatic perspectives and personae from which to view nature, those who sought to render de Barros's verse into film needed to find new filmic registers to do so: 'they compel cinematic language to change its "nature" just as nature compels Manoel de Barros to change his poetry' (Müller 2014: 195). Elsewhere, in his analysis of the films of Lisandro Alonso, and in particular *La libertad*, Gonzalo Aguilar writes of a 'poética de la indeterminación' [poetics of indeterminacy] (2008: 61) at work in the portrayal of the character Misael, a solitary woodcutter whom the film follows for its entire length. 'This indeterminacy allows each of us to project, on that trace, his or her own idea of liberty and to respond to Alonso's provocation' (61), in a fashion that turns the film's protagonist into something of a sage for the viewer.

The works mentioned above might constitute examples of what Laura Marks (2000) calls 'hybrid cinema'. Marks notes the importance of hybrid cinema for certain filmmakers operating away from the major centres of cinematic production, and in particular for cinema-practitioners in the developing world or who form part of diasporic communities therefrom:

> The term 'hybrid cinema' also implies a hybrid form, mixing documentary, fiction, personal, and experimental genres, as well as different media. By pushing the limits of any genre, hybrid cinema forces each genre to explain itself, to forgo any transparent relationship to the reality it represents, and to make evident the knowledge claims on which it is based. (2000: 8)

This hybridity has been an important feature of many Latin American works in recent years — from Albertina Carri's autofictional documentary *Los rubios* (2003) and her later semi-autobiographical fiction film, with its incorporation of a variety of mixed media, *La rabia* (2008), through to Gustavo Fontán's use of intervened found material in his 2008 *La orilla que se abisma* (a film, after all, partly about the life of the poet Juan L. Ortiz) or his incorporation of his family home and relatives in *El árbol* (2006) and *La casa* (2012). One might also cite the Brazilian Eduardo Coutinho's films, in particular *Jogo de cena* (2007), with its understated yet at times unsettling blending of film documentary, theatrical performance, and anthropological research.

In her study, *Mundos en común*, Florencia Garramuño analyses what she identifies as a recent trend toward *non-specific* art. Her corpus includes Brazilian contemporary installation art, poetry from Argentina, the prose of Clarice Lispector, and a series of multi-media art works, including that of Jorge Macchi, for example his *Buenos Aires Tour* (2004), which incorporated intervened maps, texts, sound, visuals, and chance actions such as shooting a pane of glass. Garramuño argues that such works call into question ideas of belonging, pertinence, individuality and specificity in art. They do not belong to a specific genre, and through breaking with ideas of suitable forms and sites for particular types of work, strike a connection to both spectator/reader and the wider world, calling for a move from aesthetic to ethical considerations of art: 'abriendo un espacio en el que lo común, lo en común y la comunidad se definen ya no por esencias compartidas o características propias — específicas — , sino por la apertura de ese espacio hacia lo otro de sí mismo' [opening a space in which the common, the in-common, and community are defined now not by shared essences or their own — specific — characteristics, but by the openness of that space towards its other] (Garramuño 2015: 155).

In response to Garramuño's assertions, above, with regard to a tendency to non-specificity in contemporary Latin American art, Jens Andermann comments thus on Santiago Mitre and Juan Onofri's *Los posibles* (2013):

> the film transforms the 'original' spectacle into something else by bringing into the equation the essential elements of cinematic language, such as frame composition, depth of field, camera movement, and so forth. Different from the audience point of view of the original dance production, the camera literally takes to the stage, almost — but not quite — becoming yet another of the dancers swirling around one another, touching, clashing and separating again. But this intermediate position of the cinematic apparatus vis-à-vis the dance troupe is key here, as not quite another member of the ensemble yet also no longer merely an external viewer, and thus also held in the balance between 'documentation' and 'adaptation', between cinema as register of something else and as the medium of the latter's recreation. (2018)

Los posibles messes up our conceptions of what we are seeing: what looks like a rehearsal cannot be, with the camera in amongst the dancers; and the filming records a performance that took place *after* the original theatrical run of Onofri's dance work. The film plays with notions of time, genre, and the documentary function of film. It raises again, too, the important question of medium specificity:

in a work that seems to refuse to occupy a particular genre or form, analytical tools drawn from film and dance, which reference specific features of these forms, are nevertheless required for detailed analytical work. The capacious, promiscuous nature of film is key to many of the works analysed in this volume; but the existence of particular features that characterize film and poetry is central to this analysis.

The Poetry–Film Nexus in Theory and Practice

The chapters in this volume range across the length of Latin America and span almost its entire filmic history, from proto- and early cinematography to films from the 2010s. The corpus is as varied as the time-frame is extensive, including early silent cinema and what is often called 'pre-cinema'; experimental works of the avant-gardes; political cinema from the 1960s; and recent projects, from independent shorts through to big-budget productions. The chapters are united in their exploration of what we have called the 'poetry–film nexus', but their subject matter and methodological approaches are richly diverse. Aesthetic and technical questions around the presence of poetry on screen abound; with it are ethical debates around the filmmaker's relationship to the material being employed. What is more, a number of the pieces note the urgent political issues addressed in poetry-films and raised by directors who screen poetry.

Two pieces focus on some of the earliest cinematic tendencies in the region. Chrystian Zegarra offers a pioneering reading of the work of the Peruvian poet José María Eguren and its engagements with the earliest forms of cinema. Eguren is widely regarded, along with César Vallejo, as the founder of modern poetry in Peru, a bridge between late Spanish-American *modernismo* and the twentieth-century avant-gardes. Zegarra adds a new angle to readings of Eguren: his engagement in two collections from the 1910s with early cinema, via Gunning's influential concept of the 'cinema of attractions'; and studies of cinema and magic including Solomon's work on the 'film trick' and 'up-to-date-magic'. Eguren can thus be seen as a pathbreaker for the 'cinematic' poetry of the 1920s and beyond (Oquendo de Amat, Abril, Westphalen), drawing on the technical feats of early cinema pioneers, such as Méliès, Guy, or Chomón, to feed the original design of his poetry.

Nicolás Suárez similarly focuses on the legacy of turn-of-the-century and early twentieth-century literature and film, specifically the figure of Faust as reimagined in Argentina within the *gauchesca* or *criollista* tradition. From the seminal literary reworking of the Faust legend by Estanislao del Campo in 1866, Suárez reads through a series of its film incarnations, *Fausto* (1922), by Ernesto Gunche y Eduardo Martínez de la Pera; *El Fausto criollo* (1979), by Luis Saslavsky; and *El Fausto criollo* (2011), by Fernando Birri. The gaucho is one of the most keenly contested and politicized figures in Argentine literary culture; curiously, in all three cases, their rendering of Faust was the director or directors' last film. Suárez thus mixes considerations of political cinema with questions of 'late style' (Adorno, Said) to offer a historical reading of the development of the gaucho figure and the long afterlife of del Campo's poem.

Erica Segre's piece moves the volume into mid-century explorations of the legacy of the avant-gardes, in both film and poetry. While Mexico's Juan Rulfo is rightly famous for his prose fiction, little attention has been paid to his poetry, and still less to a filmic adaptation of his poem 'La fórmula secreta', by the Mexican filmmaker Rubén Gámez, in a reading by the poet Jaime Sabines. Segre examines the experimental assemblage of free verse and cinematographic aesthetics, which allows Gámez to reconceive film as a discrepant instrument of altered and haunted vision, capable of unlocking what Luis Buñuel called 'the liberating world of poetry'. Rulfo himself qualified the film as an 'ANTI-film [...] anti everything', including lyric poetry itself, depersonalized and redeployed in Gámez's provocative and dizzying work.

The Brazilian filmmaker and theorist Carlos Adriano adds a unique perspective on the poetry–film nexus through his exploration of the poetics of found-footage films, drawing on a series of philosophical reflections on questions of recycling, collage and reuse, including the Brazilian Anthropophagist (or Cannibalist) Manifesto, while at the same time analysing his own practice as a filmmaker. With an approach that mirrors Adriano's magpie-like enthusiasm for found material, he offers, if not an exhaustive theory of this particular 'subgenre', then a series of historical and aesthetic hypotheses that demonstrate how found footage is a singular field of poetic operation in cinema and how the found-footage 'cine-poet' can create artistic 'constellations' from the encounter between visual and sonic material and the written word.

Two of the pieces look at more commercially minded productions, but nevertheless highlight the destabilizing work that poetry can carry out and the unsettling aesthetic results for the viewer. Eduardo Paredes Ocampo examines two films by the Mexican director Guillermo del Toro, with a specific focus on the use of narration within his modern-day reworkings of the fantasy ghost story and the fairy tale. Paredes's narratological approach enables a thorough unpicking of del Toro's use of narrators in the films' prologues and epilogues. Both *The Devil's Backbone* and *The Shape of Water* draw on poems, converting the narrator into a poet in a gesture that not only tests the formal constraints of the (literary) genre but also expands the limited language of the media in question. The narration offers not only a self-referential reflection on the nature and possibilities of cinema, but also a poetic means of incorporating undecidability and ambiguity into otherwise more conventional screen narratives, with the poet, the ghost, and the monster working together to destabilize our understanding of the stories we are told.

Adam Feinstein is renowned as Pablo Neruda's biographer, and as such was closely involved in the development of Pablo Larraín's film of the Chilean poet's life, in particular the latter's dramatic escape from political persecution in the late 1940s. Feinstein's piece draws on more traditional adaptation- or fidelity-studies approaches to ask: can the dangers of artistic freedom with a real life sometimes prove greater than the perils of excessive reverence to the facts of a biography? If Larraín happily accepts the 'anti-realist' moniker — despite a trilogy of films exploring some of the darkest moments of Chilean history — does he make too many sacrifices in his effort to employ the poetry of cinematic language to create a Borgesian meta-fictional labyrinth? Feinstein's close reading of the historical tweaks and tricks played by *Neruda* allows a broader exploration of Larraín's aesthetics and engagement with the history of poetic cinema, in particular the strong presence of Andrei Tarkovsky's work and ideas, not least the Russian's very personal take on poetry as a non-linguistic or non-verbal substrate of artistic creation.

Several of the chapters in this volume address more directly political or even activist filmmaking. Camila Gatica explores the work of Sergio Bravo, one of the most productive members (and founders) of the Cine-Club of the Universidad de Chile. From 1956 onwards Bravo enjoyed a fruitful career making short documentaries that focused on everyday elements of popular culture; but one particular film, *Láminas de Almahue* (1961), a documentary about the construction of the titular rims of cart wheels in a rural Chilean town, employs a poem by Efraín Barquero to voice a sense of 'the popular' that was central to both the New Chilean Cinema of the 1960s and Bravo's own political filmmaking. Like Bravo, Barquero often used items from the popular world as his inspiration; thus *Láminas de Almahue* brought together Bravo and Barquero's interest in Chilean national culture, giving depth to the circularity (and physicality) of the images through the poet's words. Gatica explores what she calls 'the cinematographic poetics' of Sergio Bravo, understanding *Láminas de Almahue* as the centre of Bravo's attempt to find in poetry a corollary for his exploration of popular culture in Chile.

Irina Garbatzky explores the legacy of 1960s New Latin American Cinema in Jesús Díaz's documentary film *Cincuentaicinco hermanos* (1978). Díaz's film and accompanying book explore the lives and experiences of a group of Cuban exiles who had left as children for the USA in the wake of the Revolution and returned to the island with the blessing of its government in the 1970s as part of a radical activist group known as the Antonio Maceo Brigade. Garbatzky combines a consideration of the poetic mode of documentary filmmaking (*pace* Bill Nichols) with an exploration of the iconic figure of José Martí, whose own poetic rendering of exile and dreams of return, in an earlier and very different political context, informs Díaz's film.

Ben Bollig's piece looks at the question of how to screen the life of a poet, via two very different projects: María Luisa Bemberg's 1990 biopic about the seventeenth-century Mexican poet-nun Sor Juana Inés de la Cruz and Nicolás Pereda's 2009 fragmented and playful screening of a performance based on Sor Juana's important long poem, *Primero sueño*, by the activist and theatre-practitioner Jesusa Rodríguez. While Bemberg's film employs a series of intermedial techniques and genre-bending references — baroque portraiture, Golden Age theatre, other contemporary films — to make a feminist point about the life of Sor Juana, Pereda's aesthetic of failure, a ludic variant on so-called 'contemporary contemplative' or 'slow' cinema, uses Sor Juana's work as the basis for an urgently political interrogation of activism and feminism in contemporary Mexico.

Jessica Wax-Edwards similarly explores a highly necessary intervention into contemporary Mexican politics with her analysis of two stylistically divergent films centred on the Movement for Peace with Justice and Dignity, a civil protest movement founded by the Mexican poet and essayist Javier Sicilia who, after the murder of his son Juan Francisco as a direct result of drug war violence, announced his 'retirement' from poetry and convened a massive protest march against the violence, as well as rallies across the country. The first of the films, a PBS documentary entitled *El poeta* (Kelly Duane de la Vega and Katie Galloway, 2012) follows Sicilia on his journey across Mexico, in an experiential and often visually poetic representation of the poet/activist, despite its largely conventional TV documentary format; a visually poetic register co-exists with the traditional didactic mode of expository documentary. Sicilia's final poem, as well as his personal struggle, form the basis for the second film, Pablo Orta's short *El hijo del poeta* (2012). Here the relationship between poetry and violence is interrogated through a form of visually poetic filmmaking. Despite its brevity, its topic of representation is ambitious as well as pertinent to Mexico's current crisis. In both visual texts the titular poet constitutes a 'microcosmic node' where the effects of sustained national violence and collective loss intersect. Wax-Edwards explores the characterization of the poet figure onscreen in both documentary and fiction narratives and examines the capacity of poetic language (both visual and verbal) to contend with violence and trauma.

The variety of poetic and filmic techniques on display in these analyses is testament to the vibrancy and dynamism of the poetry–film nexus in Latin America. It is also striking that from what may seem initially purely aesthetic concerns, many of the pieces move into questions of ethics and politics, highly revealing of the cultural context in contemporary Latin America. The authors demonstrate that an awareness of the multiple ways in which engagements between screen and page may blur the limits between the two forms does not preclude close readings and analyses that are sensitive to the — always historicizable — specificities of film and poetry. Implicitly they trace, too, connections in theme, method, and forms of political engagement, across the region and over the length of the film century, and beyond. The poetry–film nexus defines a constellation of artistic practices that creatively explore, exploit, and at times explode, the connected and multiple resources of image, sound and text.

Works Cited

ABRAMS, M. H. 1993. *A Glossary of Literary Terms* (Fort Worth, TX: Harcourt Brace Jovanovich)

AGUILAR, GONZALO. 2008. *New Argentine Cinema: Other Worlds* (New York: Palgrave Macmillan)

ANDERMANN, JENS. 2018. 'Argentine Cinema after the New: Territories, Languages, Medialities', *Senses of Cinema*, 89 <http://sensesofcinema.com/2018/latin-american-cinema-today/argentine-cinema-after-the-new-territories-languages-medialities> [accessed 16 June 2020]

BAZIN, ANDRÉ. 1967. *What Is Cinema?*, vol. 1 (London: University of California Press)

BELLOUR, RAYMOND. 2018. 'Arrested Images and "the Between-Images"', in *Raymond Bellour: Cinema and the Moving Image*, ed. by Hilary Radner and Alistair Fox (Edinburgh: Edinburgh University Press), pp. 130–44

BERG, WALTER BRUNO. 2002. 'Literatura y cine: nuevos enfoques del concepto de inter-medialidad', *Iberoamericana*, 2: 127–41

BOLLIG, BEN. 2012. 'Filming Fierro: Aesthetics and Politics in Film Adaptations of National-Epic Poetry', *New Cinemas: Journal of Contemporary Film*, 10: 63–80

—— and DAVID M. J. WOOD. 2014. 'Film-Poetry/Poetry-Film in Latin America. Theories and Practices: An Introduction', *Studies in Spanish and Latin American Cinemas*, 11.2: 115–25

BUÑUEL, LUIS. 1958. 'El cine, instrumento de poesía', *Revista de la Universidad de México*, 13: 1–2; 15

CANUDO, RICCIOTTO. 2014 [1911]. 'The Birth of the Sixth Art', in *Film Manifestos and Global Cinema Cultures: A Critical Anthology*, ed. by Scott MacKenzie (Berkeley: University of California Press), pp. 595–603

CERESA, CONSTANZA. 2014. 'Velocidad y desorientación en *Punctum* de Martín Gambarotta y *Silvia Prieto* de Martín Rejtman', *Studies in Spanish & Latin American Cinemas*, 11.2: 179–91

CLAYTON, MICHELLE. 2012. *Poetry in Pieces: César Vallejo and Lyric Modernity* (London: University of California Press)

COCTEAU, JEAN. 1985. *Two Screenplays: The Blood of a Poet. The Testament of Orpheus* (London: Marion Boyars)

—— 1994. *The Art of Cinema*, ed. by André Bernard and Claude Gauteur (London: Marion Boyars)

—— 2015. *Poética del cine* (Buenos Aires: El cuenco de plata)

COLERIDGE, SAMUEL TAYLOR, HENRY NELSON COLERIDGE, and WILLIAM PICKERING. 1836. *The Literary Remains of Samuel Taylor Coleridge*, vol. IV (London: William Pickering)

D'ARGENIO, MARIA CHIARA. 2014. 'A Poetic *cine urgente*: Experimentalism and Revolution in Santiago Álvarez's Documentary Films', *Studies in Spanish & Latin American Cinemas*, 11.2: 127–45

—— 2015. 'Modernidad, escritura nueva y cine mudo en el Perú', in *Cine mudo latino-americano: inicios, nación, vanguardias y transición*, ed. by Aurelio de los Reyes and David M. J. Wood (Mexico City: Instituto de Investigaciones Estéticas-UNAM), pp. 191–207

DELGADO MOYA, SERGIO. 2017. *Delirious Consumption: Aesthetics and Consumer Capitalism in Mexico and Brazil* (Austin: University of Texas Press)

EISENSTEIN, SERGEI. 1949. *Film Form: Essays in Film Theory*, ed. by J. Leyda (London: Dennis Dobson)

—— 2014 [1937–41]. *El Greco, cineasta*, ed. by François Albera (Barcelona: Intermedio)

EPSTEIN, JEAN. 2012 [1926]. 'On Certain Characteristics of *Photogénie*', in *Jean Epstein: Critical Essays and New Translations*, ed. by Sarah Keller and Jason N. Paul (Amsterdam: Amsterdam University Press), pp. 292–96

GARRAMUÑO, FLORENCIA. 2015. *Mundos en común: ensayos sobre la inespecificidad en el arte* (Buenos Aires: Fondo de Cultura Económica)

GOLDBERG, ROSALEE. 2011 [1979]. *Performance Art: From Futurism to the Present* (London: Thames and Hudson)

GONZÁLEZ DE CANALES CARCERENY, JÚLIA. 2017. 'Japón, de Carlos Reygadas, y el haiku: poesía hecha cine', in *Ficciones nómadas: procesos de intermedialidad literaria y audiovisual*, ed. by José Antonio Pérez Bowie and Antonio Jesús Gil González (Madrid: Pigmalión Edypro), pp. 117–39

—— 2019. 'Repensar la categoría de cine poético como propuesta estética transversal en la obra fílmica de Carlos Reygadas y Lisandro Alonso', *Hispanic Research Journal*, 20.3: 272–88

VON HAGEN, KIRSTEN. 2006. Review of *Intermedialidad e hispanística*, ed. by Angelica Rieger, *Iberoamericana*, 6.21: 242–43

HEIDEGGER, MARTIN. 2001 [1960]. 'The Origin of the Work of Art', in *Poetry, Language, Thought* (New York: HarperCollins), pp. 17–86

HIGGINS, DICK. 1984. *Horizons: The Poetics and Theory of the Intermedia* (Carbondale: Southern Illinois University Press)

KANT, IMMANUEL. 2008 [1790]. *Critique of Judgement* (Oxford: Oxford University Press)

KATTENBELT, CHIEL. 2008. 'Intermediality in Theatre and Performance: Definitions, Perceptions and Medial Relationships', *Revista de estudios culturales de la Universitat Jaume I*, 6: 19–29

KOHEN, HÉCTOR, and SEBASTIÁN RUSSO (eds). 2017. *Los condenados: Pasolini en América Latina* (Buenos Aires: Nulú Bonsai)

KOZAK, CLAUDIA. 2018. 'Poesía experimental y tecnología: afinidades electivas en contextos digitales', in *Historia crítica de la literatura argentina*, vol. XII: *Una literatura en aflicción*, ed. by Jorge Monteleone (Buenos Aires: Emecé), pp. 551–79

KUENZLI, RUDOLF E. 2007. 'Man Ray's Films: From Dada to Surrealism', in *Avant-Garde Film*, ed. by Alexander Graf and Dietrich Scheunemann (Amsterdam, New York: Rodopi), pp. 93–104

LARRAÍN, CAROLINA. 2009. '11 de septiembre de 1973: trauma, testimonio y liberación a través del cine documental', *Comunicación y medios*, 20: 58–72

LESSING, G. E. 1930. *Laocoön* (London: Dent)

MAAS, WILLARD. 1963. 'Poetry and the Film: A Symposium', *Film Culture*, 29: 55–63 <http://www.ubu.com/papers/poetry_film_symposium.html>

MACCABE, C., R. WARNER, and K. MURRAY. 2011. *True to the Spirit: Film Adaptation and the Question of Fidelity* (Oxford: Oxford University Press)

MARKS, LAURA. 2000. *The Skin of the Film* (London: Duke University Press)

MARTINS, LAURA M. 2014. 'Contra la museificación del mundo: *La orilla que se abisma* (2008) y *La casa* (2012) de Gustavo Fontán', *Studies in Spanish & Latin American Cinemas*, 11.2: 167–77

MEYER, SABINE. 2019. '"Poetry [Film] = Anger × Imagination": Intermediality, the Synthesis of Poetry and Film, and Cross-Cultural Belonging in Sherman Alexie's *The Business of Fancydancing*', *The American Indian Quarterly*, 43: 36–73

MIQUEL, ANGEL. 2015. *Entrecruzamientos: cine, historia y literatura en México, 1910–1960* (Cuernavaca, Mexico City: Universidad Autónoma del Estado de Morelos, Ficticia)

MITCHELL, W. J. T. 2005. *What Do Pictures Want? The Lives and Loves of Images* (Chicago, IL: Chicago University Press)

MÜLLER, ADALBERTO. 2014. 'Manoel de Barros in Film: The Nature of Language and the Language of Nature', *Studies in Spanish & Latin American Cinemas*, 11.2: 193–202

NAGIB, LÚCIA, and ANNE JERSLEV. 2014. *Impure Cinema: Intermedial and Intercultural Approaches to Film* (London: I. B. Tauris)

Pasolini, Pier Paolo. 1976 [1965]. 'The Cinema of Poetry,' in *Movies and Methods*, vol. 1, ed. by Bill Nichols (Berkeley: University of California Press), 542–58

Paz, Octavio. 1967. *El arco y la lira* (Mexico City: Fondo de Cultura Económica)

Preminger, Alex, and T. V. F. Brogan. 1993. *The New Princeton Encyclopedia of Poetry and Poetics* (Princeton, NJ: Princeton University Press)

Prieto, Julio. 2017. 'El concepto de la intermedialidad: una reflexion histórico-crítica', *Pasavento*, 5: 7–18

Rajewsky, Irina O. 2005. 'Intermediality, Intertextuality, and Remediation: A Literary Perspective on Intermediality', *Intermédialités*, 6: 43–64

Rhodes, John David. 2010. 'Pasolini's Exquisite Flowers: The "Cinema of Poetry" as a Theory of Art Cinema', in *Global Art Cinema*, ed. by Rosalind Galt and Karl Schoonover (Oxford & New York: Oxford University Press), pp. 142–63

Rodowick, D. N. 2007. *The Virtual Life of Film* (Cambridge, MA, & London: Harvard University Press)

Rosen, Philip. 2014. 'From Impurity to Historicity', in *Impure Cinema: Intermedial and Intercultural Approaches to Film* (London: I. B. Tauris), pp. 3–20

Rowe, William. 2000. *Poets of Contemporary Latin America: History and the Inner Life* (Oxford: Oxford University Press)

Sitney, P. Adams. 2015. *The Cinema of Poetry* (New York: Oxford University Press)

Speranza, Robert Scott. 2002. 'Verses in Celluloid: Poetry in Film Form 1910–2002, with Special Attention to the Development of the Film-Poem' (unpublished Ph.D. thesis, University of Sheffield)

Stam, Robert. 2000. *Film Theory: An Introduction* (Malden, MA, & Oxford: Blackwell)

——— 2005. *Literature and Film: A Guide to the Theory and Practice of Film Adaptation* (Oxford: Blackwell)

Suárez, Nicolás. 2018. '¿Gauchos de bronce o de yeso? La martinfierrización de Juan Moreira en *El último centauro* (Enrique Queirolo, 1924)', *Vivomatografías. Revista de estudios sobre precine y cine silente en Latinoamérica*, 4: 64–87

Tarkovsky, Andrey. 2017 [1986]. *Sculpting in Time: The Great Russian Filmmaker Discusses his Art* (Austin: University of Texas Press)

Tynyanov, Yuri. 1982. 'The Fundamentals of Cinema', in *The Poetics of Cinema*, ed. by Richard Taylor, Russian Poetics in Translation, 9 (Oxford: Holdan Books), pp. 32–54

Vázquez Mantecón, Álvaro. 2015. 'Narrativa y poesía en el cine experimental mexicano: *La fórmula secreta* (1965), *Anticlímax* (1969) y *La segunda primera matriz* (1972)', *Istor: revista de historia internacional*, 16: 127–40

Verstraete, Ginette. 2010. 'Intermedialities: A Brief Survey of Conceptual Key Issues', *Acta Universitatis Sapientiae. Film and Media Studies*, 2: 7–14

Walley, Jonathan. 2011. 'Identity Crisis: Experimental Film and Artistic Expansion', *October*, 137: 23–50

Wood, David M. J. 2014. 'Nadaísmo on Film: Violence, Originality and the Archive in *Paraíso* (2006)', *Studies in Spanish & Latin American Cinemas*, 11.2: 147–65

Zaidenwerg, Ezequiel. 2018. *50 Estados. 13 poetas contemporáneos de Estados Unidos* (Buenos Aires: Bajo la luna)

Notes to the Introduction

1. It is interesting to see the resonance of this special issue away from Latin American studies: see, for example, Meyer (2019), with its attempt to 'analyze the practices of intermediality in *The Business of Fancydancing*, that is, the conjunction of poetry and film through adaptation, intermedial referencing, and media combination' (36). The article also includes a useful overview of the 'poetry film' in the USA.

2. Final ellipses in original.

3. All English translations of non-English-language sources are our own unless stated otherwise.

4. Original emphasis.

5. Italics in original.

6. Italics in original.

7. Italics in original.

8. Although Man Ray considered *Emak-Bakia* a surrealist film, his surrealist colleagues disagreed, classifying it as a Dadaist piece; see Kuenzli (2007: 96–100).

9. Cocteau refers here to the work of George M. and John Ernest Williamson, pioneers of submarine cinematography with movies such as *Thirty Leagues Under the Sea* (1914).

10. It is worth noting the virulent rejection that Deren was subjected to by the poet Dylan Thomas and the playwright Arthur Miller during the same roundtable discussion, who dismissed Deren's ideas as an excessively complex pontification on what they saw as a relatively straightforward discussion.

11. Italics in original.

CHAPTER 1

❖

José María Eguren:
The 'Cinema of Attractions' and
Modern Peruvian Poetry[1]

Chrystian Zegarra

In this chapter, I examine the work of José María Eguren from an intermedial perspective, namely, by looking at the relationship between early cinema (*c.* 1895–1907) and poetry. In doing so, I rely on Tom Gunning's notion of the 'cinema of attractions' as well as the connection between cinema and magic that early filmmakers developed through a method called 'trick film'. I see this analytical framework as especially productive because of the stylistic similarities between Eguren's poetry and both this theory and this practice. These 'attractions' tend to focus more on the spectacle of the presentation instead of a well-thought-out plot. Likewise, Eguren's poetry emphasizes the apparently arbitrary movements of people and objects and de-emphasizes narrative development. Additionally, his innovative poetic works skilfully seized on the tricks and technical contributions of some of the most renowned filmmakers of his time, like Georges Méliès and Segundo de Chomón. My analysis should further secure Eguren's place as a founder of the twentieth-century Peruvian poetic tradition and pioneer of the 'cinematic' poetry that flourished in the 1920s and 1930s.

Symbolism and the Modern Poetry of José María Eguren

José María Eguren (b. Lima 1874; d. Lima 1942) is widely considered one of the founders of modern poetry in Peru. For example, Núñez (1961: 220) has stated that Eguren gave new musical and syntagmatic dimensions to Peruvian poetic expression. Monguió (1954: 17) has called Eguren's poetry an axis of transition between the *modernista* inheritance of Rubén Darío, whose exoticism Eguren emulated on numerous occasions,[2] and the search for more personal and deeply rooted literary forms. Critics tend to credit Eguren's uniqueness to his fondness for French symbolism. For example, Anchante (2012: 227) has interpreted his work as an original take on the symbolist tradition of Baudelaire, Rimbaud, Mallarmé and Verlaine. Spikes (1966: 228) has noted that Eguren, like the French poets, avoids realistic topics, rejects traditional lyrical formulae, incorporates Orientalist elements and emphasizes subtle and suggestive atmospheres. To Lefort (2016: 186), there is a continental dimension to Eguren's symbolism that makes him unique not only within the Peruvian literary field but also within Latin American poetry more broadly. Areta Marigó (1993: 44) has argued that Eguren used this symbolist approach to move Peruvian poetry beyond the *modernista* domain: a movement that would come to its definitive conclusion with the work of César Vallejo. And Bernabé (2006: 165) has emphasized that Eguren's poetry, in overcoming the legacy of *modernismo*, can be seen as an antecedent of early twentieth-century avant-garde movements.

Beginning with his first and highly influential poetry collection *Simbólicas* [Symbolisms] (1911),[3] Eguren creates a poetic universe almost without parallel in Peruvian poetry of the era.[4] He populates this universe with enigmatic, ghostlike characters that erase the distinction between reality and imagination, carving out desolate spaces where strange and inexplicable events take place. Eguren's poetry has therefore been described as difficult, even impenetrable. While Debarbieri (1990: 26) locates this difficulty in the lack of lexical clarity that the texts convey, Higgins (1973: 60) believes that it is the result of a poetic voice that shows no interest in clarifying the events and themes described, leaving all interpretative work to the reader. According to Higgins, 'it is the characters themselves who, by the manner of their presentation, evoke the hidden world behind the poem' (1973: 60).

Critics have taken different approaches to the question of the social or political meaning of Eguren's poetry. Rebaza-Soraluz (1993: 108) has described Eguren's lyrical method as hermetic, such that the poem refers only to itself and is disconnected from any universe beyond the text. Yet, while most critics have focused on the internal elements of his poems,[5] Vich (2013: 366) has recently conducted a political reading that tries to reveal the social critique that Eguren's poetry contains. Furthermore, to Vich (2013: 374), the Peruvian poet's recurrent ghostly characters reflect the fact that the present is always a moment full of tension, and it is constantly hounded by the ghosts of the past. Similarly, Bernabé (2006: 185–86) has convincingly uncovered various social meanings beneath the apparently apolitical fabric of Eguren's work, arguing that the strange experience of reading his poems requires the reader to pay full attention, in contrast to an alienating and superficial reality that denies literature its full artistic value.[6] These critics have thus added new layers to the traditional view of Eguren as a prolific creator of enchanted scenarios that had no relevance to the broader context of his time.

In this chapter, I take the following words from Vich as a guide:

> Si tanto Eguren como Vallejo son considerados hoy los fundadores de la poesía contemporánea en el Perú debemos preguntarnos qué es lo nuevo que generaron y cuáles fueron los cambios que introdujeron frente a los lenguajes poéticos en curso. (2013: 365)

> [If both Eguren and Vallejo are today considered the founders of contemporary poetry in Peru, we must ask what they created that was new and what changes they introduced in existing poetic languages.]

I want to answer this question by demonstrating that the novelty of Eguren's poetics lies in the incorporation of late nineteenth- and early twentieth-century cinematic techniques into his literary universe. By emphasizing the intersection of different expressive media, I approach Eguren's texts as products of intermedial considerations, as Torres (2012: 142) has put it.

Photography and the Tiny Life of Toys

Before looking at the correlation between Eguren's poetry and cinema, I want to consider the fact that he was a passionate photographer. Silva-Santisteban (2005: cvii) has observed that more than any of his contemporaries in Peru, Eguren experimented with photography: a medium that, along with the cinematic image, he recognized as one of the greatest possibilities for artistic expression in his time. Núñez (1961: 207) has described a wooden camera, the approximate size of a cork and with an adapted lens, that Eguren built. Silva-Santisteban (2005: cvi) has noted that the poet used this apparatus to take hundreds of miniature images of less than three centimetres in length.[7] A number of these photographs feature dolls, alone or with other objects.

This penchant for smallness is also evident in the author's literary work. In one of his *Motivos estéticos* [Aesthetic Motifs] (a series of prose poems on a variety of artistic topics) titled 'Paisaje mínimo' [Minimal Landscape], Eguren describes his search for '[u]n paisaje filosófico que surge de lo infinitamente pequeño y cuyo postulado está contenido en una línea' [a philosophical landscape that arises from the infinitely small and whose postulate is contained in one line] (2005: 315). The most striking literary expression of this desire is the recurring representation of dolls, puppets and other toys.[8] 'Paisaje mínimo' vividly recalls a revealing episode from the author's childhood:

> jugaba en una baranda con mis carritos de hojalata pintados de rojo, amarillo y azul, llenos de paseantes de madera. [...] Yo rodaba mis juguetes con la ilusión de que la baranda larga y clara iba a la ciudad distante donde jugaban niñas y niños, y olvidaba mi paseo real, pues mi camino me parecía encantado. (2005: 312–13)

> [I played on a railing with my tin trolleys that were painted red, yellow and blue, and full of wooden people. [...] I rolled my toys, pretending that the long, straight railing led to a far-away city where girls and boys played, and I forgot where I really was, because my path was enchanted to me.]

At first glance, this anecdote seems like the work of a children's writer. Critics of Eguren's generation, however, were quick to note that the poet used childhood and children's games as a microcosm of human life with all its struggles and challenges.[9] For example, 'Paisaje mínimo' declares: 'Los juguetes son una simulación liliputiense de la vida' [Toys are a Lilliputian simulation of life] (Eguren 2005: 312). The poem 'El paraíso de Liliput' [Lilliput Paradise] from *Sombra* represents the perfection and subsequent loss of Eden in a miniaturized scene in which 'Adán y Eva primorosa, | nacieron en nítida rosa' [Dainty Adam and Eve, | were born clear and pink] (Eguren 2005: 122). Going beyond the surface of the texts, Basadre (1929: 26–27) has read in these poems a sense of frustration at the ephemerality of childhood and the inevitable loss of innocence. And according to the characteristically insightful Mariátegui: 'Eguren does not understand or know capitalist, bourgeois, occidental civilization. He is interested only in its colossal playthings' (1971: 245). Bernabé (2006: 180), in agreement with this observation, has suggested an anti-capitalist reading; by taking the toys out of the market, Eguren eliminates their exchange value and frees them from the role of mere merchandise. Thus, according to Bernabé (2006: 198), the fascination for toys establishes new relationships, outside of the economic domain, between the poet and objects, creating a model of cognition based on the trinket that serves as the foundation of Eguren's poetic world.

The poem that best and most profoundly demonstrates this use of children's games is 'Marcha fúnebre de una marionnette' [Funeral March of a Marionette] from *Simbólicas*. The text describes the funeral of a wooden doll who, surrounded by an aristocratic cortege and to the tune of solemn chords, travels to her tomb in a hearse.[10] A little girl named Paquita organizes the procession, moving the toys with a dual feeling of sadness and joy. The playful nature of the scene becomes more complicated when the poetic voice turns melancholy: 'vuelan goces de la infancia, | los amores incipientes, los que nunca han de durar' [the joys of childhood fly away, | the incipient loves that can never last] (Eguren 2005: 7). The poem comments on the fragility of love and childhood joy, and Paquita's simultaneous dancing and weeping represent the dual nature of the human experience. 'Lurking in the background of the marvelous is an ever-present threat; but the ominous, as in a childhood nightmare, is often mixed with amusement at the macabre and grotesque' (Rodríguez-Peralta 1973: 224). 'El duque' [The Duke], from the same volume, again makes reference to children's games, but this time the dolls are made out of nuts ('duque Nuez' [Duke Nut]) and spices ('la hija de Clavo de Olor' [the daughter of Clove Spice]). The poem describes the imaginary but festive and sophisticated wedding of these two characters, an event that puts bourgeois purchasing power on full display. The bride, however, is left waiting for her groom in the church because Paquita, the same little girl from the prior poem, 'se lo ha comido' [has eaten him up] (Eguren 2005: 40). Because both of these poems, and many others, feature characters from the dominant social classes, Eguren appears to be sharply criticizing the frivolity of the wealthy. To Areta Marigó (1993: 59), these representations of the bourgeoisie are a caricature of their excessive economic power.[11]

In the cinematic universe, a number of filmmakers shared Eguren's fascination with dolls and children's games. The French cartoonist Émile Cohl produced the first animated film, *Fantasmagorie*, in 1908. And the Spanish director Segundo de Chomón made dozens of movies with dolls as protagonists. In one of these, *Le Théâtre de Bob* [Miniature Theatre] (1906), three children invite the spectator to a four-act miniature puppet show that includes a fencing bout, a boxing match, a wrestling match and an acrobatic routine. The interactions between the children and the puppets recall Baudelaire: 'All children talk to their toys; the toys become actors in the great drama of life, scaled down inside the *camera obscura* of the childish brain'[12] (2012: 13). Dolls and puppets were also featured in early films by Cohl like

The Puppet's Nightmare, Drama at the Puppet's House, The Little Soldier Who Became a God (all from 1908) and *Le Petit Chantecler* (1910), in which a series of animal puppets come alive onscreen.

Eguren wrote about the relationship between poetry and technology, and especially the reproducible dimension of photography, in the *Motivo* 'Filosofía del objetivo' [Philosophy of the Camera Lens] (2005: 318). He declares that nature's essence is its ability to reproduce itself through a mysterious dualism of contradictory terms like body and soul, subject and object, life and death. In other words, these binaries allow nature to come into full existence and the universe to maintain harmony. Eguren continues, asserting that photography is a means for capturing the spirituality of natural elements: 'El retrato artístico es una afirmación y una vivencia; se llega a retratar la Naturaleza y el espíritu por medio de ella y por la magia del arte' [The artistic portrait is an affirmation and an experience; one portrays Nature and her spirit through her and the magic of art] (2005: 318). And yet Eguren (2005: 319) recognizes a relative disadvantage of photography, in that it lacks cinema's power to create an illusion of movement, an illusion that recalls the unceasing dynamism of life. In what follows, I examine the intermedial connection between Eguren's poetry and the cinema of attractions that dominated film prior to the emergence of narrative cinema around 1908.

Up-to-Date Magic and the Cinema of Attractions

In practical terms, film came to Peru shortly after its near-simultaneous beginnings in the United States and France. According to Bedoya (2013: 26–31), the first public screening of Edison's Vitascope in Peru took place on 2 January 1897 at Lima's Jardín Estrasburgo; the first screening of the Lumière brothers' Cinematograph took place a month later at the same location. On both sides of the Atlantic, the novelty of cinema quickly attracted audiences. Bedoya (2013: 57–61) has pointed out that early cinematic exhibitions in Peru took place in temporary and adapted settings, usually tents, until the Cinema Teatro was built in Lima in 1910. Low ticket prices meant that members of every social class had access to the cinema (Núñez Gorritti 2010: 62). As a result, by the time Eguren published his first book of poems, in 1911, the movies were already popular everyday entertainment. Even though Gunning's theory of the cinema of attractions relates mainly to early American cinema, I believe that Eguren's poetry is related to this particular filmmaking style, which 'dominates cinema until about 1906–1907' (1986: 64). The cinematic attraction therefore gives an illusion of constant movement, and I want to posit that Eguren used the genre as a source in developing a poetry that oscillates between exhibition and concealment of people and objects. Historically, there is evidence that films from this category were shown in Lima at the end of the nineteenth century. Bedoya (2014: 305) has reported that Peruvian audiences saw films by Edison, Lumière and the great master of the genre, Méliès, in 1898. López (2000: 52) has shown that the first films to arrive in Latin America, along with the new cinematic technology, were films of attraction. In fact, during cinema's first decade, trick films were shown around the world; a single title from the French company

Pathé could reach an estimated 300 million people through an extensive network of international distributors (Solomon 2006: 606).

On the other hand, the narrative model that remains the framework of film was not consolidated until the period between 1908 and 1913, when D. W. Griffith 'bound cinematic signifiers to the narration of stories and the creation of a self-enclosed diegetic universe' (Gunning 1986: 68). Before that development, early film — the cinema of attractions — was highly exhibitionist, consciously and directly addressing the spectator with a series of images (Buckland 2006: 49). Gunning has clarified that the attraction is not an alternative visual form, that is, it is not completely opposed to a narrative scheme. Instead, its 'drive towards display' proposes a 'different configuration of spectatorial involvement' (2006: 36–37). According to Gaudreault (1983: 312), some narrative subjects were beginning to emerge in the earliest films. And yet, before 1908, film was characterized by a narrative design that articulated 'shots in a relatively discontinuous fashion', unlike the 'continuous homogeneous narrative' that marked filmic production during and after the 1910s (Gaudreault 1983: 328). In this way, an oscillation between exhibition and narration predominates in films made between 1895 and 1913, and those films that belong to a 'system of monstrative attractions'[13] rely on a 'rhetoric of display for the viewer rather than fashioning a process of narration and absorption' (Gunning 2006: 35).

Gunning (2006: 32) borrowed the term 'attraction' from the Soviet director Sergei Eisenstein, who in the 1920s developed a notion of montage that used contrary elements to shock the spectator, much like circuses and amusement parks.[14] According to Nye, these spaces of entertainment bombard visitors with sensory stimulation. The roles of spectator and participant are made interchangeable by 'Vertigo-inducing rides such as whips, Ferris wheels, swings and slides [and] roller coasters, in particular, [which] combine real speed, simulated danger and sensory disorder and relief [...] to produce the most powerful vertiginous effect of all' (1981: 73). Musser has asserted that Gunning adopted the concept of attraction to evoke 'early cinema's affinities with Coney Island and its rides that thrill, disorient, and shock those who visit these heterotopic spaces' (2006: 391).[15] Cinematic attractions — for example, the camera tricks developed by Méliès — are key elements of the films of this period. Gunning (1996: 76–77) has characterized the attraction by brevity, a discontinuous experience of time, a sudden and surprising appearance on the screen and, most importantly, an alternation between presence and absence. The attraction, unlike narration, focuses on exhibition, such that the spectator experiences time in a non-linear way. In Gunning's words: 'Rather than a developing configuration of narrative, the attraction offers a jolt of pure presence, soliciting surprise, astonishment, or pure curiosity instead of following the enigmas on which narrative depends' (1996: 81). The attraction thus constructs a temporality out of a succession of appearances and disappearances that are unrelated to mechanisms of cause and effect and the classic scheme of past, present and future. To Gunning, '[i]n this intense form of present tense, the attraction is displayed with the immediacy of a "Here it is! Look at it!"' (1996: 76).

Eguren constructs this same kind of radical temporality in his poetry. For example, 'Lied I' from *Simbólicas* configures a temporal framework that is anchored in the present. Although the text begins in the past tense ('Era el alba' [It was dawn]) and ends in the present ('Es el alba' [It is dawn]), time does not move — it remains dawn — and the poem describes a single event, the suffering of a dying tree. This pain takes on a greater dimension when anonymous characters witness it and the whole forest groans: 'y en la bruma hay rostros desconocidos | que contemplan al árbol morir' [and in the mist there are unknown faces | that watch the tree die] (Eguren 2005: 6). 'El bote viejo' [The Old Boat] from *Sombra* plays similar tricks with the passage of time. In this poem, a boat arrives alone at a beach at sunrise. Different characters — 'gaviotas' [seagulls], 'niños' [children], 'novios' [lovers] — interact with the boat until it leaves in the night: 'partió el bote muriente | a los muelles lejanos' [the dying boat departed | for distant piers] (Eguren 2005: 131). The poem does not narrate these events so much as exhibit an unreal object that appears and then disappears from a space that does not respond to the laws of time. In a similar way, film has played a key role in representing the accelerated time of modernity since the nineteenth century. According to Doane (2002: 3–4), cinematographic technology facilitated the representation, archiving and reconceptualization of time in the modern era. Film, especially narrative film, gives the impression that it continuously reproduces time in the same way that it passes in the real world. And yet, because the viewer cannot see the empty spaces between frames and the montage cuts, this temporal representation is based on a dialectic of presence and absence (Doane 2002: 172). As Doane has noted: 'Movement takes place in the interval, in the transitions *between* states, not in their accumulation'[16] (2002: 174). In the case of the early cinema connected to Eguren's poetry, time is not configured as an apparently continuous succession of images, but rather as a 'juxtaposition of autonomous tableaux' (Doane 2002: 190). Notwithstanding the so-called flicker effect[17] evident in these prenarrative films, they manage to reproduce the temporality of the era onscreen in a fairly accurate way.

In contrast to the sequential logic of later narrative cinema, the attraction follows a simple formula: 'now you see it, now you don't' (Gunning 1996: 79). Gunning (2012: 53) has connected this dynamic of appearances and disappearances of elements to the magic shows that were popular in Europe in the second half of the nineteenth century.[18] It is worth recalling that audiences initially perceived film as magical artifice.[19] According to Solomon, film studios encouraged this perception:

> At the turn of the twentieth century, every major international moving-picture manufacturer offered a selection of what were variously termed 'magic,' 'magical,' 'mysterious,' 'mystery,' 'mystical,' 'phantasmagoric,' or 'trick' subjects for sale to its clients. The many films that fall into these categories together comprise one of the most popular genres of early cinema: the trick film. (2006: 596)[20]

Moreover, Solomon (2006: 602) has crucially distinguished between the theatrical conventions of 'modern magic' — where the audience can easily differentiate between the different roles that the magician takes on — and 'up-to-date magic' — where the audience is confused by the magician's disguises and rapid metamorphoses.

In film terms, the difference between these two ways of doing magic is whether or not film tricks are used. 'Modern magic' films, which were produced in the very first years of cinema, featured magicians who performed in front of a continuously shooting camera; in contrast, in 'up-to-date magic' films, cinematic techniques share the spotlight with the magician and enhance the spectacular power of the cinematic medium (Solomon 2006: 602–03).[21] Solomon has called 'modern magic' movies 'films of tricks,' and 'up-to-date magic' movies 'trick films' (2006: 602). I prefer the experimental character of 'trick films', which have found a place in film history through the paradigm of the cinema of attractions. Their influence goes even further, however, as 'the tricks of the trick film would become integral components of the very magic of cinema, more or less seamlessly integrated into new forms of cinematic storytelling and spectacle' (Solomon 2006: 613–14).

According to Solomon (2006: 609), audiences experienced trick films much as they did magic shows, and were left intrigued as to the meaning of the successions of juxtaposed images they had seen. Eguren's poems have a similar effect on the reader, who frequently encounters inexplicable — magical — events.[22] For example, in 'La nave enferma' [The Sick Ship] from *La canción de las figuras*, a 'vapor enfermo' [sick steamship] brings foreign men to an unidentified port. They unload merchandise from sunrise to sunset and then depart forever: 'Nunca más volvieron | los desconocidos' [They never returned | those unknown men] (Eguren 2005: 73). The poem achieves what Gunning has described as an accomplishment of film: '[c]inema not only emerged in a rich context of virtual images, it interacted with magic's traditions of deceptive and playful images — within a dialectic of the visible and the invisible' (2012: 63).

These pre-cinematic traditions include phantasmagoria shows, where images were projected by magic lantern. According to Robinson (1997: 5), the Belgian magician Étienne Gaspard Robertson invented these shows, performing in revolutionary Paris with a special lantern of his invention called a phantascope. Robertson deliberately misadjusted the lens of the lantern, distorting its focus and creating a ghostly atmosphere, and he kept the apparatus in constant motion, moving it closer to and further from the screen so that the images suddenly changed size (Robinson 1997: 6). He also used two lanterns to create an effect known as 'superimposition': 'The first lantern usually provided the background, while the other was mobile, and could produce the illusion that the apparition, often a ghost or a skeleton, was moving toward the public' (Natale 2011: 137). These manipulations added a moving dimension to the images and accentuated their impact. Natale (2016: 157) states that these tricks of lantern projection and superimposition were actually adopted into early film. Thus: 'The history of superimposition is connected not only with the photographic medium but also with the projected image' (Natale 2016: 156). In this vein, for Natale (2016: 156), magic lantern projections were similarly used to project photographs that featured the trick of multiple exposure and sometimes even spirit photographs. When cinema appeared in the last five years of the nineteenth century, this moving dimension could be produced differently. While the magic lantern used mechanical techniques, cinema resorted to the physiological phenomenon of the persistence of vision, or the fact that a 'visual impression persists in the brain for a brief but determinate interval after the object which made that impression has been withdrawn, or has changed its place' (Robinson 1997: 7).

In light of early cinema, Natale (2016: 165) points out that trick films were first created by using the 'multiple exposure' technique as well as 'stop-motion' and 'substitution splicing'; when done successfully, these darkroom manipulations produced the effects of 'dissolves', 'replication of characters or objects', 'superimposition' and 'transparency'. These widely seen trick films 'were composed of a series of apparitions, transformations, and magical attractions that aimed at astonishing the spectator with the visual wonder of complex visual tricks' (Natale 2011: 140). As has been mentioned before, and following Natale (2016: 166–67), in its earliest years cinema was not so focused on plot as much as on its magical attributes and characters. Stage magicians were often the protagonists, with fairies, devils and others of the sort being supporting characters. George Albert Smith, the pioneer of the trick film, produced a movie titled *Photographing a Ghost* (1898), 'which involved the comical and unfortunate attempt of a photographer to take a picture of a spirit' (Natale 2012: 141). Smith had a background in magic lanterns, portrait photography, and stage hypnotism which helped him exploit superimposition and he eventually obtained a patent for double exposure. That is why Natale (2016: 136) concludes that the historical account of multiple exposure and superimposition, and that of the trick film for that matter, cannot be easily understood by looking at the history of photographic or filmic images alone. Rather, it would be necessary to pinpoint the developments of these techniques in the broader context of a visual culture that encompasses diverse manifestations like 'spiritualism, stage magic, magic-lantern projection, photography, and cinema' (Natale 2016: 136).

Silva-Santisteban (2005: liii) has observed that Eguren's poetic work demonstrates this same feature, namely, the introduction of mysterious and sometimes spectral characters, whose appearance is followed by their rapid eclipse once their performance is complete. This description is accurate: Eguren's poems resort time and again to this mechanism of an intense appearance followed by a hasty disappearance. A good example of this dynamic is the poem 'El caballo' [The Horse] from *La canción de las figuras*. The mysterious, haloed ghost of a horse that perished in an 'antigua batalla' [ancient battle] returns to places that it had frequented in life. It goes through a sequence of rapid actions: it arrives, it hesitates, it slips, it neighs, it stands up and it walks slowly. Rather than narrative eagerness, the text uses this un-dead image to exhibit the horrors and devastation of war, describing 'vías desiertas' [deserted streets] and 'ruinosas plazas' [destroyed squares] (Eguren 2005: 58).[23] Similarly, Vich (2013: 368) has read the poem 'Lied III' from *Simbólicas* as staging an enigmatic ritual in which the animated spirit of a sunken ship, after hearing a bell ring, rises to the surface of the ocean for an instant, and then hides itself under water again.[24] This same dynamic of presence and absence is evident in 'La Walkyria' [Valkyrie], also from *Simbólicas*. The title character appears briefly and proclaims her musical powers; her sudden arrival, her violence and her phantasmagoric qualities shock the reader: 'Yo soy la walkyria que, en tiempos guerreros | cantaba la muerte de los caballeros' [I am the Valkyrie who, in times of warriors | sang the knights to their deaths] (Eguren 2005: 22). She then leaves the scene (the verb 'caminar' [to walk] suggests her exit in this context). The fleeting span of her appearance, that is, the actions of appearing and disappearing, confine the temporal scope of the poem. 'Lied II,' from the same collection, is another example of this mechanism of appearance/disappearance characteristic of the cinema of attractions. The first two stanzas portray a calm seascape, with a gentle breeze that flutters to the rhythm of a Schumann melody. Without warning, a 'virgen nacarina' [pearlescent virgin] suddenly emerges 'desde el submarino panteón' [from the underwater pantheon]. In the last stanza, she fades and vanishes into darkness and doubt: 'Sobre ella parado un cuervo incierto | la guía en violeta navegar' [An uncertain crow stood on top of her | guiding her violet navigation] (Eguren 2005: 26). The final lines echo the ocean scene of the opening, but they allude to a sadness that results from the woman's departure. This isolated figure — 'la virgen de nácar' [the mother-of-pearl virgin] — neatly fits Eisenstein's definition of 'attraction' as 'an independent and primary element in the construction of a performance — a molecular [...] unit of effectiveness in theatre and of *theatre in general*'[25] (1974: 78). This notion of the independence and effect of the attraction allows us to foreground the very different divinities in Eguren's 'El dios cansado' [The Tired God] from *La canción de las figuras* and 'El dios de la centella' [The God of the Spark] from *Sombra*. Isolating these gods as attractions makes the contrast between them clear; the former is a sterile and discredited creator, while the latter animates and energizes the universe: '¡Mortal, despierta, mira: tras el monte | ha lanzado una estrella!' [Mortal, wake up, look: beyond the mountain | he has launched a star!] (Eguren 2005: 94).

A particularly emblematic poem, 'Los reyes rojos' [The Red Kings] from *Simbólicas*, describes two monarchs who fight from morning to night for no specified reason. The poem follows the design of an attraction in its nonlinear configuration of time, exhibiting the battle rather than relating it. Although the text suggests the passage of time through a chromatic progression of light to dark, the two enemies remain enclosed in a single scene of unexplained conflict, a circle without escape:

> Desde la aurora
> combaten dos reyes rojos,
> con lanza de oro. (Eguren 2005: 29)

> [Since daybreak
> two red kings have fought
> with golden spears.]

The poem ends, but the conflict does not:

> Viene la noche
> y firmes combaten foscos
> los reyes rojos. (Eguren 2005: 29)

> [Night falls
> and the red kings fight on
> staunch and frowning.]

The structural elements of 'Los reyes rojos' are found in other works by Eguren.

For example, 'Los robles' [The Oak Trees], also from *Simbólicas*, shares its circular structure and focus on the instant. In seven stanzas of two lines each, the poem refers only to the weeping of the trees. The circle — and the poem — begins with: 'En la curva del camino | dos robles lloraban como dos niños' [At the bend in the road | two oak trees cried like two little boys]. It ends at the same place: 'Y en la curva del camino | los robles lloraban como dos niños' [And at the bend in the road | the oak trees cried like two little boys] (Eguren 2005: 38). In another example, the poem 'Las torres' [The Towers], again from *Simbólicas*, depicts a battle between two towers. Unlike 'Los reyes rojos,' which used a greyscale progression of light to dark to mark time, 'Las torres' indicates its passage with vibrant colour changes from 'brunas' [dark], 'áureas' [golden], 'rojas' [red] and 'negras lejanías' [black distances] as the combat proceeds through successive phases. In the last stanza, the attraction once again disappears, as the reader witnesses the death of both towers.

Eguren frequently relied on this mechanism of the vanishing protagonist. The title character of 'La Tarda' [Tarda], one of the most celebrated poems of *Simbólicas*, has a physical appearance that resembles death: 'del esqueleto madre' [skeleton's mother]. Unable to cry, this mysterious spirit inexplicably disappears from the page, leaving only traces behind: 'Va a la ciudad que duerme parda, | por la muerta avenida' [She takes the dead avenue | to the brown-sleeping town] (Eguren 2005: 37). The poem's macabre tone is emphasized by the sound of her 'ronca carcajada' [hoarse laugh] and a close-up image of her 'vacíos ojos' [empty eyes] (Eguren 2005: 37). With respect to close-ups, early filmmakers used such shots very differently to how Griffith later would, most notably in the narrative films he made for Biograph beginning in 1908. According to Gaudreault (1983: 328), Eguren's poetic close-up recalls the way that the cinema of attractions isolated relevant items and increased their onscreen size inside a 'circular matte,' a practice that contrasts with the better-known use of the close-up as a procedure that furthers a film's narrative development and characterization. Like the close-ups of the cinema of attractions, Eguren's focus on Tarda's eyes has the effect of disrupting the poem. Gaudreault has described the pre-1908 close-up as an attraction, like an image enlarged by a 'magnifying glass' without any narrative function of its own (2011: 54). According to Gunning, as Griffith gained cinematic expertise and consolidated the foundations of classic Hollywood cinema, 'the joins between shots [were] less noticeable and the enlargement of the close-up less jolting and excessive' (1991: 294).

Eguren wrote two other poems, both from *La canción de las figuras*, featuring fantastic disappearing characters. These are the 'ángeles tranquilos' [peaceful angels] of the poem by the same name and blonde women with candles in 'Las candelas' [The Candles]; these characters perform music and dance numbers and then vanish or die. These poems recall early films that feature the attraction as their primary visual strategy, such as Méliès's films *The Vanishing Lady* (1896) — where a woman fades away and a skeleton takes her place — *The Haunted Castle* (1896) and *The Bewitched Inn* (1897).

Coda: The Persistent Mobility of Inanimate Objects

By way of conclusion, I want to briefly analyse the poem 'El dominó' [The Domino] from *Simbólicas* as a final demonstration of the cinema of attractions as a lens for reading Eguren's poetry. The poem describes 'un dominó vacío, pero animado' [an empty but animate domino], borrowing a popular disguise from Carnival street parties. This solitary domino hosts a dinner party without guests in a room where objects move by themselves: 'Alumbraron en la mesa los candiles, | moviéronse solos los aguamaniles' [The lamps shone on the table, | the pitchers moved on their own] (Eguren 2005: 41). The reader thus enters a scene that obeys its own physical laws, those of the special effects of filmmakers like Méliès and De Chomón, according to which objects move around the screen but not in response to any external force. Fernández Cuenca (1972: 50) has explained that this cinematic technique, known as frame-by-frame shooting, required interrupting filming after each frame, changing the placement of the objects and then recording the next frame. Through repetition of this process, an inanimate object came to life onscreen.[26] Eguren's domino undertakes a secret mission that remains indecipherable to the reader, such that exhibition of this strange, spectral character prevails over narration. Finally and inexplicably, the domino leaves the room:

> Y luego en horror que nacarado flota,
> por la alta noche de voluntad ignota,
> en la luz olvida manjares dorados,
> ronronea una oración culpable llena
> de acentos desolados
> y abandona la cena. (Eguren 2005: 41)

> [And then horrified at hovering mother-of-pearl,
> at the midnight of an unknown will,
> in the forgotten light of golden delicacies,
> he murmurs a guilty prayer
> full of desolate accents
> and leaves the dinner.]

As noted above, critics broadly agree that José María Eguren is one of the founders of poetic modernity in Peru. In my analysis of his poetry, I have taken an intermedial approach, locating the author within the rich cultural context of the first decades of the twentieth century, when cinema became an essential art form. In the mid-1930s, Emilio Adolfo Westphalen published a sort of manifesto on the particularity of contemporary poetry: 'A la poesía de ideas, falsa poesía, absurda, de metafísicos, teólogos y escolásticos, a la poesía didáctica al igual que a la de sonidos, la poesía-mística o simbolismo [...] ha sucedido una vital, dinámica, del movimiento del ser, cinemática' [The poetry of ideas, false, absurd poetry of metaphysicists, theologians and scholastics, didactic poetry and the poetry of sounds, mystical-poetry or symbolism [...] has been succeeded by a vital, dynamic, moving poetry, a cinematic poetry] (1935: 16–17). Westphalen thus recognized — and demanded recognition of — a fact evident from reading the poetry of the era: film had exerted considerable influence on the writers of his generation. As this reference demonstrates, Eguren inaugurates a cinematic poetry in Peru that would reach its high point in the 1920s and 30s with Carlos Oquendo de Amat's *5 metros de poemas* [5 Metres of Poems] (1927), and Enrique Peña Barrenechea's *Cinema de los sentidos puros* [Cinema of Pure Senses] (1931). The modern factor that made Eguren's poetry so groundbreaking was a product of its contact with early film techniques, especially those of the cinema of attractions.

Works Cited

ANCHANTE, JIM ALEXANDER. 2012. 'Símbolo, simbólica y simbolismo en los *Motivos* de José María Eguren', *Lexis*, 36: 225–52

ARETA MARIGÓ, GEMA. 1993. *La poética de José María Eguren* (Seville: Alfar)

BASADRE, JORGE. 1929. 'Elogio y elegía de José María Eguren', *Amauta*, 21: 21–29

BAUDELAIRE, CHARLES. 2012. 'The Philosophy of Toys' in *On Dolls*, ed. by Kenneth Gross (London: Notting Hill), pp. 11–21

BEDOYA, RICARDO. 2013. *El cine silente en el Perú* (Lima: Fondo Editorial Universidad de Lima)

—— 2014. 'El cine mudo en el Perú', in *Cine latinoamericano (1896–1930)* (Caracas: Centro Nacional Autónomo de Cinematografía), pp. 301–27

BENJAMIN, WALTER. 1999. 'Old Toys', in *Selected Writings (1927–1934)*, ed. by Michael W. Jennings, Howard Eiland, and Gary Smith (Cambridge, MA: Harvard University Press)

BERNABÉ, MÓNICA. 2006. *Vidas de artista: bohemia y dandismo en Mariátegui, Valdelomar y Eguren (Lima, 1911–1922)* (Rosario: Beatriz Viterbo, Lima: Instituto de Estudios Peruanos)

BUCKLAND, WARREN. 2006. 'A Rational Reconstruction of "The Cinema of Attractions"', in *The Cinema of Attractions Reloaded*, ed. by Wanda Strauven (Amsterdam: Amsterdam University Press), pp. 41–55

DEBARBIERI, CÉSAR. 1990. *Los personajes en la poética de José María Eguren y otros textos* (Lima: Pedernal)

DELGADO LEYVA, ROSA. 2012. *La pantalla futurista: del Viaje a la Luna de Georges Méliès a El Hotel eléctrico de Segundo de Chomón* (Madrid: Cátedra)

DOANE, MARY ANN. 2002. *The Emergence of Cinematic Time: Modernity, Contingency, the Archive* (Cambridge, MA: Harvard University Press)

EGUREN, JOSÉ MARÍA. 2005. *Obra poética. Motivos*, ed. by Ricardo Silva-Santisteban (Caracas: Biblioteca Ayacucho)

EISENSTEIN, SERGEI. 1974. 'Montage of Attractions: For "Enough Stupidity in Every Wiseman"', *The Drama Review*, 18: 77–85

FERNÁNDEZ CUENCA, CARLOS. 1972. *Segundo de Chomón: maestro de la fantasía y de la técnica (1871–1929)* (Madrid: Editora Nacional)

GAUDREAULT, ANDRÉ. 1983. 'Temporality and Narrativity in Early Cinema, 1895–1908', in *Film before Griffith*, ed. by John L. Fell (Berkeley: University of California Press), pp. 311–29

—— 2011. *Film and Attraction: From Kinematography to Cinema* (Urbana and Chicago: University of Illinois Press)

GUNNING, TOM. 1986. 'The Cinema of Attraction: Early Film, its Spectator and the Avant-Garde', *Wide Angle*, 8: 63–70

—— 1991. *D. W. Griffith and the Origins of American Narrative Film: The Early Years at Biograph* (Urbana and Chicago: University of Illinois Press)

—— 1996. 'Now You See It, Now You Don't: The Temporality of the Cinema of Attractions', in *Silent Film*, ed. by Richard Abel (London: Athlone), pp. 71–84

—— 2006. 'Attractions: How They Came into the World', in *The Cinema of Attractions Reloaded*, ed. by Wanda Strauven (Amsterdam: Amsterdam University Press), pp. 31–39

—— 2012. '"We Are Here and Not Here": Late Nineteenth-Century Stage Magic and the Roots of Cinema in the Appearance (and Disappearance) of the Virtual Image', in *A Companion to Early Cinema*, ed. by André Gaudreault, Nicolas Dulac, and Santiago Hidalgo (Hoboken, NJ: Wiley-Blackwell), pp. 52–63

HAYWARD, SUSAN. 1992. 'Ahistory of French Cinema: 1895–1991: Pioneering film-makers (Guy, Dulac, Varda) and their *heritage*', *Paragraph*, 15: 19–37

HIGGINS, JAMES. 1973. 'The Rupture between Poet and Society in the Work of José María Eguren', *Kentucky Romance Quarterly*, 20: 59–74

HUHTAMO, ERKKI. 2012. 'Toward a History of Peep Practice', in *A Companion to Early Cinema*, ed. by André Gaudreault, Nicolas Dulac, and Santiago Hidalgo (Hoboken, NJ: Wiley-Blackwell), pp. 32–51

LEFORT, DANIEL. 2016. 'Simbolismo y surrealismo en Francia y en el Perú: la formación de una cultura híbrida', *Revista de Crítica Literaria Latinoamericana*, 84: 179–92

LÓPEZ, ANA. 2000. 'Early Cinema and Modernity in Latin America', *Cinema Journal*, 40: 48–78

MARIÁTEGUI, JOSÉ CARLOS. 1971. *Seven Interpretive Essays on Peruvian Reality*, trans. by Marjory Urquidi (Austin: University of Texas Press)

MERCER, LEIGH. 2007. 'Fear at the Hands of Technology: The Proto-Surrealism of the Films of Segundo de Chomón', *Studies in Hispanic Cinemas*, 4: 79–90

MONGUIÓ, LUIS. 1954. *La poesía postmodernista peruana* (Mexico City: Fondo de Cultura Económica)

MUSSER, CHARLES. 2006. 'Rethinking Early Cinema: Cinema of Attractions and Narrativity', in *The Cinema of Attractions Reloaded*, ed. by Wanda Strauven (Amsterdam: Amsterdam University Press), pp. 389–416

NATALE, SIMONE. 2011. 'The Invisible Made Visible: X-rays as Attraction and Visual Medium at the End of the Nineteenth Century', *Media History*, 17: 345–58

—— 2012. 'A Short History of Superimposition: From Spirit Photography to Early Cinema', *Early Popular Visual Culture*, 10: 125–45

—— 2016. *Supernatural Entertainments: Victorian Spiritualism and the Rise of Modern Media Culture* (University Park: Pennsylvania State University Press)

NÚÑEZ, ESTUARDO. 1961. 'José María Eguren: vida y obra', *Revista Hispánica Moderna*, 3–4: 197–274

NÚÑEZ GORRITTI, VIOLETA. 2010. *El cine en Lima, 1897–1929* (Lima: Consejo Nacional de Cinematografía del Perú)

NYE, RUSSEL. 1981. 'Eight Ways of Looking at an Amusement Park', *Journal of Popular Culture*, 15: 63–75

ORTEGA, JULIO. 1971. *Figuración de la persona* (Barcelona: EDHASA)

REBAZA-SORALUZ, LUIS. 1993. 'Tres voluntades fundadoras de una poética nacional: Edgar Allan Poe, Ricardo Jaimes Freyre y José María Eguren', *ALEPH*, 8: 99–110

ROBINSON, DAVID. 1997. *From Peep Show to Palace: The Birth of American Film* (New York: Columbia University Press)

RODRÍGUEZ-PERALTA, PHYLLIS. 1973. 'The Modernism of José María Eguren', *Hispania*, 56: 222–29

SILVA-SANTISTEBAN, RICARDO. 2005. 'El universo poético de José María Eguren', in *Obra poética. Motivos*, ed. by Ricardo Silva-Santisteban (Caracas: Biblioteca Ayacucho), pp. ix–cxiv

SOLOMON, MATTHEW. 2006. 'Up-to-Date Magic: Theatrical Conjuring and the Trick Film', *Theatre Journal*, 58: 595–615

——— 2012. 'Georges Méliès: Anti-Boulangist Caricature and the Incohérent Movement', *Framework*, 53: 305–27

SPIKES, JUDITH. 1966. 'The Aesthetic of José María Eguren', *Hispania*, 49: 228–31

TORRES, ALEJANDRA. 2012. 'José María Eguren y las imágenes técnicas: a propósito de "Filosofía del objetivo"', *Escritura y Pensamiento*, 31: 141–57

VICH, VÍCTOR. 2013. 'Robles, buques, caballos y sangre en la poesía de José María Eguren', *Revista de Crítica Literaria Latinoamericana*, 78: 365–75

WESTPHALEN, EMILIO ADOLFO. 1935. 'La poesía de Xavier Abril', in *Difícil trabajo: antología 1926–1930*, by Xavier Abril (Madrid: Plutarco), pp. 11–24

Notes to Chapter 1

1. This chapter was translated from the Spanish by Erin Dougherty. I thank Benjamin Pratley (Colgate University, NY) for his help with proofreading parts from the final version of the article.

2. An inexhaustive survey of Eguren's poetry revealed the following exotic vocabulary: *chinesca* [Chinese or Chinese-related], *papiros* [papyruses], *bayadera* [temple dancer], *druidas* [Druids], *beduinos* [Bedouins], *bizantino* [Byzantine], *loto* [lotus] and *cingalesa* [Singhalese].

3. Eguren also published three other books of poetry: *La canción de las figuras* [The Ballad of the Figures] (1916), *Sombra* [Shadow] and *Rondinelas*. *Sombra* and *Rondinelas* were published together in the volume *Poesías* [Poetry] (1929). As for formal poetic analysis, Núñez (1961: 232–33) has painstakingly studied Eguern's patterns of metre and rhyme. The poet used a variety of metrical schemes that reveal the influence of Spanish classicism, Bécquer and of course the *modernistas*, especially Darío. Although Eguren did not reproduce the metric models of his time (like the sonnet, for example), he did use traditional octosyllabic, decasyllabic, hendecasyllabic, Alexandrine and even sixteen-syllable verses. He used these verses freely, however, creating combinations that served his own rhythmic needs. With regard to rhyme, Eguren generally relied on consonant rhyme, although he also used assonant rhyme in a number of his texts.

4. Eguren's uniqueness notwithstanding, some of the poems in *Simbólicas* are strikingly similar in style and subject matter to works from *Exóticas* [Exotics] (1911) by the anarchist intellectual Manuel González Prada. Silva-Santisteban (2005: xxx) has explained these coincidences as a result of the fact that Eguren may have learned technical lessons about poetry by reading González Prada's works and discussing them with him.

5. Mariátegui may have been the first influential critic to describe, in 1928, the literary 'pureness' of Eguren's work, noting that, 'unlike most Peruvian poetry [... it] does not pretend to be historical, or philosophical, or religious, but is simply poetry' (1971: 237). Ortega (1971: 63) has disputed that assessment, arguing that Mariátegui was unduly influenced by extratextual elements like the bourgeois status of Eguren's family.

6. Higgins has also read a social critique into the poet's observations of the failings of bourgeois society: 'Eguren viewed the society of his day with a critical eye and [...] his detachment implies the assertion of a set of personal values in opposition to the negative life style of the modern world' (1973: 61).

7. The National Library of Peru conserves 525 of these photographs (Bernabé 2006: 196).

8. The following lines demonstrate Eguren's insistence on toys: 'Reír te miro, con tu sonrisa clara, | entre exóticos juguetes de cartón' [I watch you laugh, with your clear smile, | surrounded by exotic cardboard toys] ('Sayonara' from *Simbólicas*) (2005: 10); 'Linda y caprichosa la rubia ambarina | quiebra los juguetes y la mandolina' [the lovely and capricious amber blonde | breaks the toys and the mandolin] ('Colonial' from *Sombra*) (2005: 108); 'Los músicos sueños, antes de la aurora, | tocan en el piano fiesta encantadora, | los finos arpegios, rara melodía | que tiene el castillo de juguetería' [Before dawn, the dream musicians | play an enchanted party on the piano | the fine arpeggios and strange melody | of the castle of toys] ('Los sueños' [Dreams] from *Sombra*) (2005: 134); and 'La plazuela galana | simula un juguete | de pino' [The gallant plaza | looks like a toy | made out of pine] ('Témpera' [Tempera] from *Rondinelas*) (2005: 172).

9. Benjamin has described this situation: 'When the urge to play overcomes an adult, this is not simply a regression to childhood. To be sure, play is always liberating. Surrounded by a world of giants, children use play to create a world appropriate to their size. But the adult, who finds himself threatened by the real world and can find no escape, removes its sting by playing with its image in reduced form' (1999: 100).

10. In 'El pelele' [The Straw Doll], another poem from *Simbólicas*, children also laugh and cry as they stage a doll's death: 'Las princesas rubias pasaron el día | cantando placeres con la tristecía | en la rondinela de la juventud; | y en el gorigori llevando sin duelo, | del pobre pelele caído en el suelo, | el triste ataúd' [The blond princesses spent the day | singing joys with sadness | in the *rondinela* of youth; | and in the mourningless dirge, | for the poor doll fallen on the floor, | the sad casket] (Eguren 2005: 28).

11. Eguren's books feature numerous aristocratic characters, including princesses, queens, kings, marquises, emperors, *infantas*, knights, baronesses and viceroys.

12. Emphasis in original.

13. Gaudreault and Gunning both use this term to refer to films made between 1895 and 1908. According to Gaudreault (2011: 53), the emphasis on exhibiting attractions in these films overshadows narrative aspects or eliminates them altogether.

14. To Eisenstein, '[a]n attraction [...] is any aggressive aspect of the theatre; that is, any element of the theatre that subjects the spectator to a sensual or psychological impact, experimentally regulated and mathematically calculated to produce in him certain emotional shocks which, when placed in their proper sequence within the totality of the production, become the only means that enable the spectator to perceive the ideological side of what is being demonstrated — the ultimate ideological *conclusion*' [emphasis in original] (1974: 78). Gunning has traced a connection between early film and the experiments of the historical avant-garde. As shown below, those aspects of Eguren's poems that relate to the cinema of attractions also connect to surrealism.

15. Huhtamo has made the similar argument that the cinema of attractions 'inherited many of its features from forms that had thrived at fairs and fairgrounds, displays of magic, magic lantern, and variety shows, etc.' (2012: 35).

16. Emphasis in original.

17. A result of early film technology that projects intervals of blackness between illuminations of the image in frame; this phenomenon only disappeared when technological advancements that improved cranked-cameras and film projectors were 'fully regularized through electrical power and the three-blade shutter' (Doane 2002: 199).

18. Eguren's poetry also highlights magical spaces and events. For example, in one of his best-known texts, 'La niña de la lámpara azul' [The Little Girl with the Blue Lamp] from *La canción de las figuras*, the enigmatic title figure offers to guide the poet on 'un mágico y celeste camino' [a magical, celestial path] (Eguren 2005: 54).

19. Natale has noted that before cinema, photographic techniques like X-ray photographs, for example, were used to produce magical and mysterious effects and encourage belief in 'the presence of an invisible world of spirits among us' (2011: 354).

20. Mercer (2007: 88) has argued that the radicality of its technical experiments makes this genre an antecedent of the avant-garde films of the 1920s, especially surrealist films.

21. Hayward has recognized film tricks in the works of Alice Guy, an important pioneer of French cinema: 'reversing film so that, for example, a person who has just fallen from a roof is seen jumping back on to it; stop gap shooting to allow an object to be moved to a different place within the frame; fast and slow-motion' (1992: 22). And Solomon has described Méliès' use of tricks: 'Elaborately choreographed theatrical action performed in front of resolutely motionless drawn backdrops creates an odd effect. [...] The backdrops of Méliès' films are crowded with signifiers — some iconic, others symbolic, and many both — that ask to be read by the spectator. Often, they are festooned with text, with names, signs, and toponyms of all types, often in multiple languages' (2012: 322).

22. As noted at the beginning of this chapter, Eguren's poetry clearly relates to French symbolism and Hispanic American *modernismo*. It can also be argued, however, that the mysterious and

dreamlike characters that populate the Peruvian poet's work prefigure the surrealists' interest in images that originate in the unconscious. An example is the poem 'Rêverie' [Daydream], which describes a dream about two vague and enigmatic feminine figures: 'Las vi en el blasón de la poterna | azulinas y casi borradas | despierto años después, la cisterna | las mecía medio retratadas' [I saw them on the postern's coat of arms | cornflower blue and nearly erased | years later the unsleeping cistern | rocked their half-drawn selves] (Eguren 2005: 11). Further, the intermedial dialogue between Eguren's work and early cinema, especially the films of Méliès, may have influenced the creation of magical literary atmospheres that anticipated André Breton's surrealism.

23. In the poem 'Los delfines' [The Dolphins] from *La canción de las figuras*, a group of dead dolphins dance in a brilliantly lit room. These ghostlike animals apparently seek to communicate the pain of living in a world that does not value aesthetics: 'Un Saber innominado | [...] | sufrir los hace, sufrir por el pecado | de la nativa elegancia' [A nameless Knowledge | [...] | makes them suffer, suffer for the sin | of native elegance] (Eguren 2005: 71).

24. Temporally, 'Lied III' follows the cycle of appearance, action and disappearance that is characteristic of the cinema of attractions. The protagonists appear in the first stanza: 'En la costa brava | suena la campana, | llamando a los antiguos | bajeles sumergidos' [On the wild coast | the bell rings, | calling the ancient | submerged vessels]. These ships then take different actions (moving, coming closer and crying) before returning 'al panteón de los mares' [to the pantheon of the seas] (Eguren 2005: 42).

25. Emphasis in original.

26. According to Delgado Leyva (2012: 134), De Chomón used this technique in his work for Pathé, which began in 1907. One of the best-known examples is *La maison ensorcelée* [The House of Ghosts] (1908), in which three people take refuge from a storm in a house in the middle of a forest. They watch in disbelief as objects move by themselves: suitcases move across the floor, a knife cuts bread and sausages, the room tilts and spins, clothing on hangers becomes animated, etc. Another example is Cohl's *Matrimonial Shoes* (1909), in which the shoes of two neighbouring guests at a hotel move around after their owners place them in the hallway outside of their respective rooms.

CHAPTER 2

❖

The Creole *Faust* on Screen: Between Late Style and the Comedy of Development

Nicolás Suárez

From the beginnings of Argentine cinematography, gaucho-themed literature has provided a prolific repertoire of plots, characters and landscapes for cinema, at least until the late 1970s, when adaptations of this type of texts became increasingly sporadic. Works such as *Martín Fierro* (1872 and 1879) by José Hernández, *Juan Moreira* (1879–80) by Eduardo Gutiérrez and *Santos Vega* — in the versions by Gutiérrez (1880–81) and Rafael Obligado (1885) — were made into a film on eleven, five and four occasions, respectively. Almost as productive as these works, Estanislao del Campo's *Fausto* (1866) — generally known as 'el *Fausto* criollo' or the creole *Faust* — was transposed to cinema three times: *Fausto, narrado por Anastasio El Pollo* (1922), directed by Ernesto Gunche and Eduardo Martínez de la Pera; *El Fausto criollo* (1979), directed by Luis Saslavsky; and *El Fausto criollo* (2011), directed by Fernando Birri. Film adaptations of *Fausto*, however, have received practically no attention from critics — a lack of interest that contrasts with the key position that literary criticism has assigned to Del Campo's poem in the history of gaucho literature.

The fundamental device of gaucho literature is that it is not poetry written by gauchos, but it seeks to be read (or heard, rather, since its audience was often illiterate) *as if* it had been composed by gauchos. This poetry was often composed in relation to precise contexts, and pursued concrete political ends (which is why some of its authors were called *gauchipolíticos* [gauchipoliticians]). The idea was, for example, that the gaucho who read or heard those poems would feel part of a larger collective, be it the independent homeland or the independent continent. Hence, according to the classic formula coined by Josefina Ludmer (2000), the gaucho genre is defined as a *use of the voice (of the) 'gaucho'*.[1] That is to say that there is a literate use of the gaucho's voice: the gaucho's words are used; but the use of the word 'gaucho' is also in dispute. What is in question is the definition of what a gaucho is or what a gaucho should be like, who is a gaucho and who is not. Through this formula, Ludmer described the chain of uses articulated by the genre: a use of the gaucho's body by the army, a use of the gaucho's voice by literate culture and a use of the gaucho genre to integrate the gauchos into liberal state law. These uses cover a varied set of texts that can be divided into different historical stages throughout the nineteenth century.[2] Within this vast corpus of gaucho poetry, *Fausto* occupies a key position because it introduces a series of innovations that changed the history of the genre, representing its autonomization and depoliticization. The exclusion of the political, in turn, corresponded to the emergence of a new urban and cultured public whose invention constitutes, according to Ángel Rama (1982: 166), *Fausto*'s fundamental innovation.

The anecdote about the poem's origin is almost as well-known as it is quaint. On 30 September 1866, the opera *Faust*, by Charles Gounod, was staged at the Colón Theatre in Buenos Aires. Poet Estanislao del Campo and his brother-in-law Ricardo Gutiérrez attended the performance. Both were well-off members of the Buenos Aires ruling elite. Gutiérrez had garnered praise from his contemporaries by writing poems with a rural theme in a cultured language that was the opposite of the gaucho genre as defined by Ludmer. Del Campo, on the contrary, was at that time a soldier, as well as a government official and an amateur writer who had barely composed a handful of poems. He had published some poems in newspapers under the pseudonym 'Anastasio El Pollo', which evoked the gaucho newspaper writer invented by Hilario Ascasubi. During the performance at the Colón, Del Campo commented on the opera with his friend Gutiérrez, adopting the voice of Anastasio and imagining what he would have perceived. Gutiérrez was amused by the occurrence and encouraged him to turn those comments into a longer poem, which was published a few weeks later in a local newspaper under the title *Faust (Impressions of Gaucho Anastasio El Pollo during the Representation of this Opera)*. In November, the text was republished with some additions in a standalone pamphlet, and Del Campo donated the proceeds to the soldiers of the Paraguayan War.[3]

The poem dramatizes the dialogue between two gauchos, Laguna and Anastasio El Pollo, who meet in the country after returning from the city. The gaucho's visit to the city to attend patriotic festivities was a common motif in gaucho poetry, which Del Campo nevertheless modifies, since Anastasio does not travel to witness a patriotic celebration but an opera performance. Observing the patterns of the genre, the gauchos greet each other, get off their horses, and exchange tobacco and alcohol, after which the exchange of stories ensues. Laguna tells El Pollo that he tried in vain to collect a debt for a sale of wool and, as a result of a casual allusion to the devil, El Pollo tells him in turn what he saw in the city. Confusing the fiction of opera with reality and using his gaucho language, El Pollo narrates his entrance into the Colón Theatre and how he witnessed the appearance of the devil and the difficulties faced by Doctor Fausto and Margarita.

Before publishing the poem, Del Campo sent a manuscript version to various intellectuals, whose comments — not all favourable — were included, along with a foreword by the author, in the first edition in book form. Consequently, since the circulation of its first manuscript, the text has provoked a fruitful exchange with critics. In subsequent years, some negative views about the text emerged, especially since José Hernández, in the Prologue-letter to *Martín Fierro*'s first part, expressed a political critique of *Fausto*, questioning the verisimilitude of the poem and its sense of mockery towards the gaucho. From then on, new critics would follow this path, such as Paul Groussac (1939: 99) and Leopoldo Lugones (2009: 135), who disqualified Del Campo and the protagonist of the text as a 'payador de bufete' [writing desk singer] and an 'impossible gaucho', respectively. Contrary to this folkloric approach, inseparable, in Lugones's case, from his epic vision of *Martín Fierro*,[4] various empathetic readings of the poem emerged throughout the twentieth century. Jorge Luis Borges (1997) highlighted the fantastic vein and Pedro Henríquez Ureña proclaimed himself against the realistic demands of certain critics 'with a limited idea of the "real"' (1949: 148). A third critical line, which focuses on the uses of parody in the poem, was opened by Enrique Anderson Imbert, who extended the poem's ironic reach ('the bourgeois of Buenos Aires who attended the premiere of *Faust* [...] were as marginal with respect to Paris as the gauchos with respect to the Colón Theatre'), and pointed out that '[i]n order to praise *Martín Fierro*, the injustice of belittling *Fausto* was committed' (1968: 29–47). From this perspective, other critics (Domínguez and Masine 1980; Lamborghini 2003) noticed the change that the parodic bias of *Fausto* introduced into gaucho literature. Once this critical corpus had been settled, in the last two decades a set of new works have reviewed these readings and reframed the poem within the vast series of adaptations of Goethe's *Faust* (1808–32) in several media (Roman 2003; Aguilar 2009; Schvartzman 2013).

Following these new readings, I will now approach the three film versions of the creole *Faust* paying attention to the poem's intermediality and its relation to the global spectacle of the opera. The absolute lack of critical comments on these films is noteworthy not only in contrast to the abundance of readings of the poem but also because they are works directed by emblematic filmmakers in the history of Argentine and Latin American cinema. Martínez de la Pera and Gunche, who had started their careers as photographers and authors of travelogues, were awarded various prizes at the San Francisco International Exhibition of 1914. Upon returning to Argentina, they brought back a Griffithian idea of continuous montage and staging that was key to their feature film *Nobleza gaucha* (1915), which was Argentine cinema's first blockbuster. Saslavsky, by contrast, worked as a film critic and, after being sent to Hollywood in 1931 as a correspondent for *La Nación*, returned to the country in 1934 with a knowledge of classical cinema and international entertainment culture that helped him achieve a box office hit and critical acclaim with *La fuga* (1937), which incorporated Argentine nuances into a gangster storyline. Lastly, in the case of Birri, his experience as a student at the Centro Sperimentale di Cinematografia in Rome during the 1950s, as well as his intense vocation for teaching, enabled him to become a promoter of neorealism in Argentina and one of the founding fathers of the new Latin American Cinema. All of them, therefore, were important but also importing filmmakers, in the sense that after their trips to the United States and Europe, they returned to Argentina with ideas and technologies that would have a strong impact on the local cinematographic field. But why, then, have their versions of *Fausto* gone unnoticed?

I can outline two explanations. Firstly, given that they are adaptations of Del Campo's poem, these were not 'political' films, in the sense of the function that gaucho-themed films performed during the first half of the twentieth century. For decades, this kind of cinema assumed in Argentine culture the functions of *criollista* literature, which occupied the place of a rebellious discourse that offered a 'tool of integration and cohesion alternative to State propositions' (Cattaruzza and Eujanian 2003: 262).[5] However, as Matthew Karush (2012) demonstrated, from the 1930s, official efforts to forge a national identity on the basis of rural cultures progressively stripped these images of their plebeian associations and thus undermined their ability to represent the nation. Once canonized by the state, *criollismo* lost its appeal for different social groups, and was only revitalized in the 1970s, mainly thanks to the official support from military governments towards patriotic films. In this context, a parodic poem based on purely literary material such as *Fausto*, 'without political function, without possible use' (Ludmer 2000: 220), was much less suitable to being updated in cinema and to drawing the attention of the public and criticism than other gaucho texts whose political value was higher, such as *Juan Moreira* or *Martín Fierro*. Precisely for that reason, the poem's film versions trace a history of the limits of the uses of gaucho literature in Argentine culture. In other words, every time Del Campo's text is adapted to cinema, it is because the gaucho genre can no longer be used at face value, and demands to be parodied. It is at this insurmountable limit where politics, by the very fact of being denied, sometimes returns empowered. In this way, just as Ludmer (2000: 221) detects the presence of politics in Del Campo's gesture of donating the proceeds of *Fausto* to the wounded of the Paraguayan War, a guiding question for my work is this: is the politics that the adaptations of the poem seem to deny traceable in the films themselves? It is not always so, or not always to the same extent.

The second explanation for the almost total lack of readings of the films based on *Fausto* is stylistic or, I would say, authorial. A striking fact about these three films is that they are all final works: they are the last films of their respective directors. This makes them especially apt to being approached using the concept of *late style*, as formulated by Theodor Adorno (2002) and taken up by Edward Said (2007). Late style is the language that certain artists acquire when the end of their lives approaches, that moment 'when the artist who is fully in command of his medium nevertheless abandons communication with the established social order of which he is a part and achieves a contradictory, alienated relationship with it' (Said 2007: 8). For this type of artist, adds Said, artistic lateness is not the crowning of a life of aesthetic effort, it is not harmony and resolution, but intransigence, difficulty and unresolved contradiction. It is not surprising, in this sense, that this dissonance often translates into a resistance to dealing with these works, whose integration with its authors' previous creations tends to be quite difficult. In this way, the verification of this common inclination enables the introduction of a second question regarding the filmic versions of *Fausto*: why are these creators attracted to the Faustian pact at the end of their lives and works? Goethe himself did not consider his *Faust* to be complete until 1831, when he finished writing the second part of the poem, shortly before his death. Thomas Mann, author of one of the most famous reworkings of the myth of Faust in the twentieth century, was inspired by Adorno's reflections on Beethoven's late style when in *Doktor Faustus* (1947) the protagonist Adrian Leverkühn is impressed after hearing a lecture on the composer's final period (Said 2007: 8). Is there, then, any kind of affinity between the Faustian pact and late style? If so, it would be necessary to evaluate the peculiar manifestations of such affinity in each of the analysed adaptations. The case of Birri is, in this respect, remarkable, since the concept of *late style* does not seem to apply to his *Fausto* in the same sense as in Martínez and Gunche's or Saslavsky's versions. Before the creole *Fausto*, and running in parallel with his neorealist films, a number of Birri's previous works were already highly experimental and could therefore be linked to his version of *Fausto*. Although this was not the most explored facet of his filmography, Birri has had a long-standing penchant for innovative and radically experimental cinema, for instance, in *La primera fundación de Buenos Aires* [The First Founding of Buenos Aires] (1959) and *Org* (1978), among other works.

In any case, addressing these issues requires a more general reflection on the Faust myth's role in modernity. In *All That Is Solid Melts into Air*, Marshall Berman glimpsed in the figure of Faust a myth of modern experience:

> For as long as there has been a modern culture, the figure of Faust has been one of its culture heroes. In the four centuries since Johann Spiess's *Faustbuch* of 1587 and Christopher Marlowe's *Tragical History of Doctor Faustus* a year later, the story has been retold endlessly, in every modern language, in every known medium from operas to puppet plays and comic books, in every literary form from lyrical poetry to theologico-philosophical tragedy to vulgar farce; it has proven irresistible to every type of modern artist all over the world. (1988: 38)

Berman focuses on Goethe's *Faust* and on what he deems the three fundamental metamorphoses that the protagonist undergoes: first, he emerges as the Dreamer who struggles to find a way for the abundance of his inner life to overflow into the outside through action; then, through the mediation of Mephistopheles, he becomes the Lover who explores his desires and sensibilities; and finally, after the end of the tragedy of love with Marguerite's condemnation and redemption, he reaches the climax of his life as the Developer who undertakes great works to transform the world.

This point of view allows Berman to read *Faust* as a tragedy of development, which is articulated on what he calls the protagonist's 'Faustian split'. This consists of the rupture between inner and the outer life to which those who, like Faust, are bearers of a dynamic culture within a stagnant society, are exposed. For Berman, in the twentieth century, intellectuals in the Third World, bearers of avant-garde cultures in backward societies, have experienced the Faustian split with particular intensity. This is why, in short, I propose in this chapter that, if in the nineteenth century Goethe's *Faust* constitutes a tragedy of development, the film adaptations of Del Campo's creole *Faust* in the twentieth can be read as *a comedy of development and underdevelopment*, and its aesthetic and political consequences. In order to achieve this, the fact that these films are samples of their directors' late style will be explored as an interrogation of both the limits of gaucho literature and the limits of the experience of these filmmakers, who, like Del Campo, faced the problem of cultural importation in their own particular ways.

The Silent *Fausto*: Opera and Poetry in the Beginnings of National Cinema

When Del Campo attended the Colón Theatre in September 1866, Gounod's *Faust* — premiered at the Théâtre Lyrique in Paris in 1859 — had already been performed in Germany, Belgium, Italy and England, and would continue its international run in the following decades (it was chosen for the openings of the Metropolitan Opera House of New York in 1883 and of the National Theatre of Costa Rica in 1897). In the case of Buenos Aires, Del Campo himself, along with other men of letters, had played a significant part in making the show possible, thanks to the pressure he had exerted on the businessmen who were in charge of the performance of the opera. Several recent studies on *Fausto* have examined the poem's relations with the consecration of the opera as a global spectacle, which in the nineteenth century grew at the rhythm of imperialist expansion. In an insightful study of Del Campo's text, Gonzalo Aguilar refers to opera as the first global show and argues that it should not be seen only as a genre that expands from European cities to the periphery, but also as 'a genre through which different strategies of location are put into play in a work of aesthetic universalization' (2009: 41). Conceived in this way — that is, as a cultural practice rather than a lyrical musical genre — I believe that the opera assumes at an early stage some of the characteristics that Miriam Hansen (1999) later attributed to classic Hollywood cinema through the concept of 'vernacular modernism': a phenomenon through which cinema attained global and transnational circulation thanks to its capacity to become a vehicle of modernization processes and the experience of modernity that can be adopted by and adapted to different societies.

This overlapping of functions is evident in the late nineteenth and early twentieth centuries, when cinema established a fruitful relationship with opera, from which it used to take subjects, plots, characters and even actors who gave legitimacy to the new medium. These exchanges turned the protagonists of Gounod's opera (Faust, Marguerite and, especially, Mephistopheles) into recurring characters in cinema. Long before Friedrich Murnau's expressionist *Faust* (1926), the story appeared several times in the catalogues of Lumière (1898), Méliès (1898, 1903 and 1904) and Edison (1900).[6] They were, of course, abbreviated versions of Goethe's *Faust*, which concluded, like Gounod's opera, with the end of Part One of the work. This phenomenon, Berman points out, was common to most of *Faust*'s adaptations to various media, in which, after Marguerite's redemption, human interest tends to flag (1988: 60). The whole final part of Goethe's text, when Faust connects his personal impulses with the economic, social and political forces that move the world, and learns to build and destroy, was often left aside in the story's various interpretations. The remarkable thing is that, in the case of cinema, the modernizing impulse that is relegated from the plot reappears in the modernity of the medium.

In this respect, at a moment at which filmmakers were experimenting with the medium, the characters' appearances and disappearances by work of Mephistopheles particularly lent themselves to optical and scenic tricks, which explains Méliès's decision to adapt the story of Faust on three different occasions. Méliès himself must have suffered the Faustian split described by Berman, since by introducing and modernizing the tricks of variety shows, he made, in his own way, a little pact with the devil: he betrayed the reality effect the Lumières had discovered with their famous documentary views, in exchange for the plot charms of the *mise en scène*.

This split may not have been experienced as such by Méliès, who must have happily surrendered to the success of his own findings. Perhaps, it was experienced with greater scepticism by the Lumières, who are said to have come to affirm that cinema was an invention without a future. But that Faustian split condenses the situation into which, with a greater or lesser degree of awareness, filmmakers who ventured to explore with the new medium were thrown. Among them were Ernesto Gunche and Eduardo Martínez de la Pera, who made their own version of the creole *Faust* in 1922. Long before that, they had taken their first steps as amateur photographers, and then as producers of 'vistas', among which a series of landscapes of the Iguazú Falls stands out. Some years later, as already mentioned, they were hired by the national government to participate in the 1915 International Exhibition of San Francisco, where they received two prizes.[7] But their definitive consecration would come that same year with the premiere of *Nobleza gaucha*, which they co-directed with Humberto Cairo. This film became an immediate box office success and was the highest-grossing production in the entire silent period of Argentine cinema. From then on, these directors' careers followed diverging paths: on the one hand, their most innovative contributions take place in the field of short film, in which they pioneered the technique of microphotography and made scientific and educational films; on the other, victims of their own success, they dedicated themselves to trying to replicate the *Nobleza gaucha* formula, an endeavour that became a kind of habitual obsession even for other directors and producers.

The causes of *Nobleza gaucha*'s success are varied, and summarized in a foundational anecdote. Collector Pablo Ducrós Hicken (1955) said the film was first shown at a private screening, where it was coldly received. Screenwriter José González Castillo intervened, suggesting that some landscape shots be added and many intertitles replaced with literary quotes from *Martín Fierro*, *Fausto*, *Lázaro* (the 1869 poem by Del Campo's friend Ricardo Gutiérrez), and Obligado's *Santos Vega*. By Ducrós Hicken's account, these modifications were enough for 'the film to be received with an enthusiasm such that our spectators had never before expressed'. In a meticulous study of *Nobleza gaucha*, Patricio Fontana infers from this anecdote, that 'in some way, literature saved *Nobleza gaucha* from failure' (2011: 18). More precisely, I would add that what saved *Nobleza gaucha* is not so much literature in general as poetry in particular, since all literary quotations come from poetic texts, and the landscape shots that were added correspond to what Robert Scott Speranza (2002) calls 'poetic' cinema, for these shots are devoid of narrative action.

Only two fragments from *Fausto* were used in the film, both located at the beginning of the poem:

> A great young rider, whoa!
> As I believe there is no other
> Able to carry a colt
> And to rein him in at the moon.
> (Del Campo 1998: 41)

Next, the phrase 'Oh! Creole. He seems stuck to the animal' replaces the first verses of the second tenth of the poem almost verbatim. The operation is striking because, by placing Del Campo's and Hernández' gaucho verses on the same level as Gutiérrez's and Obligado's cultured rural poetry, the film softens the gaucho genre. There is no longer a literate use of the voice (of the) 'gaucho', to use Ludmer's formula: nobody speaks as if he were a gaucho. Actually, those who speak are the gauchos themselves, and nothing suggests that there is a deliberately artificial use of their voice. On the contrary, the constructive principle that seems to animate the procedure is the appeal to a veristic discourse that unifies diverse registers. The very title of the film suggests so: according to Alfonso Reyes (1997: 153), the expression *Nobleza gaucha* [Gaucho Nobility] can be interpreted as a translation or, rather, an adaptation of *Cavalleria Rusticana* [Rustic Chivalry]. This work by Pietro Mascagni, which premiered in Buenos Aires in 1891 and was repeated with great success on multiple occasions, established in the operatic field the trend of verism (as a reaction to Wagnerian idealism and an inclination to real characters and situations) and, from there, expanded into cinema.[8]

The ability to articulate in a single work multiple discourses that were in vogue (verism with gaucho literature and *criollismo*, documentary cinema with continuous montage, circus shows with cultured poetry) was undoubtedly one of the keys to *Nobleza gaucha*'s success, which Gunche and Martínez de la Pera would try to repeat — with favourable results — in the gaucho film *Hasta después de muerta* (1916).[9] Some years later, the directors would return to gaucho literature with their adaptation of *Fausto*. Throughout 1922 and 1923, the production was advertised in the press with a campaign that insistently presented the film as a 'magnificent adaptation to film by Martínez and Gunche, editors of *Nobleza gaucha*' (*Excélsior* 1923).[10]

Although Gunche and Martínez de la Pera were still young, *Fausto* was the last feature financed by their company (Mafud 2016: 413), which allows one to consider the film as a manifestation of the directors' late style and to investigate what formal elements suggest the possibility of a premature end to their work. The difficulty of adapting to the arrival of sound films in the 1930s may have had a negative impact on Gunche and Martínez de la Pera, as happened with many other filmmakers. But, considering that their last film was released in 1922, the conditions for that ending must have been operative well before 1930. In 1923, an article in *Excélsior* magazine, punning on the title of Martínez and Gunche's film *The House of the Crows*, referred to their production company as 'The House of Lawsuits', due to the multiple legal problems they faced with their projects. This situation contrasts with the bright future that magazine *La Película* traced for the company in 1917, after the premiere of *Hasta después de muerta*.

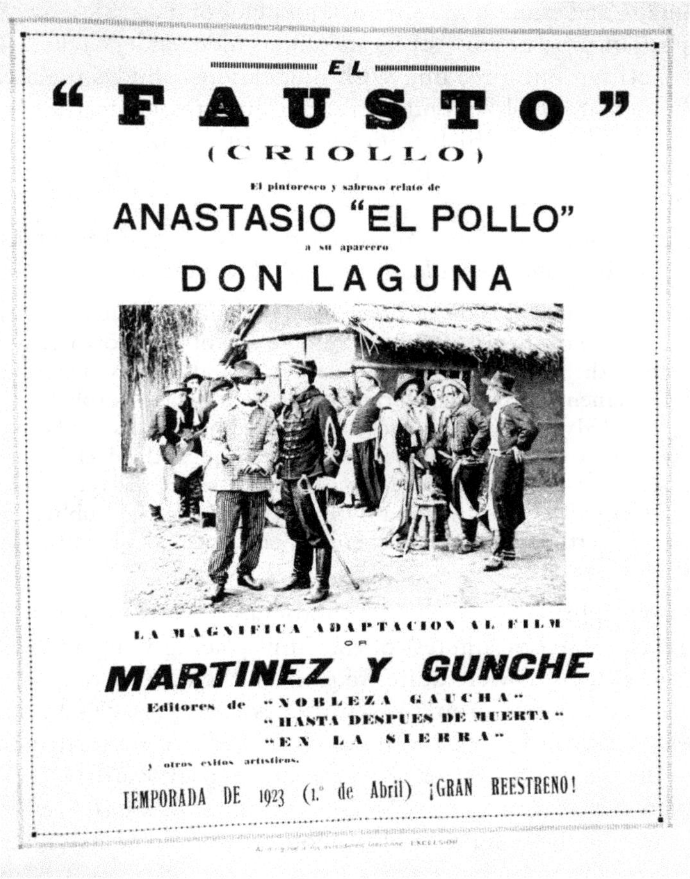

FIG. 2.1. Advertisement for *Fausto* (1922) by
Ernesto Gunche and Eduardo Martínez de la Pera (*Excélsior* 1923)

Despite the fact that their *Fausto* is currently lost, it is possible to infer from secondary sources some seemingly eccentric, unjustified or even capricious devices that correspond to the notion of late style as understood by Said. A review published in *La Nación* describes the film's aesthetic proposal in these terms:

> The legends that fully transcribe the original poem are interspersed with the action itself, in such a way that these become the primordial element of filmmaking, and thus mark the diverse times in which the scenic movement is decomposed. Hence, the film is, in fact, nothing but a reading with cinematographic illustrations of Del Campo's *Fausto*, and its development suffers from a slowness that makes it dreary at times. (*La Nación* 1922)

The commentary reveals, in its concern for the 'scenic movement' and the accusation of 'slowness', some commonplaces and critical clichés that circulated in a cinematographic field that was already autonomously constituted.[11] In this respect, although Martínez and Gunche had proved in *Nobleza gaucha* their skill in handling montage and camera movements, contemporary critics saw *Fausto* as pre-cinematographic in style because of its static and independent takes. The idea that the film was 'nothing but a reading with illustrations' alludes precisely to a more literary than cinematographic condition, according to which the 'Impressions of Gaucho Anastasio El Pollo', which completed the title of the poem, seem to become literal in its passage to cinema, as if the directors just limited themselves to *printing* on the film the poem's content.

This same aspect was also noted by the short story writer Horacio Quiroga, who reviewed the film in magazine *Atlántida* on 23 November 1922:

> As a cinematographic version of Estanislao del Campo's *Fausto*, [...] one truly would not know how to classify [this film] into any of the known genres. If one was to believe the promise in the subtitle, we would have witnessed a parody of *Faust*, the cinematographic interpretation of an opera, as told by a peasant who has attended the theatrical show. [...] But almost in its entirety the film consecrates itself to a second-hand screening of a simple third-class opera, with decorations and actors of equal value. [...] The verses of the creole *Faust* were used in the intertitles; and judging by the rejoicing of the public, the verses alone, with no further photographic commentary, would have sufficed for their plain pleasure. (2007: 302–03)

Despite acknowledging its 'excellent' photography, Quiroga then goes on to condemn the lack of artistic interest of the film, placing it at the level of a music-hall show. These criticisms were quite frequent in the cinema of the time. They do not differ much, for example, from the reproaches that Quesada's *Martín Fierro* (1923) received shortly afterwards. But the particularity of *Faust* is that it mixed typical devices of pre-cinema with some more elaborate and innovative techniques.[12] This is why Quiroga ends his review by suggesting that, although well-crafted when considered separately, the literary and the photographic elements of the film seemed not to combine in a harmonious form.

As an additional piece of information that reinforces such interpretation, it could be added that Martínez de la Pera tried to accompany the film with the complete recitation of the poem by using synchronized discs (Aretino 1980), an attempt that was apparently dismissed because it was too expensive. Nevertheless, the idea can be inserted in the context of current scholarship on early cinema sound (Abel and Altman 2001), a crucial but still little-known phenomenon that comprised a vast field of experimentation in the sound–image relations during this period. As for the staging, according to the critique in *La Nación*, 'as El Pollo's story moves forward, the interlocutors' figures appear on the screen in close-up and the description is represented in scenes that merge with the previous ones, alternately showing what El Pollo saw and what Laguna imagines through his words'. Such a procedure, which combined an idea of montage (fade-ins) with one of *découpage* (the close-ups), though complex and elaborate, would not have been easily followed by spectators.

Why, then, did this pair of directors who had demonstrated a skilful mastery of cinematographic language now make alleged beginner's errors or flourishes that seem detached from the dynamics of the work? After *Nobleza gaucha's* success in 1915, they had tried, on the one hand, to repeat their own blockbuster with their fiction films and, on the other, to flee from it with scientific and educational films. But in 1922, tired of repeating themselves and of the profusion of gaucho films that their success had triggered, and maybe also tired of the epic canonization of the gaucho that Lugones had opened with his reading of *Martín Fierro*, they decided to parody the gaucho and themselves by adapting the creole *Faust*, which showed — with the characteristic negativity of late style — that sort of Faustian split between poetic and narrative cinema to which, as in a *cul-de-sac*, their own trajectory had led them.

The Silenced *Fausto* (from 1879 to 1979)

Luis Saslavsky, who directed the second adaptation of *Fausto*, began his film career in the 1930s, standing out precisely in the area that had been most questioned in Gunche and Martínez de la Pera's version. While the 1922 adaptation had been criticized for its 'slowness' and lack of 'scenic movement', the main virtues of Saslavsky's cinema — thanks to the skills he acquired while working for three years in Hollywood — were continuity and narrative fluidity, which allowed him to avoid 'patriotic frames': a term used to stress the static, timeless quality of certain types of representations (Aguilar and Jelicié 2016: 48–49). In this sense, it can be said that Saslavsky, like Martínez de la Pera and Gunche, was (or was seen as) a bearer of a dynamic culture in an old-fashioned or stagnant cinematographic field. Regarding this experience, Saslavsky himself admitted that, when he returned from the United States, he became 'the man who had worked in Hollywood' (Barney Finn 1994: 11).

   The first time that Saslavsky applied that set of techniques to the treatment of gaucho themes was in 1949 with *Vidalita*, a film in which the well-known *Telefoni Bianchi* actress Mirtha Legrand cross-dressed as a gaucho.[13] Decades later, in a 1973 interview, Saslavsky confessed that, before filming *Vidalita*, he had tried to adapt *Juan Moreira*, but Luis José Moglia Barth beat him to it in 1948 with a much more traditionally *criollista* version than the one he imagined, in which he wanted to show 'that strange mentality of Juan Moreira, for whom [...] the woman only counts as [...] an object of pleasure and to have a child'. Speaking at the height of *criollista* cinema, while Leonardo Favio was breaking audience records with *Moreira*, Saslavsky also reported:

> Shortly after, I started to fight to make the creole *Faust*, [...] but I never found a producer who was interested. And to think that *Fausto*, together with *Juan Moreira* and *Martín Fierro*, are the three most read books of their time. *Fausto* is the story of a gaucho who goes to the theatre and sees the performance of the opera *Faust*; I thought it was beautiful to do it in cinema — and I still think so — but I never managed to raise the capital or to find a producer who was interested. (Calistro 1978: 319–20)

Following the path of demystifying the gaucho he had already explored in *Vidalita*, Saslavsky finally managed to adapt *Fausto* in 1979. He would live until 1995 but, as in the case of Martínez and Gunche, *Fausto* was also his last film. Already in the opening titles, the profusion of paratexts with quotations, dedications and thanks to different people could lead one to think that Saslavsky's *Fausto* constitutes a late work as a harmonious culmination of a life's aesthetic effort: a septuagenarian director makes his last appearance and candidly says goodbye to his friends.

However, conceived in Said's terms, late works tend to alternate massive polyphonic compositions of an abstruse sort with apparently unmotivated devices that are loosely integrated into the structure (2007: 10). This seems to be the case, in effect, with Saslavsky's *Fausto*. The film begins with an epigraph by Faustus of Mileve — the African bishop famous for having engaged in a discussion with Saint Augustine — about the unity of God and the multiplicity of the devil. Just as in Del Campo's poem Laguna confuses Dr. Fausto with 'another Fausto' (Uruguayan colonel Fausto Aguilar, popular in his time), Saslavsky presents another 'other Fausto', in a devilish and anachronistic play of references. Next, he thanks writers who collaborated in different ways in the film: Estela Canto ('with her prose'), Luisa Mercedes Levinson ('with her poetry') and Enrique Anderson Imbert ('with his advice'). I am particularly interested in the critic Anderson Imbert's contribution. His view marked a turning point in the history of the readings of *Fausto*, given that — as Schvartzman (2013: 342) states — it stripped away a 'thick layer of prejudices in order to open up to the multiplicity of the text'. Anderson Imbert perceived, in the bidirectional irony between the gauchos and the bourgeois, a 'game of perspectives that makes *Fausto* the most complex poem of all gaucho literature' (1968: 45). This multiplicity of perspectives is replicated in the film, at least at first glance, through the different quotations, thanks and debts, to which Saslavsky also adds two tributes.

The first is to Héctor Basaldúa, 'who did the illustrations of the *Fausto* published by Amigos del Arte, in 1932, which served as inspiration for the scenery and costumes.' In his works, Basaldúa depicted the premodern country, through the use of pastel colours and the infinite Pampas horizons on which the candour of typical characters was outlined. The second homage is paid to the painter Cándido López, some of whose works were used in the film, in an economic and ingenious device, to illustrate the Paraguayan War (where Laguna imagines that Margarita's brother goes when he leaves for war). López's work departed from the academic canon of battle paintings in order to achieve greater clarity in the panoramic exhibition of battles, which earned him a reputation for being a purveyor of naïve art. This produced in his paintings an effect of neutrality in the representation of war that, in the film, combined with other formal elements, translates into a lack of historical and political perspective.

The film structure and the construction of point-of-view are significant at this point. The narration is organized on three levels: the story of El Pollo in the Colón Theatre; the story told by El Pollo to Laguna (the only one observing the metrical form of the poem); and the story that Laguna imagines when listening to the words of his friend. With regard to the adaptation process, this arrangement has two main consequences. The first is that, by showing almost exclusively what Laguna imagines, the film dissolves one of the fundamental procedures of the poem, which — as Anderson (1968: 35–43) points out — consisted of the counterpoint of styles between the opera and the gaucho genre, or between what happens to El Pollo in the Colón and what Laguna understands. In the film, this contrapuntal effect only subsists in the very limited passages in which the gauchos' degradation of high culture is self-evident, as for example when Mefistófeles becomes 'Mephisto Pérez'.

The second consequence has to do with the political effects of the fact that Laguna imagines he is Faust and visualizes Mephistopheles as an indigenous man. It is through this blind spot that politics sneaks into a story that pretends to be closed and autonomous. In a context like that of 1979, when the military government was celebrating the centenary of the so-called Campaign of the Desert (which was actually the occupation of a territory already populated and the annihilation of its inhabitants), the characterization of the devil as indigenous can be read as a political gesture and an all-encompassing defence of the military institution. This was further supported by Saslavsky's attitudes throughout that year, such as when he announced the production of the film in a press conference with military officers or when he pronounced himself in favour of 'intelligent censorship', a euphemism for censorship pure and simple (*Somos* 1979).

If Ludmer read Del Campo's poem as 'a tale of apparitions' (2000: 13) that displays the modern contract between seeing and believing (El Pollo, who lacks the category of representation, *believes because he sees*), Saslavsky's gestures allow us to think of the film as a tale of the disappeared that displays the sinister reverse of that contract: *not believing because you cannot see*. It was at that same time that David Viñas positioned the repressive dictatorial practices of the 1970s in a historical series centred upon the extermination of the indigenous population in General Roca's campaign. His controversial idea was that 'the Indians were the disappeared of 1879' (2013: 16). In a less circular and teleological approach than that of Viñas, Saslavsky's *Fausto* shows that these relations between historical processes may not be so direct but do exist and express themselves in a refracted way, as ironic allegories, which is precisely the way late works apprehend death (Adorno 2002: 566). Thus, Margarita, once fallen into disgrace as a result of Fausto's actions, 'disappears' her son and throws him into a well, where he is later found by the police.

It was in this atmosphere that the film was released. Only a couple of weeks after the premiere, dictator Rafael Videla made his famous statement about the victims of forced disappearance during state terrorism:

> [...] the disappeared, as long as he remains such, is an unknown. If the man appeared, he would receive treatment X, and if his appearance proved his death, he would receive treatment Z. But while he is disappeared, he cannot have any special treatment, he is an unknown person, he is a disappeared person, he has no entity, he is... neither dead nor alive, he is missing.[14]

Finally, it is also symptomatic that this tragedy of community sacrificed for the sake of development was adapted to film in 1979, just as Jean-François Lyotard proclaimed the end of the 'grand narratives' that had legitimated the modern project for two hundred years. The gaucho genre, too, at that moment, had lost validity as a fable of national identity. This is probably why David José Kohon's *El agujero en la pared* [The Hole in the Wall] (1982), also released during the military dictatorship, returned to the myth of Faust but in very different terms.[15] This reactivation of the myth in a critical political and social context was presented in the opening credits as a film 'slightly based on the legend of Faust and the classical works on the theme'. Kohon himself has declared that he drew inspiration for his adaptation from 'classical' versions like Goethe's or Marlowe's, but omitted any reference to Del Campo's poem (Naudeau 2006: 221). Moreover, his approach of the myth can be aesthetically and ideologically set against Saslavsky's, since the film is openly metaphorical and critical of the violence and censorship that were taking place at the time: the main character is a *Porteño* Faust who amasses a fortune by doing business in the obscure and corrupt worlds of finance, press and politics. This contrast between the films of Saslavsky and Kohon shows that, after the extreme popularity and politicization achieved with films such as Torre Nilsson's *Martín Fierro* (1968) or Solanas' *Los hijos de Fierro* (1972–75), the gaucho genre returned to an autonomous and seemingly depoliticized ground, but to which politics returned more strongly. From then on, other more temperate uses of the gaucho would emerge in cinema, and the versions of *Fausto* echoed them once again.

Final Considerations: Birri's *Faust* and the Gaucho Genre in the Twenty-First Century

In 1979, while Saslavsky premiered his *Fausto* with the support of the military government, Fernando Birri — then exiled in Italy — presented the film *Org*, an absolutely atypical work, almost three hours long, with 26,000 cuts and 700 alternative soundtracks. Considering that in 2011 Birri directed a new version of *El Fausto criollo* and that this was his last film, the precedent of *Org* triggers a kind of paradox: what forms do the irreconcilability and the fragmentary nature of lateness take in the case of a creator whose previous work was already heterogeneous?

Influenced by his experience as a student in the Centro Sperimentale de Cinematografia, Birri returned to Argentina in 1955, after the fall of Perón, with the intention of applying the ideas collected in Italy. To this end, he founded the Instituto de Cinematografía de la Universidad del Litoral, where he tried to combine the precepts of Italian neorealism with the need to invent a different cinema for Latin America: 'to face reality with a camera and document it, to document underdevelopment', he would say in a text known as the Santa Fe Manifesto (2003: 456). At that time Latin American sociologists and economists of what would later be known as 'dependency theory' challenged the hypothesis according to which in order to achieve development in peripheral countries it was necessary to repeat the evolutionary phase of the economies in the central countries. In this context, Birri said that 'the cinema that becomes an accomplice of this underdevelopment, is sub-cinema', and so he struggled for a national, realist and critical cinema.

The first fruit of this experience was the emblematic documentary *Tire dié* (1958–60), for which Birri worked with more than eighty students and which would become a touchstone of the New Latin American Cinema. Like his debut film, Birri's *Fausto* was produced in his native Santa Fe, with a strong influence of regional culture and with the participation of children and students from the local film school who defined themselves as *Tire dié*'s grandchildren. With a totally unorthodox production design, the film was financed by the Government of Santa Fe, which also edited a book with the script and a shooting diary, in exchange for which Birri promised the government that he would donate his house in San José del Rincón to be converted into a cultural space. The work and life of this octogenarian director were thus intermingled in a new version of the creole *Faust* that was presented as 'a lyrical-epic vision of our "barbaric" Pampa [...] and a naïve-grotesque, humorous vision, imported from the "civilized" world' (Birri 2017: 13).

The film can be included in a series of new uses of gaucho literature in cinema that have been partly reviewed by Ben Bollig (2012) in his study of recent adaptations of *Martín Fierro*, such as *Martín Fierro: el ave solitaria* (2006) by Gerardo Vallejo, and *Martín Fierro: la película* (2007) by Liliana Romero and Norman Ruiz. The first of these films amounts to a nostalgic exercise by a director linked to the political cinema of the 1970s that returns to the figure of the primitive rebel he had already worked on at that time.[16] Meanwhile, the second — an animated film made ostensibly for children — involves the neutralization of the gaucho genre's corrosive potential to the point of turning it into a vehicle for a progressive message with educational purposes (Bollig 2012: 75). Birri's *Fausto* seems to be nourished by both tendencies: it is, on the one hand, a nostalgic exercise by a political filmmaker of the 1960s and 1970s who returns to a topic that was extremely productive in that period; and, on the other, it is a film performed by children with a markedly naïve tone. Taking this into account, it can be argued that if Saslavsky's *Fausto* was referenced in that of Basaldúa, Birri's would be closer to that of cartoonist Oski, who in 1963 had illustrated an edition of the poem with his style of simple strokes and surreal touches.[17]

Like that of Saslavsky, Birri's version is loaded with multiple references. The plate that presents the title of the film is, in fact, directly lifted from Murnau's *Faust* (1926). Immediately after, while the initial credits are still running, scenes of *Faust et Marguerite* (1904) by Méliès are shown, framed by a curtain that simulates a theatrical setting. The sequence culminates by showing once again the title of Murnau's film, but now there is a superimposed text in a light-blue font with the missing characters that transform the word *Faust* into *El Fausto criollo*, replicating the colours of the Argentine flag. Just as the poem by Del Campo made a literary use of the gaucho's voice, this procedure seems to suggest that an Argentine film can, inversely, make a 'barbaric' use of the great Western cinema tradition. In this way, using a rough and ready device, the film sets out the relationship between the creole *Faust* and the problem of cultural importation, and also adapts the poem's reflexivity into a self-referential filmic discourse.[18]

This procedure is prolonged in several moments of the film through the inclusion of fragments of *El último malón* (1917), by the Santafesino director Alcides Greca. The poem's allusions to the Paraguayan War are thus replaced by the images of another battle: the last indigenous rebellion of the Mocovíes in the north of Santa Fe, which Greca reconstructs in his film; and Rosa, one of the main characters of

El último malón, becomes — in an adaptation of the floral metaphor — a sort of alter ego for Margarita. These devices are articulated in a not very fluent account through the voice-over of El Pollo (played by an actor who reads the verses with a broken rhythm) and through a conventional use of clichés (for instance, the sound of an analogue projector when film footage is displayed). All this coexists with a mix of subtitles of different colours (yellow for El Pollo's lines, white for Laguna's, red for Mephistopheles's and blue for Fausto's) and countless anachronistic references whose role in the work seems unintegrated into the structure (just to mention a few: the devil playing the guitar in the style of Angus Young, a serenade by rock singer Fito Páez, or an altar to the popular saint Gauchito Gil). The modernism of Birri's late period thus carries out, unlike his previous films, a mythical regression to traditional forms and motifs (such as the very same story of Faust, or Méliès's films) which were complemented, without fitting into a system, by a panoply of quotations and anomalies. But it is precisely this atavistic coarseness that shows how Birri's late style makes its way into the work of an artist that was already fragmentary: everything becomes now, in Adornian terms, 'unabashedly primitive' (2002: 565).

Unsurprisingly, in this sense, the film had no commercial or festival premiere; it was only shown in a few screenings organized by governmental agencies. It is at this point that politics intrudes into the adaptation of a work that claimed to be autonomous: the gaucho genre autonomized, neutralized, lent itself to a politically innocuous official use. Therefore, if late style is first and foremost a matter of what style cannot say, just as in the cases of Saslavsky or Martínez and Gunche, Birri's penchant for a gaucho poem that admitted no political use implied, at the final limit of his work, a way to process the Faustian split that had marked a life.

Works Cited

ABEL, R., and R. ALTMAN. 2001. *The Sounds of Early Cinema* (Bloomington: Indiana University Press)

ADAMOVSKY, EZEQUIEL. 2019. *El gaucho indómito: de Martín Fierro a Perón, el emblema imposible de una nación desgarrada* (Buenos Aires: Siglo Veintiuno)

ADORNO, THEODOR. 2002. *Essays on Music* (Berkeley, Los Angeles and London: University of California Press)

AGUILAR, GONZALO. 2009. *Episodios cosmopolitas en la cultura argentina* (Buenos Aires: Santiago Arcos)

—— and E. JELICIÉ. 2016. *Borges va al cine* (Buenos Aires: Libraria)

ANDERSON IMBERT, ENRIQUE. 1968. *Análisis de 'Fausto'* (Buenos Aires: Centro Editor de América Latina)

ARETINO, DONATO. 1980. 'Hacedor de *Nobleza gaucha*, primer film de largometraje argumental rodado en el país', *Convicción*, 7 February

BARNEY FINN, OSCAR. 1994. *Luis Saslavsky* (Buenos Aires: Centro Editor de América Latina)

BERMAN, MARSHALL. 1988. *All That Is Solid Melts into Air: The Experience of Modernity* (New York: Penguin)

BIRRI, FERNANDO. 2003. 'El manifiesto de Santa Fe (1962)', in *Cine documental en América Latina*, ed. by Paulo Antonio Paranaguá (Madrid: Cátedra), p. 456

—— 2017. *El Fausto criollo* (Rosario: Espacio Santafesino Ediciones)

BOLLIG, BEN. 2012. 'Filming Fierro: Aesthetics and Politics in Film Adaptations of National-epic Poetry', *New Cinemas*, 10: 63–80

BORGES, JORGE LUIS. 1997. 'La poesía gauchesca', in *Discusión* (Madrid: Alianza), pp. 188–203

CALISTRO, MARIANO. 1978. *Reportaje al cine argentino: los pioneros del sonoro* (Buenos Aires: Abril)

CATTARUZZA, A., and A. EUJANIAN. 2003. *Políticas de la historia: Argentina, 1860–1960* (Buenos Aires: Alianza)

CUARTEROLO, ANDREA. 2013. *De la foto al fotograma: relaciones entre cine y fotografía en la Argentina, 1840–1933* (Montevideo: CDF Ediciones)

DEL CAMPO, ESTANISLAO. 1998. *Fausto* (Buenos Aires: Colihue)

DOMÍNGUEZ, N., and B. MASINE. 1980. 'El *Fausto* criollo, una doble mirada', *Lecturas Críticas. Revista de Investigación y Teoría Literarias*, 1: 20–26

DUCRÓS HICKEN, PABLO. 1955. 'Orígenes del cine argentino: una realidad apasionante', *El Hogar*, February, chapter 4

Excélsior. 1923. 18 July

FITZSIMMONS, LORNA. 2018. *Faust on the Early Screen* (Amsterdam: Amsterdam University Press)

FONTANA, PATRICIO. 2011. 'El gaucho y el tranvía: notas sobre el criollismo de *Nobleza gaucha* (1915)', *El matadero*, 7: 13–35

GARCÍA, N., and J. PANESI. 1998. 'Introducción', in *Fausto*, by Estanislao del Campo (Buenos Aires: Colihue), pp. 19–36

GROUSSAC, PAUL. 1939. *Los que pasaban* (Buenos Aires: Sudamericana)

HANSEN, MIRIAM BRATU. 1999. 'The Mass Production of the Senses: Classical Cinema as Vernacular Modernism', *Modernism/modernity*, 6: 59–77

HENRÍQUEZ UREÑA, PEDRO. 1949. *Las corrientes literarias en la América hispánica* (Mexico City: Fondo de Cultura Económica)

KARUSH, MATTHEW. 2012. *Culture of Class: Radio and Cinema in the Making of a Divided Argentina, 1920–1946* (Durham, NC: Duke University Press)

La Nación. 1922. 16 November

LAMBORGHINI, LEÓNIDAS. 2003. 'El gauchesco como arte bufo', in *La lucha de los lenguajes: historia crítica de la literatura argentina*, ed. by Julio Schvartzman (Buenos Aires: Emecé), pp. 105–18

LUDMER, JOSEFINA. 2000. *El género gauchesco: un tratado sobre la patria* (Buenos Aires: Perfil)

LUGONES, LEOPOLDO. 2009. *El payador* (Buenos Aires: Biblioteca Nacional)

LYOTARD, JEAN-FRANÇOIS. 1984. *The Postmodern Condition: A Report on Knowledge* (Minneapolis: University of Minnesota Press)

MAFUD, LUCIO. 2016. *La imagen ausente: el cine mudo argentino en publicaciones gráficas. Catálogo. El cine de ficción, 1914–1923* (Buenos Aires: Editorial Teseo)

MOLITERNO, GINO. 2008. *Historical Dictionary of Italian Cinema* (Lanham, MD: Scarecrow Press)

NAUDEAU, JAVIER. 2006. *Un film de entrevista: conversaciones con David José Kohon* (Buenos Aires: Fondo Nacional de las Artes)

PRIETO, ADOLFO. 2006. *El discurso criollista en la formación de la Argentina moderna* (Buenos Aires: Siglo Veintiuno)

QUIROGA, HORACIO. 2007. *Cine y literatura* (Buenos Aires: Losada)

RAMA, ÁNGEL. 1982. *Los gauchipolíticos rioplatenses* (Buenos Aires: Centro Editor de América Latina)

REA, LAUREN. 2013. *Argentine Serialised Radio Drama in the Infamous Decade, 1930–1943: Transmitting Nationhood* (Farnham & Burlington, VT: Ashgate)

REYES, ALFONSO. 1997. *Obras completas XIV* (Mexico City: Fondo de Cultura Económica)

Rojas, Ricardo. 1960. *Historia de la literatura argentina* (Buenos Aires: Kraft)

Román, Claudia. 2003. 'La vida color rosao: el *Fausto* de Estanislao del Campo', in *La lucha de los lenguajes: historia crítica de la literatura argentina*, ed. by Julio Schvartzman (Buenos Aires: Emecé), pp. 59–81

Said, Edward. 2007. *On Late Style: Music and Literature Against the Grain* (New York: Vintage Books)

Schvartzman, Julio. 2013. *Letras gauchas* (Buenos Aires: Eterna Cadencia)

Somos. 1979. 2 November

Speranza, Robert Scott. 2002. 'Verses in Celluloid: Poetry in Film Form 1910–2002, With Special Attention to the Development of the Film-Poem' (unpublished doctoral thesis, University of Sheffield)

Suárez, Nicolás. 2017. 'Movement and Projection in the Slaughterhouse of Argentine Cinema: *Martín Fierro* (1923) by Alfredo Quesada', *Catedral Tomada. Revista de Crítica Literaria Latinoamericana*, 9: 295–320

Tranchini, Elina. 1999. 'El cine argentino y la construcción de un imaginario criollista', in *El cine argentino y su aporte a la identidad nacional*, ed. by César Maranghello, Emilio Díaz, and Elina Tranchini (Buenos Aires: Faiga)

Viñas, David. 2013. *Indios, ejército y frontera* (Buenos Aires: Santiago Arcos)

Notes to Chapter 2

1. Unless otherwise states, all translations are by the author.
2. In this sense, after the celebrations of the triumphs of the South American armies in the independence wars of the early nineteenth century and the fall of the governor of Buenos Aires Juan Manuel de Rosas, Del Campo's work corresponds to a transition period during the internal struggles for the conformation of the Confederation and the advent of the new liberal economic order, while urban society was moving away from the countryside (Rama 1982: 60–63).
3. The Paraguayan War took place from 1864 to 1870, and pitched Paraguay against the Triple Alliance of Argentina, Brazil and Uruguay. The results were devastating for Paraguay, which suffered a severe loss of population and territory. But the consequences were also widely commented upon in Argentinian newspapers, not only due to the political relevance of the conflict but also because several members of aristocratic families took part in this war and some even lost their lives.
4. The epic and academic canonization of José Hernández's text began in 1913, when Lugones delivered a famous series of lectures on the epic meaning of the poem that would later be collected in *El Payador* (1916). By raising the story of a quarrelsome gaucho to the category of national epic paradigm, Lugones's proposal triggered many contradictions, but was arguably a powerful reading operation.
5. The vast set of stories about rebellious gauchos that were published after Eduardo Gutiérrez's *Juan Moreira* allowed Adolfo Prieto (1988) to detect the emergence of what he called *criollista* literature, and to study its role in the formation of Argentine identity in the turn of the century. According to Prieto, the tensions between the rural past and modernization processes created a sense of belonging for the creole lower classes, immigrants and elites, although the appraisals of the phenomenon by these groups had different and even contradictory meanings. In recent decades, new research has shown that *criollismo* did not disappear in the early twentieth century, as Prieto suggested, but was reconverted from literature to other practices, such as cinema and radio (Tranchini 1999), (Rea 2013), (Adamovsky 2019).
6. A detailed account of this matter is provided in Lorna Fitzsimmons's *Faust on the Early Screen* (2018).
7. One of these prizes is presumed to be for the documentary on Iguazú. I have taken this biographical information about Gunche and Martínez de la Pera from Andrea Cuarterolo (2013).
8. Mario Gallo, for instance, an Italian immigrant who was a pioneer on Argentine fiction film, directed two adaptations of *Cavalleria Rusticana* in 1908 and 1919.

9. Proof that the directors of *Nobleza gaucha* were not the only ones who tried to repeat the film's success is the fact that *Juan sin ropa* (Georges Benoît, 1919) –whose title was inspired by the character of *Santos Vega* by Rafael Obligado– was marketed, after a change of distributor in 1921, under the significant title of *Nobleza criolla* (Mafud 2016: 281).

10. The word 'editors', used in the advertisement, can be considered a proof of how fluid the work in the film industry was at the time. Both Martínez and Gunche assumed the role of directors, editors and directors of photography, among other tasks.

11. I have previously addressed, in a study of Alfredo Quesada's *Martín Fierro* (1923), the notions of movement and projection (in Gilles Deleuze's and Jean-Michel Frodon's terms, respectively) as the two main demands of the Argentine cinematographic field of the 1920s (Suárez 2017).

12. The term 'precinema' refers to different technologies and techniques that were developed under a basic notion of montage and *mise en scène*, and preceded the invention of the cinematograph by the Lumières in 1895.

13. White telephone or *Telefoni Bianchi* films were light comedies and melodramas made in Italy during the 1930s and 1940s. Often set in elegant environments, these comedies featured white telephones as part of their *décor* and used techniques from Hollywood screwball comedies. They were a response to a heightened demand for films for the home market following the withdrawal of the American majors from Italy in the wake of the fascist state monopoly on film distribution. Although highly successful among the general public and even replicated in other countries, white telephone comedies were severely disapproved of by the critics for their frivolousness and for diverting attention from political and social problems (Moliterno 2008: 340).

14. The complete testimony is available at <https://www.youtube.com/watch?v=3AlUCjKOjuc> [accessed 19 June 2020].

15. David José Kohon was a prominent figure of the so-called Generation of the 60s, which was strongly influenced by the work of avant-garde European filmmakers of the time. In 1969, he gained international prestige with *Breve cielo* [Brief Sky] and continued to make a few other films until in 1982 he directed *El agujero en la pared*. This adaptation of the myth of Faust was, just as in the cases of Martínez and Gunche and Saslavsky, his last feature film.

16. *El camino hacia la muerte del viejo Reales* (1971), a documentary by Vallejo that portrayed the exploitation of peasants in Tucumán, opened with an epigraph from *Martín Fierro*. Vallejo, who was part of the Cine Liberación group with Fernando Solanas and Octavio Getino, also took part in the production of *Los hijos de Fierro*.

17. Birri had already used drawings by Oski in his animated film *La primera fundación de Buenos Aires* (1959), based on Ulrico Schmidl's chronicles.

18. A review of repetitions, duplicities, synonyms and parallelisms in Del Campo's poem can be found in the works by Ludmer (2000: 222–24) and Noemí García and Jorge Panesi (1998: 29–31).

CHAPTER 3

❖

'Tal vez acaben deshechos en espuma' (Juan Rulfo): The Poetics of the Afterimage and the Posthumous in Rubén Gámez's *La fórmula secreta* (1964–65)

Erica Segre

Charting Contexts of Invasion: Rubén Gámez's Film and Juan Rulfo's Poem

In 1962, the experimental Chilean dramatist and visionary, Alejandro Jodorowsky (2004: 30–31) published a text in the Mexican magazine *S.NOB* that visualized a new combinatory being, a cybernetic organism, which fused human matter with a self-sustaining electronic mechanism. Written in a knowingly exalted style, vatic-like and subtly ironic, the article was illustrated with a transitional artefact, which seemed to draw on the history of western anatomical drawing to evoke a half-fused, headless sculpture as if unfashioning its natural skin and allowing the non-organic, abstract automata to emerge from its skin coils. Cast in a retrograde fashion reminiscent of late nineteenth-century commercial illustration, the monochrome drawing is literally conjoined to a mysterious mechanical support.

In a mock-religious style Jodorowsky referenced Bach's St Matthew Passion, invoking a baroque musical echo of this fantastical being as if the cybernetic organism was a 'revenant', a returning phenomenon rather than a futuristic glimpse of things to come: 'Yo me limito a rezar así (usando como música de fondo *La pasión según San Mateo de Bach*): Padre Cyborg que estás en mí: ¡bendice a la máquina, electrónico soy!' [I limit myself to praying thus using Bach's Passion According to Saint Matthew: Father Cyborg that dwells in me: bless the machine, for I am electronic!] (Jodorowsky 2004: 31). The foundational cyborg 'patriarch', whose blessing is transposed (imprecisely) to the manifestation of the inhuman and the robotic, serves to mythologize this materialization of the uncanny admixture ('esculturas-máquinas') as part of a much longer narrative of ritual and object-based worship. For Jodorowsky, this offers a critical opportunity not devoid of humour, or indeed terror, to expose commodification and materialism, to allow the cyborg being to both dehumanize the rise of electronic media as estrangement and technocracy and to posit its provocation as a measure of existential disorientation. His vintage cyborg is a catalyst for anti-bourgeois discrepant action, a conceptual

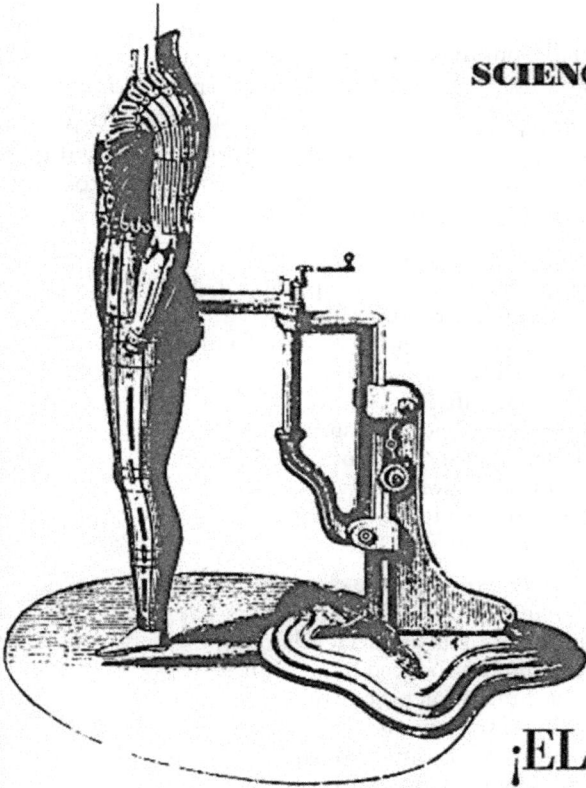

SCIENCIE-FICTION

¡EL CYBORG!

por Alejandro Jodorowsky-Prullansky

"FRIO COMO UN PEZ, BOCA SELLADA Y
GLANDULAS DE ACERO... ASI SERA EL
HOMBRE DEL PORVENIR, EL CYBORG, CON-
QUISTADOR DE LOS PLANETAS".

J.B.

¿QUE ES UN CYBORG? ES UN ORGANISMO CIBERNETIZADO

VAMOS A TRATAR aquí el tema más bello y emocionante de la ciencia actual. Este descubrimiento, el Cyborg, termina con toda una época del pensamiento humano. Durante mucho tiempo se nos enseñó, románticamente, a desconfiar de la máquina. Chaplin en *Tiempos modernos*, Kafka en *La Colonia penitenciaria*, Bradbury en *Crónicas marcianas*, Simak en *Mañana los perros*, el surrealismo en su *Manifiesto contra la ciencia* (*Los robots no pasarán*, Breton.), etc., llegaron a una especie de fobia artística contra la máquina: Ella terminaría por apoderarse del Universo, exterminando al hombre. Tinguely, Marcel Duchamp, Hiquily, Felguerez y muchos otros, como reacción, crearon una estética nueva, *las esculturas-máquinas*, llevados por una especie de amor auto-provocado hacia el mecanismo, pero sin abandonar nunca el humor y, sobre todo, *el terror*.

Cada espíritu sensible se vio en la obligación de sustituir el mito de la Araña gigante-devoradora o el de la ballena jonaseana (representativos de la Madre devoroz-madre-universal de acero y engranajes, tragando por una boca erizada de bisturíes, a la pobre humanidad-hijo para triturarla...

Este terror al crecimiento mastodóntico del acero

30

FIG. 3.1. '¡El Cyborg!' Post-impression from an anonymous original, improvised application by Alejandro Jodorowsky, 1962. Original publication *S.NOB*, Number 4, 11 July 1962.

instrument to dismantle the predominance of facile Anglophone acquisitiveness. The multimedia artist Felipe Ehrenberg embraced a similar counter-narrative in 'El nuevo Génesis' (1967), originally published in *Psicograma* no. 3 as an anti-industrial fable,[1] (Debroise and Medina 2014: 106–09). Using an interplay of multi-coloured human silhouettes and text boxes, Ehrenberg reconfigured the return of the neo-Gothic monster as a Frankensteinian embodiment. Conceived as a staged striptease, each numbered capsule advanced the detraction of civility and communality, suppressing causal links to end up with a bestial 'reduction' stripped bare:

> Día 3: La máquina cibernética cambia su
> programa de trabajo en un medio aleatorio. [...]
> Día 5: El hombre se retira a un olimpo
> artificial: se convierte en el mito de las máquinas.
> Día 6: Las máquinas olvidan al hombre
> y su programación. Sufren una distorsión
> de los mecanismos de placer y displacer.
> Se tornan sadomasoquistas, neuróticas,
> inhibidas amnésicas y agresivas.
> Día 7: Striptease de una máquina enferma:
> es el hombre 'civilizado'.
>
> [Day 3: The cybernetic machine changes
> its work programme through random means [...]
> Day 5: Man retreats to an artificial Olympus:
> he becomes the myth produced by machines.
> Day 6: The machines forget the man
> and his programmes. They undergo a distortion
> of the mechanisms of pleasure and pain.
> They become sadomasochistic, neurotic, inhibited,
> amnesiac and aggressive.
> Day 7: Striptease performed by an ailing machine:
> disclosed is a 'civilized' human being.]

In both of these counter-cultural, experimental figures, Jodorowsky and Ehrenberg, there is an appropriation of a pseudo-macabre counterpoint to expose the underlying eviscerations of conventional urbanity and the expanding domination of bourgeois appetites and mediocrity in Mexico. In a parallel vein, *La fórmula secreta*, Rubén Gámez's disruptive film, resorts to ambiguity as a recursive feature of its aesthetic to disorientate the viewer and problematize the act of looking at a non-naturalistic mediation. His disenchanted vision of contemporary Mexico relies on a similarly unhinged and 'horrifying' premise.

Originally known as *Coca-Cola en la sangre* and later converted to the more enigmatic and clinical *La fórmula secreta* (1965), the film revolves around an equivocal bio-medical process. This hidden or delinquent intervention, which is technical to the extent that it is a faceless action, seeks to revive a moribund individual: it is ostensibly intended — from the very outset — as a revitalizing transfusion, a stimulus, to rekindle a waning (yet invisible) body through a 'miraculous' exchange of life-giving serum. One might consider that what is at stake is something quasi-vampiric, a possession or occupation, with the black liquid monstrously replacing

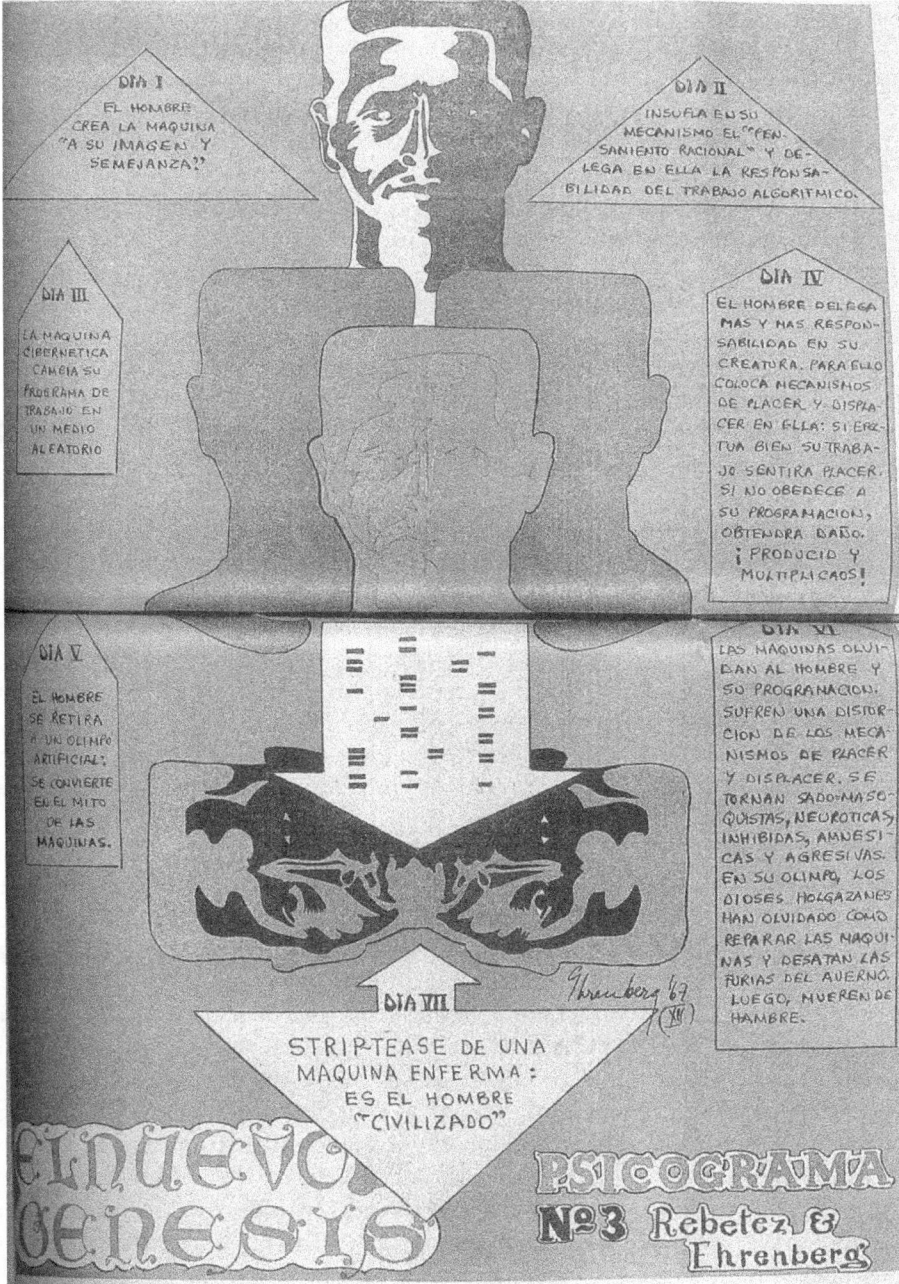

FIG. 3.2. Felipe Ehrenberg and René Rebetez, 'El nuevo Génesis', 1968. From *Psicograma*, no. 3, *El Heraldo de México*, 4 February 1968.

the natural organic fluid, supplanting a symptom of humanity with an alien admixture. It is akin to an external commonplace manifestation of the everyday while carrying this estranging feature inwardly to a corrosive outcome. The revival is consequently a false expectation as there is no virtual 'resurrection' (despite the Churrigueresque Pueblan interiors so frequently lit up in slow takes), but instead a litany of deadly foreshadowings of various types.[2] There is no transformation as such of the implied generic patient, but rather a progressive form of what Juan Rulfo would go on to explain to the bewildered viewing public as expressive of 'un país influido por el automatismo y la técnica maquinista' [a country influenced by automatism and mechanical technique] (Fell 1996: 363). Automatism and mechanistic technique de-familiarize our conventional perception, emphasizing unawareness or involuntariness as far as sentience is concerned while stressing mechanical operations devoid of human agency to distance us from the resident aliens apparently circulating in our midst. The notion that an involuntary but irresistible inclination may explain this acceptance of US imperialism's tendrils underscores the potency of visual suggestibility.

The aim of this chapter is to read Gámez's experimental film within its know-ingly alienating spectrum of effects, from conceptual premise to satirical insin-uation. I will resituate Rulfo's poem in tandem, embedded as it is within a 'película ANTI [...] anti todo' [an ANTI film [...] anti everything] (Brennan 2014: 23), thereby unlocking what Luis Buñuel had called 'el mundo liberador de la poesía' [the liberating world of poetry] in the filmic texture[3] (1958: 1). The work's oneiric (rather than neorealist) dimension may indeed open the inner eye of a radical social critique. For Buñuel (1958: 2), the film medium itself resembled the morphology of the unconscious. His film *El ángel exterminador* (1962) exploited absurd non-sequiturs, farce and the inexplicable in order to expose the pretensions of the Mexican bourgeois regime and its sacrificial violence. Rulfo's unique film-poem emerged as a response to the depopulation of the countryside and the repressive expansionism of the bourgeois city that he had caught in photographs of internal migrants tangled in the web of railway lines, living by squatting between perilous verges in the 1950s. It comprised a reactive interplay, predicated on Rulfo's witnessing existing footage before interpreting his hermeneutic monologues that accentuated discontinuity and the blurring of self and collective entities. This performative interpenetration of Gámez's texture relies on Rulfo's film-poem being subsequent, delivered in an aleatory orchestration (of voices) by a well-known poet, Jaime Sabines (1926–1999). The film-poem ventriloquizes Rulfo's poetic vein without attributing the voiceover to its source. It is characteristically indirect and resonant.

The metropolitan scenario alluded to in the works by Jodorowsky and Ehrenberg mentioned above offers a juxtaposition of straight inequality and political inequity, of a strangeness emerging from unfettered yet superficial urbanism displayed through the rise of an underground phenomenon. For Gámez, by contrast, the alien infiltration is articulated visually as a self-destructive introspective motif that is repeated throughout the opening sequence of *La fórmula secreta*: imbrications of inwardness and self-absorption exploited through the vertiginous, circular movement of the camera around the Zócalo, in the Mexican capital. The filmic revolution, synchronized to keep pace with Antonio Vivaldi's flute concerto *La notte*, introduces the revenant effect previously discussed in relation to Jodorowsky's cyborg by displacing the temporal ambient and collapsing the contemporary into a past-present — a baroque interlude. Anachronism becomes part of this revolution. Speedily cyclical, the camera turns on the space of the city's foundation, the colonial grid or street layout. The choice of Vivaldi was unlikely to have been an arbitrary musical selection: after all, the composer had explored sympathetically the role of *Motezuma* in an opera (1733) and this associative veneer might have been part of Gámez's game. The Zócalo appears to be the site of political, spiritual and economic power where the legacy of vice-regal centralization seems to persist — or at least has left its monumental architectural semblance: it is here where nation, capital, the church and commerce used to intertwine. The neocolonial matrix is, consequently, introduced as a formative conjunction with the not-so-enigmatic transfusion of the unusually prolonged *fade in* (lasting three minutes) in which 'aparece la Coca-Cola, la botella y luego la cámara por el hilo, el tubo' [the Coca-Cola appears, the bottle and then the camera following the conduit, the tube] (Pelayo 2014: 366).

This focally extended shot, starting with the bottle brand and following the meandering length of the conduit in an unbroken take, turns what for Gámez was a concept, something problematically 'muy abstracto' [very abstract], into a potential visual overlap reliant on insinuation and allusive play (Pelayo 2014: 366). Even the typeface of the title is archaic with its medieval-style letters picked out against the not-so-native grain of this site of mimicry (the Zócalo), with colonial architecture reminiscent of centuries-long superimpositions. The filmic look seems to emphasize how undifferentiated it all appears to be; masquerade, façade — a place overlooked by the silhouette of a scavenging vulture inserted as a menacing black outline. This scavenging artefact-bird, made of cardboard with an excessively long neck to displace the association with the obligatory 'Mexican' eagle, soars comically above the Zócalo transforming it into a desert-like elsewhere. We begin to sense the dust revolving in this accelerated whirlwind, as the filmic is contaminated with the rough-hewn grain of the medium itself, its filtering or mediating of the visible. We shall see later how Gámez deliberately experimented with segmentation, dissolves and rapid editing. How he dislocated the coursing of the shot itself, for instance, seeking to escape the framed human subject, such as a peasant unseated from his habitual screen terrain, his set locality. How he intercalated still images in rapid sequence to aggregate the corporate intrusion relating to industrial manufacture, evidencing the substitution of a mirage of autonomy with the reality of underdevelopment. Gámez's unusual use of flicker or blink effects is of particular interest when evaluating how he disturbs conventional film viewing: he turns to these perceptual omissions, visual gaps or reverberations in order to draw attention to an intermedial convergence — a coalescing of disturbing incongruities. A systematic imbalance emerges relating to the assemblage of photographic stills, of stencil contours or comic image (the laughing cow), of film motility, branded outline (the silhouette of the black Coke bottle) and Rulfo's stanzas. The utterance of the poem moves from the personal to the collective in the first section, and then, in the second section, to choral and intersubjective invocations of the ruinous, generating a similarly disjointed construction. Palimpsest-like in practice, with its layering of 'la misma jeringa' [the same syringe] with 'este aire lleno de cenizas' [this air full of ash], the poem revisits the scourge of age-old hunger, mediating a recessive and darkened vision of rurality — rural terrain that the film personifies, blighted by neglect yet supported by the extractive pull of economic dependence (Rulfo 2014: 28–29).

In the opening sequences of the film it becomes clear that unlike the 1920s European avant-garde (I am thinking of Hannah Höch for instance), Gámez's approach to collage and photomontage was not dependent on 'the collision of the heterogeneous'. It did not attempt to intervene 'decidedly' but without seeking harmonization or assimilation of pictorial or graphic elements in pursuit of creative revelations (Alison and Malissard 2018: 151). In later interviews, he was adamant about the structural impetus, the planning of shots; the absence of improvisation: 'todo estaba escrito' [everything was written down] he claimed — perhaps to correlate the impact of a musical soundscape that plays such a dominant role in the syncretic aesthetic of transpositions (Pelayo 2014: 366). Unfolding, despite its irregularity, through synoptic passages with interludes and episodes transitioning from section to section, the film articulates what has been termed intriguingly a 'nacionalismo defensivo' [defensive nationalism] (Jorge Ayala Blanco), predicated on a radical critique of the supposed apathy of the great mass of underdogs and lumpenproletariat (2014: 64). The inertia of unreflective labourers is often shown in close-up: an impassive blank gaze looking at an 'invisible' lens; moving on the back of an open truck, slumped like a bulky, non-sentient thing, winding through subterranean, newly designed traffic channels made in concrete. Conversely, literally unmoving peasants appear in situ impaled in dust cracks foregrounding their blurred in-betweenness, amplified temporally to mark their germinating stillness rather than productivity. As Gámez freely admitted to his interviewer, the slumbering, politically unconscious and unresponsive *pueblo* was his target:

> De alguna manera quería denunciar con ella al pueblo, no al gobierno ni al sistema, sino a nuestro pueblo 'agachón'[4]: hay una escena en la que, filmando a un individuo, lo golpeo dos veces y le hiero la cara, y el tipo se queda impávido, sin hacer nada. Eso quise denunciar, la masa informe que va a seguir comiendo raíces y yerbas y va a seguir subsistiendo, un pueblo dormido que tolera estos gobiernos déspotas que tenemos, un pueblo dormido que no sólo no tiene conciencia de la política sino que no tiene conciencia de nada.

> [I wanted to somehow denounce the people through it, not the government or the system, but that 'submissive' populace: there is a scene in which, filming an individual, I hit him twice and injured his face, and the guy remains impassive, without doing anything. That is what I wanted to denounce, the homogenous mass that is going to continue eating roots and herbs and is going to continue enduring, a dormant people that tolerates the despotic governments we've got, a dormant population that not only has no political conscience but has no awareness of anything.] (Lerner 2014: 324)

The film's disenchanted vision is certainly all-encompassing in relation to the decline of the strata of class and culture. Degeneration across social boundaries conflates margins of anxiety in a melancholy refrain where apathy confronts threatened or actual class violence. The film ends with a revelatory drama based on flight and terror. We witness a bourgeois technocrat pursued by a revolutionary *charro*, or cowboy, waiting to reel in his prey from horseback somewhere in midtown.

The use of sonority as a visual subtext or echo is something that Gámez resorts to repeatedly, we shall discover, to allude to the internal scope of invasion: there is the indecipherable 'text' delivered by a single solemn voiceover that overlays men in underground poses and corporeal interconnections. These men watchfully follow a largely apathetic lens that tends towards a frontal immobility. Even when at his most overtly playful or subversive, Gámez still tends to exploit an echo chamber sense of confinement, a subterranean imprisonment that resonates uncannily. His mysterious Ur-language with its Japanese-sounding inflections echoes weirdly to underline its strangeness, its alien infiltration in key interludes shot in dark, indoor spaces that resemble spaces of abduction. This is the depth of echo as a means of foraging inwardly; the kind of cognitive dissonance that will shape Gámez's poetics of the afterimage in his exploitation of Rulfo's play with shadows: 'Se nos regatea hasta la sombra' [They even haggle away our shadow] (Rulfo 2014: 27).

The gamut of afterimage effects, deliberately variegated in the film's experimentation, encompasses a number of optical and conceptual interpretations of image processing through filmic and still photography. If afterimage relates to an optical illusion (that is, the manifestation of an image after exposure to the original source has ceased), this may easily lend itself to ideas of reverberation and haunting. However, a lesser physiological approach might include a pathological exaggeration of such phenomena that may not be recognizable as distortions. Of the latter, illusory and hallucinatory *palinopsia* (revisitation of a visual image once the optical prompt is absent) offer contrasts in resolution and distinctness, the former being affected by ambient light and motion to a diffuse degree, while the latter may produce longer-lasting and high resolution images which may be recursive. This gamut of afterimage effects will be analysed later in relation to the embedding of Rulfo's poem in the film. The suppression of defiance, for instance, which is voiced connecting self and others seems at the very least equivocal and typically indirect ('Según parece' [Apparently]): 'No es que seamos alzados' [We are not insurgent] evokes precisely what it denies, drawing an image of a more confrontational duality. (Rulfo 2014: 27–28).

Equally prevalent as a resource is the notion of 'zombified' presences on screen, at once palpitating but wholly arrested: the living-dead motif, with actors either indifferent to the scrutiny of the lens, stalled and unaware, or returning an inscrutable gaze mindlessly when faced with the director's specular insistence. These penumbral apparitions (both shown outside in parched soil and within *cámara oscura* interiors), become the half-awake and evanescent automata poeticized by Rulfo's meditation on dissolution, whirlwinds, ruins and semi-consciousness, recited by the poet Jaime Sabines. It is here, within the liminal space afforded by intimations of environmental collapse that Rulfo's poem anticipates a kind of resistance; that is before the second instalment of the poem unfurls its darker blending of penitence and rebellion in a chorus of incantations and religious epithets. Rulfo's words signal a possible escape from such telluric dystopia; words of precarious agency that clamour for collective attention even if only from the brink of ecological disaster. A form of verbal spectrality, not unlike a posthumous trace found in an aftermath, seemingly advances an overturning of the status quo. The shift of perception is mused subtly through an inversion of tone — Rulfo evoking mourning and victimhood for a collective betrayal, a backward-looking gesture towards a receding horizon of action. As Octavio Paz acknowledged in his signature anthology *Poesía en movimiento* (1966), the interrelation between opposition and action was characteristic of his generation's kind of disenchantment: 'intentaron reunir en una sola corriente poesía, erotismo y rebelión. *Dijeron: La poesía entra en acción*' [they tried to combine in a single current poetry, eroticism and rebellion. *They said: poetry takes action*] (1983: 20). I intend here to contextualize Rulfo's super-saturated poem with reference to Efraín Huerta's layers of post-revolutionary disenchantment ('La traición general' [General Treason] of 1937) and his archaeological alienation. The comparison with Huerta's disconnection with ancient disjecta ('El Tajín' from 1963) will help to amplify the connective tissue of Rulfo's familiar imagery of absence and loss. It will also prompt a re-reading which rescues something overlooked, the 'hopeful' speculation as to future outcomes: Rulfo's elliptical interrogations seem to offer a less pessimistic view than some critics have alleged, providing at least a provocation if not a full-blown rebellion. The textual imagery (drawn from Rulfo's cadences), is embedded in the film's infra or subterranean narrative. The film's transposition of verbal vision with the 'inner', ill-defined figment of the imagination, operates as an excessive accretion, a mixed assemblage of selected image and subsequent allusions still yoked to some of the more ribald sections of the drama on screen.

Satirical episodes, for instance, such as the revolving merry-go-round with its laughing girls in flawless, devotional white; the scaffolding from which clerics fall, like life-hating crows, while the topsy-turvy children at play, in seminary dress, applaud. Shot in a sequence of alternating images staring straight at the camera with a variety of lively demeanours (unlike the impassive, plummeting clergy), the children offer a disabused 'knowingness'. Simultaneously, shots of rough boards carrying the damning statement 'censurado' [censored] repeat across the screen in an unexpected alteration of filmic segments. This passage undoubtedly exposes bourgeois hypocrisy, alluding explicitly to perversion, abuse and complicity in religious institutions. The authoritarian suppression of sexual culpability, made abundantly clear in the *mise en scène*, was, obviously, influenced by Buñuel's film satire.

Returning to the secretive drug-addiction, 'la fórmula' as a compulsive affliction, we apprehend a bizarre form of dependence. It is as if the threat of linguistic estrangement has moved manifestly forward. We may recall at this point of poetic addiction Rubén Darío's frequently anthologized anticipation of linguistic dissolution. This extraneous infiltration appears to interrogate Darío's prescient question in 'Los cisnes', echoing across the temporal divide:

¿Seremos entregados a los bárbaros fieros?
¿Tantos millones de hombres hablaremos inglés?
¿Ya no hay nobles hidalgos ni bravos caballeros?
¿Callaremos ahora para llorar después?

[Will we surrender to the savage barbarians?
Will so many millions of men speak English?
Are there no noble gentlemen or brave knights?
Will we acquiesce now to mourn afterwards?]

Published in Darío's *Cantos de vida y esperanza* (1905), the poem sought to recuperate Latin American identity during a period dominated by Anglophone colonial wars and imperialism as well as to challenge the tensions between modernity and tradition, the commercialization of art and the dominance of economic positivism (1949: 69). In *La fórmula secreta*, the threat has materialized in a sound intervention: a belaboured childish voice seeking to emulate English, mispronouncing many words reread from a manual, struggles to make palatable the indigestible otherness of an alien tongue. She provides an explicit ramification of this social phenomenon (migratory as well as localized) allying tongue and occupation in a grotesque loosening of national sovereignty.

Already in *Salón México* (1949), director Emilio Fernández had product-placed the Coke bottle in the inescapable prison-like dance hall to herald a commercial dependence. His luckless *cabaretera* protagonist is caught in a proletarian masquerade. Her oscillating duality between proletarian exploitation and bourgeois respectability seeks to camouflage the social mobility her younger sibling has gained through an exclusive education. She is shown drinking this non-alcoholic yet 'addictive' beverage insinuated within the urban paraphernalia, smuggled in as an anticipatory portent of invasions in progress — in an ostentatious shot to flag up the insidious potency of US capitalism and the openness or vulnerability of the transitional metropolis. Fernández's film combines late nineteenth-century anxiety about Anglophone hegemony in Latin America through a mythopoetic aperture with a film melodrama set in a transitional period of new alliances, in the immediate aftermath of the Second World War. In *Salón México*, we witness the disorientating effects of a nation-conscious dual urbanization that has implications for Gámez's film. Evolutionary development at once rooted, sourced in the pre-Hispanic and vernacular, yet also extraneous, deracinated and invasive, dislodges *Salón México*'s narrative ability to resolve the dramatic tensions counterpointed in the script. Reconfiguring the poetic and filmic anxiety concerning the predominance of Anglophone intervention in Latin America, we may pinpoint Gámez's anti-imperialist stance and his objection to neocolonial cultural expansion through pop and mass media infringements of unchanging models of 'Mexican' autochthony in the mid-1960s. The emblematic or rhetorical performance alluded to in Fernández's *Salón México* serves to underscore the factual incongruities and the epidermic nationalism that are later explored by Gámez, when entangling his endless hot dog across the Mexican capital's formative centre.

Gámez's key satirical motif, the epic mounted *charro* (who moves from province to capital as in a number of comical dramas from the 1950s) (Segre 2007), is akin to any *Villista* centaur: an icon that ranges from Revolutionary photo-reportage to popular film emblem. Transferred from parochial corral to asphalt pavement he is free to pursue new prey in the cityscape. The bourgeois everyman is seen hurrying and then running, terror rising with every panicked step. As the thrown coil inevitably captures him and drags him down to the ground, a directorial manoeuvre allows him to exchange a deathly stare with the camera. The *charro* strangled and immobilized, the final still shot of him loops around its own terror effect to correlate subjectivity and the idea of death in Mexican visual culture (Lomnitz 2005). As a formative visual trope, 'the charro' figure has a long syncretic history based on colonial perceptions of death rituals combining pre-Hispanic and post-Conquest conversion. Modern poetic renditions have tended to make it synonymous with structural modalities in Mexican culture thereby making deadly re-visitation a commonplace motif of hallucinatory perception. The dead man walking anticipates the ending that befalls him: the running forwards while looking over one's shoulder captures symbolically the ontological uncertainty of the bourgeois citizen during the authoritarian repression associated with the six years of Gustavo Díaz Ordaz's presidency (1964–70). The infiltration of this efficacious spectre from the mythic past, the ultra-Mexican film macho, may be regarded as Gámez's dead-ending of screen escapism. This classic personage is a familial visual presence as far as screen iconicity is concerned. His secondary menace draws together something of José Clemente Orozco's Castile-centric horses of the apocalypse (associated with the importing of alien 'monsters' by the Conquistadors), and displacing the effect of the Coca-Cola transfusion concept with its own unbidden yet equally negative 'retorno' [return].[5] However grotesque and comical the Horseman's streetwise antics may appear to be to the onlooker, he projects the long shadow of persecution linked to militia in the city (and neo-*caciquismo* in rural areas) during the clashes that took place in 1958–59 in central Mexico City. These involved massive protests by university students but also the mobilization of organized urban workers, alienated by falling living standards and repression (Navarro 2012: 51).

In the light of this rereading of contextual allusions, one might take issue with Jesse Lerner's sophisticated analysis of Gámez's film that relies on the redeployment of the 'fold' as a concept borrowed from Gilles Deleuze and his vision of the baroque. Lerner conceives the baroque palimpsest as an introverted feature of the film's *mise en scène* (with reference to theorizations by Alejo Carpentier in the 1940s and Severo Sarduy in the 1970s). However, there are alternative possibilities of interpretation linked to the use of afterimage effects that interpenetrate the filmic and the poetic dimensions — what Octavio Paz (1983: 6) celebrated as the interpenetration of closed and open, prosodic and prosaic forms: 'una arquitectura que sin cesar se deshace y se rehace' [an architecture that ceaselessly unmakes and remakes itself], predicated on experimentation and mutability. Gámez's film is not only reliant on musical editing, which carries multiple sonorities breaching containing frames; it also plays with a variety of splicing techniques to solder the moving image to poetic ambiguity. Still photographs, brand emblems, recycled industrial close-ups, and a long, unfurling list of hand-drawn, transnational private industries end the film on a slow but layered fade in which smuggled pop slogans and graffiti are also graspable: 'Kilroy was here'; 'Die Now — Pay Later'; 'Keep Going Baby'; 'Klan Sinatra'. Gámez's short film is thus less melancholy resignation as Lerner contends ('niega cualquier esperanza de cambio, reforma, evolución o revolución' [it negates any hope of change, reform, development or revolution]), and more akin to a contestatory action which 'galvanizes' the viewer and startles his facile consumption of film 'junk' (Lerner 2014: 327).

A convergence occurs in *La fórmula secreta* between disparate but secretly interrelated (multiple?) invasions completing the circular design so conscripted through the film's overt musical counterpoint. The metonymically significant revolving of the camera when in operation in the opening sequence combines with the whirlwind identity of Rulfo's imagined rural transits (delivered through the first instalment of the poem), and with intertwined animal symbolism relating to the actual butchering of a cow on screen in real time subsequently. As in Manuel Álvarez Bravo's celebrated photograph of a slaughtered protesting worker, *Obrero en huelga, asesinado* (1934), the dying cow registers its ongoing spillage (its eyes visibly becoming emptied of a sentient gaze as we watch) beyond the filmic frame. The blood in both cases, in the still and moving image, infringes a photographic boundary, in a telling meta-photo/filmic moment that implicates the viewer. What follows includes the slaughterer now cast in supplicant mode carrying uphill in some provincial corner the heavy morphing minotaur-head, shown occasionally transfigured from decapitated limb into a human death mask. A switching of faces, from animal sacrifice to human expiation, is worked in as a structural feature of montage. It is also worth pointing out that from early on Gámez's film manipulations include a crucial number of recurrent acts of heterosexual voracity apparently linked to something akin to a Thanatos impulse: wild desire is unleashed in conjunction with acts of sacrifice/slaughter. One early ritual sequence, for instance, takes place on the back of the open truck in motion: it focuses on a necrophilic transposition between the living and the dead, a facial double-take in which open mouths, one living, the other 'shrouded', appear to touch. This phantasmal switch creates a disturbing congress, an unearthly communication across physical divisions not unlike Juan Rulfo's *Pedro Páramo* (1955), where Juan Preciado carries the photograph of his dead mother as an active and vengeful memory to his ancestral village, entangling the living and the dead:

> Era un retrato viejo, carcomido en los bordes; pero fue el único que conocí de ella. Me lo había encontrado en el armario de la cocina [...] Desde entonces lo guardé. Era el único. Mi madre siempre fue enemiga de retratarse. Decía que los retratos eran cosa de brujería. Y así parecía ser; porque el suyo estaba lleno de agujeros como de aguja, y en dirección del corazón tenía uno muy grande donde bien podía caber el dedo del corazón. (1994: 10–11)

> [It was an old portrait, with worm-eaten edges; but it was the only one of her that I knew. I had come across it in the kitchen cupboard [...] From then on I kept it. It was the only one. My mother was always hostile to being photographed. She used to say that photographs were associated with witchcraft. And so it seemed to be; because hers was full of needle-point holes, and in the direction of her heart there was a very large opening where the middle finger, the finger of the heart, might have found a space.]

The photograph becomes as if invested with a transformative power. It is as if the acute receptivity of a pupil seen externally indicates an inescapable extinction of light, 'el caudal de luz que penetra el ojo y nunca retorna. Es como un sol en negativo' [the flow of light that penetrates the eye and never returns. It is like a negative of the sun], according to Margo Glantz's (2001: 18) suggestive exegesis. This transfer of perceptual darkness as a repository of internal sight remains an intermedial intervention that is characteristic of Rulfo's use of filmic and photographic effects in his fiction and which surfaces in his fluid film-poem.

The notion of a blurred interface between ecstatic desire and possession, between clandestine flesh and the devil, reappears in a later intervention in Gámez's provocative film. It involves several clutching embraces by a couple, expressive of erotic excess while the systematic slaughter of the cow is ongoing. The implied stimulus that links sexual arousal and a death act is undoubtedly disturbing.

Although the premise of Gámez's film supposedly relies on the Coca-Cola formula and the blinking-effect of the simplified bottle brand with its unsettling optical repetition, its invasive subterfuge is equally dependent on the penetration of a US sausage that creates a disjointed montage of urban fragments, fragments that it alone connects and conjugates nonsensically. This absurdist line of disparate shots makes for a heterogeneous panorama (including marching legs; a shot of the Torre Latinoamericana; a typical display of chiles from a stand; a baker decorating a cake; a switched-on television screen; a Tina Modotti-like shot of a *huarache*-wearing foot; the sausage coils climbing round a pillar in the Zócalo). Strung together by an endless hot dog, meandering its way through and entangling the activities of the capital, there is a degree of obvious artifice that is both laughable, a kind of silent-film gag, and intriguing because of what it appears to portend. Again, we discover the interconnections between lines of invasion: crisscrossing like a spider's web over the dislocated subtext of the film that interrogates and mocks *los de abajo* [the underdogs] and *los de arriba* [the masters].

'La palabra clave es indeterminación. Textos en movimiento.' (Octavio Paz): Rulfo's Poetics of the Afterimage

In Efraín Huerta's 'La traición general' [General Treason] from 1937, the disabused perspective, 'el desengaño' [disenchantment], targets the betrayal perpetrated by declamatory and civic-minded poetry 'de los que prohijaron fríamente [...] la farsa del silencio' [of those who fostered glacially the farce of silence] (Hirschman 2001: 130). The poem starts with a negative, which is repeated to expose a falsehood, a realm of affectation and fiction: 'No; no era verdad tanta limpia belleza' [No; no such thing as so much flawless beauty]. Huerta indicts those who plotted to extend the miasma of untruth and amnesia: 'Y ahora, cuando nada nos pasa desapercibido, | denunciamos a los traidores, a los huecos poetas | que nos cantaron "nanas" deliberadamente | y nos dieron calmantes y narcóticos' [And now, when nothing may be overlooked, | we denounce the traitors, the shallow poets | who sang 'lullabies' deliberately | and gave us sedatives and drugs] (Hirschman 2001: 128).

Slumber-inducing 'lullabies' are followed by chemical and narcotic substances that make for a general level of dysfunction, alluding to the neutralizing effects of a biomedical cosh. The collective, working-class somnolence decried by Gámez informs Rulfo's evasive and discontinuous narrative voices in his 1950s fiction. This dormant consciousness also provides a tendency to displace responsibility in his later film-poem. In the latter, key, telluric imagery is recycled across the first and second instalments to emphasize the impact of a whirlwind. As if swivelling into an all-absorbing funnel, it shifts local perception into something more diffuse, an actual slippage. At first a stark cataclysm is envisaged as a possibility 'como un relámpago de muertos' [a lightning-strike of the dead], which is then echoed in the second section as a visible phenomenon: 'Cola de relámpago, | remolino de muertos' [Lightning tail, | swirl of the dead] (Rulfo 2014: 29). The echo-effect moves from a potential simile to an undisclosed affirmation of a lightning tail culminating in a whirlpool of the dead as if a nightmarish vision has materialized objectively. This move from an interrogative subjective position to an impersonal actuality is characteristic of Rulfo's oscillating perspective in which a speculative opening is often matched, in the binary that is set up, by something indeterminate and ill-defined in the usually elliptical 'end'.

In Efraín Huerta's 'El Tajín' (from 1963), we encounter the disaffection with the monumental remains of an archaeological world 'resurrected' for an amnesiac present. Rulfo's syncretic view of vernacular culture was intimately linked to his labyrinthine approach to the present-past. His mythopoetic fabric in *Pedro Páramo* is disassembled and discontinuous with non-linear passages that collapse the boundaries of conventional realism and the fantastic. This ephemeral dimension, as we have seen, relies interestingly on the use of a punctured photograph as a memory object in the narrative. The soiled photograph creates instability in levels of representation, being both a dated and archival object, and a fantastic, virtual figment that escapes itself, thereby tending to infect the present with the 'murmullos' tenanted in a parallel dimension.

In 'El Tajín', the encounter with the ruin is pitiless; a stark emptiness prevails, as nobody returns from the dead. Those who seek to retrace their steps, to re-tread originary pathways, meet only immobility and blindness:

> Andar así es andar a ciegas, | andar inmóvil en el aire inmóvil, | andar pasos de arena [...] Dar pasos sobre agua, sobre nada [...] | dar pasos sobre muertes | sobre un suelo de cráneos calcinados. | Andar así no es andar sino quedarse | [...] porque nada está vivo | en esta soledad de tibios ataúdes. | [...] Ni un aura fugitiva habita este recinto | despiadado. Nadie aquí, nadie en ninguna sombra. | Nada en la seca estela, nada en lo alto. (Huerta 2014: 54)

> [To move like this is to be blinded, | to move in immobility through an immobile air, | to tread on the sand [...] To walk on water, on nothing [...] | to step over deaths | over ground covered in calcinated crania. | To move like this is not to move but to stay | [...] because nothing is alive | in this solitude of tepid coffins. | [...] Not even a fugitive aura dwells in this pitiless | enclosure. Nobody here, nobody behind any shadow. | Nothing in the parched stela, nothing upwards.]

The trope of a submerged shipwreck allows for the idea of lost illusions and of trapped air, of utter dereliction: 'No hay origen. Sólo los anchos y labrados ojos | y las columnas rotas y las plumas agónicas. | Todo aquí tiene rumores de aire prisionero | [...] No hay un imperio, no hay un reino. | Tan sólo el caminar sobre su propia sombra, | sobre el cadáver de uno mismo' [There is no origin. Only wide and decorative eyes | and the broken columns and anguished feathers. | Everything here lets out gusts of imprisoned air | [...] There is no empire, there is no kingdom. | Just walking on one's own shadow, | over one's own corpse] (Huerta 2014: 55). The asphyxiating ambience precludes an idealized return of a pre-Hispanic aboriginal cosmovision. The poet envisages a transcendent moment of abysmal silence in which, after the predicted decline of 'el país-serpiente sea la ruina y el polvo' [the ruin and dust of this snake-country], only the desolation of El Tajín's Totonac legacy, its imperfect monumentality, is glimpsed before it too is rubbed out; 'Y después, nada' [And then nothing] (Huerta 2014: 56). Huerta's thematization of the irrecuperable, of cultural inertia, is in a vein that captures Rulfo's tormented preoccupation with the extreme poverty of peasant life; a harrowing 'timeless' existence of mere subsistence, 'agarrándonos del viento con las uñas' [clutching at the wind with our nails] as expressed in the film-poem (Rulfo 2014: 27). There is a tension between the intangible, volatilized domain of dust-lands that the film-poem evokes (whereby Gámez situates his *campesinos* in the most infertile soil texture imaginable), and the sculptural plasticity of the peasant archetype captured on screen. The terrain between film-poem and visuality exploits this intermedial memory site, this dug-in space in which the poetic and filmic interpenetrate. 'El maldecido sol | que nos cunde a diario a despedazos' [The cursed sun | that spreads daily shredding us] combines the fragmenting impact of sun on anvil with the later intimation of rebellion, an arousal of a homogenous hive-like, furious buzzing 'cuando dejemos de gruñir como avispas | en enjambre' [when we cease snarling like wasps in a swarm] (Rulfo 2014: 28).

The syncretic paradigm plays a connective role between Gámez's film and Rulfo's film-poem, arguably first fictionalized by the author as a device. Rulfo had had occasion to illustrate one of the Goodrich-Euzkadi travel guides with shots of the celebrated church of Tonantzintla in Puebla State, with its highly decorated interior where the process of native conversion is palpable in the convergence of artistic styles (Guía Goodrich-Euzkadi 1960). Gámez transfigures the motif as an ancillary subtext for his anti-imperial perspective. His conflating of angelic visages from plafond detail and towards the end, more abstract and lasting shots that slowly navigate intricacies, gold leaf refracting from spot-lit darkness.

The film-poem seems to have absorbed evocative impressions from a wider set of recurrent preoccupations for Rulfo in 1964. Unusually, he found himself contributing a text for the exhibition of Pedro Coronel's paintings at the Galería de Arte Mexicano and used the analysis of pictorial features as a filter for an overlaying of visual manifestations with broader implications — especially in relation to a social critique of the bourgeois regime. Rulfo creates an allegorical insight when seeking to characterize Coronel's abstracted bodies:

Sus figuras yacen como aplastadas y gimientes en la tortura de la desesperación o huyen casi sin forma hacia un horizonte de tinta. La imagen de nuestro tiempo: el hombre cuyos goznes han sido rotos y cuyas deslavadas arterias se mueven aferrándose al vacío en contorsiones casi macabras. (Vital 2003: 169)

[His figures lie as if squashed and afflicted in despairing torment or undertake flights that are almost formless towards an inky horizon. An image of our times: a man whose hinges have been broken and whose faded arteries move by clinging to emptiness through quasi macabre contortions.]

Anguished, desperate figures almost escaping from shape itself allude to Rulfo's view of the broken-backed present circumstance. The flaying gestures describe a scenography of body language on the brink, a last grasp before disintegration. It is in these 'contorsiones', twisted like the swirls of the Tonantzintla baroque exploited by Gámez as designed formal 'revolutions', that we glimpse how Rulfo's anguished perception had a capacity to expose the macabre colour of the political situation. The invoked dislocated arteries speak eloquently of a disassembly of the corporeal self, a recurrent indeterminacy of subjectivity in which self and other are often collapsed in his writing. These parenthetical interludes create decentred visual associations. The interplay of public rhetoric, brute power and corruption elaborated in the first part of the film-poem, in a speculative way, allows the atrophying bodies shown draped on the soil on screen and the inaction described in the poem to intersect in a structural tension. When Rulfo (2014: 28) conjures a swelling chorus of grievance to be overheard, allowing the voiceless a precarious point of inception — 'Alguien tendrá que oírnos' [Somebody will have to hear us] — Gámez's camera foregrounds the way that skin and texture transfix the subaltern figure, dehumanizing his struggle and objectifying his stillness as an arrested, uncritical 'thing'. Gámez's experimentation, his oppositional provocation, was by comparison with Rulfo's organic film-poem, highly discrepant and unsympathetic when portraying Mexico's 'agachados'.

The solemnity often accorded to the collaborative embedding of Rulfo's text overlooks many of Gámez's dissensual games that surely were intended to deflate the Mexican screen sublime (Gabriel Figueroa's camerawork on adaptations of Rulfo's screenplays such as *El gallo de oro* in 1964, or *Pedro Páramo* in 1966 notwithstanding): 'una cámara que llevará al infierno' [a camera that will transport you to hell], as Gámez memorably put it. For instance, the director enjoyed showing a lack of confluence between film camera and documentary subject: 'La cámara mira hacia un campo y un campesino entra en cuadro y nuestra cámara lo rechaza, lo saca del cuadro. El campesino insiste en aparecer en la película y la cámara lo vuelve a rechazar' [The camera is directed at a field and a peasant comes into the frame and our camera rejects him, expels him from the picture. The peasant insists on appearing in the film and the camera once again rejects him] (Pelayo 2014: 367). This sidestepping of the curious subject, a tongue-in-cheek rejection on the part of the director has no echo in Rulfo's grave 'tierra pasmada | donde nos olvidó el destino' [stunned earth | where destiny forgot us] (2014: 27). In Rulfo's film-poem, the pursuit of a remedy ('nos llegue a todos el remedio', [let a remedy reach us all]), is expressed monochromatically, in earnest (2014: 29). This hope of relief from unbroken victimhood may ambiguously intimate death as well as a beneficial intervention from some unspecified quarter, creating a liminal imprecision as to its space–time location. Their 'collaboration' is consequently more random and dissonant than one may first assume, creating what Octavio Paz (1983: 11) recommended in experimental poetry: 'Abrir las puertas condenadas...' [To open bricked-up doors...]. The trope of the sealed room or the hidden 'cuarto de atrás' [backroom] reveals intimate moments in which openings in poetic utterance disclose the repressed tunnels of alternative 'inner' sight: this romantic lumber-room may coalesce sundry fantasies alongside nightmare and terror; visceral, wordless fear and reveries of hope and fulfilment. Opening such closets ushers in an ill-defined range of dichotomous possibilities. The poeticization of this trope ('puertas condenadas') however does not fully conjoin the practices adopted by Gámez and Rulfo in their respective interactions.

Jaime Sabines's voice has a declamatory emphasis filtered through a permanent echo-effect. This creates an internal disjunction at odds with the external panning shots that evidence the parched terrain in startling sunlight and the unmoving figures looking directly at the lens. The sculptural treatment of the peasants — shot to underscore the interplay of clean contrasts afforded by the quality of natural light — tends to establish an equivalence between their chiaroscuro symmetries, barely palpitating in the aura that grounds them, and the interspersed shots of cherubs from the interior of Tonantzintla. Some of the shots are repetitive and seen in close-up; others expand the remit. But the sequence is a structured interlacing, a transposition that we may describe as the effect of an afterimage. However, unlike the suppression of an image object that keeps reverberating optically, here the effect involves primarily an intermedial negotiation between a particular colonial aesthetic and its embodied 'objective' or 'material' association. In addition, it is not clear which way the transition is meant to head, whether backwards, as an unmasking in which the human skin gives way to the underlying colonial manufacture, or whether it is, conversely, the colonial artistry surfacing and supplanting the pigment of identity in a forward action. This doubt as to the direction of travel, as to the character of possession, swallowing or assimilation, is also part of what weaves its resonance as a deliriously unstable afterimage. The final sequence involves an upending of the peasants now shown in horizontal multitudes encased in the fissures of the terrain anticipating their own mortality in a scattering of limbs reminiscent of collective graves. As previously discussed, this resemblance to something deathly or interred creates a notional or virtual afterimage effect, yoking disparate elements to evaporate the boundaries between the resonant image and the verbal evocation.

The after-image effect may be reconfigured as a 'doubleness' in the sense that it conjoins an unstable dual authorship, creating an undecidable oscillation: so as the recitation of the poem sequence ends, the blinking presence of the black Coke bottle flickers repeatedly and uneasily, against a bleeping staccato soundscape which is mechanistic in its timekeeping. In the context of the diversionary tactics deployed by its avant-garde repudiation of pictorialism, the film's use of an iconoclastic opposition, and its experimentation with duo-collages, allows 'weaving', real or figural, to emerge. This is a counter-cultural trope for abstraction understood as nihilistic. Such a vituperative anti-everything grain, close to Gámez's aims as a filmmaker (as previously discussed), tends to create productive collisions and asymmetries. Nevertheless, the atomistic segmentation of his conceptual film avoids submerging the poem's distinguishing vocality: the final protesting condemnation of the culpable, with Sabines echoed by a choral chanting, makes for a sacrilegious litany. Allusions to criminals disintegrate the final parodic phrases into an indictment, delivering the darkest satire: 'Atajo de malvados, punta de holgazanes. *Ruega por nosotros.* | Sarta de bribones, retahíla de vagos. *Ruega por nosotros.* | Cáfila de bandidos. *Ruega por nosotros.* | Al menos éstos ya no vivirán calados por el hambre' [Collection of the wicked, lazy good-for-nothings. *Pray for us.* | Gallery of brigands, string of idlers. *Pray for us.* | Flock of bandits. *Pray for us.* | At least the latter will no longer have to endure hunger] (Rulfo 2014: 30).

In relation to the interplay of collaged features knitting the infrastructure of Gámez's film and Rulfo's film-poem, we witness the double of a blink as an optical disturbance and register its similitude to anticipatory gleanings as a poetic tactic. The poetic declamation, an intake that precedes utterance, shapes intermedial action across several contexts of creativity. This then situates the unwholesome formal adjacency between a loose and threadbare 'weaving' between Sabines's poetic voice, Gámez's visual interpretation of content, and a disjunct lack of screen seriality or fluency.

Conclusion: Posthumous Cages of Invention

As will be recalled, the opening sound track begins with the powerful sound of invisible marching feet. The percussive score flickers this subtext in Gámez's entangled critique. There is a reprise and amplification of this militaristic motif — from the aggressive shot of a man firing a rifle in full-blown conflagration, smoke emanating from this aggressive act, followed by an apparently random association with a fairground gallery of easy targets. This aggression is focalized so that it refracts back on the viewer who may find himself slipping into the spaces occupied by one of the targets — a shot reversal borrowed perhaps from Buñuel's *Abismos de pasión* (1954). This adaptation of Emily Bronte's *Wuthering Heights* follows the obsessive lover as he descends into the crypt for a breathless 'last' kiss. There is a comparable meta-filmic turn of the 'shot' that rings out, eliminating the tragic hero with immersive effects on the viewer who may feel trapped in the frame. Similarly constrained, the frame in *La fórmula secreta* flags up its own inventive 'cage'. Towards the end of the film, the metal cage becomes a reality with its incarcerated 'agachado', clinging to the railings in full view of the Metropolitan Cathedral in the Zócalo. This public 'encierro' [imprisonment], with its skeletal paradigm in bright sunshine, is brutally ironic as to the forces of exclusion and repression.

For Rulfo the posthumous serves as a residue, a spectre prone to return in hauntings in relation to a suppressed history of marginalization and victimhood.

In the short, explicatory text that he circulated at the film's opening at the Regis Cinema (November 1965), there is a tendency to emphasize the ironic hallucinatory nightmare idea through the recurrence of isolated moments of light, epiphanic glimpses of self-recognition cast as 'flamazos' [big flames], in which 'cada flama corresponde a una secuencia distinta, a una pesadilla diferente' [every flame corresponds to an alternate sequence, to a different nightmare] (Ayala 1993: 127–28). In this entrapment, perceptions are confusing in a penumbral world: 'como si hubiera caído en la sonda de un remolino' [as he had fallen into the depths of a whirlpool], corroding his sense of permanence, displacing any hope of earthly sanctuary. On other occasions, numinous darkness distorts ocularcentric habits: 'la oscuridad le hace percibir luces donde sólo hay sombras' [darkness makes him discern lights in the domain of shadows] (Ayala 1993: 128). Rulfo's exposition (a secondary narrative interpretation to guide the public) is only loosely connected to the specificities of his poem, or its disruptive interplay with Gámez's anti-imperialist critique of transnational corporate invasions. It forms a framing, subsequent construction that underscores the phantasmal and the oneiric as 'poetic' organizational principles. In Buñuel's defence of cinema as an instrument of poetry, he turned the neorealist glass into an empty gloss precisely because of its lack of horizontality, its inability to recognize the lateral mirage of possibilities reliant on its 'carga de afectividad' [affective charge], its subjective association making the experimental approach open-ended and heretical (Buñuel 1958: 15). Rulfo's silhouetted re-reading of the film as a whole and his film-poem's operations within the exploratory design of Gámez's geste, point to last impressions, standing in lapidary anticipation of a forthcoming ironic ending: an ending that is recycled, an anticipation of a future that is perpetually displaced by an interrogation or an enigma. The indeterminacy of Rulfo's spectres, their co-hosted straddling of celluloid and verbalization, their unknowability as screen presences, depends on inscrutability — the extent to which they inhabit a posthumous identity predicated on waiting indefinitely.

In the maze of disorientation, feeling a collective way in the 'revuelta obscuridad' [mixed-up obscurity], the deathly hoard of Rulfo's second poetic resolution face either dissolution 'en espuma' [in foam], vaporized and disseminated into infinitesimal particulars; or the fall of material detritus, 'ya son puro escombro' [reduced to nothing but debris], combining their duality as photo-mechanical composites whose impurity is part of their intermedial reverberation (2014: 29). Their experimental origin as phenomena relies on perceptual uncertainty; this discontinuity of perception, rendered as immobility by Gámez outdoors and shadowed internally through a formal transposition indoors, ossifies the possibility of action even if Rulfo's words (delivered by Sabines) rise to a climax of imprecation. Finally, what remains is an inventive notion of imprisonment, a constraint that allows anguished alternatives to be glimpsed from the shapeless dark.

Works Cited

ALISON, JANE, and CORALIE MALISSARD (eds). 2018. *Modern Couples: Art, Intimacy and the Avant-garde* (London and Metz: Barbican Gallery, Centre Pompidou-Metz)

AYALA BLANCO, JORGE. 2014. 'La alienación', in *Rubén Gámez: 'La fórmula secreta'*, ed. by Damián Ortega (Mexico City: Antítesis, Alias), pp. 60–65

—— (ed.). 1993. *Juan Rulfo: El gallo de oro y otros textos para cine* (Mexico City: Era)

BRENNAN, DYLAN. 2014. 'Sobre *La fórmula secreta*', in *Rubén Gámez: 'La fórmula secreta'*, ed. by Damián Ortega (Mexico City: Antítesis, Alias), pp. 23–25

BUÑUEL, LUIS. 1958. 'El cine, instrumento de poesía', *Universidad de México*, 13: 1–15

DARÍO, RUBÉN. 1949. *Cantos de vida y esperanza* (Buenos Aires, Mexico City: Austral)

DEBROISE, OLIVIER, and CUAUHTÉMOC MEDINA (eds). 2014. *La era de la discrepancia: arte y cultura visual en México* (Mexico City: UNAM, Turner)

FELL, CLAUDE (ed.). 1996. *Juan Rulfo: toda la obra* (San José: Costa Rica University, Colección Archivos)

GLANTZ, MARGO. 2001. 'Los ojos de Juan Rulfo', in *México: Juan Rulfo fotógrafo* (Barcelona, Madrid: Lunwerg), pp. 17–21

Guía Goodrich-Euzkadi: Caminos de México. 1960. (Mexico City: Goodrich-Euzkadi)

HIRSCHMAN, JACK (ed.). 2001. *Efraín Huerta: 500,000 Azaleas. The Selected Poems* (Willimantic, CT: Curbstone Press)

HUERTA, EFRAÍN. 2014. *Trans poética* (Mexico City: Era)

JODOROWSKY, ALEJANDRO. 2004. 'El cyborg!', in *S.NOB* (Mexico City: Aldus), pp. 30–31

LERNER, JESSE. 2014. 'Rubén Gámez: cine neobarroco en tiempos de cambio', in *Rubén Gámez: 'La fórmula secreta'*, ed. by Damián Ortega (Mexico City: Antítesis, Alias), pp. 318–29

LOMNITZ, CLAUDIO. 2005. *Death and the Idea of Mexico* (New York: Zone Books)

NAVARRO CASTILLO, RAQUEL. 2012. *Héctor García en '¡Ojo!: Una Revista Que Ve'* (Mexico City: INAH, CNCA, Centro de la Imagen)

PAZ, OCTAVIO (ed.). 1983. *Poesía en movimiento: México 1915–1966* (Mexico City: Siglo XXI)

PELAYO RANGEL, ALEJANDRO. 2014. 'Conversaciones con Rubén Gámez', in *Rubén Gámez: 'La fórmula secreta'*, ed. by Damián Ortega (Mexico City: Antítesis, Alias), pp. 362–71

RULFO, JUAN. 2014. 'La fórmula secreta', in *Rubén Gámez: 'La fórmula secreta'*, ed. by Damián Ortega (Mexico City: Antítesis, Alias) pp. 26–30

—— 1994. *Pedro Páramo* (Bogotá: FCE)

SEGRE, ERICA. 2007. *Intersected Identities: Strategies of Visualization in Nineteenth- and Twentieth-Century Mexican Culture* (New York and Oxford: Berghahn Books)

VITAL, ALBERTO. 2003. *Noticias sobre Juan Rulfo* (Mexico City: RM)

Notes to Chapter 3

1. See Ehrenberg's collaboration with René Rebetez, *Psicograma no. 3: El nuevo Génesis*, 1968, *El Heraldo de México*, 4 February, coord. by Luis Spota.
2. This relates to a late seventeenth-century Hispanic architectural style dominated by dense ornamentation. The Baroque complexity relied on stucco convolutions and illusionism. In Mexico, it is associated with colonial churches in the state of Puebla.
3. Delivered as a speech in 1953, subsequently transcribed and published in 1958.
4. The vernacular term 'agachón' means 'submissive'. There is a well-known photograph by Manuel Álvarez Bravo known as *Los agachados* (1934): it shows a line of urban workers seemingly decapitated by a deep, horizontal shadow as they hunch over a cheap meal, seen from behind.
5. See Orozco's fresco, *Four Horsemen of the Apocalypse*, 1938, in Guadalajara's Hospicio Cabañas.

CHAPTER 4

❖

The Poetics of Found Footage as Film Poetry: A Personal Case Study[1]

Carlos Adriano

There are innumerable forms of poetry in cinema, as many as there are forms of poetry in literature. Limiting myself to the field of experimental cinema and restricting myself to short films, I might cite a few random examples: there is the poetry of *Anemic Cinema* (Marcel Duchamp, 1926), of *Rainbow Dance* (Len Lye, 1936), of *Mothlight* (Stan Brakhage, 1963), and of *Unsere Afrikariese* [Our Trip to Africa] (Peter Kubelka, 1966).

Here I will address the poetry of found footage films, a subgenre of experimental film that recycles archival images. Still restricted to shorts and a few other random examples, I could cite: the poetry of *Berlin Horse* (Malcom Le Grice, 1970), of *Eureka* (Ernie Gehr, 1974), of *Opening the Nineteenth Century: 1896* (Ken Jacobs, 1990), and of *Instructions for a Light and Sound Machine* (Peter Tscherkassky, 2004).

Without claiming to outline an exhaustive theory, I will try to feel my way through historical and aesthetic hypotheses that demonstrate how found footage is a singular field of poetic operation in cinema. In an expanded panorama, I privilege literary examples from Brazil that contribute to my argument. In the narrow confines of this text, I do not seek to provide an exploration designed to be applied definitively, nor to build a consolidated argument (according to a teleological logic). I comment on aspects of some of my own found footage films as possible, personal and specific examples of processes and procedures.

I follow Goethe and understand the poet as a genus and the artist as a species (Cicero 2012). And, in order to read the poetry in (and of) cinema, I understand poetry as a form of language with a specific function and efficacy (Jakobson 1987) and as a structuring technique with singular criteria (Chklovski 1996). At the limits of my exploration are reflections that address this theme according to particular contexts and injunctions (Pasolini 1976), (Sitney 2015).

As the text of an artist, aware of academic protocols, it is necessary to warn the reader about my method of writing, which takes the montage of found footage as its principle. It may seem that none of the sources cited lead to a comprehensive argument. As in a found footage film, the mobilization of heterogeneous materials wagers on unexpected connections, on the supposition that resonances are both counterposed and shared, at the service of serendipity. And it wagers on the 'contaminated' form of its criticism of its object; Pound once said that the best criticism of a poem was its translation. Rather than guiding the reader down a set path, the accumulation of references lends itself to *dérives*. As an introduction to his *Histoire(s) du cinéma* [Histories of Cinema], Godard suggests: 'Don't show all aspects of things. Leave a margin of indeterminacy.'

A Tropical Method: Cultural Anthropophagy

'Scripts. Scripts. Scripts. Scripts. Scripts. Scripts. Scripts.' (Andrade 1970: 15). This phrase, which suggests a draft schedule for, or the pre-production of a film, is from the *Manifesto Antropófago* [Anthropophagist Manifesto], launched by the Brazilian writer Oswald de Andrade (1890–1954) in the '374th year since the Ingestion of Bishop Sardinha'[2] (Andrade 1970: 19). Printed in the first edition of the *Revista de Antropofagia* [Review of Anthropophagy], in May 1928, its tasting menu begins as follows: 'Only Anthropophagy unites us. Socially. Economically. Philosophically. The world's only law. Masked expression of all individualisms, of all collectivisms' (Andrade 1970: 13).

Anthropophagy is one of the most original and fertile artistic contributions that Brazil has ever produced. A strange species of aesthetic ideology and of radical cultural intervention, Anthropophagy's proposition was, in short, the ingestion of foreign influences and repertoires in order to produce a new, renovated and innovative art of local, modern originality for the world. The Concrete Poetry and Tropicalist movements,[3] for example, would not have existed with the potency and resonance that marked them and propelled them internationally if they had not digested Oswald's lesson quite so well.

Subverting the myth of the 'noble savage', the movement proceeded to transplant magical indigenous practices into artistic practice, by proposing to allegorically cannibalize the Other, inspired by the ritual gesture of First Peoples who preached that the swallowing of the enemy was a means of acquiring their best values and spirits. In Oswald's scheme, the act of eating implies a philosophical synthesis: 'Knowledge. Anthropophagy'[4] (Andrade 1970: 15). The absorption of belief implies demystification and desacralization as an act of devo(ur)tion:[5] 'Science codification of magic. Anthropophagy. The permanent transformation of taboo into totem' (Andrade 1970: 15).

I think that it is appropriate to invoke Anthropophagy as a Brazilian poetic invention that offers an original contribution to the cinema of archival reappropriation. The *Anthropophagist Manifesto* contains various allusions that can be read in the light of found footage: 'I am only interested in what is not mine. Law of man. Law of the anthropophagist' (Andrade 1970: 13) — is almost a declaration of the principles of someone looking to satisfy their own desires with outside images.

'Tupy, or not tupy that is the question' (Andrade 1970: 13) — is almost a pure manifestation of found footage: European doubt (Hamlet) transformed into indigenous affirmation (Tupy) through the carnivalesque parody (à la Bakhtin) of poetic sonic paronomasia ('to be' becomes 'tupy'). In the *Manifesto da Poesia Pau-Brasil* [Manifesto of Brazilwood Poetry] (1924), in his syncopated way, Oswald was explicit: 'All digested. Without cultural meetings. Practical. Experimental. Poets' (Andrade 1970: 10). In another excerpt, the reference to reappropriation figures clearly: 'The richness of balls and ready-made phrases' (Andrade 1970: 5). The key phrase 'tupy, or not tupy' from the 1928 manifesto had an equivalent in the 1924 manifesto, directed towards the very 'act of seeing oneself with one's own eyes' (that so guided Stan Brakhage): 'See with free eyes' (Andrade 1970: 9).

The poems of Oswald de Andrade were made as operations of reappropriation and reassembly, 'of common-places [that] transform into uncommon places' (Pignatari 1973: 153). In the preface to the book *Brazilwood Poetry* (1925), Paulo Prado fixed upon this discovery: 'Brazilwood poetry is Columbus's egg' (Andrade 1971: 67). In the section entitled 'on the occasion of the discovery of Brazil', with the poem 'Escapulário' [Scapular], Oswald converts the 'Our Father' into poetic belief through the observation of nature: 'On Sugarloaf Mountain | Daily | Give us, Lord | Poetry | Daily' (Andrade 1971: 75). In the section, 'História do Brasil [History of Brazil], a reassembly of texts by travellers who docked in the country occurs; under the caption 'Pero Vaz Caminha', the poem 'A Descoberta' [The Discovery] reads: 'We followed our path through this distant sea | Before the octave of Easter | We came across birds | And we sighted land' (Andrade 1971: 80).

Oswald also engaged in parody, remaking classic poems from his national literature, like 'Canto do regresso à patria' [Song of Return to the Homeland] (a parody of 'Canção do exílio' [Song of Exile] by Gonçalves Dias) and 'Meus oito anos' [My Eight Years] (parody of 'My Eight Years' by Casimiro de Abreu). Oswald's farce-çade[6] would recall, in a lesser and burlesque tone, the masks (*personae*) that Pound created to recite the Provençal troubadours (Campos 1983). For the concrete poet Décio Pignatari (1927–2012), 'the poetry of Oswald de Andrade is a ready-made poetry' (Pignatari 1973: 154); his formulation is pure found footage: 'it is a poetry of possession against property' (Pignatari 1973: 153).

A Clandestine Seism: A Montage of Attractions

Considered an 'anthropophagist of romanticism',[7] the poet Sousândrade (Joaquim de Sousa Andrade, 1832–1902) from the state of Maranhão, located in Brazil's northeast, chose an indigenous Colombian (on a sacrificial pilgrimage to the New York Stock Exchange) as the protagonist of his radical epic poem *O guesa* [The Guesa] (1888) and as the pariah *persona* of the poet himself.

Underestimated as a representative of the second generation of Brazilian literary Romanticism, Sousândrade was saved from oblivion by the book *ReVisão de Sousândrade* [ReVision of Sousândrade] (1964), by Augusto and Haroldo de Campos. The *ReVision* of this 'clandestine earthquake' (Campos 2002: 21) is a critical work of vitality and renovation as it puts the poetry of a marginal author back into circulation and situates it at the heart of modernity.[8] The Campos brothers' first study was rightly called 'Montagem: Sousândrade' [Montage: Sousândrade] (published on the 'Invention Page' of the newspaper *Correio Paulistano*, between February

FIG. 4.1. Frame from *Sem título #5: a rotina terá seu enquanto* (2019),
digital video, property of Carlos Adriano.

1960 and February 1961) — the cinematic collage of the poet is enunciated in the title.

'I've already heard twice that "*The Guesa* will only be read fifty years from now"; I grew sad — the disillusion of one writing fifty years too soon': so the author saw it in *Memorabilia*, from 1877 (Introduction to Canto X) (Campos 2002: 197). Facing poverty, at seventy years old, the poet had to sell parts of the wall of his farm, Quinta da Vitória[9] — in ironic reference to the name of the property and in metaphorical reference to his enduring difficulties, the poet declared: 'I am eating the stones of victory' (Campos 2002: 653).

Sousândrade's modernity manifests itself in his composition of words ('gil-engendra' [gil-engenders]) and sonorous textures ('o raio ora cai' [the beam now falls]). Its construction on the basis of references anticipates the ideogram-mosaic of citations with which Ezra Pound (1885–1972) elaborated his monumental *The Cantos* (1904–72). *The Guesa*'s montage of allusions is constituted as allegory, by bundling together episodes, images and temporalities of diverse natures, on mythical and historical levels to compose a mobile of actions and stagings, akin to those assembled by Michel Butor or Alexander Calder, that refer back to Ovid's *Metamorphoses* and that, furthermore, influenced another cultivator of the plasma of words: Joyce and his *Finnegans Wake* (1939).[10]

His most ambitious and aesthetically impactful work is *The Guesa* and above all its sections 'O inferno de Wall Street' [The Wall Street Inferno] (Canto X) and 'Tatuturema' (Canto II), both inventive in their elaboration of forms (composition of words, structure and elliptical epigrams, juxtaposition of times and disparate characters). Sousândrade's poem is already cinema (like *The Cantos* and the *Metamorphoses*) through the cut of its verses, its citation of real references, montage of images and allusions, movement through time and serial enumeration of motifs. 'Tatuturema' can be compared to *Macunaíma* (1928, year of the *Anthropophagist Manifesto*), by Mário de Andrade, a book that reappropriates and collages indigenous legends. Mário called his novel a rhapsody, as the combination of heterogeneous materials belongs to this genre. Composed of thirteen cantos, *The Guesa* consumed around thirty years of Sousândrade's work: he processed the collage of literary myths and reports from the newspapers of the era.[11]

If we understand the newspaper — which so interested Mallarmé during the confection of his poem *Un coup de dés* [A Roll of the Dice] (1897), the inaugural throw of the dice of literary modernity — as a kind of 'predecessor' of cinema (in its simultaneity of diverse facts drawn from reality and printed in its daily pages), it is not difficult to understand Sousândrade as the post-production editor (Bourriaud 2009) of a cinema that reappropriates the archive, that collects and juxtaposes unconnected images in a new context, resignifying this information.

Sousândrade's relations with Pound are fruitful: 'Much of the conversational fragmentism, of that kind of atemporal journalism that would come to typify *The Cantos* of Ezra Pound is already present in two infernal Sousândradian circles' (Campos 2002: 64). 'None of Pound's predecessors [...] could exhibit something as close to the author's conception of *The Cantos* as the "The Wall Street Inferno" by the poet from Maranhão' (Campos 2002: 123). The short prose texts that precede the stanzas function as theatre or film captions: 'The characters — like Poundian masks — assume the initiative of the discourse. And they interpellate. And they interpolate. All is matter in dialogue: [...] lines from *dramatis personae*' (Campos 2002: 64). An example from the first stanza of the poem: '(Guesa, having crossed the Antilles, believes himself rid of the *Xeques* and enters the New-York-Stock-Exchange; the Voice, from the wilderness:) | — Orpheus, Dante, Aeneas, to hell | Descended; the Inca must ascend... | = *Ogni sp'ranza lasciate,* | *Che entrate...* | — Swedenborg, do future worlds impend?'[12]

Of *The Guesa*, scholars of Sousândrade explain: 'it can be spoken about in terms of montage of shots or takes, of collage' (Campos 2002: 65), of 'stupendous flashback' (Campos 2002: 68), and '[yet] within this cinematographic technique, an analysis of montage in terms of Eisenstein's notion of the ideogram remains present' (Campos 2002: 67).

Appropriation in Other Arts: Rarefied Points of a Constellation

The 'ready-made poetry' of Oswald de Andrade borrows its defining term from the readymades 'invented by' Marcel Duchamp. This gesture consisted of dislocating already existing prosaic objects from everyday life to the context of artistic exhibition and thus giving them another meaning. Among Duchamp's emblematic pieces are *Bicycle Wheel* (1913) and *Fountain* (1917). Man Ray also (re)produced readymades in conglomerates, such as *Cadeau* [Gift] (1921) and *Obstruction* (1920/1961).

Collage is understood as the first antecedent of and procedure closest to a cinema of found footage. Among its pioneers and masters are George Braque, Kurt

Schwitters and Max Ernst. Through the common thread of photographic content, photomontage is also an important reference for found footage film montage. Raoul Hausmann, Aleksander Rodchenko and the Brazilian Geraldo de Barros are among its key names.

The 3D assemblages of which the box-works of the Brazilian Farnese de Andrade are composed can be put into dialogue with the assemblages of Joseph Cornell, who, what is more, produced the film that is considered the precursor of a language of found footage associated with the American avant-garde: *Rose Hobart* (1936). Coming from the arts of collage and assemblage, Bruce Conner (1933–2008) became a pioneer of that language with *A Movie* (1958); in a pop vein, he made the music film *Mongoloid* (1978) for the band Devo.

The recycling-collage of sounds found in nature, then recorded and reprocessed, has George Antheil and Edgard Varèse as precursors of so-called concrete music: Pierre Schaeffer, Pierre Boulez, Karlheinz Stockhausen. The 1990s had remix and sample music courtesy of John Oswald (*Plunderphonics*, 1996), John Zorn (*Godard/Spillane*, 1999) and Paul Miller aka DJ Spooky (*Optometry*, 2002).

In the 1960s, remix literature, the literal and literary *détournement* of the Situationist International by Guy Debord & Co. and OuLiPo (Ouvroir de Littérature Potentielle), a group led by Raymond Queneau and François Le Lionnais, of which George Perec and Italo Calvino were part. The entire work of authors such as Jorge Luis Borges and Enrique Vila-Matas is built upon citations, pastiche, allusions and appropriations. In the shift between the verbal and the non-verbal, the cut-ups (1959) of William S. Burroughs paved the way for the poems built of unconnected lines and visual collages of John Ashberry and for the 'uncreative writing' of Kenneth Goldsmith underpinned by the Duchampian concept of the detour.

Found footage cinema is part of this wide field of artistic manifestations that find an *analogue* logic in the appropriation and recycling of techniques and aesthetics of language associated with a kind of non-discursive or non-utilitarian articulation, based on allegorical, contrapuntal relations of correspondences, of metaphors — that is, the configuration of a poetics.

Reappropriation Cinema: Methods and Poetics of Found Footage

Found footage cinema is defined by montage — it is a singular type: associative, disjunctive, parametric, paratactic. Montage is that expedient of cinematographic language in which the act of cutting has a double meaning (simultaneous, paradoxical): separate to unite. By cutting an image in movement, the moments in which it starts and ends are decided, where it stops and continues. Found footage is a form of cinematographic production that recycles, re-edits, and resignifies unrelated images, filmed in other times and contexts, through the manipulation of image (plays of texture, reframings, speeds, granularity) and of montage (associations and dissociations through rhymes, disjunctions of disparate motifs, discontinuity of form and meaning), challenging expectations and conventional codes.

As a genre or procedure that handles archival images in an experimental language and by means of intervention in film material, found footage is guided by a notion

FIG. 4.2. Paulo Emílio Salles Gomes, 1966; frame from *Festejo muito pessoal* (2016), digital video, property of Carlos Adriano.

of composition based on *poetic* motives and structures, provoking tensions in the illustrative use often made by narrative compilation documentary, for example. Precisely by taking the world as a database and through a continual critical process of mediation and transformation of filmic material, found footage becomes a form of operational procedure that allows images to be understood as history and to transform images into residues of history — or ruins of history, as the degradation of images makes possible the history of cinema (Usai 2001).

The English term 'found footage' is adopted in Portuguese. The very difficulty of translating 'found footage' into Portuguese indicates the difficulty of conceptualizing it appropriately and warns of its irreducibility, or the irreproducibility of its formulation. Found footage is a mode of production that allows the articulation of images to be read and operated in the domain of 'intertextuality' (Iampolski 1998) and 'intermediality' (Pethö 2011). Furthermore, it now possesses a historical and theoretical corpus that is reasonably consistent and established: Leyda (1971); Wees (1993); Russell (1999); Brenez (2002, 2012); Baron (2013); Blümlinger (2013).[13] As it would be impossible to deal with found footage in its full theoretical complexity in the narrow confines of this chapter, I point to the exhaustive taxonomy by Brenez and Chodorov (2002) and the unprecedented and little-known treatment of audiovisual dissonance by Rogers (2017).

Holly Rogers starts out from the Surrealists' notion of automatic writing and the Situationists' concept of literary *détournement* to show how found footage builds meaning through audiovisual deconstruction, generating dissonances. She pays particular attention to soundtracks that, kept or replaced, trigger an activating disjunction of new forms of materiality, bricolage and juxtaposition in the manner of Eisenstein's vertical montage that contests alienating mainstream images.

Using various terms with literary roots, Brenez and Chodorov's cartography proposes two principal forms of appropriation: 'intertextual', that is, the refilming of an original — according to Chomon, *Le Voyage dans la lune* [A Trip to the Moon] (1909) follows the homonymous 1902 film by Méliès, whilst in *Psycho* (1999) Gus Van Sant remakes Hitchcock (1960) — and 'recycling', which can take two forms. The first is 'endogenous' and applies to the trailer and self-citation of a film (*Un film* [A film], Marcel Hanoun, 1983). The second is 'exogenous' and applies to three forms of allusion: (1) stock footage — B films with takes from other productions to compensate for mistakes or absences; (2) montage films — critiques of current events (*The Fall of the Romanov Dynasty*, Esther Schub, 1926) or essays (*Our Century*, Artavazd Pelechian, 1982); and (3) found footage — work of intervention and filmic autonomy using new spheres of montage. In a Mallarmeic bid for the prismatic subdivision of ideas, the pair propose five uses for found footage: elegiac, critical, structural, materiological and analytic.

'Elegiac' use of found footage fragments the original in order to keep the fetish object (*Rose Hobart*, Joseph Cornell, 1936). 'Critical' use employs four operations: anamnesis, misappropriation, variation/exhaustion, and readymade. Through anamnesis, found film images exhibit their latency (*A Movie*, Bruce Conner, 1958). Misappropriation refers to the *détournement* of the Situationist International (*La Société du spectacle* [The Society of the Spectacle], Guy Debord, 1973). Variation/exhaustion dwells on a single object and drains its potential (*Lettre de Sibérie* [Letter from Siberia], Chris Marker, 1958). The readymade returns to Duchamp's gesture and appropriates the untouched object (*Perfect Film*, Ken Jacobs, 1986).

'Structural' use means that a film is made following a protocol (*Berlin Horse*, Malcolm LeGrice, 1970). 'Materiological' use explores the substance of film (the emulsion of Carl Brown; the decomposed frame of Cécile Fontaine). 'Analytical' use consists of four modes of operations of visual study: gloss, layered montage, analytic variation, and synthesis between layered montage and analytic variation. In the case of gloss, *Erich von Stroheim* (Maurice Lemaître, 1979) offers verbal praise of the images of *Foolish Wives* (1922) to the director. Layered montage is practised by Godard (*Histories of Cinema*, 1978–98) and Gustav Deutsch (*Film ist* [Film is], 1998). An analytic variation is the treatment of images as images (*Tom Tom the Piper's Son*, Ken Jacobs, 1969–71). The synthesis of layered montage and analytic variation restores the historical nature of film images through aesthetic intervention (films by Yervant Gianikian and Angela Ricci Lucchi). For Brenez and Chodorov, *Outer Space* (Peter Tscherkassky, 1999) is an agglomeration of all these uses. Curiously, the production company of Tscherkassky is called P.O.E.T., an acronym of the full name of the artist.

Found footage operates using the remnants and shadows[14] of images, images that have remained — as reticence, lapse and silence — articulated in constellations. Ruins are evidence of the remains of time. A cinema of reappropriation of the archive re(in)states the experience of ruins. To find a filmed image is to reprocess recovered time. To think about time as montage of heterogeneous elements: a distinctly poetic position. When approximating two distinct realities: 'the more distant and distinct the relationship between two realities that are brought together, the stronger the image — the greater its emotional potential and poetic reality will be' (Reverdy 1918: 1). The beauty, wonder, or enchantment of the encounter results from this.

Here, I cite a happy formulation generated from an analysis of the film *Nostalgia* (Nostalgia) by Hollis Frampton that functions as an allegory of both metahistory (Frampton 2009) and found footage: 'creating ruins is the work of survival' (Moore 2006: 67). One of the most inspiring and original approaches to history as reimagination (reconfiguration) of memory — and, therefore, a basic reference for the cinema of found footage — comes from Walter Benjamin and his pivotal formulation: 'Allegories are in the realm of thoughts what ruins are in the realm of things' (Benjamin 1998: 178).

Benjamin gathered the wrecks of history to de/construct a monument in ruins; he articulated the notion that knowledge in the gaps of an image could configure a moment of memory as constellation, history as montage of discontinuities, and citations without quotation marks. The term and terms of the equation of the dialectical image, of another archaeology, illuminate the relation between heterogeneous times: 'It's not that what is past casts its light on what is present, or what is present its light on the past; rather, image is that wherein what has been comes together in a flash with the now to form a constellation' (Benjamin 1999: 462). The way in which Benjamin deals with the dialectical images of memory, of the ruins and montage of time, is congenial to the forms of production and conception of found footage film.

The 'dialectical image' (Benjamin 1999) is allusive (it aspires to make present an absence), elusive (it operates using the pieces of a ruin), and evasive (it restricts experience to a promise of incompletion). Through its shadowy folding together of the double (present and remains of the past) and the ringing of bells (and spells) in spite of the sorrow of loss, the dialectical image is an allegory for cinema, given its very condition of existence: a fleeting and ephemeral image that tries, in the transitory instant of now, to retain time in a flash and grasp the (flee)ting[15] moment; a be(t)witching[16] image of the flicker that configures the spell of a provisional provision and crystallizes thought. In the configuration of a constellation, the past and present are articulated in fulguration, in a fertile and inaugural allegory — 'Ideas are to objects as constellations are to stars' (Benjamin 1998: 34). An archive or database comprises a constellation of films ready and waiting to be reappropriated.

Reappropriation, as the montage of temporalities in found footage cinema, contains indices and indications that lead us to 'anticipatory plagiarism'[17] (Bayard 2009). This occurs when the author is inspired by a later author, by works produced (in truth, not yet produced) in a time ahead of that in which the appropriation takes place. That is, it would be possible to say that Sophocles plagiarizes Freud, Fra Angelico plagiarizes Pollock, Laurence Stern plagiarizes Joyce and Virginia Woolf in *Tristram Shandy*. The notion of 'anticipatory plagiarism' originates from OuLiPo and finds expression under the auspices of Borges who shows how each writer creates his predecessors through 'retrospective influence' (Bayard 2009: 61). This is the Borgesian notion that books differ from one another not in the way that they are written but in the way in which they are read. The borrowing

FIG. 4.3. Frame from *Sem título #5: a rotina terá seu enquanto* (2019),
digital video, property of Carlos Adriano.

of works 'through' a dialectical time-image is at the heart of found footage, as it
propels images backward or forward. These acts of appropriation are differentiated
according to the interpretation of the filmmaker.

'Os Colombos' [The Columbuses], by Fernando Pessoa, seems to be a poem
that praises found footage: 'Others must yet possess | What we must lose. | Others
empowered to find | What in our find | We found or left unfound, | As Fate
allowed or disallowed. | But what they shan't possess | Is that magic of remoteness
| Which makes history. | In consequence, their glory's | The fair proffered
bright- | ness of a borrowed light' (Pessoa 1998: 189–90). The poet of heteronyms
(appropriating personae) evokes a happy encounter with the 'found', with its
enigmas and signs, inherent to the process of found footage cinema.

Another Tropical Method (and Lost Ruin of a Seism): Plagiarism

There was no cinema in the *Semana de Arte Moderna* [Modern Art Week], focused
as it was on literary and musical presentations and an art exhibition. Modernism,
understood as a movement around 1922, was never really represented in the
Brazilian cinema of the age, unlike in the plastic arts, literature and music. The
specific conditions of its cinema meant that it was somewhat culturally out of step.[18]
Nonetheless, the principal ideologue and theorist of Brazilian modernism, Mário de
Andrade (1893–1945), wrote film criticism between 1922 and 1943.

Poet and polymath, romanticist and polemicist, musicologist and ethnographer,
multidisciplinary critic and first culture secretary of Brazil (1935), the author of poetry
books *Lira Paulistana* [São Paulo Lyre] and *Pauliceia Desvairada* [Hallucinated City]
published thirteen pieces on cinema in magazines and newspapers that formulate

a singular argument during a period of the establishment and transformation of cinema on a global scale that is nonetheless inserted into the local context of São Paulo. Mário was one of the first film critics in Brazil as well as one of the most inspiring. His first review was specifically about a Brazilian film (*Do Rio a São Paulo para casar* [From Rio to São Paulo to Get Married], José Medina, 1921; now lost). It was the first and last time that Mário published on national cinema, which, more than simply curious, is intriguing.

To write *Macunaíma*, Mário de Andrade copied indigenous legends from the German ethnographer Koch-Grünberg and other specialists on Amazonian themes, such as his Brazilian compatriot Raimundo Moraes, who defended the poet from accusations of plagiarism when he published his indigenous rhapsody. More of a copier than a compiler, Mário confesses to profligate reappropriation and professes his right to plagiarize in the letter-chronicle *A Raimundo Moraes* [To Raimundo Moraes] (*Diário Nacional*, 1931).

In an article about *Fantasia* (Walt Disney, 1940), published in two parts in the newspaper *Diário de São Paulo* (1941) and then in one part in the magazine *Clima* [Climate] (1941), Mário de Andrade articulates a precise and *avant la lettre* notion of found footage cinema:[19] 'the forms and movements derive from one another, through associations and constellations of images of all kinds, and, as unexpected as it may sound to us, follow an irrefutable logic' (Andrade 2010: 73).

The Birth Myth of Brazilian Cinema: A Hypothesis

My first found footage film is *Remanescências* [Remainiscences] (1994–97), made using a fragment of eleven frames of what is supposedly the first shot filmed in Brazil, recorded in 1897 by Cunha Salles. The image, whose projection lasts less than a half second, shows a wave that beats a pier once (the sea is used as a metaphor for poetry). In my doctoral thesis (Rosa 2008), I expressed my dissatisfaction with the disregard that historians show towards the figure of Cunha Salles and his founding role in Brazilian national cinema. I also produced a meta-historical reparation.[20]

As Cunha Salles was an illusionist, doctor, bookmaker, market seller and exhibitor of attractions (including films), historians do not recognize or admit that the fragment of film that Salles deposited in the Section of Industrial Privileges (Ministry of Agriculture), now in the National Archive (Rio de Janeiro), on 27 November 1897,[21] along with the patent process for a whole cinema-system, could have been filmed by him, which would lead to him being credited as the author of Brazil's first national film.

If the debate were based on a technical examination of the film (the format of its perforations, the division of its frames, its aspect ratio, gauge, and chemical process), then I might be able to accept the contention about whether Cunha Salles was the 'author' of these mythical images. But not because his multidisciplinary pursuits are taken to testify to a lack of seriousness, character or credibility, as if to prove our supposed atavistic *Tupiniquim*[22] condition as eternally condemned Macunaímic entities. Ultimately, it does not particularly matter whether he filmed it or not.

Instead, I prefer to consider how this supposed birth (a debatable, mythical notion) of Brazilian cinema took place by means of found footage. If the authorship of the film is questionable, Cunha Salles's eventual appropriation of this fragment of film is incontestable, as there is in the National Archive a record of a patent request in which he affirms that he has attached a film sample and, indeed, there is also the fragment of film from which the eleven frames reemployed in *Remainiscences* are taken.

Cunha Salles might have been lying and the film might not have been made by him — if this is the case I, for my part, would love him to have 'stolen' Marey's film, *La Vague* (1891), that depicts a pier in a way strikingly similar to that of the fragment, granting another meaning to the waves whose essence remains.[23] The hypothesis of this artist-metahistorian would thus be: the first Brazilian film was not filmed but rather reappropriated according to the code of found footage.

My investigation and argument take place against the background of Hollis Frampton's (1936–1984) metahistory. In 1971, he produced two seminal works: an essay (*For a Metahistory of Film: Commonplace Notes and Hypotheses*) and a film (*Nostalgia*). Curiously, the text does not mention found footage.[24] Axiomatically, the film is comprised of material from the filmmaker's photographic archive. It would thus be possible to read these works together to formulate a metahistory of found footage.

Metahistory is an ethical-aesthetic artifice that would allow the artist to continue composing works as a justification of their personal project and belonging to his or her artistic medium. Through an imagined poetic language, as 'theorized' by Borges (2007), the formative parameters of a poetic programme are chosen. New works would be articulated with old works in a constellation of invention, an infinite archive of images and sounds destined to inseminate the process of production with resounding consistency. According to the filmmaker-theorist-rhetorician, '[the] metahistorian of cinema [...] is occupied with inventing a tradition [...]. Such works may not exist, and then it is his duty to make them, or they may exist already, somewhere outside the intentional precincts of the art [...]. And then he must remake them' (Frampton 2009: 136).

In an essay on metahistory, Frampton elaborates on the key concept beyond the technical and institutional system of film — of an 'infinite cinema' (Frampton 2009: 134) that projects its materiality as the constitution of empty and emptied frames, which are, therefore, available to be filled with images. In my vision-intervention, this notion would accommodate the ideal of an infinite archive — a concept appropriate to found footage.

In his essay about posthumous fame, called Heróstrato [Herostratus] (*c.* 1930), Fernando Pessoa, who appreciated the occult arts of metempsychosis, seemed to foresee the metahistorical method of Frampton, in an act of 'anticipatory plagiarism': 'the true novelty that lasts is that which gathers all the threads of tradition and weaves them together in a pattern that tradition would be incapable of creating' (Pessoa 2000: 91). I can hear here an echo from Ezra Pound's Canto 81: 'to have gathered from the air a live tradition' (Pound 1975: 522). By means of its

Borgesian gift for inventing predecessors, the devouring (digestion and devotion) of Frampton's metahistory was made possible by Oswald's anthropophagic method, an artifice that allowed the official history of the inauguration of Brazilian cinema to be reread.

For filmmakers working with found footage — artist-metahistorians — metahistory would act as a passcode to filmic signs that rotate in constellations, like a skeleton key to repositories of unknown or forgotten images in archives. Applied to found footage, metahistory would provide a critical and poetic treatment of the archives of cinema history. As a *Structural Constellation* (to borrow the Benjaminian title of Josef Albers' work), it is kind of articulation that maintains points of contact with poetry and its paratactic structuring.

Early Cinema, Cinema of Attractions: A Pedagogy

Santoscópio = Dumontagem [Santoscope = Dumontage] (2007–09) is a film which forms part of my doctoral thesis. It is a film in the so-called structural vein of experimental cinema. One possible definition, which attempts to make sense of this characteristic (Sitney 1974), is that this kind of film prioritizes the materials, properties and essential structures of cinema through a materialist approach in which cinema becomes more like thought, in which film is a metaphor or allegory for consciousness (Michelson 1971).

Santoscope = Dumontage recreates the universe of the 'cinema of attractions', a concept coined by Tom Gunning and André Gaudreault, informed by 'new cinema history', which, starting from the FIAF Conference in Brighton (1978), evaluated 'early cinema' in other terms, not just as texts (films) but through its contexts (exhibition documents) (Rosa 2008). Under the rubric of an 'aesthetic of astonishment' (Gunning 1989), the 'cinema of attractions' (Strauven 2006) is a cinema that directly relates to the spectator, that interpellates without recourse to narrative absorption or diegetic illusion. Its triumph lies in the power that surrounds its basic act: showing, not narrating, thereby inciting visual curiosity.

The subject of my doctoral research was the discovery and restoration of a rare and extraordinary protocinematographic artefact (Adriano 2018). I found, in the Santos Dumont collection of the archive of the Paulista Museum of the University of São Paulo, a hub with 1339 photocards whose titles, authorship, place, time and method of production were unknown. I discovered that it was a Mutoscope reel, in which photographs were reproduced from frames of a 68mm film. The film was shot by the British subsidiary of the American Mutoscope and Biograph Co. and was first exhibited in the Palace Theatre, in London, on 3 December 1901: *Santos Dumont explaining his airship to the Hon. C. S. Rolls.* However, far from simply explaining the steering mechanism of his balloon, Santos Dumont (1873–1932) is also explaining the invention of his very thought.

In *Santoscope = Dumontage*, two formal and conceptually foundational parameters that are unique to the Mutoscope as a device are defined in terms of a poetic methodology for the structuring of the work's images:[25] the loop and the flicker.

FIG. 4.4. Frame from *Santoscópio = Dumontagem* (2010), 35mm film,
property of Carlos Adriano. Mutoscope hub, 1901;
source: Acervo do Museu Paulista da Universidade de São Paulo.

The exhibition mechanism, necessary for the visual mechanics of the Mutoscope, that alternates photographic and black and white (imageless) cards to produce a flickering effect, generates structural dimensions of refractions, illusions and projections of movements in *Santoscope = Dumontage*. The exhibition mechanism keeps going in a 'closed circuit', facilitated by the ring-like format of the 1901 reel that means its movement continues in a circular action, and inspires the rotations, chains and cadences of reiteration and repetition of the movements and gestures of this reappropriation film.

Santos Dumont's actions are a performance (for the Biograph camera, for his fellow aeronaut and the future founder of Rolls-Royce, and for the spectator): he makes marked gestures in the air and in the frame during his demonstration that are demarcated by his body's contact with instruments (sheets of paper, a set square, a T-square and slide rule) and, in our reappropriation, he enters a dance (as we say people 'enter a trance'), in the sequence set to the music of the song 'De Babado' [Frilled] (Noel Rosa and João Mina, 1936).

The discovery, restoration and reinvention[26] of this Mutoscope film of Santos Dumont allows us to configure a hypothesis about the artist-metahistorian in a Brazilian context. Just as the Brazilian inventor and aviator worked with leftover materials to make his machinery (tinplate, bamboo, clocks), the artist-metahistorian uses forgotten or unknown vestiges of a culture of artefacts, not only in the sense of rescuing them for history's sake, but also reinventing them to bring them to life in the same gesture and impulse (of research and creation), inseminating the fields of art and history with 'resonant consistency' (Frampton 2009: 136). The fact that this Mutoscope film of Santos Dumont is a rare Brazilian specimen of — a missing link in? — the early 'cinema of attractions' only underscores this hypothesis about the resonance of the artist-metahistorian.

The loop is a rotation that repeats itself and, in so doing, differentiates itself, like a wave in the sea. In the etymological origins of the word poetry we find the word that returns. In Latin, the first person singular of the verb 'to return' is *vertere*, and its past participle is *versus*; which allows poetry to be understood as work in verses, and its structure of rhyme and stanzas as repetitions, recurrences and reiterations. In the revolutions of the turns of the loop, returns, returns, returns (to return to the 'scripts, scripts, scripts' of the *Anthropophagist Manifesto*).

Fossils and Pearls: A Found Treat

From the dance of Santos Dumont (just one shot of just one film), we move to a dance extracted from a single shot of just one film. *Sem Título #1: Dance of Leitfossil* [Untitled #1: Dance of Leitfossil] (2013–14)[27] appropriates a scene from *Swing Time* (George Stevens, 1936) in which Fred Astaire and Ginger Rogers dance to the sound of *Pick Yourself Up*. However, the original music is replaced by a song in a 'fado' style (a traditional Portuguese musical genre) called 'Desfado' [Un-fado], composed by Pedro da Silva Martins and performed by Ana Moura.[28] Two distinct realities (a Hollywood scene and a Portuguese fado) are brought together through the 'poetic justice' of an unexpected poetic reality, as Reverdy wished (1918).

Untitled #1: Dance of Leitfossil was inspired by Aby Warburg (1866–1929), who understood the history of art as the survival of forms (in his case Antiquity in the Renaissance). Warburg has two key concepts: 'the surviving image' — the survival of ancient motifs in the art of posterior times (Didi-Huberman 2017) and 'the pathos formula' — visible manifestations of psychic states fossilized in images (Gertrud Bing *apud* Didi-Huberman, 2004). In the formulation of the *leitfossil* — the survival of the image as psychic memory that is incorporated and becomes corporeal (Didi-Huberman 2017) — and of the surviving image, Warburg works with buried times, the fossil as a living being, despite the dormancy of its form (Bachelard 1988), (Didi-Huberman 2017).

In the curiosity cabinet of the found footage filmmaker, there is no dead archive; only living archives, their forms dormant. It is, therefore, a step or *pas de deux*, in the dance of reappropriation. Warburg spoke of 'appropriation through incorporation' (*apud* Michaud 2004: 325), in relation to his reflections on mythic thought and the capacity of man to manipulate things and establish links and separations. In addition to Greek antiquity, his research also explored the First Peoples of America. This takes us back to bricolage as a material and symbolic operation of savage thought as studied by Claude Lévi-Strauss (1908–2009). In Warburg's approach are gestures of listening to and auscultating images, recuperating 'the timbre of those unheard voices' of images (*apud* Didi-Huberman 2017: 20). They are gestures which hold various analogies with found film footage and its probing of the survival of a time–image dialectic that is buried, or dormant in its fossil form.

As in the unsettling Freudian uncanny (*unheimliche*) that returns what was once familiar, the 'tenacity of what remains, even if it is buried through the action of petrification; and the tenacity of what returns, even if it is forgotten, through the action of breezes or by phantom movements' (Didi-Huberman 2017: 221) seems appropriate to the cinema of found footage. For Warburg, 'images [...] suffer from reminiscences' (Didi-Huberman 2017: 202) and unconscious memory is apprehended as a 'knot of anachronisms' (Didi-Huberman 2017: 33) — writing about psychic archaeology and history of art, Warburg seems to theorize about found footage.

A convulsive and compulsive archivist, Warburg treated the organization of knowledge as an archive. The images collated by him in *Mnemosyne* — boards where he compared reproductions of works of art and documents from diverse eras to produce a new way of doing art history — would come to be engrams.[29] An engram maintains a mnemonic energy (Gombrich 2015: 230) and can also be read as a 'memory-image' (Didi-Huberman 2017: 197) and as a photogram (Michaud 2004). With his atlas of images, *Mnemosyne*, Warburg would institute the application of a method of montage typical of cinema to the history of art (Michaud 2004), that would dialogue at a distance with the montage of attractions represented both in early and Eisensteinian films. Warburg himself called his operational procedure an 'iconology of the intervals' (*apud* Michaud 2004), which echoes (in 'anticipatory plagiarism'?) Dziga Vertov's theory of montage.

I evoke, or invoke, the allegory used by Hannah Arendt in reference to Walter Benjamin and by Didi-Huberman in reference to Aby Warburg. The allegory of the pearl fisher is appropriate to the operations of a cinema that reappropriates the archive. To this allegory, I add another metaphor (about the desire to communicate, the ultimate gesture that, in the end, is also that of art): throwing a message in a bottle into the sea. Rather than a researcher in the style of a detective or head-hunter, Warburg was a researcher of the pearl-fishing kind (Didi-Huberman 2017). The cine-poet of found footage films also fishes for hidden treasure in the sea of memory — be they the eleven inaugural frames of Brazilian national filmography, Santos Dumont's lost Mutoscope, or the hook of a fado to guide the steps of Fred and Ginger.

This allegory would be sung as prophecy by Ariel in Shakespeare's *The Tempest* (Act 1, Scene 2): 'Full fathom five thy father lies; | Of his bones are coral made; | Those are pearls that were his eyes: | Nothing of him that doth fade | But doth suffer a sea-change | Into something rich and strange.' After a dive in which he finds a pearl, the fisherman, satisfied with and deluded by the triumph of his trophy, mounts it in a display case until he realizes, by chance, long afterwards, that the pearl was the eye of his dead father. Obsessed, the fisherman is impelled to carry out ever more dives, attracted by the proliferation of the sea's strange treasures, algae and waters of meaning and time until he is possessed by the desire to remain there for good.

At the end of a conference in 1912 in Rome, Warburg made a declaration that was as enigmatic as it was inspiring, which evidently has repercussions for those looking to find resonances with found footage cinema: 'My fellow students, I need hardly say that this lecture has not been about solving a pictorial riddle for its own sake — especially since it cannot here be illuminated at leisure [*ruhig beleuchten*], but only caught in a cinematographic spotlight [*kinematographisch Scheinwerfen*]' (Michaud 2004: 38).

A Kino Haiku for the Wizard of Ozu

Sem título #5: a rotina terá seu enquanto [Untitled #5: A Tune of None at Noon] (2018–19) recycles materials from the last film of Japanese director Yasujiro Ozu (1903–1963), *Sanma no aji* (1962). Released in the English-language market as *An Autumn Afternoon*[30] and in French as *Le Gout du sake* [The Taste of Sake], *Sanma no aji* literally means *Taste of Sanma*. In Brazil, the film was distributed under a title that offers a perfect summary of the work of this extraordinary filmmaker of everyday life, especially as this film is the last testament of the Japanese director: *A rotina tem seu encanto* [The Routine has its Charm]. After the original (untranslated) title cards in Japanese from Ozu's film and the image of a rising sun filmed in Salvador (Bahia, 2018), a haiku by Basho appears on the screen: 'here again today | on a rock adoring | the rising sun'. A haiku by Takahama Kyoshi then installs itself as a cine-haiku, after images of Ozu directing shots of *Sanma no aji* and of the filming of a train journey between Ouro Preto and Mariana (Minas Gerais, 2018): 'the rainbow appears | for a moment it is | as if you are here'. The presence of the above poems[31] is not mere citation, nor a free and circumstantial resource.

The haiku are perfectly integrated into the motifs of the film: Basho's poem is juxtaposed with the image of a Japanese man, his back to the camera (and the spectator), photographing the rising sun; the poem by Kyoshi follows the movements of the same man, in a train carriage, photographing waterfalls in Brazil's Minas Gerais. The haiku make themselves present in the very structure of the film. This poetry-form is a structuring paradigm of cinema-form; films organize their form as does poetry, here understood as the elaboration of a discourse governed by its own parameters, unconnected to phatic, factual and prosaic functions of language (Jakobson 1987), (Chklovski 1996), (Pasolini 1976).

There are three structural axes to the classical Japanese poetry form of haiku: 'kire' (the cut — of verse and images), 'teikei' (the form — lines of 5, 7, and 5 syllables) and 'kigo' (the weather — reference to the seasons of the year). Such elements can all in some way be found in the wizard of Ozu's final testament-film and *Untitled #5* seeks to show how to perceive them by recycling its images and interfering with its material. The horizontal sliding doors typical of Japanese houses literally slide across the screen as horizontal images in *Untitled #5*, which rhyme with the band of film which runs vertically down the screen. The duplication of portions of Ozu's original frame, by means of decomposition and recomposition, demonstrate the visual predicament of the Japanese director and imagine him in the constructivist lineage of Mondrian (1872–1944) and Malevich (1878–1935).

Passing through the sieve and into the crucible of Ozu, these painters whose names begin with the letter 'm' have been cannibalized by the anthropophagic method and, transferred to Japan, acclimatized to local colour (the sun of Bahia, the waterfalls of Minas Gerais). The poet Pierre Reverdy (1889–1960) was associated with surrealism and cubism and carried forward Apollinaire's theoretical propositions about the transposition of those plastic techniques to literature. By extension, the pictorial sign of Mondrian and Malevich, the cultural philosophy (anthropophagy) of Oswald de Andrade and the cinematic architecture of Ozu converge, become interchangeable and revert to a short circuit of artistic transmigrations.

An Imaginary and Marginal Film Archive

Festejo muito pessoal [A Very Personal Celebration] (2016) is a film commissioned for the official celebration of the centenary of the birth of Paulo Emílio Salles Gomes (1916–1977), a pioneering and seminal intellectual of Brazilian national cinema — a critic, historian, professor (University of São Paulo) and one of the founders of the Cinemateca Brasileira [Brazilian Cinematheque]. This cine-poem is inspired by Paulo Emílio's homonymous article: in his last, posthumously published text (1977), the author offers a balanced assessment of his relationship with Brazilian cinema and the urgency of film preservation, in the face of the innumerable losses throughout and on the margins of history.

To compose this commemorative piece, fragments of Brazilian films were appropriated from the silent period (1924–31) outlined by Paulo Emílio in the article mentioned above and films by Jean Vigo (1929–34), a filmmaker whose work the Brazilian critic brought to prominence in his 1957 book. The soundtrack employs music taken from the Folkloric Research Mission, organized by the poet Mário de Andrade in 1938, in one of his last acts as director of the Department of Culture of the city of São Paulo.

By using associations between images and sounds of poetic montage, *A Very Personal Celebration* attempted to make sense of Paulo Emílio's comment that 'returning lost and forgotten films to life is more exciting for never being conclusive'. The need to construct and preserve memory is accompanied by evidence of the irremediable decomposition and disappearance of this memory. One of the most urgent and contemporary moments of the article is when its author reflects on lost films by envisioning an imaginary film library.

Cited as an expression of anthropophagy (tending towards plagiarism), Mário plays the role of magnet and isthmus in the tribute-film to Paulo Emílio. Fundamental and central to the work was the notion of *poetry* as a structural paradigm, the character and factor of poetry as 'making': *poiesis* — the operational procedure (outside of discursive patterns) that draws associations between motifs. One of Mário de Andrade's most enigmatic poems, not yet deciphered by his exegetes,

FIG. 4.5. Giuseppe Ungaretti, 1963; frame from *Sem título # 3: e para que poetas em tempo de pobreza* (2016), digital video, property of Carlos Adriano.

is 'Silêncio em tudo' [Silence in All] (from *Lira paulistana* [São Paulo Lyre], 1945). The poem contains a stanza that baptizes and closes *A Very Personal Celebration* both unconditionally and structurally: 'Paulo Emílio like the sound | Collapsed, the train derailed | In the bad screenplay... | But the rats | The rats gnaw over there.'

Sound is one of the grains of deteriorated films, like the irreversible deterioration of the images of *Limite* [Limit] (1931) — the word 'noise' in Portuguese (*ruído*) contains the past participle of the Portuguese verb '*ruir*' (to collapse). The *ruir ido* (gone): the noise/collapse that is gone; that was/went. The 'train derailed' evokes a reel of film, with its perforations and division into frames (if, for Humberto Mauro, 'cinema is a waterfall', cinema is also a train — an allusion expressed in *Untitled #5* through the film's images of perforation and shots of the photographed waterfall).

A Very Personal Celebration begins and ends with rare documentary images of the personality it evokes, extracted from the film *Paulo Emílio encontra Giuseppe Ungaretti* [Paulo Emílio Meets Giuseppe Ungaretti] (David E. Neves, 1966). A visiting professor at the University of São Paulo, Ungaretti is a central presence in the film *Sem título #3: e para que poetas em tempo de pobreza* [Untitled #3: And What Are Poets for in a Time of Poverty?]: his image was extracted from an interview with Pasolini.

And What Are Poems For?

Untitled #3: And What Are Poets For in a Time of Poverty? (2015–16) is unashamedly and declaredly a manifesto, engaging and engaged in multiple senses, that deals with poetry and found footage in an explicit way.[32] The film expresses this in three ways: a) interviews with and testimonies from poets; b) poetry recitals and readings; and c) poetic reconfigurations and metaphors (imagistic, musical and artistic associations). The collection of interviews is interspersed with fulgurations of images about poetry.

As a counterpoint to debates and statements about the function and craft of poets, documentary images from two situations of human misery separated by an abyss of two decades were chosen: the town of Las Hurdes (*Las Hurdes: Tierra sin pan* [Las Hurdes: Land without Bread], Luis Buñuel, 1933) and Syrian refugees (TV reports, 2015). The verses of the poet Antonio Machado set to the music of Joan Manuel Serrat in the song 'Cantares' [Song] are assembled with the documentary images of all the poets who appear in the film, from *Las Hurdes* and of the Syrian exodus, by means of syncopation, ellipsis and cutting. Benjamin's notion of history, from the point of view of the defeated and ruins, is translated in this sequence, in which the disinherited from distinct eras (as in Reverdy's motto on the 'approximation of distinct realities') — the wretched of Las Hurdes and Syrian refugees — march to the same anthem of courage and dignity of the Spanish poet, author of 'El mañana efímero' [The Ephemeral Tomorrow].

The lines from the poem by Hölderlin recited by Fritz Lang (*Le Mépris* [Contempt], Godard, 1963,) are printed on the image in a tonal scale, the design of the poet fused with the filmmaker's scene. The verses of another poem by Hölderlin, recited by Danièle Huillet (*Schwarze Sünde* [Black Sin], Straub-Huillet, 1988) appear over the image in a chromatic scale, exploring the disposition of words strung together in clusters ('quandoelaseabrirá' [whenwillsheopenup]; 'onda/árida' [wave/arid]). Mallarmé's poem is read by Huillet (*Toute révolution est un coup de dés* [All revolutions are a throw of the dice], Straub-Huillet, 1977), with its translated verses thrown across the screen as the poet made them available on the page in 1897.

Untitled #3 employs a poem (a tribute to Concrete Poetry[33]) by myself the filmmaker. It is a poem composed of two words, that appear on the screen letter by letter, over the image of a cliff from the film by Buñuel, in a typology that turns 'b' and 'p' and 'M' and 'E' into graphically equivalent signs, discovering a perfect anagram for a poetic program, a filmic manifesto — 'abyss poetry' (in the original, 'poesia abismo').

The poets that appear in the film are: Antonio Machado (1875–1939), Blaise Cendrars (1887–1961), Ezra Pound (1885–1975), Federico García Lorca (1898–1936), Giuseppe Ungaretti (1888–1970), James Joyce (1882–1941), Jean Cocteau (1889–1963), José Lezama Lima (1910–1976), Stéphane Mallarmé (1842–1898) and Vladimir Maiakóvski (1893–1930). The poets that appear in the interviews are: Pound, Ungaretti, Cocteau, Joan Brossa (1919–1998) and Pier Paolo Pasolini (1922–1975).

All of the images are of poets either giving interviews for television or documentaries, or of poets acting in fiction films — Cocteau in his *Le Testament d'Orphée: ou ne me demandez pas pourquoi* [The Testament of Orpheus, or Do Not Ask Me Why] (1960); Pasolini as Chaucer in *I Racconti di Canterbury* [The Canterbury Tales] (1972) and as Giotto in *Il Decameron* [The Decameron] (1971); and Maiakóvski in *Baryshnya i khuligan* [The Lady and the Hooligan] (1918). The images of Mallarmé were extracted from *Stéphane Mallarmé* (Éric Rohmer, 1966), in which the actor Jean-Marie Robain plays the role of the poet.

The notions of 'Anticipatory Plagiarism' (Bayard 2009) and 'Anthropophagy' (Andrade 1970) can be seen in the sequence in which different poets converse in different eras (different styles and generations). Cocteau: 'many extraordinary things have been done throughout the century, but we have lost its secrets' (images of Cocteau being interviewed and in a scene from *The Testament of Orpheus* as if his speech had been dubbed; scenes from *Las Hurdes* — a cliff and children at school). Pasolini: 'my vision of the things of the world is not natural, not secular; I see each object as a miracle' (image of Pasolini in an interview and scenes of children playing with stones in a well in *Las Hurdes*). Mallarmé: 'everything sacred, that wishes to remain sacred, must envelop itself in mystery' (an actor recites a speech and a scene of funerary urns in *Las Hurdes*). Brossa: 'things wear out, in literary poetry; throwing yourself into the unknown is interesting, above all when the poet has a concrete world to give' (two scenes from *Las Hurdes*: a woman carrying a basket on her back and walking with her back to the camera in the forest, and a horizon with clouds passing; superimposition of Brossa giving an interview and Ungaretti opening his arms with a smile of satisfaction). Cocteau: 'that is an excellent definition of the poet' (Cocteau in *The Testament of Orpheus* but edited as if the speech of the interview were dubbed).

In the coda, a kind of manifesto of poetic art is configured. Phrases spoken in the film are superimposed onto close-up and negative shots of the hands of the poets. These hands enunciate movements like indicative and interrogative punctuation. The negative images suggest what is projected, what is still inaugural, the thrust of the discovery. The reiteration of hands in the final sequence, its cadence of rhymes and rhythms, emphasizes the 'making' character of poetry: *poíesis*. In Greek, *poíesis* (ποίησις) refers to the act of making or creating, originally applied to the arts and crafts in general. The *poietés* (ποιητής) was a creator, one who makes. And it did not necessarily or specifically mean poet. The archaic word to speak of a poet is *aedo* (ἀηδώ), which, in etymological terms, refers back to *aedon* (ἀηδών): ode and nightingale.

The phrase that lends itself as a title to *Untitled #3*, 'and what are poets for in a destitute time?' is by Friedrich Hölderlin (1770–1843) and appears in the poem 'Bread and Wine', begun in 1880, completed throughout the life of the author and published posthumously.[34] In one of the testimonies included in *Untitled #3*, a Mallarmaic enunciation is offered: 'take an object and extract from it a state of the soul through a series of decipherments'. Such an assertion is a kind of manifesto for a poetic method of found footage.[35] The poem that opens *Untitled #3* also functions as a manifesto: on a black screen, we hear the hoarse voice of Ezra Pound reading a fragment from his Canto 81 (translated into Portuguese by Augusto and Haroldo de Campos and Décio Pignatari): 'What thou lovest well remains, the rest is dross | What thou lov'st well shall not be reft from thee | What thou lov'st well is thy true heritage' (Pound 1975: 520–21). And then a stela, a gravestone on the screen (to mourn the companion to whom the film is dedicated: Bernardo Vorobow, who also appears in Untitled # 1: Dance of Leitfossil).

A poet and filmmaker, Pasolini is the author of one of the most cited texts on the topic of poetry and cinema and from his indispensable work/ds[36] comes one of

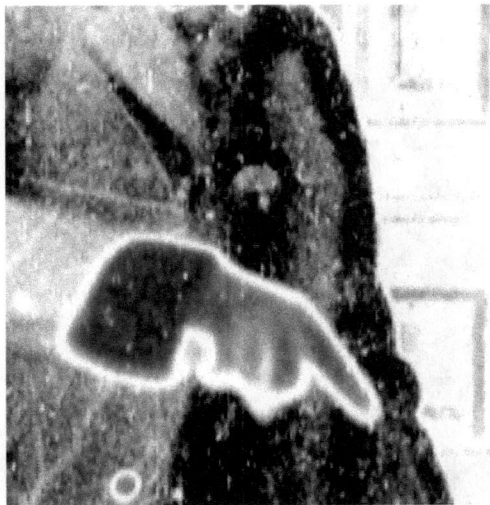

FIG. 4.6. Frame from *Santoscópio = Dumontagem* (2010), 35mm film, property of Carlos Adriano.

the most cited concepts of these studies: the 'cinema of poetry' (Pasolini 1976). I understand found footage cinema as a radicalization of Pasolini's 'cinema of poetry'. In a supposedly renovating take on the widely cited and debated term, I understand this Pasolinian notion as a promulgation of the formal autonomy of filmic texture and materiality beyond diegetic discourse, as a liberation from the parametric qualities of the normative and functional obligation of the narrative.

In found footage, by working in the pure domain of the image, sanctioned by the archive of an infinite cinema, filmic material (its elements, its structure, its form) although in ruins, pronounces itself. It is a poetic strategy to handle archival material in its materiality, exploring the poetic composition (and decomposition and recomposition) of the structure of its images. By means of operations of estrangement and dislocation, belonging to the procedures of reuse and recycling in the reappropriation of images, it would not be out of place to find correspondences between these and the literary figures of synecdoche, prolepsis and ellipsis.[37]

An archive (or database) of images and sounds is a repository for the found footage filmmaker, just as a dictionary is a resource for a poet. A good found footage film is composed within the parameters of poetic invention; understood to be an 'irreducible' form of art and language. Poetry is constructed through an associative, non-linear, allegorical and non-normative narrative structuring, of a different order to the pragmatic discourse of emphatic communication, to the utilitarian discourse of phatic communication.

In one of the most notable testimonies of *Untitled #3*, Pasolini comments on an expression of Provençal poetry, *ab joy* — 'the nightingale[38] sings *ab joy*, through jubilation'; in the sense of 'poetic ecstasy, poetic rapture'. He thus affirms, in footage that I reused in *Untitled #3*, as a poet, he writes *ab joy*: 'for all my cultural determinations and definitions, the sign which dominates all my production is this

FIG. 4.7. Frame from *Sem título # 3: e para que poetas em tempo de pobreza* (2016), digital video, property of Carlos Adriano.

kind of nostalgia for life; this sense of exclusion, which, however, does not reduce, but increases love for life.' This is a testimony that comes from an encounter with a beautiful definition of poetry: that which one wants to learn by heart ('imparare a memoria') (Derrida 1992).

Making with jubilation, nostalgia for life, poetic rapture, the permanence of that which is loved as true heritage: all are elements that could define a way of working with the reappropriation of the archive. As a poetic method for cinematographic production and cinema studies, found footage contemplates historical and aesthetic criticism — as meta-method. Above all, found footage aims — like criticism in verses, in reverse — at a reconfiguration of the very notion of the archive, and, by extension, a reconfiguration of the life of sounds and images as a promise of (another) history.

The words in a dictionary are available for the poet's reappropriation; in their reemployment, in still uncodified configurations and recombinations, resides one of their possible re-enchantments. On occasion, poets invent new words that do not exist in a 'dictionary state', as Drummond says in a poem fittingly entitled 'Procura de poesia' [Search for Poetry] (Andrade 2012: 218). For the filmmaker, images and sounds in an archive (film library, database) exist in this dictionary condition.

According to Augusto de Campos, a 'fundamental postulate of Ezra Pound's poetic-critical thought is encapsulated in the Dichten = Condensare formula' (Campos 1983: 22). Pound explains this formula as follows: 'Basil Bunting, fumbling about with a German–Italian dictionary, found that this idea of poetry as concentration is as old almost as the German language. "Dichten" is the German verb corresponding to the noun "Dichtung" meaning poetry, and the lexicographer has rendered it by the Italian verb meaning "to condense".' (Pound 2010: 36).

Ezra Pound's motto — 'make it new' (Campos 1983: 22) — is a mantra-matrix for the found footage filmmaking. The cine-poet of found footage exercises condensation and concentration: multiple times (synchronistic or disjunctive), fossil images, losses, dust and points that define a periphery — constellations, poetry.

Works Cited

ADRIANO, CARLOS. 2018. 'O mutoscópio de Santos Dumont e a poética do found footage', *Anais do Museu Paulista: História e Cultura Material*, 26 <http://dx.doi.org/10.1590/1982–02672018v26e08>

ANDRADE, CARLOS DUMMOND DE. 2012. *Antologia poética* (São Paulo: Companhia das Letras)

ANDRADE, MÁRIO DE. 2010. *No cinema*, ed. by Paulo José da Silva Cunha (Rio de Janeiro: Nova Fronteira)

ANDRADE, OSWALD DE. 1970. *Do pau-brasil à antropofagia e às utopias: manifestos, teses de concursos e ensaios* (Rio de Janeiro: Civilização Brasileira)

—— 1971. *Poesias reunidas* (Rio de Janeiro: Civilização Brasileira)

BACHELARD, GASTON. 1988. *A poética do espaço: os pensadores* (São Paulo: Nova Cultural)

BARON, JAIMIE. 2013. *The Archive Effect: Found Footage and the Audiovisual Experience of History* (New York: Routledge)

BAYARD, PIERRE. 2009. *Le Plagiat par Anticipation* (Paris: Les Éditions de Minuit)

BENJAMIN, WALTER. 1998. *The Origin of German Tragic Drama* (London: Verso)

—— 1999. *The Arcades Project* (Cambridge, MA: Harvard University Press)

BLÜMLINGER, CHRISTA. 2013. *Cinéma de seconde main: esthétique du remploi dans l'art du film et des nouveaux medias* (Paris: Klincksieck)

BORGES, JORGE LUIS. 2007. 'Kafka e seus precursores', in *Outras inquisições* (São Paulo: Companhia das Letras), pp. 127–30

BOURRIAUD, NICOLAS. 2009. *Pós-produção: como a arte reprograma o mundo contemporâneo* (São Paulo: Martins Editora)

BRENEZ, NICOLE. 'Montage intertextuel et formes contemporaines du remploi dans le cinéma expérimental', *Cinéma Revues d'Études Cinématographiques/Cinema Journal of Film Studies*, 13: 49–67

—— 2012. *Cinéma d'Avant-Garde: mode d'emploi* (Tokyo: Gendaishicho-shinsha Publishers)

—— and PIP CHODOROV. 2002. 'Cartographie du Found Footage', *Tom Tom the piper's son: Exploding*, # hors série: 97–109

CAMPOS, AUGUSTO DE (ed.). 1983. *Ezra Pound: poesia* (São Paulo and Brasília: Hucitec, Universidade de Brasília)

—— 2002. 'Carlos Adriano', *Festival do Rio,* September: 189

—— and HAROLDO DE CAMPOS. 2002. *Re Visão de Sousândrade* (São Paulo: Perspectiva)

CHKLOVSKI, VICTOR. 1996. 'Poésie et Prose dans l'art cinématographique', in *Les Formalistes russes et le cinéma: poétique du film*, ed. by François Albera (Paris: Nathan)

CICERO, ANTONIO. 2012. *Poesia e filosofia* (Rio de Janeiro: Civilização Brasileira)

Clima. 1941. October

CONDE, MAITE. 2018. *Foundational Films: Early Cinema and Modernity in Brazil* (Oakland: University of California Press)

Diário de São Paulo. 1941. 9, 12 September

Diário Nacional. 1931. 20 September

DIDI-HUBERMAN, GEORGES. 2004. 'Foreword', in *Aby Warburg and the Image in Motion*, ed. by Michaud Philippe-Alain (New York: Zone Books)

—— 2017. *The Surviving Image* (University Park, PA: Pennsylvania State University Press)

DERRIDA, JACQUES. 1992. 'Che Cos'è la Poesia?', in *Points de Suspension* (Paris: Galilée)

ELSAESSER, THOMAS. 2016. *Film History as Media Archaeology: Tracking Digital Cinema* (Amsterdam: Amsterdam University Press)

FARIAS, JOÃO PAULO RABELO DE. 2018. 'O que amas de verdade permanece: a poética da memória no cinema de Carlos Adriano' (unpublished master's thesis, Universidade Federal de Minas Gerais, Faculdade de Filosofia e Ciências Humanas)

FRAMPTON, HOLLIS. 2009. 'For a Metahistory of Film: Commonplace Notes and Hypotheses', in *On the Camera Arts and Consecutive Matters*, ed. by Bruce Jenkins (Cambridge, MA, and London: Massachusetts Institute of Technology Press), pp. 131–39

GOMBRICH, ERNST HANS. 2015. *Aby Warburg: une biographie intellectuelle* (Paris: Klincksieck)

GUNKEL, DAVID J. 2016. *Of Remixology: Ethics and Aesthetics After Remix* (Cambridge, MA: MIT Press)

GUNNING, TOM. 1989. 'An Aesthetic of Astonishment: Early Film and The (In)Credulous Spectator', *Art and Text*, 34: 31–45

HEIDEGGER, MARTIN. 2018. *Hölderlin's Hymn Remembrance* (Bloomington: Indiana University Press)

IAMPOLSKI, MIKHAIL. 1998. *The Memory of Tiresias: Intertextuality and Film* (Berkeley: University of California Press)

JAKOBSON, ROMAN. 1987. *Language in Literature* (Cambridge, MA: Harvard University Press)

LA FERLA, JORGE. 2014. 'Arrêt ton cinéma', in *El fin de los medios masivos: el debate contínua*, ed. by Mario Carlón and Carlos A. Scolari (Buenos Aires: La Crujía), pp. 135–59

LEYDA, JAY. 1971. *Films Beget Films: A Study of the Compilation Film* (New York: Hill and Wang)

MACDONALD, SCOTT. 2015. 'A Sudden Passion: Carlos Adriano's Sem Título # 1: Dance of Leitfossil', *Film Quarterly*, 69: 45–51. Reprinted in 2017: *Tropicália and Beyond: Dialogues in Brazilian Film History*, ed. by Stefan Solomon (Berlin: Archive Books, University of Reading), pp. 179–89

—— 2019. 'Carlos Adriano', *The Sublimity of Document: Cinema as Diorama (Avant-Doc 2)* (New York: Oxford University Press), pp. 337–55. Reprinted in *Found Footage Magazine*, 5: 124–37

MACIEL, KATIA. 2017. 'La Mer Larme', in *Trailer* (Rio de Janeiro: 7 Letras)

—— 2019. 'Desfado ou / Ai Que Tristeza Esta Minha Alegria', in *Conversa infinita: Carlos Henrique Schroeder, Katia Maciel*, ed. by Davi Pessoa and Manoel Ricardo de Lima (Rio de Janeiro: Mórula)

MATOS, OLGÁRIA. 2016. 'A poética das imagens e do tempo do cineasta Carlos Adriano', *Folha de S. Paulo* <http://www1.folha.uol.com.br/ilustrissima/2016/04/1758883-a-poetica-das-imagens-e-do-tempo-do-cineasta-carlos-adriano.shtml>

MICHAUD, PHILIPPE-ALAIN. 2004. *Aby Warburg and the Image in Motion* (New York: Zone Books)

MICHELSON, ANNETTE. 1971. 'Toward Snow', *Artforum*, 9: 30–37

MOORE, RACHEL. 2006. *Hollis Frampton: (nostalgia)* (London: Afterall Books)

PARENTE, ANDRÉ. 2007. 'Cinema em trânsito: do dispositivo do cinema ao cinema do dispositivo', in *Estéticas do digital: cinema e tecnologia*, ed. by Manuela Penafria and Índia Mara Martins (Rio de Janeiro: Livros Labcom), pp. 3–31

PASOLINI, PIER PAOLO. 1976. 'The Cinema of Poetry', in *Movies and Methods*, vol. 1, ed. by Bill Nichols (Berkeley: University of California Press), pp. 542–58

PETHÖ, ÁGNES. 2011. *Cinema and Intermediality: The Passion for the In-Between* (Newcastle: Cambridge Scholars Publishing)

PESSOA, FERNANDO. 1998. *Poems of Fernando Pessoa*, trans. and ed. by Edwin Honig and Susan M. Brown (San Francisco: City Lights Books)

—— 2000. *Heróstrato e A Busca da Imortalidade*, ed. by Richard Zenith (Lisbon: Assírio & Alvim)

PIGNATARI, DÉCIO. 1973. 'Marco Zero de Andrade', *Contracomunicação* (Sao Paulo: Perspectiva), pp. 141–55

—— 1982. 'Oswald de Andrade psicografado por Décio Pignatari', *Folha de S. Paulo*, 27 June: 3–6

PIGNATARI, DÉCIO. 1999. 'Carlos Adriano: he's reel!', *Folha de S. Paulo*, Ilustrada, 18 April: 1

POUND, EZRA. 1975. *The Cantos of Ezra Pound* (London: Faber and Faber)

—— 2010. *ABC of Reading* (New York: New Directions)

REVERDY, PIERRE. 1918. 'L'Image', *Nord-Sud: revue littéraire*, 13: 1–5

ROGERS, HOLLY. 2017. 'Audiovisual Dissonance in Found-Footage Film', *The Music and Sound of Experimental Film*, ed. by Holly Rogers and Jeremy Barham (New York: Oxford University Press)

ROSA, CARLOS ADRIANO JERONIMO DE. 2008. 'O mutoscópio explica a invenção do pensamento de Santos Dumont: Cinema experimental de reapropriação de arquivo em forma digital' (unpublished doctoral thesis, Universidade de São Paulo, Escola de Comunicações e Artes)

ROTHENBERG, JEROME, and JEFFREY C. ROBINSON, 2009. *Poems for the Millennium*, 3 (London: University of California Press)

RUSSELL, CATHERINE. 1999. 'Archival Apocalypse: Found Footage as Ethnography', in *Experimental Ethnography: The Work of Film in the Age of Video* (Durham, NC, and London: Duke University Press), pp. 238–72

SITNEY, P. ADAMS. 1974. *Visionary Film* (New York: Oxford University Press)

—— 2015. *The Cinema of Poetry* (New York: Oxford University Press)

SKOLLER, JEFFREY. 2005. *Shadows, Specters, Shards: Making History in Avant-Garde Film.* (Minneapolis: University of Minnesota Press)

SOUSA ANDRADE, JOAQUIM DE. 1986. 'The Wall Street Inferno (From 'O Guesa') (Sousândrade) (1832–1902)', *Latin American Literary Review*, 14: 92–98

STRAUVEN, WANDA (ed.). 2006. *The Cinema of Attractions Reloaded.* (Amsterdam: Amsterdam University Press)

USAI, PAOLO CHERCHI. 2001. THE DEATH OF CINEMA: HISTORY, CULTURAL MEMORY and THE DIGITAL DARK AGE (London: The British Film Institute)

VELOSO, CAETANO. 2002. 'O cinema que faz do espectador um artista', *Festival do Rio*, September: 188

WEES, WILLIAM C. 1993. *Recycled Images: The Art and Politics of Found Footage Films* (New York: Anthology Film Archives)

XAVIER, ISMAIL. 1978. *Sétima Arte: um culto moderno* (São Paulo: Perspectiva)

—— 2019. 'Tema e variações: dois diálogos do pós-cinema com os Philosophical Toys do século XIX', in *Pós-fotografia, pós-cinema: novas configurações das imagens*, ed. by Beatriz Furtado and Philippe Dubois (São Paulo: Sesc), pp. 30–41

Notes to Chapter 4

1. This chapter translated from Portuguese by Victoria Adams, including all quotations unless otherwise stated.
2. Whose name translates into English as Bishop Sardine.
3. Concrete Poetry was inaugurated in 1958 by Augusto and Haroldo de Campos and Décio Pignatari. Emerging around 1968, Tropicalism was an eminently musical phenomenon (Caetano Veloso, Gilberto Gil, Tom Zé, Mutantes), with inflections in the plastic arts (Hélio Oiticica), theatre (the piece *O rei da vela* [The King of the Candle], by Oswald de Andrade, produced by the Grupo Oficina [Workshop Group] and directed by José Celso Martinez Corrêa, 1967) and in films like *Terra em transe* [Entranced Earth] (Glauber Rocha, 1967), *O bandido da luz vermelha* [The Red Light Bandit] (Rogério Sganzerla, 1968) and *Macunaíma* (Joaquim Pedro de Andrade, 1969).

4. The *Manifesto Pau-Brasil* [Brazilwood Manifesto] reads: 'Poetry for poets. The joy of those who don't know and discover' (Andrade 1970: 6). His poem 'may 3rd': 'I've learned with my ten year old son / That poetry is the discovery / Of things I've never seen'. (Andrade 1971: 104).

5. In the original Portuguese 'devo(ra)ção', a combination of the words 'devoração' [devouring] and 'devoção' [devotion].

6. In the original Portuguese 'dis-farsa', a combination of the Portuguese words 'disfarce' [disguise] and 'farsa' [farce].

7. Edgard Cavalheiro, in his article 'O antropófago do romantismo' [The Anthropophagist of Romanticism] (O Estado de São Paulo, 1957) (Campos 2002: 27). Sousândrade is enthroned in the anthology *Poets for the Millennium: The University of California Book of Romantic and Postromantic Poetry* (Rothenberg 2009).

8. Beginning the 1960s, the concrete poets (Augusto, Haroldo, Décio) also undertook a recuperation of Oswald's work, in articles and editions.

9. Whose name translates into English as Victory Farm.

10. Lewis Carroll also created portmanteau words, as in 'Jabberwocky', a nonsense poem from *Through the Looking-Glass* (1871).

11. By working with news reports, Sousândrade is a predecessor of Santiago Álvarez (1919–1998).

12. English translation by Robert E. Brown (Sousa 1986: 92).

13. And also related studies, such as those by Skoller (2005), Elsaesser (2016), and Gunkel (2016).

14. In the original Portuguese 'so(m)bras', a combination of the words 'sombras' [shadows] and 'sobras' [leftovers].

15. In the original Portuguese '(perd)ido', a combination of the words 'perdido' [lost] and 'ido' [gone].

16. In the original Portuguese 'bruxa-bruxuleante', a combination of the words 'bruxa' [witch] and 'bruxuleante' [flickering].

17. In this kind of plagiarism, a writer from the present appropriates the work of (or borrows motifs from) a future writer (and not a past writer, as in classic plagiarism). Curiously, I see a counterpoint of the 'anticipatory plagiarism' in the psychographic-semiotic plagiarism by Décio Pignatari, who did an Anthropophagist metempsychosis of Oswald de Andrade's poems: 'People are not psychographed, but language is. Mystery is not minor due to this. We psychograph signs and we are constantly psychographed. In some grave beyond, there will be some deceased author, in the ways of Machado de Assis and Brás Cubas, who is psychographing me' (Pignatari 1982: 3).

18. A pioneering study of Brazilian cinema and modernism is that of Xavier (1978). Readers of English will find an introduction to early Brazilian cinema, containing revealing analysis of filming in both an urban setting and the Amazon and questions of identity and modernity, in Conde (2018).

19. Writing in 1939 about the photomontage of Jorge de Lima (*Pintura em pânico* [Painting in Panic]), Mário seems to speak about found footage: 'It only consists of people arming themselves with a good number of magazines and books with photographs, cutting out images and reorganizing them in a new composition' (Andrade 1992: 71); 'our most hidden tendencies, our most recalcitrant instincts and desires, our ideals, our culture, all is revealed in photomontage' (Andrade 1992: 73); 'photomontage must not only be a variety of over-realist poetry [...], it is an art of light, like photography, cinema [...] — it is a kind of introduction to modern art' (Andrade 1992: 75).

20. *Remainiscences* is intended as a kind of 'mesmerizing "reelization" of filmic thought [...] its very process-structure of iconic thought in its sober, mnemonic excess' (Pignatari 1999), a kind of film 'made for the artist-spectator. That is: it makes the spectator see themselves as an artist [...] and thus makes a difference to the critical perspective of all our cinema' (Veloso 2002).

21. Among innumerable events that could be catalogued in the mirage-like year of 1897, I cite the fact of J. J. Thompson having found the first fundamental particle (the electron) and Mallarmé having released his seminal poem 'A Throw of the Dice'; in Brazil, we had the Canudos War.

22. An indigenous people of Brazil.

23. In *Sem título #2: La Mer larme* [Untitled #2: Sea of Tears] (2009–15), I composed with the waves of Marey and Cunha Salles.

24. One of Frampton's films (not made of found footage) is called *Poetic Justice* (1972).

25. On the device, see Parente (2007).
26. On the relations between *Santoscope = Dumontage* and the contemporary art of Peter Kubelka and Tacita Dean, see La Ferla (2014); and on its relation to the 'philosophical toys' of the nineteenth century, see Xavier (2019).
27. MacDonald (2015) offers an unsurpassable analysis of the film. See also MacDonald (2019). The film artist and poet Katia Maciel composed a poem for/about the film (Maciel 2019: 17).
28. In the exhibition *E para que poetas em tempos de pobreza? Cinepoemas de Carlos Adriano* [And What Are Poets for in a Destitute Time? Cinepoems by Carlos Adriano] (Instituto Tomie Ohtake, São Paulo, 2019), the installations for *Untitled #1* and *Untitled #4* offered a singular experience. A large projection with open sound, *#4 Apesar dos pesares, na chuva há de cantares* [#4 Despite the Sorrows, Sing in the Rain] (2017–18) exhibits scenes of rain from 99 films produced from 1903 to 2014 accompanied by 'Singin' in the Rain'. On the wall on the side, a smaller screen with sound via headphones, the pair Astaire and Rogers mutely fluctuate — by putting on the headphones to listen to the music to which the two dance, the spectator is surprised to find that the Hollywood choreography is synchronized to a fado. The spatialization of the screens allowed for various ill-fated juxtapositions and coincidences between the dances: without headphones, Fred and Ginger danced to the sound of 'Singin' in the Rain'.
29. An engram is the trace left by an event that affects living material, according to the definition of Richard Semon, disciple of the psychologist Ewald Hering, whose article 'Memory as a General Function of Organised Material' so enthralled Warburg.
30. For the English title of my film I tried to make a similar pun to that in my original Portuguese title: 'a tune' puns on 'autumn' and 'none at noon' puns on 'afternoon'. When shown abroad, my film is 'A Tune of None at Noon'.
31. *Untitled #2: La Mer Larme* (2009–2015) is composed of images of the sea filmed between 1891–1900 and, as an epigraph, contains verses from: 'Le Bateau ivre' [The Drunken Boat] (1871) by Rimbaud, 'Un coup de dès' [A Throw of the Dice] (1897) by Mallarmé, 'Cimitière marin' [The Graveyard by the Sea] (1922) by Valéry, 'Olhando o mar, sonho sem ter de quê' [Looking at the Sea, Dreaming of Nothing] (1933) by Fernando Pessoa, 'When Serpents Bargain for the Right to Squirm' (1944) by Cummings, 'As if the Sea Should Part' (1863) by Emily Dickinson, 'L'homme et la mer' [Man and the Sea] (1861) by Baudelaire (1821–1867), and 'The Garden of Proserpine' (1866) by Swinburne. The dialogue with poetry became a return, an interdisciplinary palinode: the artist Katia Maciel wrote a poem defining film as the 'trailer of trailers' (2017: 33). In another poem, she states, 'memory is trailer' (2017: 109). This leads us to think about the articulation between trailer and found footage.
32. Due to the limits of this text, I cannot comment on *Das ruínas a rexistência* [From Ruins to the Rexistance] (2007), a cine-poem about unfinished films (1961–62) by the poet Décio Pignatari.
33. The dedications of the poet Augusto de Campos are revealing: in the book *Poesia da Recusa* [Poetry of Refusal]: 'To | C.A. | your cinepoems/ of refusal' (2011); in *Marianne Moore Dez Poemas* [Marianne Moore Ten Poems]: 'to | C.A. | my favourite cinepoet' (2019). See the poem by Campos (2002).
34. In the poem 'Andenken' [Remembrance], Hölderlin articulates loss, memory, sea and love (motifs dear to *Untitled #2*), but it is in the final verse of the stanza that we find a manifesto of foundation and permanence appropriate to *Untitled #3*: 'Yet what takes | And gives memory is the sea, | And love, too, fixes with intensity our eyes. | Yet what remains, the poets found.' English translation by William McNeill and Julia Ireland (Heidegger 2018: 18).
35. On *Untitled #3*, see Matos (2016) and Farias (2018).
36. In the original Portuguese '(pa)lavra', a combination of the words 'palavra' [word], 'pá' [a tool] and 'lavra' [work].
37. Frampton, who made the found footage film *Public Domain* (1973), honed his craft by playing with filmic language, as in *Palindrome* (1969).
38. In the game of anticipatory plagiarism, here we could return to the line 'gil-engendra em gil-rouxinol' [gil-engenders gil-nightingale's call] (Sousa Andrade 1986: 95), from the 72nd stanza of 'The Wall Street Inferno' by Sousândrade. This verse was appropriated by Caetano Veloso in the song 'Gilberto misterioso' [Mysterious Gilberto'] (disc *Araçá Azul* [Blue Araçá [Cattley guava]], 1973).

CHAPTER 5

❖

Timeless Monsters and Ghosts:
A Poetic Reading of
Guillermo del Toro's Narrated Epilogues

Eduardo Paredes Ocampo

Prologue: The Return of the Voice-over

> ¿Qué es un fantasma? Un evento terrible condenado a repetirse una y otra vez. Un instante de dolor, quizá. Algo muerto que parece por momentos vivo aún. Un sentimiento suspendido en el tiempo, como una fotografía borrosa, como un insecto atrapado en ámbar. — Guillermo del Toro, *El espinazo del diablo* [The Devil's Backbone]

> [What is a ghost? A tragedy condemned to repeat itself time and again. A moment of pain, perhaps. Something dead which still seems to be alive. An emotion suspended in time. Like a blurred photograph. Like an insect trapped in amber.]

> If I spoke about it — If I did — what would I tell you, I wonder? Would I tell you about the time...? It happened a long time ago — in the last days of a fair Prince's reign... Or would I tell you about the place? Or would I tell you about her? The princess without voice... Or perhaps I would just warn you about the truth of these facts and the tale of love and loss and the monster that tried to destroy it all. — Guillermo del Toro, *The Shape of Water*

The opening scenes of Guillermo del Toro's first and most recent international films, namely *El espinazo del diablo* (2001) and *The Shape of Water* (2015), are accompanied by the words set out above, narrated in voice-over. In both cases they are pronounced by secondary characters: Dr Casares (Federico Luppi) and Giles (Richard Jenkins), respectively. The primary function of these verbalized prologues is to establish *sequentiality* at the very beginning of the films: a narratological category in which, 'while watching narrative film, the spectator takes as one goal the arranging of events in temporal sequence' (Bordwell 1988: 33).

From the prologue on, our role is set as learning about ghosts, in the first film, and about princesses and monsters, in the second. As we do that, we join all the remaining elements in the stories to these initial ideas following temporal and causal logic. The narrators, however, disappear from the development of the stories only to appear again at the very end, by way of epilogues. This is a technique that the director reproduces throughout his filmography (thus, the conclusions expounded here can be extended to del Toro's style in general).

Regarding these epilogues, at the close of *The Devil's Backbone*, Casares repeats the same words as in the prologue. However, he significantly adds 'un fantasma: eso soy yo' [a ghost: that's what I am], as a conclusion. In *The Shape of Water*, on the other hand, Giles's last statement reads:

> If I told you about her... what would I say? That they lived happily ever after? I believe they did. That they were in love? That they remained in love? I'm sure that's true. But when I think of her... of Elisa... The only thing that comes to mind is a poem whispered by someone in love hundreds of years ago: 'Unable to perceive the shape of You, I find You all around me. Your presence fills my eyes with Your love. It humbles my heart. For You are everywhere.'

The reintroduction of the voice-over in the epilogues opens up at least one semiotic problem regarding the interpretation of the films. The problem is related to the aforementioned narrative sequentiality and causal logic. In opposition to the epilogues, the narrated prologues possess the value of the premise: they are an initial statement, a presentation of causality, from which another, secondary statement is inferred to follow as conclusion or effect. This is a constant to film and to all 'representational systems such as narrative [that] work to facilitate the recognition of such phenomena as sequence and causality' (Fludernik 1996: 36).

Since the verbal prologues constitute our first encounter with the characters and actions, they build our expectation of the conflict to come. The prologues' question–answer structure hints at this *transitive* feature. For *The Devil's Backbone*, we have 'What...?' followed by 'A...' and 'Something...'. For *The Shape of Water*, there is 'Would I...?' followed by 'I would...'. A logical and rational order is established between question and answer. However, when the films reach their end, sequentiality as a technical and aesthetic tool ceases to hold its functional pre-eminence: its agglutinating value, which helped the logical and narrative development of the pieces, is not needed any more. When Casares's and Giles's voices return, everything in the films has already been told, the questions have been answered — cause to effect (more or less) tightly connected. Temporality has also ceased to possess organizational pre-eminence as the story comes to an end.

Likewise, as we will see, rational logic disappears as the fantastic and supernatural elements fully kick in: the metamorphosis of Elisa and the appearance of Casares's ghost. Reality becomes logically 'unutterable'. Thus, narration and the narrator, semiotic features dependent on sequential, temporal and rational logic, become redundant, un-functional. Why, then, bring the *narrated* voice-over back in the epilogue — a rhetorical element than performs a conclusive and recapitulative, rather than an introductory, function?[1]

To solve the semiotic problem presented by the voice-over intervention in the films' epilogues, I argue that the spectator needs to interpret the nature of such structural elements differently. To do so, the language of poetry becomes the best alternative to that of narrative, since 'when narrativity can no longer be recuperated by any means at all, the narrative genre merges with poetry' (Fludernik 1996: 36). Del Toro's epilogues do 'not trigger a narrative experience but a lyrical one' (Kiss 2015: 5).

The reading presented here — the change from a narrative to a poetic understanding of the semiotic nature of an element in a film (such as an epilogue) — represents a methodological novelty. This is due to the fact that the influence of poetry in film has been partially ignored by critics. Additionally, the language used to describe and analyse poetry — intransitivity, timelessness, and iconicity, for example — is yet to be adapted and adopted in the methodological toolkit of film studies.

To return to the epilogues, a poetic understanding, rather than a narrative one, comes in the absence of sequential and logic transitivity as 'if we had to contrast narrative and poetry (or epic and lyric), we might focus, in the first place, on the *transitive* or the *intransitive* character of the sign', respectively (Todorov 1990: 35). In this case, I argue that the intransitivity of the epilogues' semiotic nature relates them to poetry, instead of to narrative. This is because, as poetry, the epilogues lack temporal and logical causation, and narration is characterized precisely by its transitivity, causality and rational logic. The differentiation between the prologues' transitive (that is, sequential) character and the epilogues' intransitive (un-sequential) nature will be the main focus of the formal analysis of this work.

Thus, in the following pages, taking the formal concept of intransitivity as a starting point, I will propose a poetic reading of the epilogues to *The Devil's Backbone* and *The Shape of Water*. Following Todorov, I understand intransitivity as the lack of temporal and logical sequentiality in the semiotic sign — particularly in the poetic one. Furthermore, as a thematic consequence of such lack of formal causality, I will correlate intransitivity to the concept of 'timelessness' broadly understood as 'the quality or state of being timeless', 'the quality or state of being timeless', 'of being eternal, as opposed to temporal', 'of being unaffected by the passage of time or changes in fashion' (Oxford English Dictionary 2020).

I argue that *timelessness* represents a fundamental characteristic of the world of del Toro's monsters and ghosts. In general, fantastic creatures, such as monsters and ghosts, live in a special zone outside the normal scope of 'possible' or 'natural' time.[2] This unusual approach to time is specially thematized in the film's epilogues, where the characters reflect on *how* the events just witnessed came to happen. The narrators' chronological interpretation is a central part of this reflection. Due to this thematic connection, in this reading, timelessness belongs to the meaning-side, rather than the form-side, of the semiotic sign.

Additionally, the close interrelation between form and meaning in the movies' epilogues will bring me to explore poetic iconicity. This is the fundamental semiotic tool used by del Toro to conceive a poetic conception of the epilogues. In cognitive terms, 'iconicity is the principle of form miming meaning, language miming the world' (Freeman 2006: 408). Thus, the link between intransitivity ('form') and timelessness ('meaning'), through iconicity, will become the centre of this study. What are the — semiotic and aesthetic — consequences of the collapse of the distinction between form and meaning in the epilogues, brought about by iconicity?

Thus, each part of this essay, concerning one of the two films, is divided into two sub-sections that focus on the verbal content (literary strategies) and the visual content (cinematic strategies) of the epilogues. More specifically, the process of analysis of *The Shape of Water* and *El espinazo del diablo* starts with the formal character of the sign (intransitivity), then centres on its thematic consequences (timelessness), relating to meaning, and finally returns to the interaction between form and meaning through iconicity. By way of conclusion, in this chapter's own 'Epilogue', I centre on the main reason behind the poetization of del Toro's epilogues: the accessibility of the portrayed phenomenon to the viewer.

The Epilogue of *The Shape of Water*

To analyse the formal and thematic causes and consequences of the poetization of the two films' epilogues it is convenient to start with *The Shape of Water*. Although it was conceived fourteen years after *The Devil's Backbone*, the analytical pre-eminence of del Toro's last movie lies in the fact that the narrator explicitly quotes a poem in the voice-over epilogue and precisely the poetization of this kind of rhetorical resource is the central focus of this study. A contextualization of the 2017 Academy Award winner for best film should help us establish the reasons why the epilogue is to be read through (poetic) intransitivity, timelessness and iconicity, rather than through (narrative) sequentiality and causal logic.

Against the background of the Cold War, *The Shape of Water* tells the love story of Elisa (Sally Hawkins) — a deaf-mute woman who works as a janitor in a secret US military facility — and an amphibious creature (Doug Jones). The story is witnessed mainly by Giles (Richard Jenkins) — a middle-aged advertising illustrator, as obsessed with his baldness as he is with cinema. The monster has been captured by the government and is coveted by the Russians. Due to this dispute, the decision is made by Richard Strickland (Michael Shannon), the antagonistic U.S. colonel in charge of the project, to dissect the creature to explore his potential military use. Knowing this, Elisa and Giles come up with a plan to save the monster's life and free him into a canal that connects to the ocean.

At the end, Strickland corners the lovers by the canal and shoots both of them. The creature, who has the supernatural power of regeneration, survives and, after killing Strickland, takes the unconscious Elisa and dives into the water in order to save her. This is the moment in the film where rational (narrative) explanation escapes both the story-teller and the spectator, and ambiguity fully kicks in. Immersed in the dreamy atmosphere of the underwater, the monster drives his claws over Elisa's neck and opens a set of wounds that, after a kiss, will become gills from where she will breathe again. I argue that the illogical and 'unutterable' nature of this ending triggers semiotic intransitivity — and the consequent thematization of timelessness — in *The Shape of Water*'s verbalized epilogue.

Timeless Love: Literary Strategies

To begin with, it is interesting to read what Richard Jenkins, the actor playing Giles, said when asked about his role of narrator in the film in a 2017 interview:

> Narration is hard. It's really hard. I'll tell you what, I didn't have the final narration until about two weeks before I stopped shooting, and Guillermo came up to me and he said, 'I found this poem in a bookstore today. It's written by a man hundreds of years ago,' which I say in the narration. He said it was his love letter to God and we're gonna use it. So that's how that came to be (Jenkins: 2017).

Two important issues should be highlighted from Jenkins's interview before we begin our analysis. First, the fact that the poem is a 'love letter to God' connects with the thematization of timelessness in the epilogue. This is because, in canonical Western theological thought, timelessness is a temporal characteristic of the divine and of God.[3] Although the divine is never mentioned in the quoted poem, this temporal specification (or, more precisely, the specification of the lack of time) is implicitly conveyed by Giles' voice-over words. Furthermore, after seeing the monster coming back from the dead and before being killed by it, Strickland recognizes its divine nature with the following words: 'Fuck, you are a god'. In order to highlight this divine sub-text, I have maintained the capitalization of the 'You' in the transcription of the epilogue.

Second, as was shown in the introduction, implied by Jenkin's affirmation that 'narration is hard', is the fact that the causal logic proper to this literary form becomes semiotically 'absurd' when inserted into an epilogue — characterized by its conclusive and recapitulative aspects. This is because, traditionally, the end of a film lacks sequentiality and transitivity, basic characteristics of narration: after the last scene, there is not much more to tell. This is a formal problem that del Toro might have faced when thinking about *The Shape of Water*'s ending and the sense of timelessness that the director wished to convey there.

The way to solve this epistemological issue is to read the epilogue through a vocabulary which somehow differs from narration. Del Toro provides the viewer with a semiotic 'key' — the poem casually 'found in a bookstore' — which allows her to open the door to a poeticized interpretation of the voice-over in the films' epilogue. This poetic 'key' will be used to analyse both *The Shape of Water* and *The Devil's Backbone*.

The Form

We should start by analysing the prologue in order to understand the structural (transitivity/intransitivity) and thematic (time/timelessness) contrast established with the epilogue. At the start of the film, the narrator of the prologue informs the viewer that 'I would just warn you about the *truth* of these facts'. Sequential, causal, and transitive logic are bestowed on the audience precisely due to the veracity of the events to be exposed: here, we are not expected to transgress *our* rules of possibility and realism to understand the (temporal) elements of the story. From the beginning of the film, 'facts' are presented to be concatenated into a truthful, 'utterable', and temporarily rational statement. The questions in the prologue open up as premises for the viewers to connect them sequentially to what is to be shown.

However, by the end of the film, Giles has lost the ability to vouchsafe for the veracity of the action narrated so far. He is overwhelmed by the implausibility and irrationality of the facts. Thus, his language abandons the transitivity presented in the narrative beginning. During the prologue, this transitivity was conceived as sequential or as implying a concatenation of cause and effect — in order for the audience to 'tie up' the discrete elements of the story. An example of the absurdity of the facts — that produces the eventual loss of narrative transitivity by the end — is the discovery of the monster's supernatural healing powers: in a previous scene we see it touching Giles's bald head and, the next morning, hair growing back from it.

I argue that the absurdity and ambiguity behind the facts presented throughout the film — and especially at the end — has consequences in the form of the epilogue and in our reading of it. Left almost speechless by the illogical nature of what has happened, Giles's words seem sequentially broken. Thus, the speaker presents the premise through a question (a causation): 'If I told you about her... what would I say? That they lived happily ever after?' This question has an intransitive answer (a consequence), rather than a transitive one: 'I believe they did'. The uncertainty of the last statement (based on belief) is problematic as it is anticipated by a question: it is a speculative and/or hopeful answer, instead of a truthful and logical one.

Thus, Giles's explanatory method consists of constructions which rely on contingency and faith, rather than on veracity — the consequence is not a fact but a hypothesis. The sequential and rational knowledge implicit in narrative disappears from the epilogue leaving space for a poetical explanation from the audience. Semiotic intransitivity is, thus, read from Giles's hesitancy and on the way in which he constructs his statements. I argue that this lack of concatenation brings the statement closer to poetry than to narrative. This is due to the fact that the poetic sign is characterized by its lack of causal and logical connection.

In Giles's epilogue, the causal outcome of his questions is utterly static. As in the poetic sign, information and facts do not 'move' anywhere. The hypothetical answers are not a contribution to furthering the audience's factual and causal knowledge of the world. The story-teller's intention is not 'additive' — presenting a conclusion to a premise. Instead, he is interested in presenting the fact (the 'thing') itself, in all its ambiguity and fantastic illogicality.

The Meaning

Having established a poetic reading of the form of The Shape of Water's epilogue (its intransitivity), we can now turn to the theme (timelessness), denoted by such formal elements. Focusing on the quoted poem, we can see that, by accepting that 'You are everywhere', the 'original' poet (the 'man [who wrote the poem] hundreds of years ago') is alluding to the timelessness of omnipresence. In the spatio-temporal conception of the divine, the sense of everywhere also conveys that of every moment. This poet's first intention is to reflect on a love so deep and so para-logical — as the divine one — that it exists outside the limitations of time.

Thus, by quoting this poem, Giles is, first, deifying the love he has just witnessed (between an already deified monster and Elisa). Second, the storyteller is assigning the notion of timelessness to the supra-logical feeling experienced by a fantastic creature and a human. Time is an insignificant category for an affection possessing the hints of the eternal — such as divine love. With this, del Toro, through Giles's quotation, conceives a truly 'happily-*ever-after*' ending for the protagonists of his film.

Iconicity

The timelessness read in the poem's theme also corresponds to the intransitivity of the poetic sign for 'poetry does not relate any events [i.e. temporal sequentiality], but is very often limited to the formulation of a meditation or an impression' (Todorov 1973: 8). Giles's hesitant and hypothetical speech in the epilogue could be defined as a 'formulation' or an 'impression' — thus, closer to poetry than to narration. Additionally, a 'meditation' is a static mental moment, a temporal conceptual liminality that is related to the chronological fixity of eternal love or the ever-after of Paradise — as Elisa and the monster's romance.

With this semantic resemblance between poetic meditation and the theme of timelessness, we are faced with a case of poetic iconicity: of form mimicking meaning. The intransitivity proper to poetic meditation (the form) mimics the meaning of the 'original' poem and the quotation of such poem — timeless (divine) love. Additionally, Giles's impressionistic and static way of describing the witnessed facts corresponds to the spatio-temporal quietism of timelessness.

What is the reason behind the breaking of the form–meaning divide in the poeticized epilogue — of making, through poetic iconicity, the interaction between (formal) intransitivity and (thematic) timelessness explicit? The immediate answer (which will be further explored in the conclusion of this essay) is to include us, the spectators, actively in the film's communication. This is because

> the effect of poetic iconicity is to create sensations, feelings, and images in language that enable the mind to encounter them as phenomenologically real. In this way, poetic iconicity bridges the gap between mind and world. (Freeman 2006: 408)

Thus, poetry substitutes narration in its cognitive objective to give shape to reality. This happens in order for us to understand the 'thing' itself more directly. By the time the epilogue starts, the inexpressibility of the events pushes the narrator to leave logical and temporal sequentiality behind and to find some less mediated method of communicating the illogicality and ambiguousness of the witnessed phenomenon. Giles finds such a method in poetry, since poetry — specifically, poetic iconicity — opens a direct door between the spectator and reality, between 'mind and world'. To make us understand an unutterable reality, the narrator conceals the mediation of the form as, in this case, it limits the audience's *direct* access to the world — to the immediate confrontation to the timelessness of love and the divine.

The Dream: Cinematic Strategies

The same interaction between the formal intransitivity of the poetic sign and thematic timelessness can also be appreciated in the cinematographic resources which visually accompany the words of the epilogue. This iconic relationship — form miming meaning — is encompassed in the oneiric atmosphere proper to the film's end. For '*The Shape of Water* is a deep dive into a dream state, like a two-hour episode of *The Twilight Zone* written by Puccini' (Bradshaw 2018). Indeed, the film begins with the camera focusing on Elisa sleeping, making the audience believe that the whole story could be one of the character's dreams.

The connection between poetry and the dream is evident as 'to poetry is attributed the sphere of the imagination, of dream, of unreality' and 'poetry precedes the distinction between real and unreal' (Croce 1966: 282). Following this quotation, the unreal (un-sequential, illogical, ambiguous, unutterable) and the intransitive nature of the aesthetic treatment of the dream pushes it towards poetry, rather than narrative. But specifically, in the epilogue of *The Shape of Water*, how is the dream connected to poetic intransitivity and timelessness, made one through iconicity?

The Form

As with the literary strategies, we should begin with the visual sequence that accompanies Giles's words in the prologue. The scene reveals its sequentiality from the start as the camera moves in one long sequence shot. The spectator is guided, step by step, through a space cognitively constructed by the logical linking of the different revealed elements.

With the frame, we see, *first*, a submarine cave. *Then*, we move towards it. It *soon* becomes an underwater corridor from a 1950s apartment. *Afterwards*, we slowly pace through it. *Finally*, we walk into Elisa's flat — which is full of water — and find her sleeping (dreaming?).

The sequential lexicon has been highlighted purposely to show the logical and sequential concatenation achieved by camera movement. Thus, the feeling that we, as spectators, advance in time and space corresponds to the cause-and-effect dialectic of narrative causality.

In contrast, while Giles recites the poem in the epilogue, del Toro presents his characters suspended in water as if flying in ethereal and oneiric supra-reality. The contemplative stability of the camera in the epilogue contrasts with the inquisitive movement of the one in the prologue. The only real — sequential, narrative — movement perceived in the film's last moment is when Elisa lyrically loses her shoe (Fig. 5.1). Thus, it can be said that the audience witnesses a state of liminality that corresponds to the intransitive nature of poetry.

Additionally, the palette of colours, between green and blue, shows a chromatic indifference that triggers a spatial one: are they in heaven or in the sea? We are not walking through a clearly identifiable corridor as in the prologue: human logic, and the architecture that comes with it, has abandoned the epilogue. This indeterminate state should remind us of the intransitivity of the poetic sign. Indeed, in this scene

FIG. 5.1. Still taken from the final scene of *The Shape of Water* (2017) by Guillermo del Toro (Cinespace Film Studios). The lovers hold each other as in a timeless, un-sequential reality.

the viewer witnesses neither an event nor a sequence of events, but the (absolute) duration of a state or liminality. The indirect light, shining from above and shaded by layers of water, contributes to the semantics of the a-temporal, para-logical angelic reverie. Finally, a melancholic piano plays the movie's main motif (by Alexandre Desplat): a score characterized by dreamily and temporarily unspecified nostalgia.

The Meaning

These formal details — which create the epilogue's oneiric atmosphere — have deep temporal connotations. Through them, del Toro manages to communicate visually what he has explicitly put in Giles's mouth: 'that they lived happily ever after'. Thus, the hint of the eternal, of timelessness, is conveyed through the character/narrator's words and echoed by the images and sounds.

The undefined colours, the muffled sounds and the slow movements of the camera in the underwater reality are formal elements that point to the spatio-temporality not only of dreams but also of Paradise. If we believe that Elisa did die from Strickland's gunshot, we can read the formal immobility of the ending as a projection of the eternity — i.e. timelessness — of the ever-after. In both cases, the formal elements allude to a timeless moment and place of lovemaking — be it the dream or Paradise. The dream and Paradise readings belong to the meaning-side of the sign. Thus, through poetic iconicity, the elements of form and content become indistinguishable in *The Shape of Water*'s final moment.

Iconicity

Additionally, the near-immobility of Elisa and the monster alludes to a certain sense of intransitivity — intransitivity that is related to poetry. This meaning-related presentation of *intransitivity* corresponds with the film's form at large, for it happens precisely when formal *transitivity* and sequentiality have partially ceased to be functional: at the ending. As the film comes to an end, the spectator is not expected to build temporal, transitive causality from the oneiric scene. It is a 'happily-ever-after' kind of ending, without any new narrative paths opening up for the characters — Elisa being dead or alive.

Conventional conceptual tools — such as those formerly presented by narrative — fail to explain such a para-logical and ambiguous notion of time. The idea only becomes conceivable through the direct — that is, cognitively unmediated by concepts — experience of it. I argue that in order to imply the timelessness of eternal love (the meaning), del Toro decides, formally, on the intransitivity of poetic presentation. The tool that bridges this gap is iconicity — where meaning and form merge.

Thus, the pre-rational, unreal, and ambiguous aspect of the dream allows del Toro to explore such fantastic or 'unutterable' topics as timelessness or divine love. The formal resource which he uses to mimic them is the — temporal and sequential — intransitivity of the poetic sign inserted or adapted to the format of the film. However, this only shows us the *how*, but not the *why*.

The reasons, I believe, rest on the fact that, in cognitive terms, poetry (and by extension this poetic interpretation of cinema) 'opens up the possibilities created by the gaps between our conceptualization and our experience of the world' (Freeman 2006: 416). As spectators, through the poetic presentation of timelessness and through the formal aid of semiotic intransitivity, the director grants us access to the direct and unmediated experience of the characters' unutterable and quasi-divine love in the film. Again, in the case of the epilogues, the causal logic behind narrative sequentiality and transitivity represents an obstacle, rather than a cognitive aid, to understand what has happened on the screen: the depth of Elisa and the monster's timeless emotions.

The Epilogue in *The Devil's Backbone*

Now that we have established the poetic 'key' to study del Toro's epilogues (in the literary and cinematic strategies), we can turn to *The Devil's Backbone*. Del Toro's first international film is set against the backdrop of the Spanish Civil War. It tells the story of two children, Carlos (Fernando Tielve) and Jaime (Íñigo Garcés), and of their contact with two ghosts. The first is the ghost of Santi (Junio Valverde), a child who mysteriously disappeared the night a fascist bomb fell into the orphanage's patio. Later on, we learn that his disappearance is not due to the bomb: it was the porter Jacinto (Eduardo Noriega) who actually killed the child. The second ghost is Casares, one of the teachers at the orphanage, who will lose his life protecting the children from Jacinto.

The plot presents a constant flux between the evil powers of mankind (embodied by the character Jacinto) and the misinterpreted evil of the supernatural creatures (embodied by the ghosts of Santi and Casares). As in Giles's narrative mediation, Casares becomes the witness of the events taking place: the arrival of Carlos, the presence of the fascist forces in the nearby town, Jacinto's violent rebellion against the heads of the orphanage due to his avarice and, finally, the escape of the children. His death, added to his narration of the epilogue, presents a particular semiotic inconsistency: can ghosts narrate?

I argue that this inconsistency is solved with the poetic interpretation of the epilogue. Although poetry is not the only genre that permits ghosts to produce statements, the ambiguous and para-rational nature of poetry allows us a more direct interpretation of an equally ambiguous and para-rational phenomenon — i.e. narrative ghosts. As was said before and will be further highlighted in the conclusion, the mediated nature of narrative hinders the audience's immediate contact between mind and world.

Thus, although radically different in their final conception, the fantastic, unreal and illogical elements of the film connect it with *The Shape of Water*. As we will see, the specifications of the genre — the onscreen presence of a ghost as a narrator — will push the film towards a poetical explanation, rather than a narrative one. Intransitivity, as a formal element, and timelessness, as a meaning-related one, stand out in Casares's epilogue for both are methods to convey — poetically — the unutterable.

Perennial Presence: Literary Strategies

The epilogue of *El espinazo del diablo*, narrated by Casares, is verbally identical to the prologue except for the last sentence. In this sentence, the narrator accepts his supernatural character. I argue that, by addressing the fact that 'un fantasma: eso soy yo' [A ghost: that's what I am], Casares changes the semiotic nature of the sign from narrative to poetry.

Critics have alluded to the poetization of the narrator's ending saying that *The Devil's Backbone* has 'un final *poético* y estremecedor: mientras los niños abandonan el hospicio, él [Casares] queda allí, como un guardián *perenne* de ultratumba' [a poetic and shocking ending: while the children abandon the orphanage, he stays there, like a perennial guardian of the afterlife] (Díaz 2016: 57). Thus, the language of poetry ('poético') and timelessness ('perenne') are conceived as mutually influential. In this critical appreciation, iconicity is hinted at as connecting the formal discourse of poetry with the particular nature of the character — his perennial self.

In the pages that follow, I describe both the literary and the cinematographic strategies through which the poetization of the epilogue's narrator happens. As in the case of *The Shape of Water* examined above, I centre — formally — on the intransitivity of the poetic/cinematic sign and — thematically — on the timelessness hinted at in the characteristics proper to the ghost of Casares. Iconicity will be read as the poetic feature which will tie both together to allow the audience an unmediated contact with the reality.

The Form

First of all, we must assume that the change of context in which Casares's words are spoken determine their reading, even if prologue and epilogue are practically identical in their verbal expression. In the prologue, when the spectator possesses almost no information regarding the characters and the plot of the movie, there is an innate inclination towards reading all forms presented *transitively* in terms of narrative causation. In the very first moments of the movie, the viewer is constantly trying to connect the diverse premises — the presentation of a character, for example — to their predicate — his/her personality; his/her actions, etc.

Thus, the narrator mimics such sequential and logical rhetoric. The question 'What is a ghost?' presents a causality. To this premise, he instantly answers with a predicative that closes the previous causal statement: 'A tragedy condemned to repeat itself...' Although answered in highly metaphoric terms, the prologue is characterized by the sequentiality and causality — that is, the transitivity — proper to narration.

However, the introduction of the statement 'A ghost: that's what I am' in the epilogue changes the way the sign is read. If hypothetically removed from its context of utterance, Casares's intervention would still follow the narrative rule of sequence and transitivity. However, if we focus on the pragmatics of its utterance, the narration falls into a paradox which shifts it towards poetic intransitivity. This has two causes: one focuses on the producer of the message, the second on the receiver.

First of all, the presence of the supernatural element, the ghost, contradicts the causality behind the rationalized 'laws of nature' (Todorov 1975: 25). This causality is replicated in the logical sequentiality proper to narration. Thus, the rational transitivity behind narration cannot thoroughly explain a (talkative) ghost. I argue that, due to its irrational and ambiguous intransitivity, the language of poetry is equipped to deal semiotically with such a fantastic phenomenon.

Second, even if the spectator accepts a new kind of logic — but a *logic* nonetheless — when faced with a supernatural event ('and the laws of the world then remain what they are'), it becomes unclear who the receptor of Casares's messages is (Todorov 1975: 25). Thus, without a receptor, the statement is reduced to linguistic absurdity. Who is the ghost speaking to — if it is possible for a ghost to maintain a conversation in the first place? The images that accompany the poetic intervention show an abandoned orphanage, with no interlocutors except the ghosts themselves. The lack of real (flesh-and-blood to flesh-and-blood) communication makes the statement intransitive.

Consequently, two formal (linguistic) elements are in charge of the twist towards intransitivity: 1) the paradoxical nature of the utterer of the message; and 2) the lack of (logical) receptor for this message. These two formal impositions oblige the viewer to forgo the logic of narrative causality and embrace another set of decoding rules. I argue that these rules are the ones proper to poetry (and particularly of its iconic character) because

> a basic, essential requirement of the poem [is that] it can only exist as a poem on condition that it restores the longest possible durations to the 'eternal present'

of art, that it coagulates a moving process in atemporal forms [...] (Suzanne Bernard quoted by Todorov 1990: 61)

Regarding the first formal imposition (1), by accepting his status as a fantastic creature (a ghost) in the epilogue, Casares is condemning his utterance to assume an 'eternal present' form or a formulation of meditative liminality analogous to that of poetry ('of art'). This is because he is a *perennial* guardian of the afterlife, to paraphrase Díaz Maroto. Indeed, a *fantasma* does not inhabit the present, the past, or the future — it seems to dwell only in an indeterminate and infinite 'here' and 'now', in a 'coagulat[ion] [of] a moving process'. The character/ghost — and behind him, del Toro — uses the 'atemporal form' of the intransitive and poeticized epilogue to talk to us.

Regarding the second formal imposition (2), as the message lacks a real, tangible receptor, there exists no temporal anchoring (again we cannot assume that ghosts communicate with each other — actually, their communication appears to happen between *them* and *us*; the immaterial world connecting with the material). The lack of a human witness makes the logical temporality of the statement absurd. This is because humans are the only entity capable of rationally and sequentially measuring time and giving it meaning. In a sense, the utterance could be explained in the same terms as the dilemma presented by a tree which falls in a forest when no one is around to hear it. Without the measuring of it, *time* becomes a useless category to define reality, rendering the space of the ghost's utterance to somewhere 'outside time' — that is, somewhere characterized by timelessness.

The Meaning

Now that we have explored these two formal aspects (regarding the utterer and the receiver) which support a poetic reading of the epilogue, we can analyse the content of the words — the meaning-side of the sign. I argue that the content of the poeticized utterance in the epilogue reflects both on poetry's a-temporal or perpetual presence and on its correspondence to the ontological nature of the ghost. Indeed, Casares describes the ghost's nature (that is, his own) in temporal terms when he says that a ghost is 'a tragedy condemned to *repeat itself time and again. A moment* of pain, perhaps. [...] An emotion *suspended in time*'. The timeless quality shared by the nature of the ghosts and poetry alike, is evident in the paradox of an entity described as undergoing an eternal and recurring repetition: time ceases to exist or to be meaningful in infinite liminality.

Iconicity

Finally, we can consider the iconic character of the epilogue as a factor that distances it from the prologue. The phrase 'A ghost: that's what I am' lexically separates the ending from the beginning. Thus, it is fundamental in establishing the distinction between the iconic and the non-iconic and between the poetic and the narrative. Without this final line, the prologue speaks of an external entity, its subject being other than itself.

In the first moments of the film, the audience is still unaware that the person speaking about the nature of the ghost is none other than a ghost himself, Casares. Up until the end, meaning and form are still two separate entities. This is due to the fact that the form — the verbal expression, Casares's voice — has not been related to the meaning of the words produced by such verbal expression or voice — the ghost. The intransitivity of the sign (form) is still unattached to the timelessness proper to the perennial ghost (meaning).

The epilogue, however, reveals the speaker's identity. This is through the explicit statement: '[a ghost] that's what I am'. Thus, the intervention becomes iconic: form (the voice) and meaning (the ghost, alluded to by the voice) start mimicking each other. This is due to the fact that the form — the voice-over utterance — ceases to refer to something other than itself. Consequently, it comes closer to absolute self-signifying autonomy.

Thus, the voice, the utterance itself, *becomes* the meaning. Paraphrasing the ghost: '*I am all* the things I have mentioned.' In this last moment of the statement, the intransitivity of the poetic sign perfectly aligns with the timelessness of the ghost's nature. This iconic collusion produces the epilogue's particular revelatory nature — we realize that it was Casares who was charged with speaking to us from the very start of the film.

In conclusion, as in *The Shape of Water*, the poetic turn of the epilogue can be read as an element that brings the audience closer to the direct experience of the 'thing' itself. The conceptual mediation which separates form and meaning (and which is proper to narration) disappears — through iconicity — leaving us with the most essential characteristics of the ghost. Timelessness and intransitivity clash to put us, as it were, in Casares's ghostly shoes and experience another — non-sequential, non-human, non-narrative — perception of time. Timelessness per se becomes directly available to us. The supernatural, the unutterable is, to del Toro, better discerned through the scope of poetry than through that of narrative.

Casares's Look: Cinematic Strategies

How is the iconic merging between these elements — intransitivity and timelessness, form and meaning — expressed in *The Devil's Backbone*'s cinematic strategies? How is the poetization of the epilogue expressed visually in the film's ending? Firstly, although verbally Casares's narration is practically identical in the prologue and the epilogue, there is an evident disparity in the nature of the images selected to accompany the set of words in both parts of the movie.

The Form

In the prologue, while Casares speaks, we see the portal where Santi's ghost makes his spectral apparition, the bomb falling from an airplane onto a patch of land which looks like the orphanage, Jaime finding Santi dying on the floor from a wound on his head, Santi's body sinking underwater and Jaime crouching and crying over the water tank where Santi's body was dumped. Then, there is a cut and the opening title sequence begins: *El espinazo del diablo*.

This set of events is presented through the causal and temporal logic of narrative. It is shown for the viewer to establish the 'emplotment' or 'storification' as

> narratives acquire form through structuring the available information into a more or less *coherent sequence* of actions and events. This creative act of emplotment or storification traces out the actual form of plot. (Kiss 2015: 49)

The particular show of events in the prologue — its discontinuous presentation — forces the viewer to imprint sequentiality, causality, and temporal transitivity onto the images in order to start building up, by way of suppositions, the supra-structure of the plot. In this case, the 'normal' reading of the diverse and discontinuous scenes represents a hypothetical story in which Jaime was partially responsible for Santi's death — although the showing of the falling bomb adds to the narrative ambiguity. It will not be until the film's very end that these sequential suppositions are clarified — Jacinto becoming the person directly responsible for the tragedy. However, the important fact is that we proleptically build rational logic and create a signifying and coherent sequence that is part of the plot.

In contrast, the shots that constitute the epilogue show the following: the portal where the ghost of Santi makes his apparitions, the ghost of Santi levitating over the water tank where his body was sunk, the room in the orphanage full of rubble and dust and a significantly silent gramophone, Jacinto's body inside the underwater tank where Santi's body rested, the black and white photograph of Jacinto as a baby floating on the water's surface, the bomb in the middle of the orphanage's patio and, finally, the troupe of kids exiting the building while the ghost of Casares — as a perennial guardian — observes them from behind. The end.

As in *The Shape of Water*, the final intervention does not add any additional information for the audience to build up suppositions or to tie up causal and coherent relations to cognitively construct the plot: emplotment becomes unnecessary. Thus, in purely formal terms, time at the end of del Toro's movie cannot be interpreted in a narrative sense. Our sequential discernment becomes useless as the images possess no strong contextual link with each other: they are (poetic) shots of different pieces from an already solved 'puzzle'. The semiotic intransitivity — which, so far, we have heard from Casares's words — can be read also in the form of the visual strategies.

The Meaning

Apart from this formal specification, timelessness appears as a consequence on the meaning-side of the sign. The reading which is presented to the viewer at the end of the film is that of reality outside time. Without any real inhabitants — since the children, through whom the whole drama evolved, have vacated the building — the orphanage of the last moments of the movie seems like a site condemned to perpetually repeat the past in the present: a space of eternal liminality. Additionally, the separate scenes of the epilogue seem to be shot with the same unchanging twilight. When there is no witness to rationalize time, its passing becomes meaningless — and, with it, temporal sequentiality disappears from the form.

Regarding the meaning-side of the sign, the images of a destroyed and abandoned

FIG. 5.2. Still taken from the final scene of *El espinazo del diablo* [The Devil's Backbone] (2001) by Guillermo del Toro (Canal+España). The children leave the orphanage.

FIG. 5.3. Still taken from the final scene of *El espinazo del diablo* [The Devil's Backbone] (2001) by Guillermo del Toro (Canal+España). The silhouette of Casares appears after the children have abandoned the orphanage.

building metaphorically represent a state outside the logical rules of time, a state where phantasmagorical presences defy logical causality and sequentiality. Another example of the absence of transitivity in the content is the image of the floating black-and-white picture. This image may be read as a symbol of this *timelessness* (in both meaning and form). The graphic representation of the past (a photograph) lies in a liminal zone between the air and the water, without being able to sink or fly off and enter into oblivion. This liminality can be interpreted as a formulation of an atemporality.

Iconicity

The disappearance of the gap between form and meaning can be more clearly appreciated if we consider that, at the end of the movie, one of the only two 'inhabitants' of the orphanage is Casares (the other being Santi). If we match this detail to the verbal expression of the epilogue, it would seem that the images presented by the camera — a formal element 'told' to us or selected from the range of Casares's point of view — constitute an element from the meaning-side of the sign. The very fact that the frame focuses on Santi as one of these selected images of the visual scope makes it evident that the eyes through which we are looking at the destroyed and abandoned building must belong to Casares. The camera has merged with the character's vision.

Consequently, we can interpret through iconicity: 1) the voice-over (the form) as the ghost's psychological insights (the meaning) made verbally explicit; and 2) the camerawork (the form) as Casares's own view of reality (the meaning). However, there is another example of how form and meaning merge: the film's ending. In the last scene, we see the band of children crossing the massive doorway of the orphanage, entering the wild and dry Spanish plateau (Fig. 5.2). A moment later, the shape of Casares's body appears in the composition (Fig. 5.3).

The change introduced by Caseres's entrance into the frame helps to emphasize the fact that the ghost's gaze — the meaning — becomes retrospectively equivalent to the movie's frame — the form. Moments before his appearance, the space his 'body' occupied matched with that of the camera. Precisely because the ghost comes into the frame from behind, we realize that, all throughout the epilogue, we have been looking through the ghost's eyes. This is one of the most explicit examples of the way in which del Toro achieves poetic iconicity.

Finally, this scene's iconicity can be further explored with the intertextual interpretation of the departing children in the last scene of *The Devil's Backbone*. I argue that this scene can be read as a quotation and as an example of how cinema signifies through cinema, that is, of how it *means* through its own form. The reference comes from the last scene of Roberto Rossellini's *Roma, città aperta* (Italy, 1945). In a similar fashion to the ending of del Toro's film, after witnessing the execution of the Catholic priest Don Pietro Pellegrini, the children walk hopelessly towards Rome (Fig. 5.4).

The children's departure in *The Devil's Backbone* can be read as a case in which the meaning very explicitly takes the aspect of the form by quoting another film inside the film's content. With a film–inside–a-film construction, the epilogue stops signifying anything other than itself: it is the visual equivalent to Casares's acceptance of 'un fantasma: eso soy yo'. Thus, the epilogue ceases to be a transitive sign, as cinema *means* cinema. The consequence of this quotation regarding the meaning of the epilogue is that the idea of timelessness is reinforced: the temporal difference between both films becomes insignificant.

In conclusion, this case of iconicity helps del Toro to achieve a disconnection from narrativization. This is because 'narrativization' 'is our embodied rationalization strategy that naturalizes *mediated stimuli*' (Kiss 2015: 59). In the causality and

FIG. 5.4. Still taken from the final scene of *Roma, città aperta* (1945) by
Roberto Rossellini (Minerva Film). The children walk towards Rome.

sequentiality implied in the rationalization behind narrative film there is a sense
of mediation, of separation from the 'thing' itself. Poetization, then, happens when
the reader tries to bind the gap between the (formal) conceptualization and the
(meaningful) experience per se to approach the latter, that is, unmediated reality.
Iconicity helps to achieve such contact as it pushes away the differentiation in the
dual components of the sign: what we have, at the end, is the pure experience
of intransitivity/timelessness without its semiotic rationalization into the form–
meaning dichotomy.

Epilogue: The Return of the Audience

In this chapter, I have shown how Guillermo del Toro poeticizes the narrative
voice of *The Shape of Water*'s and *The Devil's Backbone*'s epilogues in comparison
to the narrative prologues. Two strategies are followed: literary and cinematic.
These strategies introduce the content of timelessness to the audience by resorting
to the formal strategies of poetic intransitivity. Iconicity comes as a consequence
of the resemblance of content — timelessness — and form — intransitivity — and
works to present an unmediated access to the thing 'itself': the ambiguous world of
monsters and ghosts.

Thus, the main focus of this chapter has been on *how* the director achieved it,
rather than on the *why*. I would like to use this last section to briefly suggest a
possible cause for his directorial decisions. In order to do this, we need to establish
two ideas related, first, to poetic cognition and, second, to the placement of the
audience in cinema.

First of all, through poetic/cinematic strategies — mainly through the iconic
resemblance of form and meaning — del Toro has achieved, in a certain way, the

goal of

> the ideal poets [: to] attempt to achieve breaking down the barrier to bridge the gap between stimuli (sensory, emotional) and conceptualization, to access as far as possible [...] precategorical experience [...], the blurring of distinct categories and forms to capture that which cannot be directly perceived [...] 'suchness,' anything immediately but not directly perceived. (Freeman 2006:409)

As was seen above, form represents a mediation between 'suchness' — or the 'thing' itself — and us, between the perceived and the perceiver. By eliminating this cognitive barrier, by merging form and meaning, through iconicity, the poet-filmmaker brings his audience closer to the emotional stimuli of Elisa and the monster's timeless and divine love and to the sensorial atemporality of being a ghost. We gain direct access to the world of the unutterable.

Additionally, in cases such as those presented by the two epilogues, narrative explanation and its transitive presentation of temporality actually hinder, rather than assist, our connection with the monster's and the ghost's reality. This is because narration is an artificial and logical construct consisting of a cognitive rationalization of cause and sequence. Thus, due to its a-logical, ambiguous, and un-sequential understanding of reality, poetic intransitivity is sought for in order to grant the audience access to the underwater world of *The Shape of Water* and the haunted orphanage of *The Devil's Backbone*.

Furthermore, it must be assumed that, in traditional — i.e. narrative — film semiotics, the film 'impute[s] a fundamental passivity to the spectator' (Buckland 2000: 13–14). The exclusion of the viewer from film semiosis is partly due to film narration's hierarchical causality and sequentiality as

> the teller of a story carefully structures it in terms of a hierarchy of cause and effect relationships [i.e. sequentiality] in order to *limit* the number of possible interpretations by a receiver of the story. The receiver of the story is therefore not free to assign arbitrary [sequential or logical] meaning to the events. (Anderson 1996: 148)

However, the strategies followed by Guillermo del Toro to poeticize the epilogues might point to the opposite process. With this, del Toro challenges, first, conventional filmmaking and, second, traditionally conceived notions of cinema — considered in criticism, for example, closer to narrative and prose than to poetry.

Indeed, by resorting to poetic language, rather than to narrative, a movie can allow spectators to 'assign arbitrary meaning to the events', in Anderson's words. Due to the fact that poetry is not limited by the sequential, causal, and hierarchical order imposed by the author/filmmaker, it allows the spectator/reader to introduce her own arrangement (logical or a-logical) into her reading of reality. Additionally, the connection with the 'thing' itself, with 'suchness', brought about by poetic iconicity, allows for a form of communication democratically available to a diversity of receivers. With it, the epilogues from the movies cancel out conceptual — logical, causal — mediation and grant *any* spectator — no matter what her 'perceptual culture' might be — access to the filmed phenomena. They allow the spectator to put forward unlimited and non-hierarchical readings of the text/film.

Works Cited

ANDERSON, JOSEPH D. 1996. *The Reality of Illusion: An Ecological Approach to Cognitive Film Theory* (Carbondale and Edwardsville: Southern Illinois University Press)

ALBER, JAM. 2012. 'Unnatural Temporalities: Interfaces between Postmodernism, Science Fiction, and the Fantastic', in *Narrative, Interrupted: The Plotless, the Disturbing and the Trivial in Literature*, ed. by Markku Lehtimäki, Laura Karttunen, and María Mäkelä (Berlin and Boston, MA: De Gryuter), pp. 174–93

BERISTÁIN, HELENA. 2003. *Diccionario de retórica y poética* (Mexico City: Porrúa)

BRADSHAW, PETER. 2018. 'The Shape of Water review — an operatic plunge into Guillermo del Toro's immersive cinema', *The Guardian*, 15 February <https://www.theguardian.com/film/2018/feb/15/the-shape-of-water-review-guillermo-del-toro> [accessed 1 May 2020]

BORDWELL, DAVID. 1988. *Narration in the Fiction Film* (London: Routledge)

BUCKLAND, WARREN. 2000. *The Cognitive Semiotics of Film* (Cambridge: Cambridge University Press)

COBLEY, PAUL. 2014. *Narrative* (London and New York: Routledge)

CROCE, BENEDETTO. 1966. 'Expression Pure or Otherwise', in *Philosophy, Poetry, History: An Anthology of Essays* (London: Oxford University Press)

DENG, NATALJA. 2018. 'Eternity in Christian Thought', in *The Stanford Encyclopedia of Philosophy*, ed. by Edward N. Zalta <https://plato.stanford.edu/archives/fall2018/entries/eternity/> [accessed 30 April 2020]

DÍAZ MAROTO, CARLOS. 2016. '*El espinazo del diablo*: de la esencia de los fantasmas', in *Las fábulas mecánicas: Guillermo del Toro*, coord. by Juan A. Pedrero Santos (Madrid: Calamar)

FLUDERNIK, MONIKA. 1996. *Towards a 'Natural' Narratology* (London: Routledge)

FREEMAN, MARGARET H. 2006. 'The Fall of the Wall between Literary Studies and Linguistics: Cognitive Poetics', in *Cognitive Linguistics: Current Applications and Future Perspectives*, ed. by Gitte Kristiansen et al. (Berlin and New York: Mouton de Gruyter)

JENKINS, RICHARD. 2017. 'Richard Jenkins (*The Shape of Water*) on incredible arc, secrets behind his poetic narration' <https://www.youtube.com/watch?v=vQLWRvCqJQo&feature=youtu.be&t=3m47s> [accessed 1 May 2020]

KISS, MIKLÓS. 2015. 'Film Narrative and Embodied Cognition: The Impact of Image Schemas on Narrative Form', in *Embodied Cognition and Cinema*, ed. by Maarten Coëgnarts and Peter Kravanja (Leuven: Leuven University Press)

Oxford English Dictionary. 2020. (Oxford: Oxford University Press) <https://www.oed.com/view/Entry/295728?redirectedFrom=timelessness#eid> [accessed 1 May 2020]

TODOROV, TZVETAN. 1975. *The Fantastic: A Structural Approach of a Literary Genre* (New York: Cornell University Press)

—— 1990. *Genres in Discourse* (Cambridge: Cambridge University Press)

TODOROV, TZVETAN, LYNN MOSS, and BRUNO BRAUNROT. 1973. 'The Notion of Literature', *New Literary History*, 5: 5–16

Notes to Chapter 5

1. Contrary to the prologue 'que es una introducción, una inauguración del discurso que rompe el silencio', 'el epílogo es una clausura recapitulativa del discurso' [that is an introduction, an inauguration of the speech that breaks the silence, the epilogue is a recapitulative closure of the speech] (Beristáin 2003: 158–59).

2. Indeed, 'when we read fantasy or science-fiction narrative, impossible timelines do not strike us as being odd, strange, or defamiliarizing because they can be explained through the conventions of the genre. [...] In the case of fantasy narratives, impossible temporalities can be explained

through the use of magic or through other supernatural interventions...' (Alber 2012: 185). In this study, I argue that one of these 'impossible temporalities' in del Toro's film is timelessness.

3. Indeed, 'timelessness views may involve both the claim that God is not located in time/spacetime, and the claim that God's life is atemporal' (Deng 2018).

CHAPTER 6

❖

How Free is Free? Pablo Larraín's *Neruda* and the Art of the 'Anti-biopic'

Adam Feinstein

The Chilean director Pablo Larraín has frequently described his loose and lyrical movie, *Neruda* (2016), about the Nobel Prize-winning poet, as an 'anti-biopic' (Dargis 2016). If we are to accept this assertion at anything like face value, we need to understand the nature of the biopic — and why its limitations impel Larraín and other filmmakers to seek an 'antidote'. George Custen (1992: 5–6) has defined the biopic (or biographical picture) as a film 'minimally composed of the life, or the portion of a life, of a real person whose real name is used'. For Custen (1992: 4), despite their claims to historical authenticity, films in this genre are of limited value as historical representations, because they create an interpretation of history 'based on the cosmology of the [Hollywood] movie industry'. Marcia Landy (1996: 153) disagrees with Custen's emphasis on the monolithic Hollywood studio as the origin of the biopic: 'The biopic is a crude and stratified expression of motifs that are plundered from official history and memory as embedded in other literary forms, film genres and artistic forms such as painting and music.' For Landy (1996: 153), the biopic does not present 'one history' but rather multi-layered 'sheets of history'.

The biopic, as Belén Vidal (Brown and Vidal 2014: 2) has noted, is indeed a 'troublesome genre. Often cavalier in its handling of historical fact and mired in its own sense of self-importance, [it] commands as much critical derision as industrial visibility.' Dennis Bingham (2010: 3) has called the biopic 'a respectable genre of very low repute'. One director, Todd Haynes, poured scorn on the genre: he has called the biopic 'a formula, almost more nakedly so than any other film genres, because whatever the life is has to fit in this one package' (Axmaker 2008). Roger Daltrey, lead singer with The Who, was similarly dismissive when he declared: 'I don't want to make a biopic [about the band's late drummer, Keith Moon] — I want to make a drama' (Lewis 2019).

Writing in 1992, George Custen insisted that the biopic was fading as a genre. Yet between 2000 and 2009, twelve of the twenty Oscars awarded in the Best Actor and Actress categories were handed to actors playing real-life figures. As Vidal puts it (Brown and Vidal 2014: 2), the biopic is often seen as 'a throwback to old-fashioned modes of story-telling, a sort of heavy armour that constrains filmmakers'

FIG. 6.1. Luis Gneccho as Pablo Neruda in Pablo Larraín's *Neruda*

creative movements'. Perhaps it is the attempt to shed these shackles that explains the growing trend in recent years for filmmakers to focus on a single period of a person's life. This restriction of a film to a particular moment of a life, so the paradoxical theory goes, is not constricting but liberating. Martin Barnier (2010: 23–24) has observed that the biopic deals with the transformation of an image, not its stability.

Pablo Larraín is the son of right-wing politicians, members of Pinochet's supporting political party, the Independent Democratic Union (UDI). This is important because he did not inherit a disturbing memory resulting from a stressful event that affected his family. Nevertheless, in his films, Larraín assimilates a traumatized collective memory, articulating a remarkable narration of the darkest years in Chilean history. *Neruda* is set in Santiago in 1948, at the outset of the Cold War. In that year, Neruda, already renowned for his *Twenty Love Poems and a Song of Despair* and *Residence on Earth*, stood up in the Santiago Senate (where he represented the Communist Party) and condemned Chile's then-president, Gabriel González Videla, for turning against the Communist Party that had helped bring him to power and for behaving as thuggishly as Franco in Spain.[1] Following his courageous outspokenness, Neruda was deprived of his parliamentary immunity and forced into hiding with his second wife, the Argentinian painter Delia del Carril. For a whole year, which the poet himself later called 'a year of blind rats', they were rushed from one safe house to another, sometimes in the middle of the night, to avoid being captured. Had he been, he might well have been taken to the concentration camp at Pisagua in the northern Atacama Desert (where the commandant was a certain Augusto Pinochet — twenty-five years before he led the military coup against President Salvador Allende). Although we do not see this in the movie, Neruda eventually escaped across the Andes on horseback into Argentina and made his way to Europe using the passport of his fellow writer, the Guatemalan novelist Miguel Ángel Asturias.

Gabriel García Márquez called Neruda 'the greatest poet of the twentieth century in any language' (Mendoza 1983: 49). Carlos Fuentes said he was 'the King Midas of poetry: everything he touched turned to gold' (Anon., 1982). Larraín, however, is not interested in reverentially reinforcing such reputations, but rather in capturing a bigger picture. As he told one interviewer: 'I'm Chilean. Neruda is in the water, in the earth, in the trees [...] This is a movie about the Neruda cosmos' (Brown 2016). For Larraín, Neruda should not be a sacrosanct icon. It is therefore entirely legitimate, in the director's eyes, to subvert not only the many myths surrounding the poet but the very aesthetics of the biopic. A playfully free narrative line and a dream-like creativity with the biographical truth are appropriate, Larraín feels, because it is essential to flout cinematic conventions in order to deflate the legend Neruda himself insists on perpetuating.[2] Larraín has certainly avoided the criticism handed out to a film like Julie Taymor's *Frida* (2002) for being too respectful to its subject — although Taymor's latest biopic of Gloria Steinem, *The Glorias* (2020), is far less conventional.

At the same time, Larraín is perfectly aware of the poet's stature. He reminds us, as President González Videla declares in the movie, that Neruda was a man who 'could pull a piece of a paper out of his pocket and ten thousand workers would go silent to hear him recite poetry in that voice of his'. Indeed, Neruda is such a well-known figure that any actor playing him will run into what the *Cahiers du Cinéma* critic, Jean-Louis Comolli (1978: 44), termed the 'body too much' — namely, the difficulty this actor faces in depicting both the character and the sum of all the previous representations (and historical meanings) evoked by the character. For Comolli, the actor's challenge is to enact the demeanour of his subject as accurately as possible while, in actual performance, emphasizing his own separateness from that character.

In fact, Larraín's movie tells much of the story from the perspective not of the poet but that of the fedora-wearing police inspector, Óscar Peluchonneau (Gael García Bernal), who is leading the manhunt. After Neruda's senatorial immunity is lifted and it is decided that Neruda must flee Chile, the poet (impressively played by Luis Gnecco) exclaims: 'I'm not going to hide under the bed. This has to become a wild hunt!' And wild it certainly becomes.

Delia, in a touching performance by the remarkable Argentinian actress, Mercedes Morán, says of her husband: 'He wants to go down in history.' The truth, however, is that both Neruda and his pursuer crave fame. Both want to be remembered — one as a poet, the other for capturing a poet. But both come reluctantly to realize, especially in the film's increasingly elegiac second half, that they are, in some way, validating each other. At one point, Delia tells Peluchonneau that he is merely a secondary character in a story created by Neruda. Neruda leaves novels behind at each location he visits during his escape as clues for Peluchonneau. Neruda appears to believe he can influence the detective if Peluchonneau could only open his mind to new words, ideas and forms. But it is Peluchonneau who narrates the film. Indeed, as Stephen Borunda has noted (2016), Larraín's decision to allow Peluchonneau's non-diegetic and sonorous narrations to reveal both his mind and Neruda's is crucial: 'Even the sculpting together of juxtaposed shots suggests a symbiotic relationship between Neruda and Peluchonneau. As Peluchonneau smokes, Neruda drinks; as Peluchonneau walks down city streets, Neruda walks on a city roof.'

Larraín would presumably agree with Giles Hardie (2013), for whom biopics can work 'if they are also great thrillers [...] They can't work if their makers don't choose a genuine story-telling genre that makes their mark on the reality. Biography is the shelf you might find the book on, but it isn't itself a narrative style.' Larraín has indeed insisted that *Neruda* 'is a noir film. It has elements from the 1940s and the 1950s movies. It is also a chase movie, it has thriller elements. It's a cat-and-mouse. It's a road movie. It's a black comedy. It's a Nerudian cocktail. That's what inspired us' (Betancourt 2016).

It also indulges in Buñuelesque surrealism, which Neruda had (temporarily, at least) rejected after the Spanish Civil War (Feinstein 2013). In the opening scene, the poet is seen pissing in the chamber of the Santiago Senate, which mysteriously doubles as an opulent urinal, a scene that could have come straight from Luis Buñuel.[3] Elsewhere, Larraín injects Hitchcockian artifice: for example, the use of an obvious back projection during a car chase. Indeed, the hunt for Neruda could, in itself, be seen as a Hitchcockian 'MacGuffin'. Federico Jusid's discordant but florid Bernard Hermann-style score provides a further echo of Hitchcock.

After Larraín read the text of Neruda's 1971 Nobel Prize acceptance speech, he was struck by the moment when the poet was describing his escape from Chile and declared that he was not sure whether he had lived, written or dreamed this point in his life. That was when Larraín decided to play with Guillermo Calderón's initial screenplay, which had been more conventional:

> We discovered that we were making a Nerudian movie about his cosmos, his world, more than about Neruda himself. You just can't put him in a box; it's impossible [...]. He was a diplomat; he was a senator, a political leader, and one of the greatest poets ever. He created a very sophisticated and complex cosmos, and that's what we worked with. The movie is very cubist — Picasso is like a hiding key. He is a character who's in the movie very little, but for us he is essential in terms of the work. It's more just building little pieces, that then you put in a larger frame, and it creates something different — another image somehow. (Brown 2016)

In a sense, this concept of the filmmaker piecing together the world to produce a series of fresh images does reflect the way many poets see their own creative process. The American poet, Robert Duncan (2014: 144), wrote: 'The poetic imagination faces the challenge of finding a structure that will be the complex story of all the stories felt to be true, a myth in which something like the variety of man's experience of what is real may be contained.' But instead of making films himself, Duncan took under his wing a young movie-maker, Lawrence Jordan, who shared his view that true artists had shamanic powers and could transmit knowledge beyond their direct experience. And film, they both ultimately agreed, was the most effective art form in which to do this.

Larraín has never described himself as a shaman. And it is interesting that the Mexican co-star of *Neruda*, Gael García Bernal, has specifically affirmed that Latin

America has suffered — and learned from — its turbulent history of revolutions, dictatorships and messianic leaders: 'We are more mature, in the sense that we know there is no shamanic answer to things' (Carroll 2016). However, Larraín notes: 'When there's crisis, there's art; when there's pain, there's art; when there's suffering, there's art. When we struggle, we create things, as a humanity' (Carroll 2016). He has frequently declared that he wanted *Neruda* to be as lyrical and dream-like as a poem. (Intriguingly, James Nolan [1994], in an entirely different context, while striving to distinguish historical poets from their famous poetic personae, wrote that Neruda and Walt Whitman were 'not impersonating shamans' but were 'shaman-like' in their poems.) There is nothing new, of course, in trying to reproduce a literary form on celluloid. In his 1944 essay, 'Dickens, Griffith and the Film Today,' Sergei Eisenstein described the way in which D. W. Griffith translated the literary devices and conventions of novelists like Dickens into their film 'equivalents'. What Eisenstein attempted to demonstrate was that such devices as cross-cutting, close-ups, flashbacks or dissolves all had literary parallels. Eisenstein (1949) felt that Griffith's problem lay in his misunderstanding of the nature of the editing process, so that a shot of Lilian Gish rocking a cradle in *Intolerance*, inspired by a Walt Whitman poem, remained fixed as an isolated, life-like cradle and lacked the original poem's 'harmonic recurrence of montage expressiveness'.

Eisenstein frequently demonstrated his contempt for the simplest requirement of film as narrative: namely, the ability to create the illusion of events unfolding in a logical way. Eisenstein (1949) himself declared that his aim in breaking away from conventional narrative methods was to direct 'entire thought processes' as well as emotions. By liberating the action from the traditional definitions of time and space, he hoped to free himself from conventional limitations. For his part, Larraín shows himself to be highly eclectic in his choice of film syntax, in order to achieve the lyrical rhythm of his film. While he shares Eisenstein's lack of interest in the simple mechanics of story-telling, Larraín is prepared to employ both the long takes so intimately associated with one of the directors he most admires, Andrei Tarkovsky, and Eisensteinian editing (which Tarkovsky abhorred).

What makes a film poetic? It is insufficient to call attention to the beauty of the imagery or the dreamlike quality — although Larraín's regular cinematographer, Sergio Armstrong, does achieve some stunning shots, not just of the naturally photogenic Andes but also of the dark, repressive interiors where Neruda is concealed. Paintings can also be lyrical. But the difference in the cinematic medium is the passage of time — we move in time from one image to another in poetry and film (in this, they are both more like music). Moreover, poetry (and poetic film) also juxtapose images in time. Armstrong's camera is constantly on the move, in a conscious effort to mirror the inquisitive restlessness of Neruda's poems. '[His] poetry has many, many elements and layers, and, of course, one of them is the rhythm', says Larraín:

> So we tried to deliver that rhythm to the screen and to the way the movie was shot. If you read Neruda's poetry, you will find there's a specific tone and speed and pace, and we tried to create a reflection of that in the film. That's why the camera is moving all the time, and it's just sort of looking and tracking

the main characters wherever they are. It's a movie where people [are] moving from one side to another, from one idea to another, from one life to another. (Slater-Williams 2017)

But *which* poetry? Neruda's work is far from monolithic. He himself insisted that he was a love poet, not a political poet, and I myself have consistently argued that those who attempt to drive a wedge between these two types of poetry in Neruda's work are forging a false dichotomy. On the other hand, Eugenio Di Stefano claims that Larraín's *Neruda* is happy not only to accept the existence of such a schism but to play on it. For Di Stefano, the film openly dismisses, and even mocks, Neruda's 'sentimental' poetry and celebrates his political poetry. Significantly, Larraín has confirmed, in the DVD commentary to *Neruda* and elsewhere, that he wanted audiences to begin to read Neruda's political poetry after watching the film. In his year in hiding in the late 1940s, Neruda was writing much of his 1950 epic, *Canto General*, and the film shows poems from this book such as 'The Enemies' and 'Let the Woodcutter Awaken' being recited by workers and inmates — as Eugenio Di Stefano (2018: 23) has rightly pointed out — not in theatrical settings but rather in factories and prisons.

In one scene in *Neruda*, the poet, dressed as Lawrence of Arabia, recites his famous Poem 20 from the *Twenty Love Poems and a Song of Despair* to a crowded room as people listen admiringly. Later in the film, Neruda will again deliver the same poem in a brothel/theatre after a performer begs him to recite it. 'In both examples, Larraín emphasizes the theatrical quality not only of the settings where the poem is performed but also of the emotional appeal that poem elicits from the beholder' (Di Stefano 2018: 23). Here, at least, Larraín's film does reflect Neruda's true constituency. What Larraín's movie does not show is Neruda's own antagonism to Poem 20, which he came to see as part of his protracted post-adolescent anguish, precisely the type of poetry he turned against after his experiences in Spain in the 1930s. (At one reading; in Lima in 1970, Neruda actually refused to recite Poem 20, except that the audience went on strike and would not leave the auditorium until he did so. That 'cinematic' episode indicated both Neruda's rock-star status and his reluctance to read this particular poem, a reluctance which we could not possibly suspect from watching Larraín's *Neruda*.) So while Di Stefano is correct to note the film's mockery of the love poetry, the mockery is ill-directed in the true biographical context. For Di Stefano (2018: 23), Larraín's 'unenthusiastic' depiction of Neruda's love poems is 'a response both to their lack of political content as well as their theatrical appeal to the sentiments of the beholder. As such, the theatrical representation of the love poetry in *Neruda* is considered a continuation of the critique of the commercials already established in [Larraín's earlier film] *No*, which places too much emphasis on the beholder at the expense of the work of art.'

Larraín told one interviewer: 'I think cinema is about capturing time. So there's something about the speed that I tried to bring from Neruda's work [...] He has a rhythm. He has a speed. I tried to grab [Neruda's] poetic rhythm and bring it to the camera movement, put it into the way the actors walk or move. The camera moved faster with somebody and slower with somebody else. It's very handcrafted' (Buder 2016). His aim, he said, was to create an illusion, to adopt a more emotional approach, rather than a broader, intellectual one:

> That's why we shot in scope [Cinemascope], so that the environment would be relevant. We were always very close to the characters. The medium or close-up shots have a lot of information in the background that would continue to change. We were looking for some type of lighting that would be intentional. Sometimes, the lights are in the frame, and we're creating super-strong flares. It could be the sun or artificial light. We would set up very long shots — sometimes I cut it in the movie, but they're usually very long shots. We would go through different spaces and have different lights and atmospheres. (Buder 2016)

The film's colour scheme is also significant. The purples and blues, by Larraín's admission, come from the colour palette of the late-1940s. 'We were looking for a very distinctive look that would bring personality to the film. And also there's a very simple connection with Neruda's poetry and life. He lived many, many years of his life in front of the sea and wrote about the sea and the sky and the blue. Blue was an important colour in his work. And he was also a Communist, and that's red. And if you combined blue and red, you would get purple' (Slater-Williams 2017). Interestingly, Larraín's colour scheme is more closely related to the poet's work and environment than his particular mood, unlike, for example, in Julie Taymor's *Frida*, in which the director relies on colours to convey Frida Kahlo's point of view: when Frida is happy and energetic, the screen is dominated by the bright colours she wears and those that surround her; when she is sad and immobilized, the screen is dominated by much subtler greys, greens, and browns.

There can be no question that Larraín enjoys the playfulness of time. It is scarcely a coincidence that three of his favourite films are Alfred Hitchcock's *Vertigo*, Billy Wilder's *Sunset Boulevard* and Andrei Tarkovsky's *Ivan's Childhood*: all three toy imaginatively with time. Tarkovsky is perhaps the most interesting choice. He saw filmmakers as true poets, because they created new worlds. He believed that filmmakers did not need to recreate the real world, because film itself was doing that for you. He saw himself as 'sculpting in time'. Both he and his father, the poet Arsenii Tarkovsky, shared Henri Bergson's conviction that all our memories remain with us and that time is not a linear sequence. Frank Kermode (2000: 179), echoing Gilles Deleuze, the influential philosopher and film theorist, declared: 'It is on change, between remote or imaginary origins and ends, that our interests are fixed [...] in a freedom which is the freedom of a discordant reality. Such a vision of chaos or absurdity may be more than we can easily bear.'

Larraín does not find the freedom and chaos unbearable at all. He revels in it. He is an admirer of realist filmmakers such as Mike Leigh, but says he is incapable of making such movies himself: 'I love those movies, but I can't do that. I'm just not interested. I'm trying to find tools that would create an atmosphere that would support storytelling in an undetermined direction', he told one interviewer (Buder 2016). Stylistically, Larraín has always professed to prefer the illusionism of Georges Méliès to the realism of the Lumière brothers (Feinstein 2017). Of course, this schism is excessively stark. Most filmmakers would reject any such un-nuanced opposition. After all, what is imaginary and what is real? Gilles Deleuze (2005)

FIG. 6.2. Gael García Bernal as Óscar Peluchonneau in *Neruda*

wrote that cinema was able to move from one level of reality to another so that 'we no longer know which is imaginary or real [...] not because they are confused, but because we do not have to know'. Robert Rosenstone (1995: 71) believes that invention does not necessarily violate historical truth:

> We must recognise that film will always include images that are at once invented and true: true in that they symbolise, condense or summarise larger amounts of data; true in that they impart an overall meaning of the past that can be verified, documented or reasonably argued. And how do we know what can be verified, documented or reasonably argued? From the ongoing discourse of history; from the existing body of historical texts, from their data and arguments.

Larraín has stated that he sought a structure more akin to a story by Jorge Luis Borges: 'I realized it could work as a meta-fictional labyrinth. All these characters — Neruda, Óscar the detective, the narrator who narrates himself into the story — are creating each other because they need each other to tell the story. The film is about storytelling and how we need to tell stories in order to survive life' (Ashton 2017). This would appear to fall into line with Belén Vidal's claim that, beyond the postmodernist movement, the biopic has become a genre 'that intently reflects on its own forms of life writing' (Brown and Vidal 2014: 15). As Eugenio Di Stefano (2018: 23) has also pointed out, there is a strong Latin American tradition that uses crime fiction to abstract from reality, as seen in Borges's essays on crime fiction. And the books that Neruda ostentatiously leaves behind for Peluchonneau to find before escaping to his next hide-out are from Borges and Adolfo Bioy Casares's 'Séptimo Círculo' series of crime novels.

So, is Larraín's film a ludic exploration of the nature of fiction, with Neruda as its driving-force, or an overly inventive examination of a key episode in the extraordinary life of one of the central figures in twentieth-century literature? It is certainly true that Neruda could be an avid self-mythologizer, and Larraín evidently feels justified in establishing his own myth of a poet somehow coming to welcome his policeman pursuer as a mutual 'creator', a fellow artist. At one point, Neruda calls Peluchonneau 'my phantom in uniform. I dream of him and he dreams of me.' Yet, this can lead to absurdities. Peluchonneau comes across a book ostensibly by Neruda, called 'The Woman at the Zoo' (no such book exists), which Neruda has dedicated, adapting the great line from his 'Heights of Machu Picchu': 'Sube a nacer conmigo, hermano policía' [Rise and be born with me, policeman brother]. And when Peluchonneau says of Neruda in the voice-over: 'The poet has the fever of artistic spirits who tend to think the world is something they imagined', this simply does not reflect Neruda's credo. It is more akin to Neruda's arch-enemy and fellow Chilean poet Vicente Huidobro's *creacionismo*. Neruda, in stark contrast, felt he was depicting the world as it really was, as he felt it.

As I have pointed out elsewhere (Feinstein 2017), Larraín does allow genuine details from the poet's life to slip in. Neruda requests textbooks, especially on natural history, to help him in writing his epic work, *Canto General* (with its twin themes of betrayal: the personal betrayal by President González Videla and the savage betrayal of pre-Columbian civilization by the Spanish conquistadors). Many of the people who harboured Neruda in hiding assured me that he often made requests for such books at this time. He did disguise himself as a heavily bearded ornithologist to escape the clutches of the authorities. (It was a wonderfully apt choice — Neruda was exceptionally knowledgeable about Chile's birdlife and would go on to write a delightful collection, *The Art of Birds*, in 1966.) And Neruda's close friend, Pablo Picasso, did give his one and only public address in support of the fugitive poet.

The question that needs asking is whether Larraín over-indulges his delight in the imaginary over the real. Would the sixty-three-year-old Delia — attractive as she still was — really have beckoned to Neruda, saying: 'Give me a child'? You could tentatively make a case that she was living in yet another of the dream worlds summoned up by Larraín. But later, Delia tells Neruda: 'You'll go off on your own, as always.' As always? Neruda and Delia were very close, ever since they first met in Madrid in 1934. She had been a Communist long before him and he also trusted her as a literary critic, showing her his manuscripts. They travelled everywhere together. Neruda had not yet fallen in love with Matilde Urrutia (and even after he did so, he would continue to find it impossible to choose between the two women he adored and was forced to separate definitely from Delia only in 1955 after the Chilean Communist Party intervened and urged him to avoid a scandal.) Neruda's real-life emotional and intellectual intimacy with Delia explains why it seems pointlessly crude to depict him fondling his typist's breasts as he dictates a passage from his *Canto General*, with Delia standing just a few feet away. It also jars when Larraín's screenwriter, Guillermo Calderón, has the poet argue bitterly with Delia, insisting that he is 'the real artist' and then add, appallingly: 'You suffocate me all day long [...] I used to be a prince. Look what you've turned me into [...] Kill yourself. That way I'll write about you for another twenty years.' Later, he tries to recant by (correctly) informing her that he would not even have become a Communist without her (Delia was instrumental in firing his political commitment during the Spanish Civil War) — but the damage, for many viewers, is already done.

Perhaps it was these scenes between Neruda and Delia that prompted Víctor Pey — one of those who harboured the couple for a few weeks at his apartment near the Plaza Italia in Santiago during their year in hiding (he is played by Pablo Derqui in the movie) — to declare that the film 'no tiene ni pies ni cabeza' [makes no sense whatsoever] (Morales 2016). Amidst the preening in Larraín's film, you would hardly guess that Neruda could be a heroic man of action: he had saved Pey's life back in 1939 by including him among the more than 2300 Republican refugees from Franco's fascism on board the *Winnipeg*, the fishing boat he chartered to take them from Bordeaux to Valparaíso. Pey, who died in 2019 at the age of 101, was adamant that any resemblance between Larraín's portrayal of Neruda and the real man was 'pure coincidence' (Morales 2016).

There are many other anomalies. Peluchonneau did exist (despite many other writers' claims to the contrary) — which lends an irony to his on-screen question: 'Am I fiction?' — but his son, Jorge Peluchonneau Cádiz, has stated that his father emerges unrecognizable in the film. He certainly never met Neruda, in the snow or elsewhere, and his father had not been a national police chief nor his mother a prostitute — although this latter invention neatly puts him at ease in the brothels where he looks for Neruda. It is true that President González Videla brought Neruda's first wife, Maria Antonia Hagenaar (Maruca), to Chile from Europe to contest his marriage to Delia on grounds of bigamy. But Maruca was not stupid. She would not be likely to say, without a trace of irony, as she does here: 'Pablo has lots of money because he writes very long poems.'

Larraín does show us, with directorial pep and panache, Neruda's huge influence, as a Communist poet, over his natural constituency: the ordinary working man. One of the formative experiences in Neruda's life took place in Santiago's central market in 1938 (ten years before the action in the film), when the leader of the porters' union approached him at the end of a poetry recital with a sack around his waist and tears of gratitude in his eyes. In the movie, this same commitment to the workers and the poor is echoed by the detective when he declares: 'The poet gave them words to talk about their lives, and these words gave meaning to their nightmares. That's why he did it, to give them voice. They will quote him each time history tramples them. They don't remember the love poems. They remember the poems of rage. Unrecognizable poems. Poems of an imaginary future.'

But what we do not see in the film is the immensely moving capacity of poetry to break down barriers between people of diametrically opposed political beliefs. This is odd, because Larraín has stated that the way Latin Americans, and specifically Chileans, think is forged by poetry: 'We in Chile have a way of thinking and talking that is very particular. The way we speak our Spanish is through metaphor [...] I'm sure people are reading less poetry than before, but I'm also sure that the way we think has been shaped by poetry. It's in our bloodstream' (O'Sullivan 2017). His film is partly concerned with the power of poetry to move and influence. It is specifically here that Larraín makes too many sacrifices in his determination to flee the facts. According to the poet's memoirs, when Neruda hid on the estate of the right-wing mill owner, Pepe Rodríguez — a friend of President González

Videla, who would have been expected to hand over Neruda to the authorities —
Rodríguez was so entranced to meet Chile's greatest poet that he urged his workers
to ensure Neruda escaped. In the film, however, the mill owner glibly announces
that it would be more fun to help a Communist than the police. Of course, we
have only Neruda's account, which he may well have embellished, and that of Jorge
Bellet, one of the key figures in organizing the poet's escape from Chile, but the
interesting question is why Larraín preferred his own version to Neruda's more
poignant one.

Larraín is well aware of Neruda's habit of self-aggrandizing. From his own
declarations, the director appears to prefer to tell his own, Borgesian stories rather
than Neruda's:

> Borges had an idea of overlapping fictions. *Neruda* is a Nerudian story
> overlapping with a Borgesian process. Well-known people throughout
> history at some point become concerned with managing their own legacy or
> iconography [...] People want to project a certain idea of themselves, to twist
> history so that it regards them in a specific way [...] We know where they were
> at such and such time. But once they close the door, that's where the fiction
> starts, the imagination starts. We make a little hole in the door, we slip a camera
> through that hole, we find out what we can see. I'm a storyteller. I don't want
> to relay facts. I want to play. And to create a problem. (Teodoro 2016)

It is instructive to compare Larraín's depiction of Pablo Neruda with the two other
principal fictional cinematic representations of the poet. They also take liberties,
but in different ways. The better known of these is Michael Radford's delightful *Il
Postino* [The Postman] (1994). Based on Antonio Skármeta's novel, *Ardiente paciencia*
[Burning Patience], and set on an unnamed Italian island, the movie begins like the
neorealist Luchino Visconti's great 1948 fishing drama, *La Terra trema*. The titular
postman, Mario Ruppuolo, played beautifully by Massimo Troisi, has a cold.[4] Then
we learn, from a cinema newsreel, that Neruda is in Rome. The year is 1952 —
towards the end of Neruda's European exile (the period immediately after the time
depicted in Larraín's film). Unlike Larraín's use of archive footage in the third film
in his 'political trilogy', *No* (2012), the newsreel in *Il postino* is not genuine — we see
the superb French actor, Philippe Noiret, as Neruda. But the newsreel voice-over
correctly notes that Neruda's Communist declarations on Italian soil have caused
him problems — in fact, he would be chased down a Venice canal by gondola and
was saved from expulsion from the country only when Elsa Morante, the wife of
Alberto Moravia, attacked a policeman with her umbrella at Naples. It should be
recalled that Neruda was still in hiding from the Chilean authorities and had found
a haven for himself and his lover, Matilde Urrutia, at the home of Erwin Cerio on
Capri (having sent Delia back to Chile to prepare his return from exile).

The screenplay is by Radford and Troisi but also Anna Pavignano, Furio
Scarpelli and Giacomo Scarpelli. Neruda is just as much a celebrity in *Il postino* as
he is in Larraín's film. However, as Ellen Cheshire (2015: 49–50) has pointed out, of
all the creative arts, writing is the one that directors often find difficult to convey
on screen: 'How often have you seen the clichéd montage sequence of writing,
screwing up paper into balls, cuts to overflowing waste-paper basket full of failed

attempts?' But it is the potency of poetry which constitutes one of the main themes (and charms) of Radford's movie: Mario wants to learn how to write poetry to woo the woman he loves, Beatrice Russo, played by Maria Gracia Cucinotta. The role of poetry, the film eventually shows us, is not just to woo but as a weapon for social and political justice. In contrast, we do not see much of this specific role in Larraín's *Neruda*, even though it was crucial to the poet's work after its dramatic metamorphosis in the wake of Lorca's murder in August 1936. Poetry has power. In *Il postino*, Beatrice's mother visits Neruda and warns him that she will shoot Mario if he keeps using metaphors on her daughter! Mario subsequently blames Neruda for his falling in love — and for 'teaching him to use his tongue for more than licking stamps'.

Il postino, for all its many enticing qualities, is a curious hybrid. Michael Radford actually began as a documentary maker but here he creates his own myths and takes considerable chronological liberties: on screen, for example, Neruda is already married to Matilde Urrutia, whereas, in fact, he was still married to Delia. He looks much older than forty-eight — more like the sixty-two he was when he actually married Matilde in 1966. (Noiret was sixty-four when he made the film.) One of the letters Mario brings him announces that he has been nominated for the Nobel Prize, although he was not officially nominated until 1964 (when Jean-Paul Sartre won but rejected the award). Neruda did not actually win the prize until 1971. (The title of Skármeta's original novel, 'Burning Patience,' is taken from Neruda's Nobel Prize acceptance speech in Stockholm — but Neruda himself borrowed the expression from one of his beloved French poets, Arthur Rimbaud.) *Il postino* also shows Neruda indulging in two of his least favourite activities, dancing and swimming. But the true spirit of Neruda is there on screen: Neruda was extremely generous to younger budding poets. Many of his friends confirmed this to me in Chile, but we have evidence from many other, more impartial sources. For example, the Spanish poet Gabriel Celaya showed one of his poems to both Neruda and Lorca, in Madrid in 1935. Lorca made some brief comments about the structure of Celaya's poem, whereas Neruda generously took the time and care to go through each line of the poem meticulously and, according to Celaya (1972), 'in total contrast to Lorca, showed himself to be, as in his own poetry, more concerned with the minimal units of the poem, the right adjectives, no wasted images, functional sounds than with the form and overall structure of the poem. The accumulation of correct words or lovely details takes precedence for him, like a primitive, over the general concept.' One of the most moving scenes in *ll postino* has Neruda and Mario sitting on the beach and Mario finding that he has been using metaphors without realizing it. In the end, the postman acknowledges that 'poetry doesn't belong to those who write it, but those who need it'.

Skármeta directed his own celluloid version of his novel eleven years earlier, in 1983. Understandably, *Ardiente paciencia* stays far more loyal to its source material — and to the chronology of the events depicted. It is set in Chile, for a start, not on an Italian island. And most of the cast and crew are Chilean. Neruda is played by the Chilean actor Roberto Parada, looking less like the poet than either Noiret or Gneccho (except, oddly, in the black-and-white TV pictures of him reading his Nobel Prize speech). In real life, however, Parada had been a friend of the poet and, as a result, successfully captures his way of moving. Indeed, the movie opens with Neruda strolling along the beach in front of his Pacific Coast home at Isla Negra in 1969 — the year the poet stood as 'pre-candidate' for the Presidency of Chile. (The political backdrop of the entire film is the 1970 Presidential election, at which Neruda renounced his candidacy in favour of Salvador Allende who, as we know, became the first democratically elected Marxist head of state anywhere in the world.) Then we meet the postman, Mario Jiménez (interpreted by Óscar Castro Ramírez, the Chilean actor, theatre director and playwright). He is supposed to be just twenty-two, but looks older, as he delivers the post to Neruda. The first letter the poet opens announces his candidature for the Nobel Prize. Then the dialogue between the two men erupts in similes, rather than metaphors. 'Everyone's a poet', Neruda tells Mario when he hears of the postman's career ambition. 'It's much more original to be a postman.' The dynamic of the friendship between them is very similar to that in *Il postino* — Mario needs Neruda's help in employing the appropriate language to court Beatriz González (Marcela Osorio) — and then to pacify her mother. We see him reading a genuine Neruda book, *Aún* — unlike the invented titles from Larraín's film. As in *Il postino*, Beatriz's mother is fully aware of the danger of poetry: she tells her daughter: 'I'd prefer a drunkard who grabs hold of your backside. At least he wouldn't say your smile flew like a butterfly.'

Neruda's wife, Matilde, is curiously absent — a startling omission. Another jolt comes when we see Neruda dancing (to The Marvelettes' 'Please Mr. Postman'). Significantly, Skármeta (1983) himself declared: 'I didn't want to tell the story of the great Neruda. I am not the kind of writer who [...] praises, creates myths or fabricates [...] I am a writer of the quotidian. I was interested in the everyday Neruda whom I got to know in his house by the sea at Isla Negra in 1969.' This produced a very different approach from Larraín's or Radford's. And for all Skármeta's admiration for Neruda, his vision stemmed from a very personal identification with the postman, not the poet: 'As a twenty-four-year-old, I used to fall hopelessly in love every other day, but I could never find the words to seduce the girls. Then I whispered lines from Neruda's *Twenty Love Poems and a Song of Despair* in a girl's ear, as if they were my own. I have Neruda to thank for soon losing my innocence' (1983).

Skármeta (1983) added: 'There is another person in the film, someone without a face: a poetic charm, an expression of tenderness and humour which coloured the mood of Chilean society until democracy was destroyed.' The mood of the film does indeed darken, firstly with Neruda's illness and culminating in Augusto Pinochet's military coup. The scene when Mario visits Neruda and the poet begs to be allowed to go to the window to witness the truth of what is happening to his beloved homeland is profoundly affecting. But while Beatriz's mother appreciated the threat from verse, Skármeta could have reinforced this message with a genuine incident: when Pinochet's soldiers arrived to arrest Neruda at his Isla Negra home after the coup, he told them from his sickbed: 'Look around you: the only thing of danger to you here is poetry.' At which point, the young soldier leading the raid retreated shame-faced.

All three films are about people playing roles. Bingham (2010: 378) has written that biopics are a 'form of celebrity culture. They are made [...] to find truth out of invention.' He adds that, as a form, the biopic is not just about self-identification and self-invention but about identification with others. 'The best biopics [...] are about people who play roles and about how they feel within these roles' (2010: 378).

It has been pointed out that this was one of the superficial similarities between *Neruda* and the other biopic Larraín released in 2016 — *Jackie*. He was well aware that both Neruda and Jacqueline Kennedy were constantly attempting to shape their image.

> But there's something that is out of their control. There is what they try to do in terms of public image, and there's a final public image, and I'm focused on that gap — that part that they don't control, even if they tried to [...] Their intentions are very important. That's what creates humanity and fragility. That's what also creates the essence of the cinema that I'm interested in, which is a combination of love, rage, and curiosity. Sometimes it's hard to see those intentions, or maybe it's hard to portray them on film in a way that doesn't sound too preachy or irrelevant. So instead of saying it out loud, you say it multiple times in the movie by hiding it. You get a sensation after you see the whole film throughout yourself [...] I try to have an active audience that are thinking and feeling for themselves. (Brown 2016)

Most of Larraín's films contain characters who find it difficult to distinguish between fantasy and reality. In his superb *Tony Manero* (2008), his favourite actor, Alfredo Castro (he takes the role of President González Videla in *Neruda*), plays Raúl Peralta, a man impervious to the political climate around him and so obsessed with his ambition to impersonate the John Travolta character in John Badham's *Saturday Night Fever* that he becomes a serial killer. But Larraín also knows how dramatic and poignant real life can be cinematically — Asif Kapadia's trio of documentaries, *Senna* (2010), *Amy* (2015) and *Diego Maradona* (2019), provides marvellous evidence. The action of the second film in Larraín's own 'political trilogy', *Post Mortem* (2010), takes place during the final days of Salvador Allende's presidency. Mario Cornejo (Alfredo Castro) is an employee at a morgue who falls for a dancer, Nancy Puelma, who then mysteriously disappears. Typically, the employee really existed. Moreover, as Alfredo Castro told me, the morgue where *Post Mortem* was shot was the very room where the autopsy took place on Salvador Allende's body in 2011 to ascertain whether he was murdered or committed suicide on 11 September 1973.[5] Mario, like Raúl in *Tony Manero*, is a ghostly, almost vampiric figure — in the world but not of it. And Larraín shot the third in his trilogy, *No* (2012) — about the rival 'Yes' and 'No' television campaigns for the historic 1988 national referendum, which, to Pinochet's enormous surprise, rejected the extension of his dictatorship — with a rebuilt U-matic video camera, the standard format of Chilean television in the 1980s. This gives the film a blurry, grainy period look, making it easier to switch between the fiction and the documentary sections which are spliced in. Larraín himself declared: 'It breaks my illusion when I'm looking at a film that is shot in high resolution and they cut to archival footage that is made in video or on old resolution film stock. [In *No*] [w]e were able to create the illusion in a way that fiction became documentary and documentary became fiction' (Wilkinson 2013: 3). Larraín's technique provoked considerable debate. But Di Stefano (2018) is right to state that the blurring of the line between fiction and documentary 'is a product of choices made with an eye to asserting the film's status as an "illusion". Larraín, in other words, chooses this technology as a means to insist on the film's status as fiction.' It is worth recalling that there is a long and honourable tradition in Chilean filmmaking of fusing reality and fiction within a non-linear narration. The most striking feature of Miguel Littín's magnificent *The Jackal of Nahueltoro* (1969) is the way the film splices events together from different time periods as it tells the true story of a man who murdered a homeless woman and her five children in an apparently motiveless crime fuelled by drunken violence. The movie begins with a sequence depicting his arrest and then tracks back into the events of his early childhood. The film is framed as a documentary reconstruction offering differing layers of competing information.

A significant, and intriguing, influence on Larraín was Maurice Pialat's 1991 movie, *Van Gogh*: 'Pialat used the paintings as a mirror. That's how I approached Neruda. We used his poetry to create the structure. Nothing is entirely serious. It is more based on poetry than anything else. Neruda's poetry was a virus that infected us all' (Feinstein 2017). As in Pialat's film, Larraín stages certain set-pieces in a claustrophobic demi-monde of prostitutes entertaining the respectable. Yet Pialat, unlike Larraín, is usually, if problematically, classed as a realist. Unlike Vincente Minelli's *Lust for Life* (1956), starring Kirk Douglas, Pialat condenses the whole of Van Gogh's adult life into his film, dramatizing key episodes to create the sense of one crisis crashing after another. His narrative lacks a specific emphasis. He keeps his subject at a distance — indeed, Van Gogh is often marginal to, or even absent from, entire scenes.

Ingmar Bergman associated poetry with the dissolution of narrative, the freedom from story-telling. When writing about the genesis of *Cries and Whispers*, his remarkable 1972 film about three sisters in Sweden at the beginning of the twentieth century, Bergman (2017: 70) declared: 'I believe that the film — or whatever it is — consists of this poem: a human being dies but, as in a nightmare, gets stuck halfway through and pleads for tenderness, mercy, deliverance, something [...] I believe this is the poem or the invention, or whatever.'

Nevertheless, it is Andrei Tarkovsky who seems ultimately, to me, to be the key reference point for Larraín's approach in *Neruda*. 'In my view, poetic reasoning is closer to the laws by which thought develops, and thus to life itself, than is the logic of traditional drama [...] The usual logic, that of linear sequentiality, is uncomfortably like the proof of a geometry theorem', Tarkovsky (1989: 20–21) wrote in *Sculpting in Time*. 'As a method, it is incomparably less fruitful artistically than the possibilities opened up by associative linking, which allows for an affective as well as a rational appraisal [...] The method whereby the artist obliges the audience to build the separate parts into a whole, and to think on, further than has been stated, is the only one that puts the audience on a par with the artist in their perception of the film.'

In a startlingly similar vein, Larraín has stated:

> I prefer to make films which provoke questions and then it is up to the audience
> to complete and answer these questions. It is up to the audience to decide what
> works and what doesn't, based on their own biographies, their own perspectives.
> But to achieve this, you have to invent a cosmos within the film which is not
> merely narrative, which is not simply a dramatic structure. There has to be an
> atmosphere and a tone and these must travel through both shadow and light,
> because if there is just a single tone, there can be no music. (SensaCine 2016)

If Larraín's playful dissolution of the narrative line can indeed be seen as
Tarkovskian 'time-sculpting' or Bergmanesque lyricism, the question remains: how
much of Pablo Neruda the man has been lost in this 'music'? For some, the sacrifice
has simply been too savage. For others, the film constitutes a new poem in itself,
Larraín's own cinematic 'translation' of the truth.

Works Cited

ANON., 1982. 'Carlos Fuentes at UCLA', *Mester* <https://escholarship.org/uc/item/23d8h6w9>
[accessed 15 June 2019]
ASHTON, STEPHEN. 2017. 'Pablo Larraín puts poetry on the screen with *Neruda*', *The Desert Sun*
<https://eu.desertsun.com/story/life/entertainment/movies/film-festival/2017/01/09/
pablo-larran-puts-poetry-screen-neruda/96251416/> [accessed 19 June 2019]
AXMAKER, SEAN. 2008. 'Todd Haynes and a Whole Slew of Dylans', *Green Cine* <https://
www.greencine.com/central/toddhaynes> [accessed 15 June 2019]
BARNIER, MARTIN. 2010. 'Biographie filmée et historiographie', in *Les Biopics du pouvoir
politique de l'antiquité au XIXe siècle: hommes et femmes de pouvoir à l'écran*, ed. by Martin
Barnier and Rémi Fontanel (Lyon: Aléas), pp. 23–24
BERGMAN, INGMAR. 2017. *Images: My Life in Film* (New York: Arcade Publishing)
BETANCOURT, MANUEL. 2016. 'Pablo Larraín on his "Anti-Biopic" about Pablo Neruda &
Gael García Bernal's Mysterious Face', *Remezcla* <https://remezcla.com/features/film/
interview-neruda-pablo-larrain-gael-garcia-bernal-new-york-film-festival/> [accessed
4 September 2019]
BINGHAM, DENNIS. 2010. *Whose Lives Are They Anyway? The Biopic as Contemporary Film
Genre* (New Brunswick, NJ: Rutgers University Press)
BORUNDA, STEPHEN. 2016. *Neruda* (2016). Reviewed by Stephen Borunda', *Film Matters
Magazine* <https://www.filmmattersmagazine.com/2017/08/25/neruda-2016-reviewed-
by-stephen-borunda/> [accessed 1 March 2020]
BROWN, EMMA. 2016. 'Pablo Larrain's examination of two icons', *Interview* <https://www.
interviewmagazine.com/film/pablo-larrain> [accessed 4 September 2019]
BROWN, TOM, and BELEN VIDAL (eds). 2014. *The Biopic in Contemporary Film Culture* (New
York and London: Routledge)
BUDER, EMILY. 2016. 'Neruda: How Pablo Larraín "Discovered the Movie While Making
It"', *No Film School* <https://nofilmschool.com/2016/10/pablo-larrain-interview-
neruda> [accessed 1 March 2020]
CARROLL, RORY. 2016. 'Gael García Bernal and Pablo Larraín: "Trump has the nuclear
codes but we have a camera"', *The Guardian* <https://www.theguardian.com/film/2016/
dec/09/gael-garcia-bernal-pablo-larrain-donald-trump-we-have-a-camera> [accessed 1
March 2020]
CELAYA, GABRIEL. 1972. 'El poeta del Tercer Día de la Creación', *Revista de Occidente*, 106:
97

CHESHIRE, ELLEN. 2015. *Bio-pics: A Life in Pictures* (London: Wallflower)

COMOLLI, JEAN-LOUIS. 1978. 'Historical Fiction: A Body Too Much', *Screen*, 19: 41–54

CUSTEN, GEORGE F. 1992. *Bio/Pics: How Hollywood Constructed Public History* (New Brunswick, NJ: Rutgers University Press)

DARGIS, MANOHLA. 2016. 'Why the Movie "Neruda" Is an "Anti-Bio"', *The New York Times* <https://www.nytimes.com/2016/05/19/movies/cannes-pablo-larrain-interview-neruda.html> [accessed 1 March 2020]

DELEUZE, GILLES. 2005. *Cinema 2: The Time Image*, trans. by Hugh Tomlinson and Robert Galeta (London: The Athlone Press)

DI STEFANO, EUGENIO. 2018. 'Forms of Freedom in Pablo Larraín's *No* and *Neruda*', *Open Library of Humanities*, 4: 23 <http://doi.org/10.16995/olh.361>

DUNCAN, ROBERT. 2014. *Collected Essays and Other Prose*, ed. by James Maynard (Berkeley: University of California Press)

EISENSTEIN, SERGEI. 1949. *Film Form: Essays in Film Theory*, ed. by Jay Leyda (New York: Harcourt)

FEINSTEIN, ADAM. 2013. *Pablo Neruda: A Passion for Life* (London: Bloomsbury)

—— 2017. 'Fast, loose and lyrical: Pablo Larraín's Neruda anti-biopic,' *The Guardian* <https://www.theguardian.com/film/2017/apr/06/neruda-pablo-larrain-biopic> [accessed 15 June 2019]

HARDIE, GILES. 2013. 'Big names, big flops: Why the biopics have failed in 2013', *Sydney Morning Herald*, 25 October

KERMODE, FRANK. 2000. *The Sense of an Ending: Studies in the Theory of Fiction, with a New Epilogue* (New York: Oxford University Press)

LANDY, MARCIA. 1996. *Cinematic Uses of the Past* (Minneapolis: University of Minnesota Press)

LEWIS, REBECCA, 2019. Untitled article, *Evening Standard*, 14 June, p. 13.

MENDOZA, PLINIO APULEYO. 1983. *Fragrance of Guava: Conversations with Gabriel García Márquez* (London: Verso)

MORALES, MAURICIO. 2016. 'Víctor Pey: La película Neruda "no tiene pies ni cabeza"', *elciudadano.com* <https://www.elciudadano.com/reportaje-destacado/victor-pey-la-pelicula-neruda-no-tiene-pies-ni-cabeza354/12/23/> [accessed 15 June 2019]

NOLAN, JAMES. 1994. *Poet-Chief: The Native American Poetics of Walt Whitman and Pablo Neruda* (Albuquerque: University of New Mexico Press)

O'SULLIVAN, MICHAEL. 2017. 'Q&A: Pablo Larraín, director of *Jackie* and *Neruda*, talks about the anti-biopic', *The Washington Post* <https://www.washingtonpost.com/lifestyle/qanda-pablo-larrain-director-of-jackie-and-neruda-talks-about-the-anti-biopic/2017/03/03/61b3d57c-fde4–11e6–8ebe-6e0dbe4f2bca_story.html> [accessed 4 September 2019]

ROSENSTONE, ROBERT A. 1995. *Visions of the Past: The Challenge of Film to our Idea of History* (Cambridge, MA: Harvard University Press)

SensaCine. 2016. 'San Sebastián 2016 — Pablo Larraín: "La mezcla entre la poesía y el cine es peligrosa"' <http://www.sensacine.com/noticias/cine/noticia-18546263/> [accessed 4 September 2019]

SKÁRMETA, ANTONIO. 1983. 'Das Fernsehspiel', *ZDF*, 42

SLATER-WILLIAMS, JOSH. 2017. 'Pablo Larraín rethinks the biopic with Neruda', *The Skinny* <https://www.theskinny.co.uk/film/interviews/pablo-larrain-neruda> [accessed 10 July 2020]

TARKOVSKY, ANDREI. 1989. *Sculpting in Time* (Austin: University of Texas Press)

TEODORO, JOSÉ. 2016. 'The State that I am In', *Film Comment* <https://www.filmcomment.com/article/pablo-larrain-jackie-neruda-interview/> [accessed 1 March 2020]

WILKINSON, A. 2013. 'Man in the *No*', *Eye for Film* <http://www.eyeforfilm.co.uk/feature/2013–02–07-pablo-Larraín-talks-about-his-oscar-nominated-film-no-feature-story-by-amber-wilkinson> [accessed 4 September 2019]

Notes to Chapter 6

1. Neruda had witnessed Franco's brutality — and was especially appalled by the murder of his friend and fellow poet, Federico García Lorca — while Chilean consul in Madrid in 1936.
2. Neruda informs one of his young underground protectors, Álvaro Jara, that he wishes to be a 'popular giant'. To which Jara replies: 'I ask that you be more humble.'
3. There is a similarly incongruous scene in Buñuel's 1974 movie, *Le Fantôme de la liberté* [The Phantom of Liberty]: a typical bourgeois dinner party at which the dining table is ringed not by chairs but by toilet seats.
4. Tragically, in real life Troisi was suffering from a severe heart defect — he was too ill to ride the bike around the island and the man bringing Neruda his post is a body double — and Radford told me there were two doctors on set and an oxygen tent. Troisi died the day after shooting was completed.
5. It was finally determined that Allende had killed himself.

CHAPTER 7

❖

Cinematographic Poetics in Sergio Bravo's Documentary *Láminas de Almahue* (1962)[1]

Camila Gatica Mizala

Between 1955 and 1973 Chilean cinema flourished. The film production of these years is known as the New Chilean Cinema, a cultural movement and project promoted by artists and intellectuals of that period in Chile, and part of a wider cinema movement, the New Latin American Cinema. It is hard to establish a clear moment when the movement began, although most scholars would set its starting date in the early 1960s (Cortínez and Engelbert 2014), (Mouesca 1988). In this context, 1957 is a key year, since that was when a group of film enthusiasts founded the *Centro de Cine Experimental* [Centre for Experimental Film] at the Universidad de Chile, headed by Sergio Bravo.[2] The Centro also emerged as a more practical expression of a love for (and interest in) cinema that had moved them to start, in 1954, the *Cine Club Universitario* [University Cinema Club], which later played an important role in the development of the first film archive in 1961 (Lema 2005), (Mouesca and Orellana 1998), (Mouesca 2005), (Pick 1984), (Vega 1979, 2006).

This essay seeks to link Chilean cinema and poetry in the 1950s and 1960s through the work of Sergio Bravo and Efraín Barquero. The relevance of this artistic encounter was that it put together two forms of poetics — the making of a film and poetry — while, at the same time, creating a new experimental cinematic idiom in the form of cinematographic poetics. When we look at poetry in 1950s Chile, a number of themes mark authors' works, most notably a criticism of the modern individual and the bourgeoisie (Nómez 2007, 2008, 2014). This poetry represents a return to the origins of the world. Perhaps one of the most important concepts that can be used to define the type of poetry of this decade is *Larismo*, a form of poetic practice founded by poet Jorge Teillier (n.d.), and characterized by its 'return to the past, a paradise lost in which the quotidian and kindness contrast against the dominant backdrop of modernity'.[3]

This chapter looks at the connections between cinema and poetry through an analysis of *Láminas de Almahue* by Sergio Bravo (1962), a film that shows the making of the metal rim (the *lámina* of the title) that protects the wheels of the wagons in the town of Almahue. The documentary brings together film and poetry, not only through Efraín Barquero's verses accompanying Bravo's montage (which were written for the documentary), but also through Bravo's cinematographic poetics. I argue that it is in his own poetics that an idea of *lo popular* is projected in the image. The chapter is divided into three parts. First, a section that provides historical context, which will be key to understanding the concepts of cinematographic poetics and *lo popular*, which will guide the second section. Although cinematographic poetics will be explored further in this second section, this concept will be understood as the coming together of a historical context and the ability to create films that are able to represent that particular context. The third section will focus on an analysis of the documentary.

Methodologically speaking, the analysis draws on a literary approach that intertwines Barquero's poetry with the images in order to construct a direct dialogue between the two. In terms of visual analysis, the piece follows an aesthetic perspective that builds from film studies and technical aspects of the documentary. Moreover, throughout the article, there will be a historical perspective guiding the analysis in order to contextualize the elements specified before. It is in the intersection between images and poetry that the poetics of the *Láminas de Almahue* appear.

Contextualizing Bravo's Experimental Filmmaking and Barquero's Poetry

To understand the changes in both Chilean cinema and poetry taking place from the late 1950s onwards, Cortínez and Engelbert state that it is essential to look back to the 1930s and the consequences of the Great Depression (Cortínez and Engelbert 2014: 53–54). In response to the economic issues brought about by the depression, the Chilean state implemented an import substitution industrialization model in order to develop national industries (a policy adopted by many other countries in the region). The depression allowed economic and political nationalism to take centre stage, mainly through policies developed by the *Frente Popular* (Popular Front, 1936–41) and the Radical Party governments (1941–52) that followed (Silva Avaria 2018). The state sought to improve the quality of life through more schooling, which in turn translated into an accumulation of human capital (Loveman 2001), (Meller 2007). Moreover, mortality rates declined (through health provisions and better access to medicine), allowing a demographic explosion to take place (Correa et al. 2001).

Politically, the period between the 1930s and 1960s saw the inclusion of more people in the political processes through electoral participation. This also meant that political parties had to transform in order to represent those new voters and their interests. Perhaps the best example of the latter was Democracia Cristiana [Christian Democracy], founded in 1957 to support the presidential bid of Eduardo Frei Montalva (who would become President in the 1964 election). Democracia Cristiana was a party made up of young people (mainly men) who were strongly influenced by Jacques Maritain's ideas and Christian Humanism. The party had a strong sense of social responsibility and of the need to include those previously marginalized by politics and economics. The entry of Democracia Cristiana into Chilean politics reshaped society's structure around three socio-political projects: 'a right-wing project (technocratic and economically liberal), the Democracia Cristiana project (a revolution in freedom that aspired to establish communitarianism in Chile), and the left-wing project (that searched for a total replacement of capitalism by socialism)' (Bowen Silva 2008).[4]

By the 1950s Santiago had undergone accelerated urbanization. Many people saw the capital city as a space that could offer better opportunities, prompting an exodus from the countryside in search of a better life. The result of this migration was the emergence of *poblaciones callampas* or shanty towns. These settlements housed migrants from the countryside, workers from small industries whose salaries were very low, and anyone who could not afford rent.[5] Democracia Cristiana began to think about ways of including these newcomers in politics, alongside rural peasants.

In short, from the 1930s onwards, Chile experienced a turn towards state-led industry, with the newfound relevance of the middle classes in national politics, the power of unions, and the importance of agriculture and its workers. All these elements highlighted a series of changes in the national culture where the popular classes had a space. Culturally, *criollismo* had played a key role since the late nineteenth century, focusing on the countryside as a space that preserved all things Chilean.[6] *Criollismo* also appears as a reaction against ideas of the city as a privileged space for the arts and intellectual activity at the turn of the twentieth century (Subercaseaux 1992, 2007). In the 1940s the state took on an active role in attempting to open spaces for culture, which went hand in hand with the role it needed to have in the economy. One of these efforts was Chilefilms, a state-led studio that during the 1940s began to produce its first films (Peirano and Gobantes 2015). Besides the state, universities began to have a more active role in the development of culture and education (Correa et al. 2001: 233). Particular emphasis was given to branches of culture that could have a social impact and reaffirm Chilean national identity in a positive way.

Amongst the factors that led to the emergence of New Chilean Cinema in the 1950s was a desire to challenge traditional themes and ways of making films. This was the decade in which the social documentary movement developed, which experimented with new ways of subverting the traditional omniscient narrative in documentary films, introducing democratization and plurality to the way filmmakers addressed their topics (Burton 1990: 49–84). As Julianne Burton outlines, the latter meant rethinking how documentaries were defined, using folk song lyrics and the self-presentation of social actors or introducing their voices as narrators, alongside other elements (Burton 1990: 50). These stylistic choices also represented a form of empowerment, not only by filmmakers finding innovative ways of documenting and addressing new topics and themes, but also through the topics themselves, which highlighted the challenges that society was facing at the time. In short, these were films that constantly emphasized the connections between politics and society, both in theory and practice; but also the different ways in which these interactions could be enacted.[7]

Following Cortínez and Engelbert, between the 1920s and the 1970s Chilean culture developed by including social practices coming from urban and rural backgrounds, traditional as well as technologically and ideologically advanced mediums; oral and written forms; and popular and scholarly knowledge (Cortínez and Engelbert 2014: 61). Moreover, the socio-political developments described above gave way to a change in sensibility that allowed the development of two groups, the Instituto Fílmico of the Universidad Católica and the Centro de Cine Experimental at the Universidad de Chile, to capture these changes on film (Vega 2006: 39). Those working with film showed a privileged historical consciousness, which the Instituto Fílmico and the Centro Experimental were able to represent on film. The latter enabled them to

> get inside shanty towns, travel with the Navy to southern zones; the filmmakers acted as reporters, penetrated mines; infiltrated street demonstrations; recorded Senate sessions, attended complicated surgeries in university hospitals; went with *organilleros* and many craftsmen on their daily routines; in the field they filmed the inside of huts, the dynamics of the threshing season, and the long process of construction of tools used in labour and transport. (Corro et al. 2007: 30–31)

The two documentaries filmed by Bravo in 1957 and 1958, *Mimbre* [Wicker] and *Trilla* [Threshing], respectively, led to the establishment of the Centro de Cine Experimental in 1958. The two productions 'looked to innovate in traditional themes and present a certain degree of aesthetic experimentation' (Salinas Muñoz, Stange Marcus, and Salinas Roco 2008: 17). The presence of the word 'experimental' in the name of the Centre is not gratuitous. According to Pedro Chaskel, one of the founding members of the Centro de Cine Experimental, their model was Teatro Experimental of the Universidad de Chile, a group that offered an alternative to the more conventional theatre being staged at the time. Moreover, Chaskel mentioned that 'experimental' was a word that was part of the university culture. In this sense, there was 'an intention to break a little with traditional Chilean cinema [...] and we chose precisely documentary to register the "national reality", culture, social classes, etc.' (Salinas Muñoz, Stange Marcus, and Salinas Roco 2008: 42). In short, the 'experimental' element was there to challenge commercial films, to highlight a difference in the way of making movies. It is not what is being filmed that is experimental per se, but its motivation, thematic focus, and political stance. These interests pushed the filmmakers of the Centro de Cine Experimental to 'insert themselves into themes linked to national identity, social and political reality', and become active filmmakers within reformist and revolutionary political projects (Salinas Muñoz, Stange Marcus, and Salinas Roco 2008: 44). In Bravo's case, he experimented with filmmaking through the incorporation of poetry.

As stated in the introduction, a useful concept that guided 1950s poetry is the *lar*. *Lar* means home, and perhaps more specifically it relates to the stove, the fire at the centre of the house, the kitchen (the hearth of the home in rural communities).[8] By using this word to define their style, poets highlight that search for this seemingly lost rural world. Nostalgia could possibly be another value attached to *larismo*, as the poet writes by 'reconstructing memory through an affective withdrawal due to a world that seems adverse' (Nómez 2017: 137). What lies beneath this return to the *lar* is, ultimately, the need for community, and rites linked to those rural communities.

As Naín Nómez states, these themes hark back to the rural world for inspiration, instead of looking at modern life and new artistic trends, in a style that was used by some poets in the beginning of the twentieth century. Furthermore, this return to the rural world turns it into a refuge that allows poets to reconnect with nature, a space often seen 'repressed by new ways of inhabiting the world' (Nómez 2017: 134). The work of poets such as Violeta Parra, Jorge Teillier, and Efraín Barquero, amongst others, marked a shift in focus not only towards the rural world, but also towards everyday practices.[9] According to Nómez, this retreat towards the rural sphere was in many respects a response to the international context (the Cold War), as well as the national background of economic tensions (such as high inflation), and the push by previously overlooked social sectors for more political participation (including from women and urban workers). In short, 1950s Chile was a place of tensions during which the country experienced a need for reorganization. The poetry and cinema of that decade took up those tensions and rethought themselves, turning to experimentation as a way of presenting the shift in idioms. In this context cinema and poetry will meet in the work of Bravo.

Cinematographic Poetry and *lo popular*

There is a further connection between the shift towards the rural in poetry, and the cinematic aesthetic of the New Chilean Cinema as it turned towards everyday life. The possibility of capturing reality on film, meaning the opportunity of showing 'the truth', became an exercise in reaching something that was perceived as hidden in the depths of the Chilean people. In addition, films coming from Italy had an impact on Latin American productions, particularly on the young Chilean filmmakers of the 1950s, who were part of both the Centro de Cine Experimental and the Instituto Fílmico.[10] Italian neorealism created a new type of image, which Bazin called 'image facts', and had a documentary quality that could not be separated from the idea of the film or the script (Bazin 2005: 16–40). There was a political element, as well as a practical one, linked to the neorealist aesthetic. Moreover, the adherence to actuality and facts was both explained and justified by an attachment to the particular period in which neorealism emerged (i.e. the post-war period).

Firstly at the Universidad de Chile's Cine Club, and later at the Centro Experimental, members would meet and watch documentaries from Canada's National Film Board (particularly those of John Grierson), as well as European cinema, such as Russian and Italian post-war cinema, particularly neorealism. They were especially keen on films like *Orphée* [Orpheus] (Jean Cocteau, 1950), *Blinkity Blank* (Norman McLaren, 1955), and *Nuit et Brouillard* [Night and Fog] (Alain Resnais, 1956) (Salinas Muñoz, Stange Marcus, and Salinas Roco 2008). An exception to this European influence was Fernando Birri, who in 1956 founded the first Latin

American documentary school in Santa Fe, Argentina.[11] This film school was influential for both Chilean filmmakers and the New Latin American Cinema. In the case of Chile, some members of the Centro Experimental went on to study at the Instituto de Cine de la Universidad Nacional del Litoral with Birri and were exposed to his particular style of neorealism (Salinas Muñoz, Stange Marcus, and Salinas Roco 2008: 44). It was only in the late 1960s, thanks to the international cinema festivals in Viña del Mar, that Cuban, Argentine and Brazilian cinema would begin to have a presence in Chile and an impact on Chilean filmmakers, creating the consciousness that a New Latin American Cinema existed (Salinas Muñoz, Stange Marcus, and Salinas Roco 2008: 53).

In this sense, it was not so much a film style that Chilean filmmakers wanted to emulate, but the emotions that that style evoked, that powerful ability of the stories to allow the audience to identify with the characters. Chilean directors took key elements of neorealism, like filming on the street and not using professional actors, as well as its ability to develop a national cinema without studios, as a way of capturing their reality (Giovacchini and Sklar 2014: 11). Furthermore, these were experimental cinema groups, meaning that, although they aimed to show social and political events taking place in 1950s and 1960s Chile through everyday life, they did so through experimenting with cinematographic language, and through trial and error.

Accessing reality was for these filmmakers a way of breaking the alienation of years of neocolonialism in national culture. It was only through representing social reality and bringing to the forefront values and customs associated with what they perceived to be national identity (like the countryside and *criollista* themes), that cultural liberation could be attained.[12] In short, this turn towards social reality meant finding 'true Chilean culture', where *lo popular* and *el pueblo* [the people] gained a particular significance within the arts and the academic world. The way of achieving the latter was not through technical perfection, but through a particular approach to the social environment. To achieve that 'realism without borders', filmmakers needed to accept the 'multiple and contradictory details' and to make 'those beings and their surroundings' seem alive within the reality evoked by art (Román 1973: 109–10). In short, it was the 'capacity to search for a particular reality [...] to integrate it in a narrative that gives us essential moments' (Román 1973: 110). For Chilean filmmakers of the 1960s, it was the ability to capture these particularities on film (with both their multiplicity and their contradictions) that made the realist narrative unique.

In the particular case of Bravo, his search for reality translated into his experimental documentaries, where the worlds of cinema and poetry merge. Sergio Bravo often asked other artists (poets, musicians, narrators) to collaborate in his endeavours. A clear example is Violeta Parra's collaboration in *Mimbre* (1957), for which the artist composed an original song that accompanies the documentary, becoming an integral part of the film by providing through music a distinct rhythm to that of the images (almost in counterpoint). The melody follows the movement of wicker onscreen with guitar melodies that are reminiscent of her song *Gavilán* (1959) (Guerrero and Vuskovic 2018).

For his documentary *Láminas de Almahue* (1962), Bravo enlisted poet Efraín Barquero in order to create a film about everyday life in the rural town of Almahue.[13] As in the case of *larismo*, the early documentaries of Sergio Bravo allowed the viewer to enter a world where the rural space was at the centre. At the same time, his documentaries were not a perpetual idealization of rural or traditional life, but an entry point to another way of living, other rhythms (or cadences, thinking of poetry) of experiencing the world, other ways of approaching the interactions between social and political aspects of 1950s–1960s Chile. In this context, *Láminas de Almahue* stands out as a piece that brings together not only the social and the political, but actually two kinds of poetics: Bravo's own cinematographic poetics and Efraín Barquero's verses. These two poetics will showcase the interrelations between the social and the political, as well as rural tradition and new technologies. These tensions are the truly revolutionary aspect of Bravo's documentaries, in that everything we see is in perpetual motion.

A key element here is the connection between poetry and film, and the different ways in which they connect, particularly in Chilean cinema.[14] In the words of Aldo Francia (one of the key figures of Nuevo Cine Chileno), 'it [Nuevo Cine] is profoundly nationalistic, in the good sense of the word. It values what is distinctly national, even if it is poor or "ugly" (in the bourgeois meaning of the word)' (1990: 40). In this sense, following John King, for Latin American filmmakers, their cinema was to be 'lucid, critical realist, popular, anti-imperialist, revolutionary [...] which would break with neocolonialist attitudes and the monopolistic practices of North American companies' (2000: 66). In order to accomplish the latter, no formula was stipulated, as 'flexibility would be needed to adapt to different social situations' (King 2000: 66). This characteristic is precisely what can be appreciated in Bravo's body of work.

In relation to the narrative aspect of cinema, Raul Ruiz, a key filmmaker of the New Chilean Cinema, stated that 'it is the type of image produced that determines the narrative, and not the other way round' (2000: 14). Ruiz was also one of the few Latin American filmmakers of that period to think about the possibilities of cinema in terms of creation. Ruiz built his definition from the word *poiesis*, understood by Plato as the creative process, and invited filmmakers to modify their way of making films which, in turn, entailed developing a new style, a new form of narrative. What Ruiz was discussing was the human race's ability to copy, create and provoke emotions which, in Bravo's case, would be through poetry and film, allowing a cinematic idiom to appear in the form of cinematographic poetics.

David Bordwell (1989) approached the question of film poetics, identifying the 'historical poetics' of cinema. For Bordwell, historical poetics was 'an account of how, at various times, films have been put together and have elicited particular effects', linking the definition of poetics to semantics and meaning (1989: xiii–xiv). While Bordwell (2008) focused on how films are made to elicit certain reactions, Ruiz concentrated on the creative possibilities that cinema offers (Sabrovsky 2003: 11–41). Taking into consideration these ideas on film and poetics (as seen by Ruiz and Bordwell), I understand 'cinematographic poetics' as the conjunction of the possibilities given by the historical context and the ability to create films that are able to represent everyday life.

One of the key influences, not only on Bravo's cinema, but also on many of the young filmmakers who attended experimental film schools in Chile in the 1950s (and later the New Latin American Cinema), was socially motivated cinematic realism. This meant filming people who remained on the margins of traditional institutions, 'as it provided a close representation of the life of the working class' (Corro et al. 2007: 8). The crucial element was to be true to what was there, using the streets, natural light, non-actors, etc., in order to achieve a sense of reality. In this context, the question of how to portray lo popular became a source of debate, although conceptualized as the need to represent reality (Lema 2005). There is an important clarification to be made here: lo popular can be translated into English as 'popular' (meaning 'well-known' or 'common', 'pop'), but it can also be translated as 'working class' (Jordán González and Lema Habash 2018: 255–77). The perils of translation of the term are not minor, as the relevance of lo popular and the world it encompassed would be a significant topic that filmmakers in Chile constantly tried to capture and contain in powerful images both in fiction and documentary (Silva Escobar and Raurich Valencia 2010: 67–69). This rediscovery of lo popular and its meaning by both the art world and academia was attached to the need to develop an identity that brought together the people's imaginary with a political project linked to the left.

Stuart Hall offers an interpretation of 'the popular' that allows us to explore certain key elements of the concept. For Hall (2016), popular culture is linked to questions of tradition, which is why its 'traditionalism' has so often been misinterpreted as a product of a merely conservative impulse. Moreover, popular culture represents a tension: containment and resistance. Rowe and Schelling emphasize the complexities of popular culture through a brief analysis of the role folklore has played in Latin America, as the term is often equated with the idea of popular culture. Folklore is often linked to ideas regarding a country's identity in relation to a national culture and the specific ways of life to that particular territory (Rowe and Schelling 1991). Moreover, it allowed rural societies to be integrated — albeit partially — as urban spaces grew and nations sought to modernize following European and US models at the beginning of the twentieth century. In the Chilean case, with the work of Violeta Parra in the 1950s, folklore and traditional songs would achieve a central cultural role, particularly with the development of the Nueva Canción Chilena [New Chilean Song] (González, Ohlsen, and Rolle 2009), (Palominos Mandiola and Ramos Rodillo 2018).

Chiara Sáez proposes another way of understanding this process, in which it was the development of an educated working class that was introduced within popular culture from the nineteenth century onwards. The result of this was that, within the process of modernization taking place in Latin American cities at the beginning of the twentieth century, popular culture was made absent by being left between working-class culture and mass culture (Sáez 2019). The popular culture that emerged between the mid-1950s and the coup d'etat in 1973 represented a conjunction of lo popular that emerged from the coming together of different elements developed in a long historical process, where modernization (of the city, the state, culture and the market) played a key role.

Throughout his work, Bravo was interested in *lo popular*, but his treatment and aesthetic approach to the concept changed over time. The topic of *lo popular* in Bravo's work can be organized into two aesthetic approaches: while his work between 1957 and 1964 was representative of a more poetic approach,[15] his films from 1964 onwards were more politically militant, although he later went back to bucolic themes. In a way, Bravo's aesthetic evolution evokes those same tensions. His earlier period was marked by a containment through images that are beautiful and take the viewer back to ideas of *lo popular*, as well as traditions and practices. His later phase was defined by resistance through political activism. From poetry, an answer to the question of *lo popular* is attempted from the standpoint of *poesía lárica*, where the accent is placed on 'the value of landscapes, villages and provinces', accessed through simple and unaffected writing (Teillier, n.d.).

The Poetics of *Láminas de Almahue* (1962)

Almahue is a small rural town in central Chile. Although the documentary centres on this town, it is not meant to promote the location or its economic activity (producing the metal rim that protects the wood of the wheels of the wagons). *Láminas de Almahue* is about a day in Almahue, from sunrise to sunset, a timeframe that evokes the style of the city symphony films, particularly in the way time is represented.

City symphony films were a popular genre in the 1920s–1930s, and offered audiences the chance to take part in one day in the life of a city from sunrise to sundown. Cinema presented an alternative language to cope with the hectic life of the city where perceptions of time were beginning to change and a need for standardization began to emerge (Bui 2014).[16] In a way, city symphony films worked as a translation of city life for audiences around the world, who could follow the rhythm of the modern city through the rhythm of the film (Levin 2018). For Ori Levin, these rhythms are indubitably attached to those of the human body (particularly breathing and heartbeats), as highlighting the contraposition between body and machine. In a way, *Láminas de Almahue* can be understood as a rural symphony film, where the contrast between machines and bodies is represented as Bravo captures people working the land (by hand, with horses); the forge, making wheels for wagons; and communal work. These images of technology intersect with the rhythms of nature.

Barquero's poetry also echoes the passing of time, as his words overlap the images with the poet's particular declamatory style. The poem, as conveyed through the voice-over, constantly makes a connection between human beings and nature, as well as time passing (through the movement of the sun): '¿Quién reúne al hombre con la tierra con más delicadeza que el sol naciente?' [Who unites men with the land with more delicacy than the rising sun?] and later 'Sol y hombre encadenados a un orden | El agua corre y recibe un sol inmemorial cuyos rayos son los brazos de los hombres' [Sun and men chained to an order | The water runs and receives

an immemorial sun whose rays are the arms of men] (Bravo 1962). Moreover, the
constant reminder of the importance of the body when working the land (both for
food and labour) is a reminder of Levin's aforementioned reference to the human
body and its rhythms. However, in Barquero's poetry (1962), it is not the sun, but
water that marks those rhythms, perhaps highlighting the common idea that water
is life:

> ¿quién lleva al hombre a su labor con más persistencia que el agua de la
> noche?
> [...]
> Tierra, antes de convertirte en alimento eres dura y pesada,
> y los cuerpos se gastan como maderos arrastrados por el agua.
>
> [who carries men to his labour with more persistence than the water of the
> night?
> [...]
> Land, before becoming sustenance you are tough and heavy,
> and the bodies get spent like woods dragged by water]

Furthermore, the sensibility emerging during the 1950s and 1960s allowed poetry to
present a direct connection to a sensibility that aims to reveal an image of *lo popular*,
which is particular to the language projected in the image. Barquero's poetry (as
well as Bravo's images) highlighted the role that the countryside played as a suitable
environment for the search of an autonomous language. It is in this sense that
poetry becomes the link between film and the sensibility of *lo popular*, where a new
form of expression of reality emerges. For Alicia Vega, this documentary constitutes
a 'formal-poetic experience' where perception guides and establishes the rhythm of
film, with no hypothesis to be proven (Vega 1979: 254).

The images captured by Bravo evoke the words spoken by Barquero. The
camerawork is reminiscent of Nichols's description of the poetic mode, particularly
in the exploration of 'association and patterns that involve temporal rhythms and
spatial juxtapositions' (Nichols 2010: 162). Furthermore, in *Láminas de Almahue*
people and objects are both used as raw materials by Bravo, and then selected and
arranged through montage into patterns and associations.[17] The poetic mode allows
an alternative language to arise, as it stresses 'mood, tone, and affect much more
than displays of factual knowledge or acts of rhetorical persuasion' (Nichols 2010:
162). The language that emerges is that of affect and feelings, where image and
words come together in poetry made by a combination of elements (the spoken
word, the montage, and the experience of the viewer).

The documentary is linked from the very beginning with one of Bravo's
cinematographic tropes: light. It is perhaps in this particular aspect that the Bauhaus
influence coming from Bravo's training in architecture appears most clearly. The
work of Laszlo Moholy-Nagy is a good example of the latter, where more than
the object of sculpture itself, what is of concern is the way light passes through it,
making this the focus of camera movement and what is being filmed. To highlight
the relevance of light Bravo strategically places the camera in direct relation to the
sun, to be able to capture the rhythms of the day as spoken by Barquero.

FIG. 7.1. Screen grab from *Láminas de Almahue* (1962) by Sergio Bravo

Besides light, water is another ever-present trope in Bravo's work, along with its ability to reflect nature. Pablo Corro (2010) offers a general analysis of the early work of Sergio Bravo. Bravo uses metaphors of vegetation and water throughout his work, albeit in a less obvious way in his more militant films. In *Teorías del cine documental chileno, 1957–1973*, Corro, Larraín, Alberdi and Van Diest (2007) also attempt to offer a general reading of Bravo's corpus of documentaries, asserting the importance played by movement, light and colour — which Corro (2010) calls raw materials that come from natural phenomena: elements that relate to Bravo's interest in the Bauhaus movement (Corro 2010: 94). These materials are key in linking Bravo's usage of nature's movement and a cinematographic poetics that deeply depends on the natural movement of nature, and the qualities of *lárica* poetry that are present in Barquero's writing, but particularly in the text recited (by Barquero himself) in *Láminas de Almahue*.[18] The following extract of Barquero's verses in *Láminas de Almahue* (1962) emphasizes the rhythms of nature's movements, and the relationship between nature and technology, as well as the action of humankind in relation to nature and the passing of time:

> Agua del Almahue que 'declara' haber formado el pan y el grano,
> ahora se vuelve mineral y arde como el combustible
> y mueve la gran rueda de la tierra donde el hombre escucha la voz de sus antepasados.
> Gira la rueda y alguien canta,
> es el agua el que disuelve al hombre y lo entrega más puro,
> y los rostros golpeados por la tierra y por el tiempo

> [Water from Almahue that 'declares' having formed bread and grain,
> now it turns mineral and burns like fuel
> and moves the great wheel of the land where the man listens to the voice of his ancestors.
> The wheel turns and someone sings,

it's the water that dissolves men and delivers him purer,
and the faces stricken by land and by time]

Light in particular plays an articulating role in *Láminas de Almahue*. In his use of light, Bravo plays with intensity and movement, and marks the passing of time and levels of narrative, as I discuss below. The movement of light is present through different elements: back–lit images, as well as overexposure through filming the light source directly, but also the way light passes through objects, and how water reflects nature because of the light. The use of light is accompanied by Barquero's poetry, which marks the tempo with the light of the sun that rises and reaches midday, when men are recognized as 'el hijo del fuego' [sons of fire] (Bravo 1962). There is an interesting connection to make here with light as one of the main requirements to be able to film, but also to project movies: one needs to expose film to light in order to capture the images, and, in turn, a darkened room is best for projecting said images onto a screen using a bright light.

Throughout the documentary, there is a dialogue between the cinematographic language proposed by Bravo and the language of the poetry being recited by Barquero. Although both have their own meaning, it is only when the two of them come together that a new language emerges: the representation of habits and everyday life in Almahue. It is in the relationship between nature and human beings that everyday life is expressed and captured through metaphors projected both in images and words.

Perhaps the theme for which Barquero's lyric poetry and Bravo's cinematographic poetry come together most clearly is in the description and usage of space in relation to their mediums. Space becomes a key element of movement in both the filmic and recited aspects of *Láminas de Almahue*. Here, Bravo and Barquero used their respective mediums to transport the viewer/listener to a landscape. This resource was common in the *lárica* style of poetry. Barquero's poem, written for the documentary, uses language in order to create a recited landscape, and connects Barquero's work with the style developed by Jorge Teillier. Bravo's use of images to create a landscape works by alternating shots that go from the specific to the general. The narrative presented in the documentary is achieved through the movement of what is being shot: whether it is the water of a stream, a horse moving, or the furnace where metal is prepared. As in the case of the poetry, there is a simplicity in what is captured that allows a direct relationship to be formed between viewer/listener (in the case of this particular documentary), and what is shown. The montage allows the film to present the length of the day and the length of the documentary simultaneously.[19] Bravo also uses the idea of time by including images of clocks fading into an image of the sun, which slowly sets, evoking the end of the day; which in turn reminds us that all we have seen will begin again the next day, with the rising of the sun (which is how the film begins). The movements of the sun are also clearly highlighted in Barquero's text, as he is able, through his own poetic rhythm, to have his own simultaneous experience, which reflects on the visual experience presented by Bravo.

As Vega notes, Barquero's poem is divided into two parts. In the first section the narrative is presented through the circularity of themes that he will develop in the

FIG. 7.2. Screen grab from *Láminas de Almahue* (1962) by Sergio Bravo

second part (ideas such as the balance between nature and human beings and time as a cyclical element). In the second half, Barquero moves onto universal themes, such as liberty and sovereignty, as well as historical consciousness expressed in the knowledge of the passing of time and the awareness of our place in history. This sense of circularity is echoed by the constant circular movement within Bravo's shots, from the round elements on-screen to the wheels and the metal rim being made to protect them, as well as movements made by people working the land (and making wheels). The circular movements captured by the camera remind the viewer of the importance of nature's cycles and natural rhythms. Although less common in this documentary, besides capturing circular movements (of a wheel, a watermill, a horse going in circles), at times the camera itself also moves in a circular manner in order to emphasize the relevance of cycles (through superimposing shots, one that is static in the background, and another that moves, creating the effect of circularity).

A further level of circularity is provided by reflections of light on water and other surfaces. A text by Raúl Ruiz can help in understanding the uses that Bravo makes of reflection in his work, but particularly in *Láminas de Almahue*. Ruiz did not like the idea of using mirrors in film, because mirrors give an inverted sense of reality. For Ruiz it was much more interesting to use 'a deforming mirror', as one sees reality with one's eyes, and cinema 'through distortion, may help me capture elements of reality that escape me' (Ruiz 1972: 9). In this sense, the use that Bravo gives to reflective elements (water, metal), as well as elements that cloud the image (steam), is not gratuitous. Although Bravo might not be making a comment on the idea of cinema as a mirror, he is certainly making a statement regarding the uses of distorting elements in order to capture and evoke emotion.

There is a deeper level to Barquero's poem, which bonds the surface (the text being recited) with the images (cinematographic poetics) and the universal elements. This deeper level is what gives both Barquero's poetry and Bravo's

FIG. 7.3. Screen grab from *Láminas de Almahue* (1962) by Sergio Bravo

cinematographic poetics meaning, as it ties both forms of poetry to an effort to render the documentary understandable to people beyond Almahue. The three levels stated before are present throughout the documentary, and they move along in connection with the images. In other words, in Barquero's poetry there is a sense of time and simultaneity that generates a dialogue with the images. It is this bond that allows the viewers to connect with the different levels of poetry being addressed in *Láminas de Alamahue*.

Conclusion

Bravo's *Láminas de Almahue* does not simply offer passive observation of everyday activities in Almahue. Rather, it is a poetic representation that brings together Barquero's words with images through the elements of light, water and rural life. The dialogue between these two artists consists not just of the putting-together of two forms of poetics (creation in the sense of making a film, and poetry), but of the emergence of a poetic language that mixes images and words in order to produce a visual poem. The poetry emerges because of the simultaneity of image and words, but also because of the simultaneity generated between viewer and film. Bravo and Barquero are able to capture the rhythms of everyday life in Almahue within the time of the documentary through image and poetry. It is here that the technological language of cinema, the montage that allows the cinematographic poetics to work, comes together with poetry.

The question of *lo popular* in the work of Bravo and Barquero goes beyond showing and writing about a rural town in the O'Higgins region of Chile. It is in their own poetics that the popular is projected in the image. The documentary presents a discourse that engages with nature, but also with the everyday practice of working the land, and being in communion with the land. Although the documentary might show a particular economic activity, it is more about the creation of a balance and communion with nature.

Appendix 1: Efraín Barquero's text[20]

Misteriosa, en el sueño del hombre está despierto el árbol de la especie.

¿Quién reúne al hombre con la tierra con más delicadeza que el sol naciente?
¿quién lleva al hombre a su labor con más persistencia que el agua de la noche?

Agua y fuego gravitante que esta tierra necesita,
la rueda gira buscando su redondez fecunda.

Tierra, antes de convertirte en alimento eres dura y pesada,
y los cuerpos se gastan como maderos arrastrados por el agua.
Mientras el sol sube, sube y sube, el hombre se inclina en su puesto original.

Sol y hombre encadenados a un orden.

El agua corre y recibe un sol inmemorial cuyos rayos son los brazos de los hombres.

Parece que el sol viviera en estas manos oscuras.
El hombre no mira el cielo, ni siquiera a la copa de los árboles.

Porque hay un momento en que todo, tierra, agua, aire, esperan una revelación,
y es el mediodía en que el hombre es reconocido como el hijo del fuego.

Entre el humo y el vapor, la respiración ardiente de la bestia,

el herrero padre y el herrero hijo se inclinan sobre el potro rojo que mueve la tierra.
Agua del Almahue que "declara" haber formado el pan y el grano,
ahora se vuelve mineral y arde como el combustible
y mueve la gran rueda de la tierra donde el hombre escucha la voz de sus antepasados.

Gira la rueda y alguien canta,
es el agua el que disuelve al hombre y lo entrega más puro,
y los rostros golpeados por la tierra y por el tiempo,
tienen ese silencio de las cosas eternas,
de las manos encadenadas a la rueda donde el agua destruye y da vida.

Viento de la tarde que es como el presentimiento del espacio,

y como el pensamiento invencible del hombre.

[Mysterious, in the dream of men lays awake the tree of the species.
Who unites men with the land with more delicateness than the rising sun?
who carries men to his labour with more persistence than the water of the night?
The importance of water and fire that this land needs,
the wheel turns searching for its fertile roundness

Land, before becoming sustenance you are tough and heavy,
and the bodies get spent like woods dragged by water.
While the sun rises, rises and rises, men tilt in his original place.

Sun and men chained to an order.
The water runs and receives an immemorial sun whose rays are the arms of men.
It looks like the sun lives in these dark hands.
Man does not look to the sky, not even the treetops.

Because there is a moment in which everything,

land, water, air, await a revelation, and it is midday in which men are recognized as the sons of fire.
Between smoke and steam, burning breath of the beast,
father blacksmith and son blacksmith bend over the red foal that moves the land.
Water from Almahue that 'declares' having formed bread and grain,
now it turns mineral and burns like fuel
and moves the great wheel of the land where the man listens to the voice of his ancestors.
The wheel turns and someone sings,
it's the water that dissolves men and delivers him purer,
and the faces stricken by land and by time,
Have that silence of eternal things,
of hands chained to the wheel where water destroys and gives life.

Wind of the afternoon that is like premonition of space,
and like the invincible thought of men.

Appendix 2: Technical details of *Láminas de Almahue*[21]

Documentary short, 16 mm, black and white, 23 minutes.
Director and editor: Sergio Bravo
Photography: Enrique Rodríguez and Sergio Bravo
Text: Efraín Barquero
Music: Gustavo Becerra
Film Assistant: Leonardo Martínez
Production: Centro de Cine Experimental de la Universidad de Chile
Date: 1962

Works Cited

Bazin, André. 2005. *What Is Cinema?* (Berkeley and Los Angeles: University of California Press)
Benjamin, Walter. 2002. *The Arcades Project* (London: Harvard University Press)
—— 2009. *One Way Street and Other Writings* (London: Penguin)
Bordwell, David. 1989. *Making Meaning: Inference and Rhetoric in the Interpretation of Cinema* (Cambridge, MA, and London: Harvard University Press)
—— 2008. *Poetics of Cinema* (New York: Routledge)
Bowen Silva, Martín. 2008. 'El proyecto sociocultural de la izquierda chilena durante la Unidad Popular: crítica, verdad e inmunología política', *Nuevo mundo, mundos nuevos*, 8 <https://doi.org/10.4000/nuevomundo.13732> [accessed 5 April 2019]
Bui, Camille. 2014. 'L'Invention d'une rencontre entre le cinéma et la ville: la "symphonie urbaine" au tournant des années 1930', *Annales de Géographie*, 695/96: 744–62

BURTON, JULIANNE (ed.). 1990. *Social Documentary in Latin America* (Pittsburgh, PA: University of Pittsburgh Press)

CORREA, SOFÍA, ET AL. 2001. *Historia del siglo XX chileno: balance paradojal* (Santiago: Editorial Sudamericana)

CORRO, PABLO. 2005. 'Devenir secular de la simultaneidad en el cine', *laFuga*, 1 <http://www.lafuga.cl/devenir-secular-de-la-simultaneidad-en-el-cine/223> [accessed 5 April 2019]

—— 2010. 'Sergio Bravo y tendencia del montaje', *Aisthesis*, 47: 83–99

CORRO, PABLO, ET AL. 2007. *Teorías del cine documental chileno, 1957–1973* (Santiago: Pontificia Universidad Católica de Chile, Facultad de Filosofía, Instituto de Estética)

CORTINEZ, V., and M. ENGELBERT. 2014. *Evolución en libertad: el cine chileno de fines de los sesenta* (Chile: Editorial Cuarto Propio)

DE LOS RÍOS, VALERIA. 2011. 'Vicente Huidobro y el cine: la escritura frente a las luces y sombras de la modernidad', *Hispanic Review*, 79: 67–90

FRANCIA, ALDO. 1990. *Nuevo cine latinoamericano en Viña del Mar* (Santiago: CESOC Ediciones)

GARCÍA HUIDOBRO, CECILIA (ed.). 2000. *Vicente Huidobro a la intemperie: entrevistas, 1915–1946* (Santiago: Editorial Sudamericana)

GIOVACCHINI, S., and R. SKLAR. (eds). 2014. *Global Neorealism: The Transnational History of a Film Style* (London: SAGE)

GÓNGORA, MARIO. 1981. *Ensayo histórico sobre la noción de Estado en Chile* (Santiago: La Ciudad)

GONZÁLEZ, J. P., O. OHLSEN, and C. ROLLE. 2009. *Historia social de la música popular en Chile, 1950–1970* (Santiago: Ediciones UC)

GUERRERO, C., and A. VUSKOVIC. 2018. *La música del Nuevo Cine Chileno* (Santiago: Cuarto Propio)

HALL, STUART. 2016. 'Notes on Deconstructing "the Popular"', in *People's History and Socialist Theory*, ed. by Raphael Samuel (London and New York: Routledge & Kegan Paul)

HUIDOBRO, VICENTE. 2003. *Cagliostro* (Paris: Indigo)

JORDÁN GONZÁLEZ, L. and N. LEMA HABASH. 2018. 'Raúl Ruiz's *Now We're Gonna Call You Brother* and the Problem of the People's Sonic Representation', in *Soundings: Documentary Film and the Listening Experience*, ed. by Geoffrey Cox and John Corner (Huddersfield: University of Huddersfield), pp. 255–77

KING, JOHN. 2000. *Magical Reels: A History of Cinema in Latin America* (London and New York: Verso)

KUHN, ANNETTE, 1978. 'The Camera I: Observations on Documentary', *Screen*, 19: 71–83

LARRAÍN, JORGE. 2001. *Identidad chilena* (Santiago: LOM)

LATCHAM, RICARDO. 1956. *El criollismo* (Santiago: Universitaria)

LEMA HABASH, NICOLÁS. 2005. 'Pensamientos sobre un nuevo cine: los cineastas de izquierda en el contexto revolucionario de la Unidad Popular (1968–1973)', in *Seminario Simon Collier 2006*, ed. by Martín Bowen [et al.] (Santiago: Pontificia Universidad Católica de Chile, Instituto de Historia), pp. 149–83

LEÓN FRÍAS, ISAAC. 2013. *El nuevo cine latinoamericano de los años sesenta* (Lima: Fondo Editorial, Universidad de Lima)

LEVIN, ORI. 2018. 'The Cinematic Time of the City Symphony Films: Time Management, Experiential Duration and Bodily Pulsation', *Studies in Documentary Film*, 12: 225–38

LOVEMAN, BRIAN. 2001. *Chile: The Legacy of Hispanic Capitalism* (New York: Oxford University Press)

MELLER, PATRICIO. 2007. *Un siglo de economía política chilena (1890–1990)* (Santiago: Andrés Bello)

MOUESCA, JACQUELINE. 1988. *Plano secuencia de la memoria de Chile: veinticinco años de cine chileno (1960–1985)* (Santiago: Ediciones del Litoral)

—— 2005. *El documental chileno* (Santiago: LOM Ediciones)

MOUESCA, J. and C. ORELLANA. 1998. *Cine y memoria del siglo XX: cine en Chile: cine en el mundo: historia social y cultural de Chile: historia social y cultural mundial cuadros sinópticos (1895–1995)* (Santiago: LOM Ediciones)

NICHOLS, BILL. 1981. *Ideology and the Image* (Bloomington: Indiana University Press)

—— 2010. *Introduction to Documentary* (Bloomington: Indiana University Press)

NÓMEZ, NAÍN. 2007. 'La poesía de los cincuenta en Chile y España: escorzo y aproximaciones', *Campo de Agramante. Revista de Literatura*, 7: 85–101

—— 2008. 'Sobre *El pan y el vino* de Efraín Barquero: por una liturgia de la solidaridad', *Atenea*, 498: 143–51

—— 2014. 'La poesía de los cincuenta: aproximaciones a una modernidad en disolución', *Taller de Letras*, 34: 85–96

—— 2017. 'Imaginario alimenticio y comunidad rural en la poesía chilena de los años cincuenta del siglo XX', *Literatura y Lingüística*, 35: 133–58

OSTROV, ANDREA. 2011. '*Cagliostro*: una novela-film de Vicente Huidobro', *Revista Iberoamericana*, 77: 1051–60

PALOMINOS MANDIOLA, S., and I. RAMOS RODILLO (eds). 2018. *Vientos del pueblo: representaciones, recepciones e interpretaciones sobre la Nueva Canción Chilena* (Santiago: LOM Ediciones)

PANIZZA, TIZIANA. 2011. *Joris Ivens en Chile: el documental entre la poesía y la crítica* (Santiago: Cuarto Propio)

PAZ-SOLDÁN, EDMUNDO. 2002. 'Vanguardia e imaginario cinemático: Vicente Huidobro y la novela-film', *Revista Iberoamericana*, 68: 153–63

PEIRANO, M. P., and C. GOBANTES (eds). 2015. *Chilefilms, el Hollywood criollo: aproximaciones al proyecto industrial cinematográfico chileno (1942–1949)* (Santiago: Cuarto Propio)

PICK, ZUZANA. 1984. 'La imagen cinematográfica y la representación de la realidad', *Literatura chilena, creación y crítica*, 8: 34–40

ROMÁN, JOSÉ. 1973. 'El Primer Maestro', *Primer Plano*, II, No. 5: pp. 109–12

ROWE, W., and V. SCHELLING. 1991. *Memory and Modernity: Popular Culture in Latin America* (London: Verso)

RUIZ, RAÚL. 1972. 'Prefiero Registrar antes que mistificar el proceso chileno', *Primer Plano*, I: 3–21

—— 2000. *Poética del cine* (Santiago: Editorial Sudamericana)

RUIZ STULL, MIGUEL. 2015. 'Entre *Manifiestos* y *Cagliostro* de Vicente Huidobro', *Atenea*, 511 <http://dx.doi.org/10.4067/S0718–04622015000100005> [accessed 5 April 2019]

SABROVSKY, EDUARDO (ed.). 2003. *Conversaciones con Raúl Ruiz* (Santiago: Ediciones Universidad Diego Portales)

SÁEZ, CHIARA. 2019. 'El concepto de cultura popular ausente y su aplicación al caso chileno desde una perspectiva histórica', *Comunicación y Medios*, 39: 64–76

SALINAS MUÑOZ, C., H. STANGE MARCUS and S. SALINAS ROCO. 2008. *Historia del cine experimental en la Universidad de Chile, 1957–1973* (Santiago: Consejo Nacional de la Cultura y las Artes, Fondo de Fomento Audiovisual)

SILVA AVARIA, BÁRBARA. 2018. 'La espacialidad y el paisaje en las representaciones nacionales durante el frente popular chileno. 1938–1941', *Revista de Historia Social y de las Mentalidades*, 22: 129–53

SILVA ESCOBAR, J. P. and V. RAURICH VALENCIA. 2010. 'Emergente, dominante y residual: una mirada sobre la fabricación de lo popular realizada por el Nuevo Cine Chileno (1958–1973)', *Aisthesis*, 47: 64–82

SUBERCASEAUX, BERNARDO. 1992. 'Nuestro déficit de espesor cultural', *Cuadernos hispano-americanos*, 501: 125–27

—— 2007. *Historia de las ideas y de la cultura en Chile*, vol. IV: *Nacionalismo y cultura* (Santiago: Editorial Universitaria)

TEILLIER, JORGE, *Antología poética*, <http://ciudadanoaustral.org/biblioteca/13.-Jorge-Tellier-Antologi%23U030a-Poe%23U0301tica.pdf> [accessed 5 April 2019]

VALENZUELA, ARTURO. 2013. *El quiebre de la democracia en Chile* (Santiago: Universidad Diego Portales)

VEGA, ALICIA. 1979. *Re-visión del cine chileno* (Santiago: Editorial Aconcagua, Centro de Indagación y Expresión Cultural y Artística)

—— 2006. *Itinerario del cine documental chileno, 1900–1990* (Santiago: Universidad Alberto Hurtado)

YOUDELMAN, JEFFREY. 1982. 'Narration, Invention and History: A Documentary Dilemma', *Cineaste*, 12: 8–15

Acknowledgements

I would like to express my gratitude to María Montt Strabucchi, who sent me the Call for Papers for this volume, and Ignacio López, who read many versions of this text. I also want to thank the anonymous reviewer for their generous support and constructive comments, as well as Ben Bollig and David Wood for their encouragement and feedback.

Notes to Chapter 7

1. I am grateful to Fondecyt Postdoctoral Project N° 3190267 for their support.
2. In 1955 Rafael Sánchez created the Instituto Fílmico [Film Institute] at the Universidad Católica, which was active until 1979 (when it was closed by the military authorities who ran the university during the dictatorship).
3. Naín Nómez (2017: 134) also offers a definition of *poesía lárica*. Unless otherwise stated, all translations are by the author.
4. Regarding the political restructuring of Chilean society and its debate, see Valenzuela (2013) and Góngora (1981).
5. Rafael Sánchez (founder of the Instituto Fílmico of the Universidad Católica de Chile) filmed the documentary *Las callampas* in 1958, in which he shows everyday life in these *poblaciones*, as well as the problems they posed, and the importance of solving them in an inclusive manner, instead of marginalizing the *pobladores*.
6. We can roughly define *criollismo* as a literary movement associated with themes that sought to uphold rural life, which had been looked down upon in comparison to the urban scene. *Criollismo* emerged at the end of the nineteenth century to reach its high point during the twentieth century. Some of the literary pieces that are part of *criollismo* have an epic and foundational character. In the case of Chile, one of the main authors associated with this movement was Mariano Latorre. For more on *criollismo* see Latcham (1956).
7. For theoretical readings on documentary see Nichols (1981: 170–207); Kuhn (1978); Youdelman (1982).
8. 'Lar', in *Real Academia Española* <https://dle.rae.es/?id=MvoseBV> [accessed 3 April 2019].
9. For the relation between the New Chilean Cinema and the New Chilean Song see González, Ohlsen and Rolle (2009); and Guerrero and Vuskovic (2018).
10. Recent scholarship has highlighted the importance in de-centralizing neorealism from Europe. See Giovacchini and Sklar (2014); León Frías (2013).
11. It should be noted, however, that Birri studied filmmaking at the Centro Sperimentale di Cinematografia in Rome in the early 1950s, before founding the Santa Fé School.

12. Jorge Larraín highlights the relevance of cultural representations in the process of becoming conscious of Latin America's and particularly Chile's place in the world (2001: 128).
13. This was not the only contribution of Barquero to cinema production. In 1965 he wrote the script for *Carbón* (1965), a documentary short directed by Fernando Balmaceda about the coal mining industry in Lota, highlighting the modernization (both at economic and social levels) brought to the town and Chile at large.
14. The intersection between the work of Bravo and Barquero was not the first time poetry and cinema came together. In 1934 Vicente Huidobro, a Chilean poet and founder of *creacionismo*, published his novel-film *Cagliostro* (2003). The novel had characteristics of a cinema script, and told the story of Cagliostro, an Italian magician of the 1700s, who reappears in the France of Louis XVI. For more on *Cagliostro* and Vicente Huidobro, and his relationship with cinema see de los Ríos (2011); García Huidobro (2000: 118–19); Ostrov (2011); Paz-Soldán (2002); Ruiz Stull (2015).
15. Main documentaries of the first aesthetic: *Mimbre* (1957), *Trilla* (1959), *Día de Organillos* (1959), *Casamiento de Negros* (1959), *Amerindia* (1962), *Láminas de Almahue* (1962). He also assisted and participated in a more technical capacity in *La Respuesta* (1961, photography and camera) and *A Valparaíso* (1962, assistant director to Joris Ivens).
16. From another perspective, Walter Benjamin (2002, 2009) also discusses the changes of modern life and the changing perception of time.
17. *Rain* (1929) by Joris Ivens is a great example of the above. Ivens and his films had a great influence on the young Chilean filmmakers of the late 1950s and 1960s. In 1962 Ivens visited Chile invited by the University of Chile. Regarding Ivens' visit and the filming of his documentary *...A Valparaíso* (1963) see Panizza 2011.
18. The text of the poem can be found at the end of the article, both in Spanish and English.
19. On the simultaneity of cinema see Corro (2005). On the simultaneity present in the documentary, Alicia Vega states: '"Láminas de Almahue" se organiza estructuralmente por el montaje a través de la relación del ritmo interno de los planos en yuxtaposición y una correspondencia entre el tiempo real y el tiempo cinematográfico; se logra tal perfección que este último logra dar cuenta del primero' (1979: 255).
20. Translation by the author. 'The text, originally written by Barquero in fourteen verses, was reduced to ten by Bravo for the film' (Vega 1979: 255).
21. Details extracted from Vega (1979: 195).

CHAPTER 8

❖

Lives of the Scattered Family: On Jesús Díaz's Documentary Film *Cincuentaicinco hermanos* and his Book *De la patria y el exilio*

Irina Garbatzky

In an interview with Lilliam Oliva Collman (1999), Cuban writer Jesús Díaz described his first contact with the case that would later become the object of his documentary film *Cincuentaicinco hermanos* [Fifty-five Siblings] (1978).[1] 'In 1978 — I remember it was a Friday afternoon — they told me: A group of young Cubans will arrive tomorrow, their parents took them to the United States, now they have formed a brigade and will come to our country for the very first time, and we need you to go and film a twenty-minute interview' (Collman 1999: 161).[2] The anecdote — concerning the return of the children of those citizens who migrated with their families at the beginning of the Revolution — highlights a trifling chance encounter, which would have, by contrast, a great and definite impact. The story goes on:

> I did not know anything at all about the people who were coming, or the brigade. I had never done anything similar, and it was assigned to me as one of those minor jobs that I was allowed to do back then, when we were still under censorship. [...] So the next day I go to the airport, they arrived on a Saturday afternoon. When the airplane landed (I was waiting right by the airstair), they got off singing the national anthem, and it made a huge impact on me. I decided to live with them in their camp, and the impact was bigger each day. I asked for more negative film, and permission to make a longer, more ambitious project. [...] And I remember that I knew exactly what movie I did not want to make with these members of the Antonio Maceo brigade. I did not want to use them as a pretext to show the work of the Revolution. *I wanted to show them.* (Collman 1999: 161–62; my emphasis)

There is a double discovery here: the object of a documentary story, and the unprecedented fact of meeting a group of compatriots who lived abroad but nonetheless were not identified as traitors for that reason. 'I named the movie *Cincuentaicinco hermanos*', adds Díaz, 'because I saw it clearly at that moment. It was not something I knew beforehand' (Collman 1999: 162).

Both the narration and the discovery are so consistent that, from that moment on, Díaz, who had taken up some small jobs at the Instituto Cubano del Arte e Industria Cinematográficos (ICAIC), became a filmmaker. From 1973 until then, although he had won the Casa de las Américas prize when he was very young,[3] his writing had been on hold. By 1978, Díaz had held key positions in the cultural field of the Cuban Revolution, but was then in a half-precarious, half-marginal situation.[4]

Indeed, in 1966, the same year *Los años duros* [The Hard Years] was published, Díaz inaugurated *El Caimán Barbudo*, the cultural section of the newspaper *Juventud Rebelde*, a publication of the Unión de Jóvenes Comunistas de Cuba. The magazine was presented as the journalistic organ of the cultural avant-garde. In those years, between 1967 and 1971, he was also involved in *Pensamiento crítico*, a magazine of theory, discussion and circulation of Marxist thought published by the Department of Philosophy at the Universidad de La Habana, which sought to reflect on socialism and Western Marxism from a national perspective, and also to bring on board, translate and publish texts on philosophy and sociology related to the contemporary transformations brought about by May '68, structuralism, linguistics and Marxism–Leninism. Both enterprises failed: Díaz was removed from *El caimán barbudo*, and *Pensamiento crítico* was cancelled.[5] Furthermore, in 1973 he was prevented from publishing his novel *Las iniciales de la tierra* [The Initials of the Earth] (1987), originally titled *Biografía política* [Political Biography]. Thus, during the '70s, Díaz abandoned literature and took refuge at the ICAIC, thanks to the offer of its director, Alfredo Guevara (Collman 1999: 160). Addressing for the first time the subject of those compatriots living outside the country, *Cincuentaicinco hermanos* would not only deeply shake the population of revolutionary Cuba, but also its director, who would reinvent himself:

> And so this movie becomes a full-length documentary film, and it turned out to be a success with audiences, something completely unexpected for everyone, including me. I mean, it had the same level of audience as any fiction film, even more. People cried at the cinema. There is an acknowledgement of a national unity beyond political borders. And it is this movie that changed my reputation in Cuba. (Collman 1999: 162)

The main reason *Cincuentaicinco hermanos* was so moving for the audience and the director was its perspective. Although they recount a historical event with some epic touches, in both the film and the book — a testimonial volume that brought together the materials used for the film, and was published immediately after the release of the documentary — Díaz decided to show the stories of each person ('to show them', he would say), to take their plural stories and make them singular, to expose those lives in the most direct and exhaustive way possible, trying to avoid any prejudices or jumping to any conclusions about life in exile in contrast with the revolutionary life. The effort of 'showing them' is aimed at giving an account of *one* life, or, in this case *some* lives, in a way which reminds us of the notion of immanence, which Gilles Deleuze would use years later in his essay 'L'Immanence: une vie': 'the singular life that is immanent to a man who no longer has a name and yet cannot be confused with anyone else' (2003: 362). Unlike the definite article 'the', which specifies and gathers the differences in one single abstraction, Díaz attempts to portray 'a' life — one variable life, possible among others, multiple in its vibrational and contradictory modulations.

In this work, I would like to explore the impact of both the film *Cincuentaicinco hermanos* and the book *De la patria y el exilio* [Of Homeland and Exile], which present a seismic, fragmentary and critical perspective on the new Cuban society. By using the word 'critical' I am not referring to a dissidence with the socialist regime, but to the noticing of cracks, singularities and tensions, as opposed to a totalizing, homogenizing and harmonious view — an attempt to deepen the understanding of an object in all its complexity, beyond its discursive mediation. I would also like to observe that, in order to effectively narrate those lives, Díaz recurred to a mythical constellation: that of the children and the dismembered family, condensed in the work and figure of José Martí.

The activation of Martí's poetic archive is not fortuitous, though it is not so much an aesthetic appeal as an invocation of the deep elements of Cuban culture present in his work. Its presence implies a strategy to reorder complex questions regarding identity — the ambivalent transactions with the culture of the United States, the uprooting and exile, which Martí himself lived and suffered. I use 'archive' in a Foucaultian sense; that is, not as a collection of documents or a compendium of quotes, but as a law that systematizes and makes visible a constellation of enunciations.[6] Throughout the twentieth century, but mostly since the essayists of the magazine *Orígenes* (Cintio Vitier, José Lezama Lima), and in the Revolution's ideology during the 1950s and 1960s, the figure of José Martí sustained the mythic power of an origin and a destiny — father of literary, national and revolutionary history, forger of Cuban identity, capable of reuniting its unstable and scattered elements, hero, educator and martyr. Thus, Díaz's appeal to the notions of homeland and fraternity in exile is no accident: the topic of the child yearning for their return to the island, a central motive in the life and work of Martí, turned out to be a very dear element to the canonical values of political and cultural identity. Appealing to these values would surely be fruitful, for it allowed for an 'honoured' place — to use an adjective from Martí's writing — for the children of the expatriated Cubans, who were mostly disdained by society, who treated them as *gusanos* [worms], that is to say, traitors. Through this interpretative exercise, from a perspective that saw the island as a scattered community, Díaz managed to portray the outside for the very first time, and also to reposition his own literary work in the eyes of power.

A Collective Biography

De la patria y el exilio was written by Jesús Díaz during the shooting of his documentary film *Cincuentaicinco hermanos*, which told the story of the first visit — between December 1977 and January 1978 — of the children of those who emigrated to the United States and Puerto Rico at the beginning of the Revolution. The fifty-five young people who visited the island were part of the Antonio Maceo Brigade, a movement which was born in university meetings and grew in several cities, and centred around the publications *Areíto* — founded in New York in 1974 — and *Joven Cuba*.[7] In its efforts at testimonial writing, *De la patria y el exilio*, as in other cases of the genre, was an answer to the contemporary concern of documenting the transformations brought about by the Revolution, and the resulting weakening of canonical forms, which gave rise to new formats in Latin American literature (Gilman 2013). In chronicles or ethnographic research, and through the mediation of an interviewer, the testimonial voice transmits a collective history. There is a particular use of the first person, a 'transitional form', according to Mabel Moraña, that becomes legitimate through the statement 'I represent' (1997: 46).

Díaz's documentary work is clear in this respect, and in 1978 the book received the testimonial genre award of the Unión de Escritores y Artistas de Cuba (UNEAC). It records the voices of the group in a vast textual corpus, which includes interviews, programmatic texts of the Brigade, official speeches by the government authorities, minutes of collective discussions, controversies with other Cuban immigrants published in the United States before and after their visit, and other anecdotes and personal memories, as well as a special sample of narrative and poetry by émigré writers, some of them very well known, such as Lourdes Casals, Roberto González Echevarría or José Kozer, who were not part of the Brigade, but published in *Areíto* as well.

The book not only develops the subject of the film, but also makes visible the presence of its director. In truth, he is there from the very beginning; and through a partial record of his shooting diary, he unifies the materials in a narrative flux.

> When the IL-18 [airliner] touched down at José Martí Airport, we all gathered around the glass doors, Nano with the camera, León with the microphone and the recorder, Calzadito with the cables and the lights, Pepe with the chargers, and me with the question well prepared, a question that I would not ask. (Díaz 1979: 11)

As mentioned above, the introduction of the first person in the very first paragraph works as a badge of affiliation to the testimonial genre, and strengthens the link between the self and the collective, creating at the same time an effect of suspense that gives rise to the story. It also highlights a particular avant-garde mode, which consists in removing any fictional trace and revealing its mechanisms from the very beginning, the behind-the-scenes and its technology — camera, microphones, chargers, lights, interviews.

Despite being different objects, book and film are linked in a single piece of research, which, through fragmentation and montage, replaces the classic historicist interpretation of the documentary with a certain poetic view that highlights the diversity of perspectives and subjectivities at stake — including the narrator's. Let us remember that, according to Bill Nichols (1997), as an institutional practice linked to states' need to tell their own past, the historic mode of the documentary had always been *expository*, that is to say, a mode with an economy that responds to a narrative organization of history, in terms of cause and effect, with the sole object of giving an exhaustive account of a certain piece of information. By contrast, the position Díaz assumes as a documentary maker combines different modes, which are closer to the 'participative' and 'performative' ones — also described by Nichols (2001) — in which the director's intervention gives rise to a transformational process in the subjects and the social agents involved, including himself (Piedras 2010: 3).[8] Although in *Cincuentaicinco hermanos* we cannot see him, or his gestures or body language, we do observe traces of his subjective transformations, along with marks of the author, throughout *De la patria y el exilio:* a text that records — in the form of a chronicle in present tense — the process the maker underwent. It is in the book that the narrator, in the first person, ties together each story in a great testimonial flux, giving account of his own shock, and opening himself up affectively to the case that he has been called upon to reveal:

> I remembered carefully the question that I had chosen from the list to ask without warning to the first *brigadista* that passed in front of the camera: You left this airport as a child, what do you think now, at this precise moment?
>
> The doors opened. The boys were coming towards us. I ordered the camera to start rolling. Amid the confusion of hugs and faces, I did not know at first whom to approach. Then I saw Mayra. [...] At that moment, I barely managed to move towards her tear-stained, transfigured face, I lost control and forgot the question, and could just mumble:
>
> — What's wrong? (Díaz 1979: 13)

The author hesitates and is moved, changes his plans and does not know what to do, and then includes all these difficulties as part of the testimony he is attempting to present. A few pages later, he recognizes he was overwhelmed, and, as the text moves forwards, along with the Brigade's journey, he incorporates his own associations and interpretations of the cases.

But why are the reflexions of this authorial first person, who transforms his own perspective during the shooting, allowed to appear in the written text but not in the film? It could be said that one of the first effects of the written version, in contrast with the film, is the opening of the group portrait to admit individual biographies and voices, a process that includes the narrator's voice. Thus, the book reveals something that in the film is merely hinted at: a displacement of Díaz's poetics within the testimonial genre.

The canonical value of the testimonial genre — as in a foundational example, *Biografía de un cimarrón* [Biography of a Runaway Slave] by Miguel Barnet[9] — was that the author spoke on behalf of another person who represented a social group or class, making their story an allegorical narration. In the case of *Cincuentaicinco hermanos* and *De la patria y el exilio*, although they point to a vaster social context, the testimonial link between the first-person narrator and the collective is mediated by fragmentation: not all the members of the Brigade are interviewed, and not all are interviewed to the same extent. Besides, they have individual stories, different from each other. The book is composed of sequences mostly titled with the names of some of the protagonists (for instance, 'Historia de Elián', or 'Mayra en Nueva York'), and these stories extend over several chapters, a true montage of interviews. Instead of summing up all the cases in one single example or paradigm that represents them, the stories of Elián, of Maritza, Elizardo or Marifeli are multiplied in diverse ways which are sometimes contradictory and upsetting.

Castro Avelleyra (2018) adduces that in the film *Cincuentaicinco hermanos*, the notion of identity is seen from a global viewpoint, consistent with the social discourse of the Revolution and the institution involved in the documentary (the ICAIC). Her argument is based on the complete absence of the proper names of the individuals interviewed throughout the film. However, if we compare the movie with the book, it is possible to consider Diaz's documentary perspective in a broader way, for instance, the perspective that emerges from the inclusion of the childhood stories of the brigade members, or *brigadistas*. In 'historia de Elián', the boy remembers the vicissitudes of his family when they arrived in New York, and of his mother's efforts over the years in order to pay off department store loans. The subject of the story of Maritza, which could be written as a fairy tale (Díaz 1979: 45), is the return of a daughter to visit her stepfather's factory, expropriated by the state, and to work alongside its current workers, in order to acquire a new perspective on class struggle. And there is the story of José, who fears the reencounter with his family because he was taken away when he was still a little child and cannot find a way of resuming contact with them. Or the story of Jorge, one of the children of the Peter Pan Operation, in which more than 14,000 children left the island without their parents, who sent them to refugee camps in Florida, arguing that it was like a long vacation. A biographical dimension, the effort and the attention to minute, specific narrations of each one of those lives, runs through the entire compilation of testimonies — particularly its written version — thus obstructing the idea of a homogeneity of the whole.

However, this perspective is also present at the beginning of the film, just a moment after the title appears. The movie is subtitled 'A story about the first visit to Cuba by the Antonio Maceo brigade, formed by young people who were taken out of the country as children by their parents, during the first years of the Revolution'.[10] *Cincuentaicinco hermanos* is described as an interview, and although it does not lack narrative elements and a fluid, harmonious structure, its main theme has to do with the treatment of the voice. Thus, although one cannot discern at first sight whether the one with dark glasses is Elián, or if the young pregnant woman is Marifeli, the selection of some figures and their recurring appearance in different scenes certainly ties, in a choral way, the collective to the individual.

The scenes follow their itinerary in the island, but the conversations constantly stop the action. On the return of these exiled children to Cuba, the topic of the reencounter with their country of origin is exclusively focused on instances of orality. That is to say that the subject of the film is not only the presentation of the new social dimensions brought about by the Revolution. The documentary also records the encounter, and most of all the dialogue, between the *brigadistas* and the residents of the island, to such an extent that the entire film acquires the form of a conversation: the conversations between the director and the *brigadistas*, and the conversations between the *brigadistas* and other people: workers, young people, family members, government officials.

The emphasis on the interviews turns the film's space into a true forum in which the social actors are free to talk about their situation. Each of the people who intervene, both from the inside and the outside, has a story to tell about the split Cuban family. Even the Minister of Culture, Armando Hart, tells them in a conference the story of the loss of his two nephews, who were taken to the United States, and with whom he could never resume contact. It is a revealing passage: 'After the Brigade's meeting with comrade Armando Hart', says the author in the book, '[...] we came to understand the very intricate process of emotional reflection that was taking place in front of us, and within us, regarding our homeland and exile' (Díaz 1979: 190).[11]

To sum up, if the starting point is a perspective that comes from a privileged institutional position within the cultural project of the Revolution — it should be remembered that the ICAIC was key in the convergence of the artistic and political avant-garde during its first years — this did not occlude the desire that the spectators could relate to the characters and the testimonies in all their uniqueness. It is important, in this sense, to highlight the almost complete absence in the film of a totalizing voice-over, and also of captions indicating names and ages.[12] Any claim to explain the historical event is thus minimized, and instead of a totalizing voice that closes the gaps, the microphone appears intermittently, barely hidden, as a link between the inside and the outside of the scenes, to frame the artifice through which the story is built.

Film and book intertwine and complement each other. In the former the stories are condensed and different resources are used in order to save time (for instance, the ellipses that show the volunteers going to different places on the island). Meanwhile, in the chronicles of the making of the film and all the related materials (such as the Cuban periodical publications in the United States or Puerto Rico, as well as poems, letters, etc.), the will to record and immediately publish all the interviews speaks of an attempt to show, through the fragmentation and juxtaposition of different stories, an expanded, communitarian and plural dimension of the exiles' experience.

At the same time, the fact that the book was published almost immediately after the release of the film expresses a certain questioning — very dear to Díaz — of the link between literature and cinema. In a 1980 lecture, 'Provocaciones sobre cine documental y literatura' [Provocations about Documentary Film and Literature],[13] Díaz elaborated on his concern with removing the literary burden of the documentary film. The key was rethinking the traditionally hierarchical relation between both arts, where cinema tended to be understood as a subsidiary element of the text. The problem with documentary cinema was the excessive use of words:

> [...] the long, dull narrations that make the expressivity, the length and hence the rhythm of the image subservient to the needs of the literary text; these, at times, are substituted by or mixed with previously adapted — and even rehearsed! — interviews, in which someone narrates or explains in front of the camera some subject which can be their lives, or someone else's life, or a complicated production or political process, but we are never witnessing an actual event. (2003: 474)

The metanarration, or the need to explain itself constantly, threatens the most important potential of documentary film, that is, to be 'that window on life that is "take one", unique, unrepeatable', in Díaz's words (2003: 475).[14]

Despite the evident abundance of words in *Cincuentaicinco hermanos*, Paulo Antonio Paranaguá analyses how Diaz's film attempts to treat each story and works with the emotional memory of the country of origin through its composition of such 'situations': 'Those moments in which reality acquires a dynamic that becomes independent from the director, from the crew and, in short, from everything that is not related to its own inner structure' (Díaz in Paranaguá 2003: 362). The documentary is not so much the demonstration of a thesis as it is part of an exploratory process through which it would be possible to discover and film the problems, not the conclusions (Díaz in Paranaguá 2003: 362). Thus, the task of the director — or the reporter — in *Cincuentaicinco hermanos* is understood as provoking encounters and asking questions in order to capture whatever happens there, and to transmit the variety of positions opened up after the return of those other members of the nation.

The attempt at capturing the experience without mediations had its forebears in Díaz's narrative work. His first stories followed an impulse which Alain Badiou called 'passion for the real', typical of the twentieth-century avant-gardes, which foregrounded the desire to capture the profuse, complex and singular reality of the revolutionary event in the work of art. In his first collection of stories, *Los años duros*, Díaz narrated the vicissitudes of the struggles against the dictator Batista, in a very spontaneous way that was far from the canonical, schematized and heroic narratives of revolutionary discourse, an example of which are the stories by Manuel Cofiño, another of the narrators who wrote on the same subject in those years.[15] Also, throughout the 1960s, Díaz had participated in various discussions about the values and characteristics an avant-garde piece should have in the context of the Cuban Revolution. In those discussions, published in the magazines *Bohemia* and *Gaceta de Cuba*, Díaz stressed that the critical value of avant-garde art resided in its immersion in the concerns of the Revolution: how could the tensions, the variety of actors, the divergences and the complexity of the new historical moment be transmitted if it was not through a tense, fragmentary, vibrational and multiple form?[16] Or, better, in the words of Ángel Rama, how could one achieve in an aesthetic production a direct and lived expression of the construction of the reality of a specific moment (1983: 255)? In Díaz's work — as was the case with many other Cuban filmmakers and writers (Norberto Fuentes or Tomás Gutiérrez Alea, to mention just two) — that direct way of narrating the encounter with the reality of the revolutionary event avoided the heroic, solemn or totalizing forms typical of the narrative of the Revolution, and this was questioned by some revolutionary intellectuals.[17]

Thus, *Cincuentaicinco hermanos* and *Los años duros* were different cases altogether. By taking up the declarations made in the interviews, cinema had become for Díaz a place where he could learn to narrate reality. Montage was a privileged device for that object. The emphasis on the editing and the juxtaposition of biographical pieces in the book permanently threatened the cohesion of a unique narration, and worked as a metaphor for the impossibility of social homogenization. The cuts made by the director's eye turned out to be the most suitable way of transmitting the real.

The Other Children of the Revolution

The visit of the members of the Antonio Maceo Brigade was not a vacation. This group of young people did voluntary work in factories, attended seminars on the history of the Revolution and participated in conversations and educational debates. On their return — the first, official one — the children came back to tell the community about its unstable, complex identity, composed of more than one city, and more than one language.

Their arrival foregrounded a series of strong and emotional implications for identity in revolutionary discourse. For the very first time, cinema showed an unfolded 'us' on the island, and the presence of what was our own outside the island, along with the impact of these others within the community of residents. The consciousness of the uprooting, with the evidence of the island's transcontinental links with other borders, seemed to be foundational.

Díaz's accomplishment was to look at that issue from a generational perspective. If the children of the Revolution were part of a generation in which, in the words of Che Guevara, kids were educated and instructed according to the new social values, free from all capitalist burdens, as truly 'new men' who would inhabit the future, what was the place of these other children, whose separation from their country during their childhood had put them through the afflictions of immigration, double discrimination (for being Cubans and *gusanos*), the idealization of their homeland, the criticism of their parents, the disruption of their families? Did any part of the Revolution's past belong to them? Did any part of its future?

Caught between an inside which would not accept them once and for all, and an outside that would reject them, this other generation seemed to be stranded on the margins of historical time. The Revolution's imaginary time was the future, with the revolutionary event being a zero point in the present that represented a new beginning that allowed a retelling of history, society and man. The generation born during the Revolution was thrown into a time when relations with other people, the state and work would be radically transformed. If the children of the Revolution were conscious of their participation in this new futurity, to what time did these brothers and sisters belong?

> — That is very important, because at the beginning we saw ourselves as children doomed to nostalgia, right? Like, this is it, there is nothing to be done! We used to think like that, the Cuban Revolution has gone forward and will not wait for us, right? That is, we have been sort of taken away from history. We have been taken away from history. Here, we play a sort of supporting role. (Díaz 1979: 90)

Along with the common concerns that any return home involves — the acknowledgement, the instability between two or more borders, the elaboration of oneself as an other — the impossible return of these other children is marked by the feeling of being left outside time, at least outside that unique temporality called up by the Revolution, a temporality of rupture and projection.

While revolutionary discourse established a connection between socialist futurity and the power of children as the future builders of the new world, Díaz's gaze turned to the distress of this abandoned generation, in an attempt to reincorporate them into the complex cultural fabric. What is more, he does this by passing through each of the terms of that same constellation. The figures of the child and the youth, which condensed both the sense of redemption and futurity, allow the author to trace an empathetic bridge with their interlocutors, and at the same time to smooth out the tragic nuances of any inside–outside binaries. It is no accident that the title of the film, *Cincuentaicinco hermanos*, highlights this element:

> At first, the movie had no title. The ICAIC production team chose a horrible one — as always — just to identify it: 'Volunteer Brigade'. Of course, that was not going to be the title, but then what would be the title? And why?
>
> The second project was actually a suggestion by Elisardo. While I was interviewing him, he remarked, as a sort of sad joke, that it would be a good idea to add as a subtitle to the articles that were published about the visit, 'The long holidays of '59', because that was what they were promised when they took them away — holidays. For a while, we liked the irony [...] But maybe for a movie about their parents; it had nothing to do with the children. (1979: 189)

The key was not the parents but the children. By finding this title, Díaz discovered the centre of the conflict, which is precisely the passage from the *brigadistas* to the harsh narrative of the nation as a scattered family.

In a scene of the movie, one of the members of the brigade, a young woman, talks with a Cuban resident, a young man. Like the rest of the film, this scene is made of close-ups and very few cuts (see Fig. 8.1). The camera follows them from one place to another as they have a conversation. The interlocutors introduce themselves; they are between nineteen and twenty years old. The girl, who is pregnant, tells him about her wish to come back to the island, and asks him his opinion: would he accept the return of the *maceítos* (members of the Antonio Maceo Brigade)? The young man asks her what they have done in those years, whether they had done anything transformative. She tells him that she knows about a couple of militants in the group, but that she really thinks that beyond their university education there is nothing remarkable. When he answers that there are enough technicians and professionals in Cuba, she asks if they could come back then as citizens. Very kindly, and asking her whether she is willing to listen to him, the young man answers that he believes that they are not needed, that they would not have any place in the revolutionary context. The scene captures the hesitations, the intensity, the reiterations and the silences of both, who are talking face to face, standing in the street. This moment anticipates the end of the movie; it shows the complex situation of this generation, and transmits the disappointment that is usually woven into any narrative of return.[18] None of the markers of identity that the girl uses as reasons to resume her life in Cuba are valid for the resident of the Revolution. Later, before her departure, Fidel Castro will tell them that their place is still in the United States,

FIG. 8.1. Frame enlargement from *Cincuentaicinco hermanos* (1978) by Jesús Díaz. Meeting between 'maceítos' and young men in Cuba.

because it is there that they have a political mission to carry out for Cuba — an answer given, he will say, not as a citizen but as a revolutionary man.

What is to be done, then, with identity? How can these other children — that apparently have nothing in common with their homeland — rejoin the cultural fabric? Clearly, the canonical symbols of the nation were out of reach for them. As we have seen so far, in order to weave these lives within the community, Díaz had to address, from the very beginning, the profound dilemmas of cultural tradition.

The focus on children and fraternity would surely echo in the audience's memory — it would undoubtedly evoke *Ismaelillo*, for instance, Martí's first collection of poems, that begun thus: 'Hijo, espantado de todo, me refugio en ti' [Son, frightened of everything, I take refuge in you]. In Martí's poetics, the child works as a symbol of the new poetry and the new world, having not only a poetic value, but also a political one. This creates a sense of futurity absolutely consistent with the notion of the 'new man' of the Revolution: 'I am the son of my son | he remakes me' ('hijo soy de mi hijo | él me rehace'), said Martí, thus placing in both his artistic and poetic work the future foundations for its existence. As Rama explains, the question is re-establishing filiation based on the awareness of a past that is vanishing (2015: 36–37). That dilemma, breaking with the past and assuming an identity in the process of futurity, is radicalized with the Revolution and becomes a crucial part of its conception of history. In the case of these other children, despite knowing that they do not belong to that time, they will arrive at a similar point after their journey. Their identification will not be given by marks inherited from their parents, who are linked to the pre-revolutionary culture, but by the development of the Revolution.

On the other hand, as in Martí's dilemma, the question was to make connections and big leaps that address unresolvable tensions. If in Martí these were homeland and exile, nature and technology, tradition and modernization, some of the biographies recorded by Díaz reiterate the tragedy of these tensions by telling amazing tales about the extremes that a society living in the guts of the monster can reach.[19] They also bring in the inscription of the Cuban landscape, painted by Martí in his *Versos sencillos* [Simple Verses].[20] They propose similar images to that of the two homelands — as in the title of one of the most famous poems by Martí — in order to express a feeling of extraterritoriality, clearly remembered in a poem by Lourdes Casals, 'To Ana Veltfort', included by Díaz among the testimonies: 'I carry this marginalization immune to each return, | too *Habanera* to be a New Yorker | too New Yorker to be | — even to be again — | anything' (Díaz 1979: 34).[21]

Díaz's perspective highlights these elements and makes them visible, as an interpretative matrix, a point of legibility. It is not so much an 'influence' from Martí as a deep re-articulation of that imagery, a way of making intelligible that unprecedented event which he faces: the fact that 'us' is formed also by others, that there is an outside as part of the inside, something unthinkable for the revolutionary discourse of that time.[22]

The meaning of the child as redemptive and imbued with future, the nostalgia, the uprooting, the building of a community in exile, as well as the suture of the inequalities produced by modernization — key elements in the poetics of Martí — were unrelentingly present in the Brigade's discourse and in the director's registering of its voices.

This understanding attitude, even towards the so-called *maceítos* when they realize that they cannot go back to the island, evokes Martí's pain in *Versos sencillos*, the poetry collection that redraws the landscapes of the island through memory. This sadness, according to Fina García Marruz, finds a sense of orientation in the uprooting, in the discovery of a bigger law. The final manifesto they read before leaving is a condensation of some of these topics. The young men and women understand that they cannot return, that their task is to create a group in the United States, and so they release Cuban-ness from its geographical borders and link it to a history of struggles:

> Today we are more Cuban than three weeks ago, because we have seen very closely how, after a hundred years of struggle, the Cuban people have recovered their nationality and their future, and have taken hold of their history with their own hands. We also feel happier because we understand that being Cuban is not tied to a geographical definition, but to a tradition of struggle that began with Carlos Manuel de Céspedes, Antonio Maceo and José Martí, continued with Julio Antonio Mella, Rubén Martínez Villena and Antonio Guiteras, and which our comrade Commander-in-Chief Fidel Castro, the 26th of July Movement and the other revolutionary organizations brought to its just historical continuation. (Díaz 1979: 243)

It is not by chance, then, that in the narrator's associations the figure of José Martí finally emerges. Martí is explicitly mentioned when the story of the meeting between Castro and the *brigadistas* is told (see Figs 8.2 and 8.3). It could be said that his appearance ties together the meanings that are present in the titles of the book and the movie.

FIG. 8.2. Frame enlargement from *Cincuentaicinco hermanos* (1978) by Jesús Díaz. The 'maceítos' Brigade with Fidel Castro.

FIG. 8.3. Frame enlargement from *Cincuentaicinco hermanos* (1978) by Jesús Díaz. The 'maceítos' Brigade with Fidel Castro.

FIG. 8.4. Extract from internet database.
Image of Martí in Tampa's Lyceum with a young audience in 1891.

When he said goodbye, Fidel shook hands with each one of them. I looked at the faces of the young people, the same group I had seen in the airport singing the national anthem twenty-one days before, the same faces, so different now. I knew then, although I did not turn back, that Fidel had gone and had immediately come back. He wanted to take a picture with them, a simple family picture. The group was formed, for one second they all remained still, there was a flash.

It was right then: it was the Flag, and the memory of the Anthem, and the mentions of Cuba and Puerto Rico, and the picture — Fidel at the centre, solemn, surrounded by his children — that led me to think of Martí, of his pictures, with him among the tobacco farmers in Tampa, of his conversations with the tobacco farmers in Tampa; their words, lost, had remained at the very centre of our Homeland.

I wanted to imagine — I had always wanted to imagine — how the air around those conversations had been. I felt, through time, that it must have been very similar to the air in that plain hall, that night of Friday 13 January 1978. (Díaz 1979: 220)

The reading of that picture as a family portrait and the invocation of the figure of Martí may not only be an attempt to give the *brigadistas* refuge from the poor opinion about the Cubans who lived outside the country, but it may also serve as a national framework to reinsert the problem, which allows their locating in the profuse relation of the émigrés with the United States, characterized not only by uprooting but also by cultural transactions. The image of Martí speaking to the young men and women who lived in Tampa (Fig. 8.4) — the well-known metaphor of the 'new pines' comes from that speech — became an interpretative analogy and inserted these other children in a common narrative.[23] By recovering the tutelary and heroic figure of José Martí, a decidedly social cultural reference, Díaz was sheltering the *brigadistas* beneath the values that the children have in Martí's poetry: protection, futurity, struggle and transformation.

Conclusion

At the end of the narration of one of these children's reencounter with their parents, the narrator observes: 'This is a family in tension, with its contradictions and conflicts' (Díaz 1979: 89). We may hear in that conclusion a statement about the Cuban community as a whole. The fact that this was one of the first documentary films to deal with such complex topics gives the narrator a solid critical position. During the first two decades of the Revolution, Díaz participated in several debates about the forms and functions of the cultural avant-garde. In his perspective, giving an account of the reality of the revolutionary historical process implied necessarily recognizing its dilemmas and paradoxes, although the result was far from being a harmonious and homogeneous representation of that process. *Cincuentaicinco hermanos* and *De la patria y el exilio* show, in different but complementary ways, key devices in Díaz's poetics, aimed at transmitting the revolutionary event in all its complexity, through a fragmented vision of reality, the relation between the collective and the biographical, and the acknowledgement of previously unconsidered or concealed social dimensions. In his working process, the writer found himself with the film that would relocate him in the Cuban cultural field. It also gave him a concern — diasporic Cuban-ness — that would not leave him even when, almost twenty years later, in Madrid, he created another artefact for reconnections: the magazine *Encuentro de la cultura cubana*. This was a publication that would work as a meeting point for political debate and cultural productions of Cuban intellectuals scattered throughout the world, just after the crisis of the Special Period.

Works Cited

ARTARAZ, KEPA. 2005. 'El Ejercicio de Pensar: The Rise and Fall of "Pensamiento Crítico" ', *Bulletin of Latin American Research*, 24.3: 348–66

CASTRO AVELLEYRA, ANABELLA. 2018. 'Dos viajes, *Cincuentaicinco hermanos* y una ilusión: modos de abordaje cinematográfico de la emigración cubana', *Culturales*, 6: 1–34

COLLMAN, LILLIAM OLIVA. 1999. 'Entrevista con Jesús Díaz', *Cuban Studies*, 29: 155–75

DE LA CAMPA, ROMÁN. 2006. 'Revista *Areíto*: herejía de una nación improbable', *Revista Encuentro de la cultura cubana*, 40: 137–41

DELEUZE, GILLES. 2003. 'L'Immanence: une vie...', in *Deux régimes de fous et autres textes (1975–1995)* (Paris: Minuit), pp. 359–64

DÍAZ, DESIRÉE. 2008. 'Los otros: exilio y emigración en el cine de la revolución', *Archivos de la Filmoteca*, 59: 163–83

DÍAZ, JESÚS. 1979. *De la patria y el exilio* (La Habana: Ediciones Unión)

—— 2000. 'Cuba: El fin de una ilusión", *Claves de la razón práctica*, 104: 65–70

—— 2003. 'Provocaciones sobre cine documental y literatura', in *Cine documental en América Latina*, ed. by Paulo Antonio Paranaguá (Madrid: Cátedra), pp. 472–76

FOUCAULT, MICHEL. 1972. *The Archaeology of Knowledge and The Discourse on Language* (New York: Pantheon Books)

GARBATZKY, IRINA. 2019. 'Una matriz crítica: Jesús Díaz y la vanguardia cultural en Cuba', *Caracol*, 18: 209–35

GARCÍA MARRUZ, F., and C. VITIER. 1969. *Temas martianos* (La Habana: Departamento Colección Cubana Biblioteca Nacional José Martí)

GILMAN, CLAUDIA. 2013. *Entre la pluma y el fusil* (Buenos Aires: Paidós)

GRENIER, YVONNE. 2017. 'Jesús Díaz, 1941–2002: The Unintentional Deviationist', *Cuban Studies*, 45: 115–31

MOLLOY, SYLVIA. 2015. 'Dislocación e intemperie: el viaje de vuelta', *Caracol*, 10: 18–37

MORAÑA, MABEL. 1997. 'Documentalismo y ficción: testimonio y narrativa testimonial hispanoamericana en el siglo XX', in *Políticas de la escritura en América Latina: de la colonia a la Modernidad* (Caracas: Ediciones eXcultura), pp. 113–50

NICHOLS, BILL. 1997. *La representación de la realidad: cuestiones y conceptos sobre el documental* (Barcelona: Paidós)

—— 2001. *Introduction to Documentary* (Bloomington: Indiana University Press)

PARANAGUÁ, PAULO ANTONIO (ed.). 2003. *Cine documental en América Latina* (Madrid: Cátedra)

PIEDRAS, PABLO. 2010. 'La cuestión de la primera persona en el documental latinoamericano contemporáneo: la primera persona y sus dispositivos', *Cine documental*, 1

RAMA, ÁNGEL. 1983. 'Norberto Fuentes: el escritor en la tormenta revolucionaria', in *Literatura y clase social* (Mexico City: Folios), pp. 231–61

—— 2015. 'La dialéctica de la modernidad en José Martí', in *Modernidad y latinoamericanismo*, ed. by M. F. Pampín and J. Ramos (Caracas: Biblioteca Ayacucho), pp. 3–104

ROJAS, RAFAEL. 2006. 'Jesús Díaz: el intelectual redimido', in *Tumbas sin sosiego: revolución, disidencia y exilio del intelectual cubano* (Barcelona: Anagrama), pp. 310–23

Notes to Chapter 8

1. Díaz was not only a writer, screenwriter and director — he also coordinated several periodical publications, among them *Encuentro de la cultura cubana*, a very important magazine that brought together Cuban intellectuals scattered during the Special Period crisis.
2. The original texts from Díaz's book, interview and most of the citations are written in Spanish. All the translations were made by Laura García (University of Buenos Aires). I am very thankful to her.
3. In 1966, his book *Los años duros* won the Casa de las Américas short-story prize. Díaz was twenty-five years old.
4. Yvonne Grenier observes that, far from a constant marginality, and despite the successive questionings and censures his productions suffered, Díaz always managed to put his work at the centre of the most urgent debates of his time. His strategy was to occupy the available space and to seek acknowledgement for his cultural and political leadership.
5. The story of Díaz's participation in *El Caimán Barbudo* and *Pensamiento Crítico* is long, and has been told by the author himself in an essay from 2000, and also by Artaraz (2005) and Rojas (2006). In 1967, Heberto Padilla wrote a negative review in *El Caimán barbudo* of the novel *Pasión de Urbino* by Lisandro Otero — who was then Vice-Minister of Culture — and a laudatory one of *Tres tristes tigres* by Guillermo Cabrera Infante — who was exiled at that time. The decision to publish only the latter cost him his position, and he was dismissed from the magazine. That was the last straw, along with the corrosive effect of a series of ironic, sexual and humorous articles. As for *Pensamiento crítico*, the magazine carried on autonomously for some years until it was finally closed down in 1971, after a series of interventions and accusations of anti-Sovietism and ideological deviation. Its end was literally a dilapidation, with a bulldozer dismantling the building that housed the Department of Philosophy (Díaz 2000: 70).
6. Michel Foucault proposed a particular notion of archive, one that would not represent the sum of all the texts or all that has been said, nor the institutions that guard or record, but the normative that produces its emergence: 'the archive defines a particular level: that of a practice

that causes a multiplicity of statements to emerge as so many regular events, as so many things to be dealt with and manipulated' (1972: 130).

7. Román de la Campa was part of *Areíto*. Here he describes the group: 'As I went through the pages of the magazine I found stories like mine — people who were part of the Peter Pan exodus, that left us scattered throughout the United States at the beginning of the 60s; sons and daughters of the Cuban upper middle class, who were separated from their families, and then reunited — too late in some cases — , university graduates who experienced very closely, and with sympathy, the North American spirit of political rebellion in those times' (2006: 14).

8. Piedras develops the six modes of representation in documentary cinema, as classified by Nichols: expository, observational, participative or interactive, reflexive, performative and poetic.

9. As readers may recall, *Biografía de un cimarrón* sought to gather the documents of slavery based on the story told by Esteban Montejo, and using an anthropological interview, established a relationship with history: 'History appears because the life of a man goes through it', observes Miguel Barnet in his prologue.

10. The subtitle in Spanish says: 'Un reportaje sobre la primera visita a Cuba de la Brigada Antonio Maceo, formada por jóvenes que fueron sacados del país por sus padres cuando eran niños, en los primeros años de la revolución'.

11. Hart's story is transcribed in the book: 'I want to express a personal feeling. There are many, many Cubans, who have suffered what you have suffered, and we also know many of those Cubans. Let me tell you something, let me tell you this so you know that between us there can also be a bond that allows us to understand these situations. My brother died in the Revolution. He died fighting the tyranny in a bomb explosion. He was profoundly *anti-yanqui*, he had even been to the United States once, and was profoundly *anti-yanqui*, very radical in his thinking. Although back when we were fighting we were not communists yet, he was very radical, we can even say that he was an extremist in his *anti-yanqui* thinking. He had two children, and one day, in 1960 or 1961, I don't remember exactly what year, I went to see them, but they had also taken them away, they were taken away. Had he been alive, I know that would not have happened. They live over there; I have not heard much of them. I wish some day they feel or think what you are thinking and feeling today' (Díaz 1979: 211–12).

12. Captions only appear once to indicate the year 1976, the date of a documentary film the *brigadistas* were watching, about the counterrevolutionary attack on Cubana Airlines flight 455 in which dozens of Cubans died; twenty-four of them were teenagers, members of the Cuban national junior fencing team.

13. His paper was presented originally in the seminar 'Nuevo cine y literatura en nuestra América: relaciones e interinfluencias' [New Cinema and Literature in Our America: Relationships and Inter-influences], during the second Havana festival in December 1980. The quotations are taken from *Cine documental en América Latina* (Díaz in Paranaguá 2003: 472–76).

14. The emphasis on 'take one' came from Díaz's exploration of the 1950s cinematic avant-garde, of Italian Neorealism and the French *cinéma vérité*, both of which tendencies were present in the ICAIC, particularly in the work of Tomás Gutiérrez Alea. Gutiérrez Alea's *Memorias del subdesarrollo* [Memories of Underdevelopment] can be seen, following the excellent work of Desirée Díaz (2008), as a forerunner of *Cincuentaicinco hermanos* as an early representation of exile in the cinema of the Revolution.

15. Ángel Rama explored these aesthetic and ideological debates and discussions about the writing of the Revolution in his article 'Norberto Fuentes: el escritor en la tormenta revolucionaria' [Norberto Fuentes: The Writer in the Revolutionary Storm], originally published in *Marcha* magazine in 1971. His contribution is crucial to understanding the debate that marked the Cuban narrative of those days: 'The operation of disclosing the real that characterizes original artistic creation is replaced by a set of pre-established guidelines, thus encouraging trainees to follow a codified style from a strict school, who will elaborate variations of a suggested subject' (1983: 256).

16. In my article 'Una matriz crítica: Jesús Díaz y la vanguardia cultural en Cuba', published in *Caracol* no. 18, I examine these controversies, and the particular sense of a 'cultural avant-garde' proposed by Díaz.

17. For this discussion I refer again to the previously mentioned article by Rama (1983).
18. According to Sylvia Molloy, narratives of return in contexts of migration and exile have a destabilizing effect (2015: 24).
19. 'Viví en el monstruo, le conozco las entrañas' [I have lived within the monster, I have seen its guts], writes Martí in his unfinished letter to his friend Manuel Mercado (the letter was later known as his 'Political testimony'), written shortly before he died, in 1895. Like many of Martí's sayings, this one became a famous metaphor to speak of the author's pain and his close knowledge of the U.S. enemy.
20. As he gathers from the dialogue with the young *brigadistas*, 'Seeing the landscape, I realized Cuba was a country of more palm trees than I had ever imagined. My imagination had not led me to think about that; I had already forgotten it' (1979: 40).
21. 'Cargo esta marginalidad inmune a todos los retornos, | demasiado habanera para ser neoyorkina | demasiado neoyorkina para ser | — aún volver a ser — | cualquier cosa'.
22. The astonishment produced by the visit of the Brigade can be measured in the words that the Minister of Culture, Armando Hart, addressed to them: 'It is not easy to answer that question, but we can say this: although we knew of your case, [...] this meeting has been amazing, and actually surprising' (Díaz 1979: 207–08). Castro also notices the symbolism this meeting implied: 'We have to draw our own conclusions, and you will do the same when you leave. But I think that this opens up a new possibility, and from a moral point of view, this has a huge symbolism. You will feel better and we will also feel better' (Díaz 1979: 228).
23. This is the speech pronounced by Martí for the students of the Liceo in Tampa, in 1891, known later as 'Los pinos nuevos', where the metaphor alludes to the redemption and the renewal of life ciphered in youth.

CHAPTER 9

❖

'El Mundo iluminado, y yo despierta': Screening Sor Juana in the Films of Bemberg and Pereda

Ben Bollig

Literary life has proved a popular subject for filmmakers over the years: poets in particular have become the fictionalized protagonists of biographical pictures or historical dramas.[1] The question that occupies this chapter is what happens to the literary work when the writer becomes the subject of the filmmaker's attentions. As Speranza (2002) argues, it is perfectly possible to screen such a story — particularly that of a colourful or controversial poet — without producing a 'poetic' film, in any understanding of the term. Here we compare a film from Argentina and a Mexico/Canada co-production, both based on the life and works of Sor Juana Inés de la Cruz: *Yo, la peor de todas* [I, the Worst of All] (María Luisa Bemberg, 1990); and *Todo, en fin, el silencio lo ocupaba* [All Things Were Now Overtaken by Silence] (Nicolás Pereda, 2009).[2]

The films differ in genre, style, mood and, in particular, in the role that poetry plays in their structure and *mise en scène*. Bemberg's film is a 'biopic', a relatively straightforward retelling of key moments in the life of the Mexican nun, based heavily on Octavio Paz's 1982 biography, but one that nevertheless makes significant use of intertextual and intermedial resources in its cinematography. Pereda's, in contrast, is difficult to classify, playfully evasive, 'slow' or perhaps 'contemplative', and with a cultivated aesthetic of error or even failure. How, we ask, do these films present the works in question? To put it another, more literary way, what reading of the poems do they offer?

Yo, la peor de todas

Yo, la peor de todas (henceforth *YPT*), directed by María Luisa Bemberg (1922–1995), is an account of the life of the Mexican poet and nun, Sor Juana Inés de la Cruz (Juana Inés de Asbaje, 1648–1695), adapted from Octavio Paz's biography, *Sor Juana Inés de la Cruz o Las trampas de la fe* (1982; English translation *Sor Juana, or, The Traps of Faith*, Paz 1988).[3] As John King puts it, the film is an 'exploration of a creative woman, and perhaps a woman in love with another woman, crushed by powerful men who were her patrons or confessors', and demonstrates the filmmaker's 'continued interest in transgressive women' (2000: 266). *YPT* focuses on Sor Juana's struggles with the Mexican Church hierarchy and on her amorous friendship with her patron and protector, the vicereine, María Luisa Manrique de Lara y Gonzaga, Condesa de Paredes. For Rosa Sarabia, the film offers a 'reelaboration' or 'restitution' of Sor Juana, essentially in feminist terms (2002: 121).[4]

YPT operates in the genre or sub-genre known as the biopic (or bio-pic). This is not an uncontroversial form.[5] For Belén Vidal, the genre's 'central problem' is what she calls its 'middlebrow-ness': 'its delivery of consensual pleasures related to formal conservatism and a simplified understanding of historical agency and identity' (2014: 20). There are, too, particular problems with depicting women's lives on screen. As Dennis Bingham observes, '[b]iopics of women [...] are weighed down by myths of suffering, victimization and failure perpetuated by a culture whose films reveal an acute fear of women in the public realm. Female biopics can be made empowering only by a conscious and deliberate application of a feminist point of view' (2010: 10). Denise Miller argues that 'Bemberg has taken feminist liberties with Paz' (2000: 145). In stressing her existence as a woman, Bemberg 'de-nuns' the protagonist (2000: 148) and thus, '[condenses] separate arguments [from Paz] to reinforce a feminist theme which is that the nun's betrayal is a conspiracy of misogynist men' (2000: 162–63). And while Paz's Sor Juana is a victim of local religious and political power struggles, for Miller, Bemberg's version is a victim of misogyny (2000: 152). As Sarabia puts it, 'Bemberg [vindicates] an image of an exemplary, historical, Latin-American woman, who suffered the vagaries ["avatares"] of a masculine and obscurantist society' (2002: 121). Perhaps as a result, *YPT* is structured with a falling narrative arc, from Juana's moment of greatest fame and success as a writer and intellectual, to her eventual solitude, abandonment and death. Appropriately, there is a starkness, a simplicity, to the film's *mise en scène*, with its set designs by Voytek (Wojciech Szendzikowski) and, as Nora B. Forte and Raquel Miranda (2000: 59) observe, an absence of exterior shots.

From the opening credits onwards, with their simple white-on-black letters, Bemberg foregrounds certain colour effects, such as the chiaroscuro of late renaissance and baroque portraiture, and in particular the works of Caravaggio — 'a heretical painter', in John Berger's words (2005: 82).[6] The painterly aspects of the film are obvious in the first scene, of the meeting between the viceroy (Héctor Alterio) and the archbishop (Lautaro Murúa). They are shot in profile, in a highly stylized setting, with static side-on two-shots alternating with close-ups of the two men. The close-ups feature almost totally obscured backgrounds, the faces and clothing (for example the archbishop's white amice, or the viceroy's collar) picked out against the black. In a profile shot, the bright light of the central window plays against the darkness of the rest of the frame. Overall, the scene — a discussion of the situation of religion in Europe and New Spain — cultivates a sense of artificiality, of the superficial, of the importance of appearances; it contrasts starkly to the second scene, inside the vibrant, musical community of Sor Juana's convent (Figure 9.1).

FIG. 9.1. The interior of the convent in Bemberg's *Yo, la peor de todas* (1990)

But again, in this more mobile, lively sequence, we have the intense black–white opposition of the nuns' habits, and also of the unlit arches in the background of the convent courtyard.

This chiaroscuro, what Monika Kaup calls 'the use of extreme light-dark contrasts' (2014: 230), is a constant visual motif. It occurs in two-handed scenes, accentuating the drama of exchanges between, for example, Sor Juana (Assumpta Serna) and her confessor, Father Miranda (Alberto Segado), or the meeting at the bars of the locutory between the nun and her admirer and friend, the vicereine (Dominique Sanda). The chiaroscuro effect features too in crowd scenes: as the convent elects a new Mother Superior, a line of nuns in black and white habits snakes around the interior, and then up and down stairs, recalling the fantastical scenes of M. C. Escher. We then cut to Sor Juana, alone in her cell, lit only by a candle, a skull on her desk, in a very Caravaggio-esque memento mori that draws on, for example, the latter's portrait of St Jerome (*St Jerome Writing*, 1605–06, Galleria Borghese, Rome). When the archbishop and other luminaries discuss Sor Juana's poetry, we see the black and white tiles of a floor that looks like a chessboard. Here, her poetry is as much a plot driver as an aesthetic element, motivating the intrigue that will eventually bring her down.

Bemberg uses chiaroscuro not just for visual purposes; in addition, we see scenes in which colours take on a symbolic value. Prior to the much-discussed kiss between the vicereine and Sor Juana, Dominique Sanda's character asks Assumpta Serna's to remove her veil. Under several layers of white fabric, Juana's bobbed black hair appears, a less well-coiffed version of her style as a lady-in-waiting (seen in flashback), when she enjoyed her first amorous kiss, duplicated now with the vicereine. Black, it seems, is the colour of the material, of earthly passion; white

FIG. 9.2. Sor Juana (Assumpta Serna), from *Yo, la peor de todas* (1990)

that of Juana's religious calling. Yet, as in the chiaroscuro, they are inseparable. Soon Juana is heard reading a poem, 'off', 'Detente, sombra de mi bien esquivo' [Stop, shadow of my elusive goodness] (Sonnet 165) (De la Cruz 2004: 86). This piece specifically foregrounds *shadow* in moral questions and the importance of (chaste) 'fantasy' and imagination over physical love. In its final line, 'fantasy' creates a 'prison' for the beloved — somewhat ironically given Sor Juana's eventual cloistering, as depicted in the film.

Darkness frames Juana's eventual entrapment and death — in later scenes, as the convent is beset by sickness, we see Juana alone in her cell, a crucifix and a skull on her desk, books and scientific instruments no longer visible (foreshadowing their sacrifice at the close of the film), with only the watery light from the window to illuminate the frame, as the rain falls heavily outside. In the final shot, pictured above, we see her, seated, in full habit, against the same window, in an intense chiaroscuro, the camera having panned across her empty cell, before closing on a medium shot of her seated, face blank or even traumatized, before the scene fades and an intertitle tells us she died soon after of the plague. This downbeat ending seems to counter the accusation of providing 'consensual pleasures', in Vidal's term. Instead, the film has a clear point to make about the damaging effects of patriarchy, and adopts an aesthetics based on the art and theatre of the period — Caravaggio and the *comedia nueva*, in particular.

For alongside these painterly elements, Bemberg's film also draws on theatre. One sees this in the sets — developed by a renowned stage designer — and in the inclusion in the film of part of a theatrical performance, *Los empeños de una casa* [The House of Desires] (1683), Sor Juana's play of thwarted love and mistaken identities. But it is difficult to separate out picturesque and theatrical aspects in the

FIG. 9.3. Sor Juana and the viceregal couple (Héctor Alterio and Dominique Sanda), *Yo, la peor de todas* (1994)

movie. There occurs a blurring of boundaries between forms — from painting to theatre, via an important visual resource in the film, namely the tableau. Miller states that 'Bemberg [...] keeps her camera still, rendering her tableau effect even more pronounced. This effect of an underlined emotional intensity is felt all the more strongly in a modern cinema where tableaux are rare' (2000: 158). The tableau is, one must remember, primarily a theatrical device; here it is turned to filmic purposes, with a strongly painterly feel. The camera moves as if over a canvas; the actors pose as if paused on stage. Kaup states that, '*Yo, la peor de todas* straddles the paradigmatic opposition between the actual theater stage and the illusionist space-time of cinema' (2014: 228–29).

Sor Juana's poetry features in the film, but in very particular ways, and one can argue that the aesthetics of these appearances relate to the difficulty of both screening the writing process and 'adapting' poetry for film. In an early scene, when Sor Juana meets the viceregal couple at a performance of *Los empeños de una casa* staged in their honour in her convent, the viceroy quotes from one of her most famous poems, known as 'Hombres necios' [Foolish Men] (no. 92) (2004: 71–73). With the viceroy unable to finish the quotation, Juana herself comes into shot, from a reverse angle between the viceregal couple, to continue the poem (see Figure 9.3, above). The shot, as she walks towards the camera, creates four planes: the aristocrats; Sor Juana; the actors of the play, chatting together after their performance; and the arches of the convent cloisters. It is hard to avoid seeing similarities with Velázquez's *Las Meninas* (1656, Prado, Madrid). While the camera is static, Sor Juana walks into the foreground, and into a triangle with the viceroy and the vicereine. The role of the poem here is more to move along the plot — developing in particular the relationship with María Luisa — rather than to showcase the poetry.

Poems play a particular role in the development of the relationship between Sor Juana and the *virreina*. As Sarabia notes in her study:

> The kiss [between Sor Juana and the vicereine], a suggestively erotic visual image, makes explicit/condenses the verses of amorous passion that the nun-poet had written for her vicereine, but the feelings in question are inverted and made manifest in the vicereine, who takes the initiative. (2002: 126)

Actual evidence for any romantic attachment between the two is nonexistent; within the film's narrative it is implausible for Juana to seduce or even make a pass at the vicereine. Thus the inversion of which Sarabia writes, with the effusive sentiments of Juana's admiring poetry instead ascribed to Dominque Sanda's character, as seductress, allows Bemberg to advance her idea of a physical erotic link, initiated by María Luisa, between the two women. Again, poetry is used as source for narrative and the film's feminist in(ter)vention.

Bemberg's film opts for theatre and visual arts as resources, perhaps in preference to poetry. What few if any critics have noticed, beyond Sarabia's passing reference to film history, above (2002: 121), is that, alongside its literary and painterly intertexts, *YPT* is well versed in the history of cinema. To give one example, the shot of Sor Juana after her confessor abandons her, following the violent argument with the archbishop, uses a double framing — of both the camera and the bars of the locutory. For Sarabia, this double framing 'reinforces the victimization of Sor Juana' (2002: 130). But for contemporary audiences, particularly those schooled in cinema and film criticism, there is another reason for this effect, namely that the sequence and the shot, which leave Sor Juana hanging from the bars, recall the end of a highly controversial travelling shot in Gillo Pontecorvo's *Kapo* (1960), in which a female concentration camp prisoner jumps onto an electrified barbed wire fence, thus killing herself.[7] Can we not also see, in the convent setting, in the public confessions, and in the theatrically constructed sets, references to Carl Th. Dreyer's *La Passion de Jeanne d'Arc* [The Passion of Joan of Arc] (1928), another tale of a woman sacrificed to male religious and political power? While Bemberg resists the extreme close-ups of the earlier film, the use of theatrical settings and tableaux certainly is shared across the decades.

Similarly, there are further examples, of cinematic *self*-referentiality: the confessions, the sickbed scenes, and several other sequences, are all already found in other Bemberg films, such as *Camila* (1984). The smashing of Sor Juana's glasses recalls a series of shots involving blindfolds in *Camila*; likewise the scenes of censorship and book-burning in the earlier film depicting the nineteenth-century regime of Juan Manuel de Rosas, but framed to recall events of the Argentine civic-military dictatorship of 1976–83. They also foreshadow her last film as a director, *De eso no se habla* [I Don't Want to Talk about It] (1993), where the bonfire is repeated in a darkly comic tone, as the mother of a young woman with dwarfism casts copies of *Snow White* and *Tom Thumb* into the flames.[8] The history of cinema, political cinema, and her own films, underlie the literary, artistic, and theatrical references. In a reversal of the expected order, we X-ray the surface of the baroque painting recreated in a 1980s movie to find a twentieth-century product: film.

Thus another rhetorical trope of the Golden Age appears, the chiasmus: cinema —
baroque art — cinema. As Forte and Miranda put it (albeit while making a semiotic
point about the film), 'the history represented in the film goes beyond the sources
used by Bemberg and creates its own referential object' (2000: 71).

And yet, to argue that the film overlooks Sor Juana's poetry risks slipping into
clichés about fidelity, or about faithfulness to the (poetic) 'spirit' of a work or an
artist, while at the same time overlooking the historical and cultural context of
Sor Juana's own literary creations. In *YPT*, Bemberg foregrounds the inseparability
of verse and drama for the Golden Age stage. The Calderonian theatre that Sor
Juana inherited and developed used verse just as modern film uses the soundtrack,
working with, often bending, rules set out in Lope de Vega's guide to the new
comedy, the *Arte nuevo de hacer comedias en este tiempo* [The New Art of Writing Plays
in this Age] (1609). The links between painting and Golden Age theatre have long
been recognized by critics.[9] Intermediality is not a new invention.

As noted above, *YPT* includes a brief snippet from the end of *Los empeños de
una casa*. Like many Golden Age and late-baroque comedies, it deals with the
pitfalls of a world of artifice and artificiality. A key scene of mistaken identities
and conversations at cross-purposes takes place in pitch darkness; actors would
have mimed their blindness for an audience in the light that could see.[10] Another
important moment finds the servant Castaño cross-dressed as the lover Leonor.
Similar crossings and mistaken identities are also found in Calderón, including
one of great philosophical importance: that the world is a dream that is in turn the
world — again, a chiasmus.[11] One thinks, too, in painting, of *Las Meninas*, with
its exploration of artistic self-perception, in a painting whose subject is perhaps its
own composition, and the place of this composition within the intricate political
hierarchies of seventeenth-century court life. Its background consists of portraits
owned by the king, a series of knowing artistic intertexts. The play of looks and
gazes, the sense of a court theatre being played out, are found again in *YPT*. The
overall effect in the latter is that portraiture — baroque portraiture, in particular —
comes to dominate the image, trumping poetry, to create the film's striking visual
effect.[12] At the same time, we might ask, what more baroque poetic trait is there
than literary self-reference? There is, though, an important difference: the Golden
Age worldview, found in the plays of Calderón and the verse of Sor Juana, was
underpinned by religious doctrine, debated and beset by controversies, no doubt,
but with at least some shared assumptions: the existence of God, an afterlife, and
possible salvation. These are not available to Bemberg; instead, her film rests on her
feminist convictions and support for women's struggles, historical and present-day.

Todo, en fin, el silencio lo ocupaba

Todo, en fin, el silencio lo ocupaba (henceforth, *Todo*), directed by the Mexican-Can-
adian filmmaker Nicolás Pereda (b. 1982), offers a contrasting vision of Sor Juana
and her work to that found in Bemberg's film. Pereda has a growing reputation,
in particular in film journals (especially online) and on the festival circuit, and
he is renowned for his slow, contemplative, and thought-provoking works. As

Nadin Mai (2016) writes: '[Pereda] has always favoured long-takes, *temps mort*, and a very minimalist storytelling'. Alongside this, Mai notes his use of 'an independent camera', a feature shared with other 'slow cinema' practitioners such as the Hungarian Tarr Béla or Argentina's Lisandro Alonso: 'the camera is not really following the protagonist [...] the camera has its own mind and moves to whatever place or whatever action it would like to record'. Kieron Corless (2012: 62), writing of another of Pereda's films, states that 'we're never entirely sure if what we're watching is real or fictional, or some headspinning combination of the two', a judgement that, as I shall argue, may also be applied to *Todo*.[13]

Critics have also noted the extreme minimalism of Pereda's films (e.g. Gutiérrez et al. 2012: 39). For Dan Russek the director forms part of a tendency in Mexican cinema away from melodrama — something strongly associated with its golden age of the 1940s, but also not alien to popular recent productions, such as director Carlos Carrera's *El crimen de Padre Amaro* [The Crime of Padre Amaro] (2002) — with 'the attenuation, the erasure, or the elision of emotions' (Russek 2012: 218). This is not an otiose choice, either, for, according to Russek, in Pereda's film *Perpetuum mobile*: 'the individual who, with traditional social models undermined, untied from community bonds, and orphaned from any collective project, cannot find in herself either the means to overcome their isolation' (2012: 228). Thus cinematic minimalism has a political edge to it, as shall be explored below.

Pereda is one of a number of Latin American filmmakers who produce what critics have labelled 'slow cinema' or 'slow movies', sometimes referred to as 'contemplative cinema'. Alongside Pereda, and another Mexican, Carlos Reygadas, Argentina's Lisandro Alonso is one of the region's most widely recognized practitioners of 'slow cinema'. His *oeuvre*, for Ira Jaffe, is characterized by a 'commitment to a sort of minimalism, detachment and indeterminacy' (2014: 115). There is in his works a resistance to fulfilling many of the most common expectations that spectators have of cinema, instead showing restraint: '[s]low movies [...] inhibit the expression of [...] feelings, just as they restrict motion, action, dialogue and glitter. Slow movies thus bring to the fore cheerless aspects of existence that are likely to worsen if ignored, but drape them in stillness, blankness, emptiness and silence' (Jaffe 2014: 9). What, then, is achieved by films that run so contrary to much commercial filmmaking, with its cultivation of speed, emotion, and escapism? For Jaffe, 'the mastery of form and the acuity of feeling that distinguish works of art, even when the subject matter is painful, have an uplifting rather than depressing effect on spectators alert to form and feeling' (2014: 9). What, one might ask, is 'uplifting' in Pereda?

For Tiago De Luca and Nuno Barradas Jorge 'slow films' are often characterized by 'strict adherence to realism and reality' (2016: 7). They also note the important links between contemporary slow or contemplative cinema and the availability of various digital technologies (in filming and reproducing) (2016: 11). They conclude — a point that is of particular relevance for Pereda's reworking of the work of Sor Juana — that 'a slow cinematic aesthetic [...] encourages a mode of engagement with images and sounds whereby slow time becomes a vehicle for introspection, reflection and thinking' (2016: 16).

Todo is a film that draws on, that quotes, a poem: Sor Juana Inés de la Cruz's *Primero sueño* [First Dream] (1692). *Primero sueño* has an important role in Sor Juana's *oeuvre*: it is her longest poem; it is widely accepted as one of the few pieces that she wrote out of personal choice; and, in recent years, it has been the subject of no little critical speculation, some of it sparked by Paz's biography (1982) — not least because of the seeming mystery of what the poem describes. Marked by the influence of Luis de Góngora, in particular his *Soledades* [Solitudes] (1613), it is also a poem that critics have praised for its originality, in both aesthetic and philosophical terms.[14]

The title of Pereda's film is taken from lines 147–50 of the poem: 'El sueño todo, en fin, lo poseía; | todo, en fin, el silencio lo ocupaba: | aun el ladrón dormía; aun el amante no se desvelaba' [In the end, sleep possessed everything | silence overtook, in the end, everything: | even the thief slept; even the lover was not awake]. It is a phrase marked by typical baroque features: the hyperbaton separating verb and subject; the near chiasmus that arrays 'sueño' — 'en fin' — 'en fin' — 'silencio'; and the parallelism or parison of 'aun el ladrón' — 'aun el amante'. Although the poem is a *silva* — a freely rhyming, loosely distributed series of seven- and eleven-syllable lines — here there is full rhyme patterned ABaB. As Paz puts it, '[a]lthough constructed with deliberate and rigorous objectivity, *Primero sueño* is secretly shot through with a personal note [...] a genuine intellectual confession' (1982: 496). *Primero sueño* recounts a journey: that of a soul freed from its body while the latter sleeps. Paz notes that in one aspect this is a trope typical of the era, but in others Sor Juana's differs from her models: '[t]he theme of the soul's journey is a religious theme and it is inseparable from [the idea of] a revelation. In Sor Juana's poem not only is there no demiurge: neither is there a revelation' (1982: 482). For Gerard Flynn, the poem shows that 'the soul cannot contemplate the cosmos without losing its sight. In trying to see everything the soul sees nothing' (1971: 27). This is a reading of the poem — as the story of a failure to achieve revelation through intellectual means — that is shared by many readers. As Andrés Sánchez Robayna puts it, '*Primero sueño* is the story of a failure: that which derives from the impossibility of knowledge ["conocer"]' (1991: 215). Furthermore, this is '[a] failure of knowledge ["conocimiento"], but not of vision' (1991: 217).

Paz acknowledges this sense of defeat or failure. But there is a further, feminist note to his reading: '[t]he failure derives not from her sex but from the limits of human understanding' (1982: 497) — for souls of course do not have a sex. At the same time, he is keen to avoid reductive biographical readings: '[t]here is no doubt that the sudden awakening ends the dream, not the soul's intellectual adventure' (1982: 496). And here Paz seems to wish to redeem the poem, or at least to identify something other than defeat and despair, as an example of Sor Juana's incessant, insatiable enthusiasm for knowledge. He finds its true novelty: '[i]t is a confession that ends in an act of faith: not in knowledge but in the desire for knowledge' (1982: 499). Thus *Primero sueño* goes beyond contemporary 'poesía del desengaño' [poetry of disillusionment] because of its enthusiasm for further knowledge (Paz 1982: 500): '[w]ith *Primero sueño* there appears a new passion in the history of our [i.e. Spanish-language] poetry: love of knowledge ["saber"]. [...] What was new was that Sor Juana turned this passion into a theme for poetry' (1982: 504).

Aída Beaupied takes issue with Paz's and others' reading of the *Sueño*. Whereas for Paz the poem inscribes an intellectual failure — although not one that brings despair — Beaupied, tracing the links between the poem and the hermetic tradition, argues instead that,

> In spite of the apparent absence of a revelation with which the poem seems to conclude, several clues in *Primero sueño* suggest the presence of doubly hermetic revelations; that is to say, hermetic because of their Hermeticist content, and also because they are hermetically hidden. (1996: 753)

In a longer, comparative study, Beaupied insists that 'nor is the fact that the poem does not openly declare its message a sign that it does not contain one, particularly if we are dealing with an esoteric message' (1997: 12). What is especially important is the role of the reader in completing or filling the many silences — which most critics agree are present in the work (1997: 23). Beaupied argues that the poem contains coded references to scholastic and Neoplatonic philosophy, and presents theories about knowledge and ideas of 'transgression and its punishment' (1997: 59). If there is pessimism, or frustration on display in the poem, it is not because knowledge is impossible, but because 'el saber no se puede comunicar' [knowledge cannot be communicated] (1997: 67). One might add that this is not only for philosophical reasons: it must also be related to the limits of what one in Sor Juana's position in her particular society — with the risks of religious censure or punishment at the hands of the Inquisition — might say or commit to paper.

Even if we do not agree with Beaupied's hard thesis and her somewhat esoteric reading of the poem, to regard it as recounting simply a failure of the intellectual project is to overlook its context in both biographical and socio-political terms. Here, readings that focus on aesthetic aspects of the poem can be of use, in particular when we consider its cinematic adaptation. For Paz, too, Sor Juana in *Primero sueño* 'sets out to describe a reality that, by definition, is not visible' (1982: 470). This paradox is vital for understanding Pereda's film: '[t]he poem is the story of a spiritual vision that ends in a non-vision' ['una no-visión'] (1982: 482). There is thus a 'double negation' in the poem: 'the silence of great spaces and the vision of the non-vision. Here lies the great originality of Sor Juana's poem' (1982: 482). Pereda's film aims to screen this encounter between intellectual enthusiasm, the vision that is not a vision, and the limits of the sayable — and allows us to rethink Sor Juana's 'failure'.

Todo begins with some forty seconds of darkness, in which rather indistinct voices are (just about) audible on the soundtrack. After a minute, a black and white image slowly appears — a static medium-long shot of a person lying down, still, with a circle of brightness — perhaps the moon, perhaps a spotlight — over their head. As the illumination steadily increases, we are able to see more: the figure is a woman, dressed in religious habit, and to the left, spoiling the integrity of the painterly tableau, is a member of the film crew, experimenting with a light. Voices discuss angles and lighting, while the figure remains static on a raised table or dais. Two minutes in, there is a cut, the camera angle moving 90-degrees to view what seems to be the same scene, now looking directly at the top of the actor's head. Now the light comes from one, possibly two candles and a spotlight, the former not visible in the previous shot. This opening sequence establishes some of the film's key motifs and techniques: self-referentiality; plays with light and shadow; and a very flexible attitude to continuity editing.

The film is indeed marked by a certain slowness — but not in all respects does it follow the aesthetic model of, for example, Lisandro Alonso. There are plentiful long takes — shots tend to last around a minute, sometimes longer, and there is very limited camera movement. Also, there is very little action in the shot — the protagonist, played by Jesusa Rodríguez, is often still, standing, sitting, lying down, or waiting. What movement there is — not of the camera, but of what is filmed — takes place 'backstage', behind the camera, as it were: the comings and goings of crew and others present, including janitors and security staff, as the off-screen comes on-screen.

This appearance of members of the crew and others involved in the production or staging of the work on or around the screen is part of the film's overt self-referentiality. In a sense, *Todo* is a 'making of' for a film that does not exist — rather like watching the DVD extras but without having the film itself. Throughout, what we see and hear on screen contains multiple comments about the process of filmmaking itself — acting, blocking, lighting, and camera work. Indeed, alongside Rodríguez's performed readings of the poem, the entire vocal track consists of comments about the process of staging and filming itself, either from the crew or Rodríguez herself.

Likewise, much of the action — if that is the correct word, for the film itself treats 'action'/'acción' with some irony — consists of the filming of the film itself. Equipment — particularly lights, but also cameras — is moved around and adjusted by various members of the crew. Rodríguez alters her props or costume in between those relatively brief sequences in which she performs as Sor Juana. Even these are tentative or abortive — attempting a particular movement or way of acting, to see whether it will work, and discovering, at least in Rodríguez's opinion, that it does not. Rodríguez herself divides her time in the film between three activities: reading the words of Sor Juana's *Primero sueño*; waiting quietly, patiently, and stilly, while the team make adjustments around her; and commenting on either her own performance or its *mise en scène*.

One notes also the presence of screens on screen, monitors on which we see another angle on the action — or lack of it — or the rushes of something that has been previously filmed. This, along with the strong impression that often we are witnessing a rehearsal, reinforces the feeling that as spectators we are always looking from the wrong point of view. On sixteen minutes, we see a side-angle medium shot, the lighting of which leaves the right-hand side of the frame — including Rodríguez's face and hands — in near total darkness. As she reads — 'el manjar transformado' [the delicacy transformed] (*Primero sueño*, line 838) — she appears to raise and consume a communion wafer, but this action is almost wholly obscured. Both as herself and in character as Sor Juana, Rodríguez often appears to be addressing someone other than us, the viewers; even when she performs 'to camera', it is to a camera other than the one through which we are viewing. At about ten minutes, we watch a grainier version, from a different angle, of the sequence that we have just seen, doubly mediating the image. On other occasions, when we do get to see the 'right' shot, it is mediated again, for example shown on a blurry monitor, or lit in such a way as to partially obscure the screen.[15]

The film makes use of recognizable images from what might be called the 'iconography' of Sor Juana. Just as Bemberg recreates certain tableaux, Pereda stages, or partially stages shots that mirror famous images of the nun. For example, in one sequence we see Rodríguez as Juana sitting at her desk with her papers, close to one of the most famous and oft-reproduced historical images of her — in fact it appears in Bemberg's earlier film. But at the same time, these are interrupted — by the boom mic and the monitor that intrude from the right. We also see sequences in which Rodríguez 'performs' elements of the poem: erecting the pyramids (using a tablecloth) or consuming the celestial 'manjar' — in this case a host. But these scenes too are scotched: partially or almost wholly obscured, or interrupted by the protagonist and the crew's often critical commentary. Related to this is the way sections of the poem are read and that reading filmed — the *mise en scène* of the poetic performance, as it were. For example, one sequence of around thirty seconds consists of almost total darkness on screen — broken only when a monitor flashes into view — and discussions about framing and movement are heard. Rodríguez then begins to read, from around line 540 of *Primero sueño* onwards. We see just a small image on a monitor, itself multiply reflected and lit by little more than a candle, as she declaims Sor Juana's words about 'un concepto confuso' [a confused concept] and 'el informe embrión' [formless embryo] (lines 548–49). The image has prefigured — ironically, even comically — the reading of the poem.

There is a linked tendency in the film towards moments of *mise en abîme*. In the exterior scenes that begin in the last third of the film, we see Rodríguez fully costumed in period religious habit — indeed a copy of the dress worn by the nun in the most frequently reproduced images of her. In those images, the *religieuse* is often depicted with an oval emblem, or *escudo*, on the front of her habit, including a biblical image. In *Todo*, the religious image appears to be — although given the lighting one cannot be wholly certain — that of Sor Juana herself, on the round emblem that Rodríguez wears on her chest. The image is — as one by now might well expect — not clear or large enough for us to see whether that Sor Juana has another Sor Juana depicted on her chest, and so on, and so on.[16]

As mentioned above, 'slow' movies are characterized by their apparent commitment to reality and realism — seeming to follow a line sketched out by André Bazin (1967) and Gilles Deleuze (2005) in their studies of the sequence shot and the 'time-image', respectively — both related to the oft-cited 'indexical' realist function of cinema. And yet, despite the many 'slow' features of *Todo*, this commitment to reality and realism is treated with no little playfulness. Pereda himself, quoted in Carlos Gutiérrez et al. (2012: 40), stated: 'I'm not interested in capturing reality; I'm interested in talking about it. Realism and hyperrealism have nothing to do with this.' Firstly, although what we see on screen is characterized

Fig. 9.4. Shrine from Nicolás Pereda's *Todo, en fin, el silencio lo ocupaba* (2009)

by many realist touches — diegetic sound and lighting; the presence of non-actors; errors and imperfections — it is never wholly clear *what* we are actually watching. Is this a rehearsal for a play? Is it the making of another film? If this is *real*, what is the *fiction* with which it would contrast? Contextual information makes it clear that this *real* is *also* the fiction — the making-of is the subject of the making-of (and so on — like the image of Sor Juana on the emblem on the dress of the actor playing Sor Juana, and so forth — another *mise en abîme*).

Secondly, the film has a surprising lightness of touch, incorporating ironic and humorous moments that undermine the seriousness often associated with slow movies and their realism. For example, around seven minutes in, the directorial cry of 'Acción' is followed immediately by precisely the *absence* of any action. Again, on thirty-nine minutes, the same instruction is followed immediately by a cut to black and almost complete silence. One might read these sequences as a comment on the film's status — for in a making-of, it is *not* the action of the film-proper that follows the director's instructions. But beyond such meta-filmic comment, one detects a certain, very subtle humour — the same that might be encountered in other provocative, self-referential documentaries from Latin America, such as Albertina Carri's *Los rubios* [The Blonds] (Argentina, 2003), or thinking back further, Luis Ospina and Carlos Mayolo's corrosively funny *Agarrando pueblo* [The Vampires of Poverty] (Colombia, 1977).

Part of the film's distinctive aesthetic is its presentation to the viewer of scenes framed so as to give little indication of how one might react. As with the 'deadpan' comedy of, for example, Fernando Eimbcke (e.g. *Temporada de patos* [Duck Season], Mexico, 2004) or Argentina's Martín Rejtman, there are long, inexpressive takes here that, almost as a result of the lack of any obvious reaction, inspire (quiet) laughter. One thinks of the extended shot of a slightly kitsch shrine — it seems to the Virgin Mary — including a crucified Christ alongside flashing fairy lights (see Figure 9.4, above). This is realism, and it is reality, but in the absence of indications to the spectator — through reaction shots or montage — as to how to react, one very likely response is humour.

Indeed, throughout the film, one has a sense that, subtly, something of an aesthetic of failure is being sketched, with an attendant, deadpan, sense of humour. In a film ostensibly adapted from a poem, the readings from it are worthy of comment: sections from *Primero sueño* appear in no particular order, reinforcing the impression that this is a making-of. They also start and end as if at random. This creates a strong sense of interruption, even failure. Indeed failure is a clear motif here, as lines are forgotten, lighting does not quite work, angles are wrong, and costumes malfunction. One is reminded of Jack Halberstam's reflection on failure as 'alternative ways of knowing and being that are not unduly optimistic, but nor are they mired in nihilistic critical dead ends' (2011: 24); that 'under certain circumstances failing [...] may in fact offer more creative, more cooperative, more surprising ways of being in the world' (2011: 2). Or, as Cecilia Macon puts it in her work on Albertina Carri, an aesthetic of failure allows artists to be 'willful without being optimistic' (2018: 409).

Even in those scenes that demonstrate a certain theatricality, this dramatic effect is quickly undercut. For example, at around twenty-one minutes, Rodríguez reads a section from *Primero sueño* (beginning at line 340) describing the pyramids of Egypt, having erected their form with the cloth and then taken a striking position atop the table. The tone of her voice changes — projected more, with a seriousness in the phrasing and cadence: this is clearly acting, not conversation. As spectators we can infer a dramatic performance, but the position of the camera, the combined darkness and extreme brightness of the shot, and the presence of monitors, another camera, and crew members on the edge of the scene, all distance us as spectators from those (putative subjects) fully immersed in a dramatic performance or fictional film. There is music, and dramatic music at that. And yet everything points to interruption and failure. After Rodríguez breaks off, she comments on her own performance: the pyramids take several attempts, and they do not stay up very well. She then comments on her disappointment with the results of this performance.

In another sequence, Rodríguez gets her lines wrong as she declaims from the poem. This is followed by a discussion of whether this mistake can be cut in the final version — a final version that of course does not exist. In a further sequence, on thirty-three minutes, we see her draped in a sheet, which she then waves with her arms to become the sails of a ship, accompanying or dramatizing her reading of the poem (from line 560), just as the building of pyramids had done earlier. But our view is from behind her, with much of the scene in shadow, and a bright spotlight, near the centre of the frame, obscuring much of the scene. As she casts herself down onto the stage floor, dramatic music plays from off, discordant strings, menacing percussion, and then a female operatic solo voice. But again, we are watching the action from behind, from backstage. There is a cut, to a different angle — still behind the actor, who stands up and walks towards the stage exit, while a rather threatening cello plays. But then we hear 'corte' [cut] and a discussion of how better to perform the scene, in which both Rodríguez and an invisible director give their directions. Again, the film shows and then hides its hand, as if striving to undermine itself.

Towards the end of *Todo*, as rain falls, the combination of water droplets and the bokeh effect almost totally obscure any action. On fifty-six minutes, the camera jerks and ends facing down. We hear the sound of feet and the downpour, and someone asks someone else if the camera has got wet. The closing minutes of the film show heavy rain, with the accompanying noise on the soundtrack — one assumes that filming has had to finish for the day, although of course this camera carries on recording. The final close up is of raindrops and water on the floor, and what look like discarded extension cable connectors: a striking image of a film shoot interrupted.

While the film works hard to undermine itself, the casting of Jesusa Rodríguez as Sor Juana is an important and telling decision on the part of Pereda. Rodríguez is an actor and political activist, and an elected senator for the left-wing MORENA party. She has played and impersonated Sor Juana on a variety of occasions in the past, often as politically charged theatre or as a public intervention. As Diana Taylor (2017: 78) writes, with her artistic partner (and wife) Liliana Felipe, '[t]heir performatic interventions have interrupted Mexico's social and political life with their queer, feminist performance practice and activist work over thirty years'. Rodríguez supported Andrés Manuel López Obrador (aka AMLO) — now president — in the controversial 2006 elections (Taylor 2017: 85). 'She took over the choreography of AMLO's massive recount campaign that led to a popular occupation of the Zócalo and Reforma [...]. Reading rooms, pop-up museums and art spaces, outdoor cinemas, and many other forms of public expression became active along the route of resistance' (2017: 85). Taylor also notes that '[Rodríguez] found herself using the words of the famous seventeenth-century nun Sor Juana Inés de la Cruz to talk about corruption: "robbery, repeated, is never petty"' (86). She has more than a little in common with the role that she plays in this film, as Taylor puts it: '[w]hile it seems that Mexican officials tolerate the critique from these artists, the pair have been censored, shut down, and threatened for their comments about the Catholic Church, Mexican politicians, and other corrupt or repressive forces in the country' (2017: 81).

In a film marked by its restraint and lack of, or ironic attitude towards, theatricality, this is an extraordinary performance by Jesusa Rodríguez. One sequence, lasting over a minute, sees her naked from the waist up, practicing painting on her arms and torso. She runs through her lines and nibbles on what appears to be a communion wafer. In the next shot, in close up, we see her cleaning off ink or paint, discussing the merits of dirtying a nightgown with make-up. In many sequences, it is clear that Rodríguez calls the shots, directing the staging and shooting of the action. We are implicitly watching the filming of *another* performance, one put together by Rodríguez (and her collaborators, perhaps).

FIG. 9.5. Jesusa Rodríguez as Sor Juana in Nicolás Pereda's
Todo, en fin, el silencio lo ocupaba (2009)

What, then, of the overwhelming *darkness* that characterizes so much of this film? Often nothing is shown on screen, or very little at all is visible. The lighting that is used, or is present, often does not illuminate, but rather blinds. One possible cause is that the lighting is not only diegetic, but also second-hand — not designed to light the film that we are seeing, but for *another* performance or shooting. The final third of the film moves outside, and the Torre Latinoamericana (one of the most recognizable and famous buildings in Mexico City) comes into view.[17] The camera pans to reveal Rodríguez, now in full costume as Sor Juana (Figure 9.5, above). It then pulls back to reveal a chapel or church. The evening or night-time filming is accompanied by very bright lights. The effect of these apes the chiaroscuro of her habit. The instruction from the director is that she should move so that she creates a 'gran sombra' [big shadow] as she exits. As the protagonist approaches the lights, the white on her costume turns almost fluorescent, burnt out bright on the film. After checking with the crew that the shot is to their satisfaction, she then proceeds to repeat the manoeuvre. Alongside the play with light, and with (our, the spectators') vision, again the idea of a definitive version of the film is called into question — or at least we are reminded that there is no definitive version, because we are watching it, and what we are seeing often exceeds the capacity of our vision.

A corollary to this play of light and blindness in the film is its approach to silence. In a film that portrays, or screens, a version of a poem that deals with a vision that is too powerful for us to behold, we are left with blinding illumination and a series of silences. Hence the bright lights throughout; hence also the persistent questions about how best to frame, illuminate and shoot the action; and hence the repeated — not tragic, but almost comic — failures that we see before us. But Rodríguez — like Sor Juana, perhaps — is condemned, blessed, to fail again, to fail better. This allows us to look beyond Paz and Beaupied's readings of Sor Juana and *Primero sueño*, as failure, or otherwise. This Sisyphean labour lies at the heart of this politically charged, feminist film. Perhaps not uplifting (*pace* Jaffe 2014: 9), but inspiring — a wilful failure, reflecting Jesusa Rodríguez's own career of political activism, pointing to what Halberstam called 'art without markets, drama without script, narrative without progress' (2011: 88).[18]

In conclusion, Pereda casts an important figure within contemporary Mexican feminism to make a film that constantly questions its own nature, making the viewer ask at every turn what it is that we are watching on screen. *Todo* raises the ante on the self-referentiality of Bemberg's film, being not just a film that analyses and references film and films, but a film about its own possibilities of screening a poet and their poetry, indeed of screening anything at all. Pereda also takes Bemberg's distinctive use of chiaroscuro to extremes, fitting given the importance of plays between light and dark to baroque aesthetics generally, and questions of vision to Sor Juana's long poem in particular. Pereda's film, like Bemberg's, is highly intermedial, but the difference is that it constantly undermines itself; if Bemberg uses poetry to advance narrative, at the service of a clear feminist message, Pereda does so to question the very possibility of screening verse, while at the same time hinting at a vital point about failure in Mexican politics. Again, we see another version of that baroque trope par excellence, the chiasmus: Bemberg's ostensibly feminist film makes self-reflective points about the nature of art; Pereda's ostensibly self-referential film makes a political, feminist statement. The films illustrate two different, but complementary, ways to 'read' poetry on screen, and demonstrate the rich contribution that poetry can make to film and which film can make to our understanding and enjoyment of poetry.

Works Cited

Bazin, André. 1967. *What Is Cinema?* vol. 1 (Berkeley, Los Angeles & London: University of California Press)

Beaupied, Aída. 1996. 'El silencio hermético en *Primero sueño* de sor Juana a la luz de la figura e ideas de Giordano Bruno', *Hispania*, 79: 752–62

—— 1997. *Narciso hermético: Sor Juana Inés de la Cruz y José Lezama Lima* (Liverpool: Liverpool University Press)

Berger, John. 2005 [1984]. *And Our Faces, My Heart, Brief as Photos* (London: Bloomsbury)

Bingham, Dennis. 2010. *Whose Lives Are They Anyway? The Biopic as Contemporary Film Genre* (New Brunswick, NJ: Rutgers University Press)

Brooke, Alice. 2019. Personal communication via email. In author's possession, December

Corless, Kieron. 2012. 'Free and Flexible', *Sight and Sound*, 22: 62–63

Daney, Serge. 2004. 'The Tracking Shot in *Kapo*', *Senses of Cinema*, 30 <http://sensesofcinema.com/2004/feature-articles/kapo_daney/> [accessed 18 June 2020]

De la Cruz, Sor Juana Inés. 2004. *Antología poética*, ed. by José Miguel Oviedo (Madrid: Alianza)

De Luca, Tiago, and Nuno Barradas Jorge. 2016. 'Introduction: From Slow Cinema to Slow Cinemas', in *Slow Cinema*, ed. by Tiago de Luca and Nuno Barradas Jorge (Edinburgh: Edinburgh University Press), pp. 1–21

Deleuze, Gilles. 2005 [1985]. *Cinema 2: The Time-Image* (London: Continuum)

FISHER, MARK. 2018. *K-Punk: The Collected and Unpublished Writings of Mark Fisher* (London: Repeater)

FLYNN, GERARD. 1971. *Sor Juana Inés de la Cruz* (New York: Twayne)

FORTE, NORA B., and RAQUEL MIRANDA. 2000. 'Literatura y cine: desplazamientos y transposiciones en *Yo, la peor de todas* de María Luisa Bemberg', *Anclajes*, 4: 57–74

FOUCAULT, MICHEL. 1994 [1966]. *The Order of Things: An Archaeology of the Human Sciences* (New York: Vintage)

FRUTOS ESTEBAN, FRANCISCO JAVIER, and CRISTINA GARCÍA-CAMINO MATEOS. 2003. 'La magia de la imagen', *Litoral*, 235: 20–35

GÓMEZ, MARÍA ASUNCIÓN. 1997. 'Mirando de cerca "Mujer, comedia y pintura" en las obras de Lope de Vega y Calderón de la Barca', *Bulletin of the Comediantes*, 49: 273–93

GUTIÉRREZ, CARLOS, GERARDO NARANJO, and NICOLÁS PEREDA. 2012. 'Gerardo Naranjo and Nicolás Pereda', *BOMB*, 119: 38–45

HALBERSTAM, JACK. 2011. *The Queer Art of Failure* (Durham, NC: Duke University Press)

JAFFE, IRA. 2014. *Slow Movies: Countering the Cinema of Action* (New York and West Sussex, England: Wallflower)

KAUP, MONIKA. 2014. *Neobaroque in the Americas: Alternative Modernities in Literature, Visual Art, and Film* (Charlottesville: University of Virginia Press)

KING, JOHN. 2000. *Magical Reels: A History of Cinema in Latin America* (London: Verso)

——, SHEILA WHITAKER, and ROSA BOSCH (eds). 2000. *An Argentine Passion: María Luisa Bemberg and her Films* (London: Verso)

MACON, CECILIA. 2018. 'Time Riding: Albertina Carri and the Ironic Affective Presence of the Past', *Journal of Latin American Cultural Studies*, 27: 399–414

MAI, NADIN. 2016. '*Los Ausentes* — Nicolas Pereda (2014)', *The Art(s) of Slow Cinema*, 9 June <https://theartsofslowcinema.com/2016/06/09/los-ausentes-nicolas-pereda-2014/> [accessed 18 June 2020]

MANASSERO, ROBERTO. 2013. 'Nicolás Pereda', *Cineforum*, 53: 52–53

MILLER, DENISE. 2000. 'María Luisa Bemberg's Interpretation of Octavio Paz's *Sor Juana*', in *An Argentine Passion: María Luisa Bemberg and her Films*, ed. by John King, Sheila Whitaker, and Rosa Bosch (London: Verso), pp. 137–73

PAZ, OCTAVIO. 1982. *Sor Juana Inés de la Cruz o las trampas de la fe* (Barcelona: Seix Barral)

—— 1988. *Sor Juana: Her Life and Her World* (London: Faber)

PÉREZ MARTÍNEZ, HERÓN. 2008. 'La vigencia de Sor Juana Inés de la Cruz', *Espiga*, 16/17: 59–78

PERRY, ELIZABETH. 2012. 'Sor Juana *fecit*: Sor Juana Inés de la Cruz and the Art of Miniature Painting', *Early Modern Women: An Interdisciplinary Journal*, 7: 3–32

RUSSEK, DAN. 2012. 'Soledad y solidaridad en el cine mexicano reciente: en torno a *Japón* (2000), *Párpados azules* (2007) y *Perpetuum mobile* (2009)', *Revista Canadiense de Estudios Hispánicos*, 37: 217–32

SÁNCHEZ ROBAYNA, ANDRÉS. 1991. *Para leer 'Primero sueño' de Sor Juana Inés de la Cruz* (Mexico City: Fondo de Cultura Económica)

SARABIA, ROSA. 2002. 'Sor Juana o las trampas de la restitución', *Revista Canadiense de Estudios Hispánicos*, 27: 119–38

SPERANZA, ROBERT SCOTT. 2002. 'Verses in the Celluloid: Poetry in Film from 1910–2002, With Special Attention to the Development of the Film-Poem' (unpublished PhD thesis, University of Sheffield, British Library microfilm)

TAYLOR, DIANA. 2017. 'Raging On: The Politics of Violence in the Work of Jesusa Rodríguez and Liliana Felipe', in *Performance, Feminism and Affect in Neoliberal Times*, ed. by Elin Diamond, Denise Varney, and Candice Amich (New York: Palgrave Macmillan), pp. 77–90

Vidal, Belén. 2014. 'Introduction: The Biopic and its Critical Contexts', in *The Biopic in Contemporary Film Culture*, ed. by Tom Brown and Belén Vidal (London: Routledge), pp. 1–32

Notes to Chapter 9

1. I would like to thank Alice Brooke for her help with bibliography on Sor Juana. Oliver Noble Wood read a draft of this chapter and I am most grateful to him for a number of very helpful suggestions, and also to an anonymous peer reviewer for their positive contribution. All errors and omissions are mine and mine alone.

2. There is another film of the life of the nun (played by Andrea Palma), *Sor Juana Inés de la Cruz*, directed by Ramón Peón, from 1935. *Constelaciones* (dir. Alfredo Joskowicz, 1980) deals with the figures of both Sor Juana and her compatriot and peer Carlos de Sigüenza y Góngora. Also worth noting is the recent Mexican Netflix series, *Juana Inés* (2016). These fall beyond the scope of this study. For a detailed insight into the state of Sor Juana studies, see Herón Pérez Martínez (2008).

3. On Bemberg's use of other sources, including the *Respuesta a Sor Filotea de la Cruz*, see Forte and Miranda (2000: 64–66).

4. Unless otherwise stated in the bibliography, all translations are by the author.

5. These are also known as 'biofilms'. Vidal observes the 'heavy Euro-American slant of biopic studies' (2014: 23); it is hoped that this chapter will contribute in small part to addressing this bias.

6. And see Berger (2005: 80–86) for a broader reflection on the use of chiaroscuro in his painting.

7. See e.g. Daney (2004).

8. It may be worth noting that *YPT* features a brief scene of two dwarves, wrestling in Aztec fancy dress, for the entertainment of the viceregal court.

9. As María Asunción Gómez puts it, 'the interlinking of visual arts and theatre reaches a peak in the Spanish Golden Age that is only comparable to that of today. Allusions to works of art (paintings and sculptures mainly) abound in the seventeenth-century theatrical corpus, as well as the works' creators (real or fictitious); however, Lope de Vega and Calderón de la Barca are undoubtedly those who most insistently demonstrate in their writings this unusual concern for the visual arts' (1997: 273); 'Calderón and Lope's repeated allusions to painting, and especially to female portraiture, go far beyond the purely ornamental. They constitute intertextual reflections that underline the mimetic function of pictorial art and, implicitly, of dramatic art. [...] Reflected in these works, therefore, is a constant concern (so baroque and so current) with drawing the dividing line between representation and the represented world, between appearances and reality' (1997: 289); from the earliest cinematographic records, via Orson Welles, to the works of Bemberg and Pereda, this is a central concern, too, of filmmakers.

10. This is a conjecture, but one based on Golden Age theatre practice generally (e.g. plays by law being performed during the hours of daylight) and the 2004 RSC production of the play in translation by Catherine Boyle.

11. Both the *auto sacramental* [passion play], *El gran teatro del mundo* [The Great Theatre of the World] (*c.* 1634) and the *comedia*, *La vida es sueño* [Life is a Dream] (1635), explore the possibility of life on earth as essentially illusory, the performance of a role, or at least only a preparation or test for the more important hereafter. Darkness as the cause of mistaken identity also features in *El médico de su honra* [The Surgeon [alternatively 'Physician'] of His Honour] (1637), when Pedro is mistaken by his wife Doña Mencía for the Prince, Enrique, who is surreptitiously courting her; in contrast to Sor Juana's work, terrible consequences ensue for the female lead.

12. In Gilles Deleuze's *Cinema 2*, he reflects on the links between classic cinema and baroque portraiture. For Deleuze, the key figure is Orson Welles, in whose work, in particular through his use of depth of field, one encounters a 'radical change [to] the very notion of centre' (2005: 138); he thus takes up 'a transformation of thought which originally took place in [...] the seventeenth century [...] the baroque age par excellence' (138). In Bemberg's film, it is the use

of chiaroscuro and tableaux that recall baroque portraiture. One is reminded, too, of Michel Foucault's analysis of Velázquez's painting *Las Meninas* at the opening of *Les Mots et les Choses* [*The Order of Things*] (1966), in which he writes, '[n]o gaze is stable, or rather, in the neutral furrow of the gaze piercing at a right angle through the canvas, subject and object, the spectator and the model, reverse their roles to infinity' (1994: 5); '[t]he entire picture is looking out at a scene for which it is itself a scene' (1994: 14). And yet, it is the sovereign who plays the key role: the royal couple, visible in the mirror at the back of the room, 'provide the centre around which the entire representation is ordered' (1994: 15). For Foucault, this sets the work in an earlier historical period to our own; Bemberg instead aims to show echoes and similarities between the colonial period and today.

13. See also Manassero (2013: 52).

14. And, as Frutos Esteban and García-Camino Mateos note, it has an important place in the history of the film-poetry nexus, containing — they claim — the first reference in Spanish literature to a proto-cinematic *linterna mágica* or magic lantern (2003: 27).

15. There is one further moment of simultaneous obscurity and self-reference: *Todo* appears to have been filmed in the Foro Sor Juana Inés de la Cruz, at the National Autonomous University, in Mexico City — one shot, from floor level, briefly shows the word 'Juana' printed on the floor, and what might be the rest of her name away at an angle. But it is not clear, and one can only infer this from contextual information.

16. The *escudo* was relatively common in nuns' portraiture in this period; in most Sor Juana portraits, the image is the Annunciation, with the Archangel Gabriel on the right, Mary on the left, and the Holy Spirit as a dove above them. Alice Brooke (2019) has suggested that this references the mediaeval tradition of portraying Mary at the Annunciation reading a book, as she is in all the known *escudos* in Sor Juana portraits. See also Perry (2012).

17. It is also the setting for the climax of Alfonso Cuarón's first feature film, *Sólo con tu pareja* (1991).

18. Mark Fisher (2018: 530) has written critically and quite convincingly against the ethics of failure as promoted by Halberstam et al., though with principal reference to British politics. In our case, however, we are dealing with a very different context; and while Rodríguez has encountered some political success in recent years, as a senator in AMLO's government, it would be hard to forget the experience of repeated failures against seemingly immovable obstacles and implacable opponents.

CHAPTER 10

❖

Visualizing the Poet's Struggle: Poetic Filmmaking and the Search for Peace in Mexico

Jessica Wax-Edwards

The increasingly pervasive violence of Mexico's ongoing drug war incited the renowned poet and essayist Javier Sicilia to found the peace movement *El Movimiento por la paz con justicia y dignidad* (MPJD) [The Movement for Peace with Justice and Dignity], after the murder of his twenty-four-year-old son, Juan Francisco Sicilia Ortega, in March 2011. Following his son's death, Sicilia announced his retirement from poetry and on 6 April 2011 he convened a protest march of more than 20,000 people from the city of Cuernavaca to the nation's capital city, to demand an end to the violence devastating the country (*El Universal* 2014). This first example of large-scale civic mobilization was quickly followed by a second march, known as the Silent March (5–8 May) (Casasús 2011). The rallies that followed dwarfed these first two efforts in size and ambition, collectively covering more than 40,000 kilometres and nineteen states (the Caravan of Solace (Navarro 2011), 4–10 June; the Caravan of Hope (Álvarez Icaza 2011), 9–19 September). Sicilia's personal experience of loss united families in their search for justice and recognition. Prior to Sicilia's involvement in protesting the government's role in the conflict, such experiences had been largely ignored or denigrated by the state. The rallies created a unifying thread that brought together many individuals and families suffering alone and, with its marches and demonstrations, delivered a collective mode of action, communication and grief (Goggin and Torres 2014).

Sicilia's experience of familial trauma forms the basis for two stylistically divergent films that I will analyse in this chapter. The first, a PBS documentary directed by Kelly Duane de la Vega and Katie Galloway entitled *El poeta* (2012), is an experiential and often visually poetic representation of the poet/activist that follows Sicilia on his journey across Mexico. With a keen focus on the characterization of the poet figure, the documentary conveys a personal narrative of suffering and loss that reflects the collective struggle for peace and justice embodied by Sicilia's protest movement. Despite its largely conventional TV documentary format, the film's focus on the character of the poet and his unique role in starting and leading the movement is paralleled in the film style where a visually poetic register co-exists with the traditional didactic mode of expository documentary. As part of the Voces[1] series, *El poeta* is distributed across the US and aimed primarily at Latino Americans.

The second, Pablo Orta's *El hijo del poeta* (2012), is a 5.17 minute short experimental film about loss and the search for peace protagonized by a fictionalized, nameless poet and narrated using Sicilia's final poem 'El mundo ya no es digno de la palabra' [The world is no longer worthy of the word]. As the film acknowledges in its final title sequence, its story is inspired by Sicilia's poem, and though it makes no reference to the movement he started, the relationship between poetry and violence is interrogated through a form of visually poetic filmmaking. Despite its length, its topic of representation is ambitious as well as pertinent to Mexico's current crisis. The short was chosen as winner of the 'Colima en corto' competition as part of the Festival Colima de Cine 2012 and was selected to participate in Regard sur le Court Métrage au Saguenay in Quebec, Canada (Loera 2012).

These works present the effects of the drug war on a microcosmic scale in both real and imagined narratives, generating insight into the socio-historical climate in which they were produced. As Mexican essayist and documentarian Carlos Mendoza argues, the dividing lines between documentary and fiction are often imperceptible (2009). Thus, what links the primary texts selected is the titular poet who constitutes a microcosmic node where the effects of sustained national violence and collective loss intersect. There is a longstanding trend in Mexico for artists to respond to issues of violence and trauma though visual means, and the engaged role of poetry and poets in confronting violence, particularly with regard to the contemporary drug war, is no less prevalent.[2] This chapter explores the characterization of the poet figure (Sicilia) as represented onscreen in both documentary and fiction narratives and examines the capacity of poetic language (both visual and verbal) to contend with unseen violence and cataclysmic trauma.

El poeta (2012)

From its very title, *El poeta*'s approach to the topic of a militarized drug war and the igniting of one of Mexico's most significant contemporary social protest movements is anchored in the poignant figure of the poet. Around this central figure, the documentary supplies a persuasive rhetorical framework that explores the causes of violence as well as the efforts of citizens to combat these systemic issues peacefully. From a documentary theory standpoint, the film's reliance on an informing logic, namely its didactic approach to the exposition of the subject matter, positions *El poeta* as primarily expository in its treatment of the topic. *El poeta*'s recourse to non-fiction tropes, including but not limited to expert interviews (with journalists and family members for example) and use of archival news footage as well as digitized maps that pinpoint specific locations for the viewer, all contribute to this classification. Bill Nichols (2010: 167) writes that 'Expository documentaries rely heavily on an informing logic carried by the spoken word'. Mendoza aligns the reliance on the interview as classically journalistic but suggests that its use alongside visual information renders the process original to documentary (Mendoza 2009).

In the context of *El poeta*, it is significant that this spoken word logic is limited largely to prosaic rhetoric. That is not to say, however, that the language and imagery used are not, at times, in essence affective or poetic, to use Nichols's terms, as is discussed below. Expository documentaries still rely on the use of expressive imagery and storytelling to convey the weight of their arguments (Nichols 2010: 167). There are numerous examples of this in *El poeta*, for instance the voiceover that accompanies the home footage used near the start of the film. A sound bridge is created between the extremely grainy amateur footage of a family trip to the beach and Sicilia's interview with the filmmakers by overlaying the poet's words onto these intimate images. The joining of the two sources places emphasis on Sicilia's use of language and its symbolic role. The poet's voice anthropomorphizes a Mexico that prior to the violence 'tenía sueños' [had dreams] over images of laughing young people. Using a simile, he describes the manner in which parents would wait for their children 'como una esperanza abierta al futuro' [like an open hope for the future], his words accompanied by footage of joyful children playing in the sand and sea. Finally, over a clip of a family holding hands and running towards the camera, he repeats the reference to dreams adding, 'podíamos tener un horizonte hacia donde ir' [we had a horizon to head towards]. Not only does the language here align the former dreams of Mexico with those of its young people, but the carefully selected footage complements Sicilia's word choice to produce a visually and verbally nostalgic portrayal of the past. This utopia is interrupted by the use of contemporary news footage that breaks abruptly with the calm imagery and narration of these scenes, giving way to a clear and negative image of the present, represented by the presidency of Felipe Calderón (2006–12) and the launch of his militarization strategy in December 2006. Juxtapositions such as these effectively convey the film's argument using both expository and poetic techniques without the subordination of one to the other.

While *El poeta* is largely an expository documentary, Nichols' modes are not prescriptive and most documentaries constitute a hybrid of various modes. *El poeta* embraces the evocative power of poetic association in its storytelling, but does not necessarily adhere to what Nichols terms the poetic mode of documentary filmmaking. According to Nichols (2010: 162):

> The poetic mode sacrifices the conventions of continuity editing [...] The filmmaker's engagement is with film form as much as or more than with social actors. This mode explores associations and patterns that involve temporal rhythms and spatial juxtapositions.

A key example of the filmmakers' engagement with film form is witnessed during the opening titles of the documentary. The film commences with an out-of-focus and most likely handheld establishing shot of the US/Mexican border at night; the pace of the footage is discernibly slowed with small camera movements drawing attention to the passing headlights of cars. The gentle shifting of the camera combined with the steady flow of traffic subtly vivifies the space that supplies a backdrop to the didactic white intertitles that appear across the dark blue sky. The composition of the words comprises a mix of bold block capitals and standard English type: for

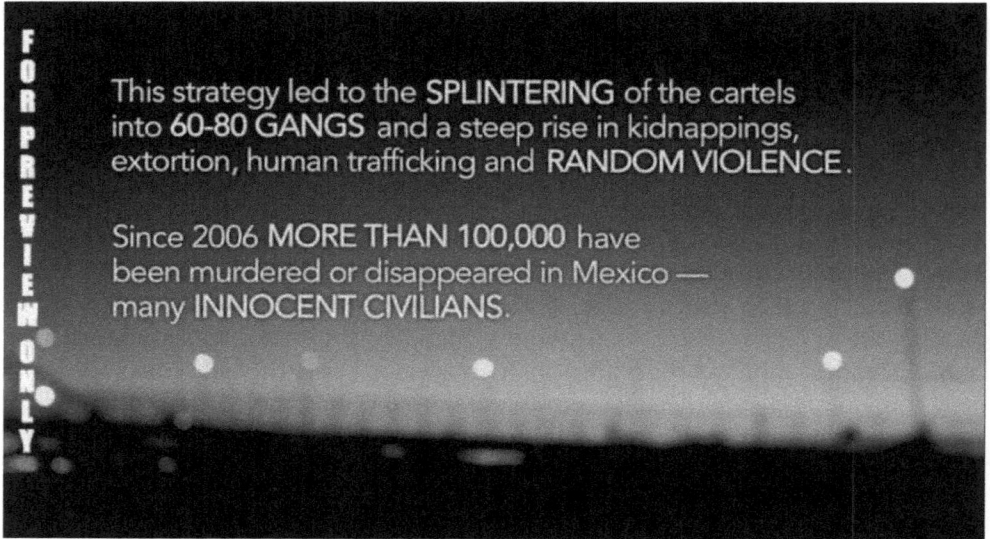

This strategy led to the **SPLINTERING** of the cartels into **60-80 GANGS** and a steep rise in kidnappings, extortion, human trafficking and **RANDOM VIOLENCE**.

Since 2006 **MORE THAN 100,000** have been murdered or disappeared in Mexico — many **INNOCENT CIVILIANS**.

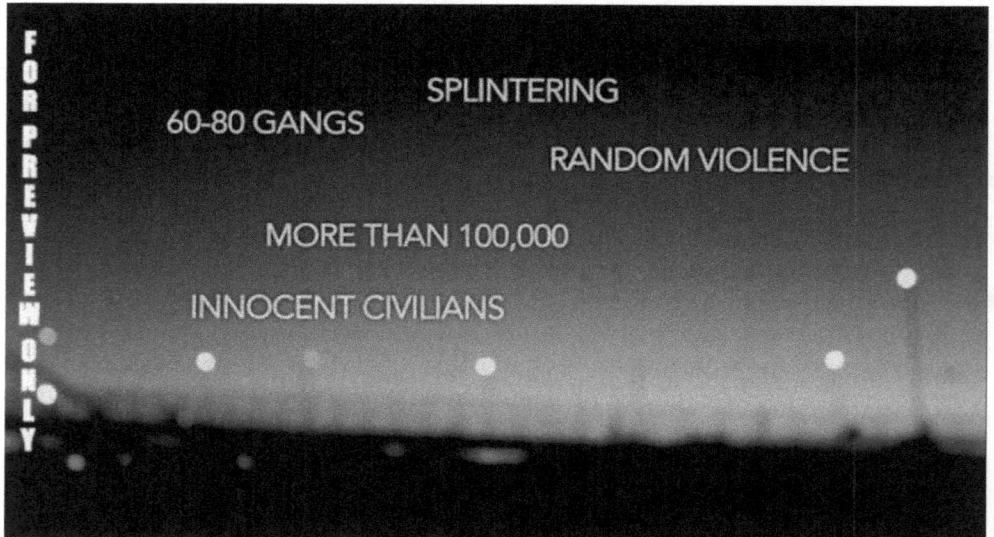

SPLINTERING

60-80 GANGS

RANDOM VIOLENCE

MORE THAN 100,000

INNOCENT CIVILIANS

FIGS. 10.1 & 10.2. Screen grab from *El poeta* (2012) by Kelly Duane de la Vega and Katie Galloway

instance the first title to appear reads 'IN 1971 President Richard Nixon declared a WAR ON DRUGS'. Alongside synthesized industrial sounds, the titles gradually swell onscreen, in the case of the first two titles, over the course of sixteen seconds. During this process, the regular type fades, leaving only the emboldened capitalized text onscreen. In its now seemingly dishevelled arrangement, the remaining text resembles a free-verse poem that simultaneously places prosodic stress on key words, while abstracting them from the formerly logical syntax. With the first two titles, for example, the emphasized words that persist are 'IN 1971', 'WAR ON DRUGS', 'A TRILLION DOLLARS' and 'INCARCERATED MILLIONS'. Thus the resounding information points to the history of the conflict, though the emphasis on the US's role in the war is somewhat de-emphasized. The next set of titles, which appear (and disappear) in the same fashion on the same background, read 'U.S. BACKED', 'WAR ON DRUGS IN MEXICO', 'MILITARY FORCE', 'CAPTURE OR KILL CARTEL LEADERS'. These titles focus on the relationship between the US and Mexico's own government, which in turns places greater significance on the aforementioned backdrop: the US/Mexican border.

In keeping with Nichols' description of the poetic mode of documentary, which 'explores associations and patterns that involve temporal rhythms and spatial juxtapositions' (2010: 162), the vast lacunae between some capitalized lines and the close proximity of others bestow new significance to the words. Likewise, the repetition of certain ideas or parties between frames further accentuates the accusatory stress of these facts.

The final set of redacted titles reads 'SPLINTERING', '60–80 GANGS', 'RANDOM VIOLENCE', 'MORE THAN 100,000', 'INNOCENT CIVILIANS'. Subtly mirroring the increasing severity of the situation that the figures depicted suggest, of the three this set of titles also has the greatest number of emphasized lines yet: five compared to the previous two sets of four. Similarly, the duration of this sequence outlasts the previous two at a total of twenty-five seconds. Pointedly, the length of time devoted solely to the emphasized lines is perhaps the most fleeting, lasting less than a second before disappearing entirely and finally the entire shot fading to black. The final two emphasized lines of this last set, 'MORE THAN 100,000' and 'INNOCENT CIVILIANS', though separated by the absence of an entire line of regular text, create a sense of poetic enjambment. Thus the ultimate emphasis of the film's introductory poem/intertitle rests on the vast number of innocent citizens caught in the crossfire of this international drug conflict, with the evanescent nature of the text visually reflective of the rapid loss of life as well as the increasing imperceptibility of the dead and disappeared in state discourse.

The style of quasi-poetic language used is notable in its historical significance. The abstracted words are vaguely reminiscent of Modernist poetry such as Stéphane Mallarmé's free-verse 'Un coup de dés jamais n'abolira le hasard' or Guillaume Apollinaire's avant-garde 'Calligrammes'. Apollinaire's collection in particular, subtitled 'Poems of Peace and War 1913–1916', is reflective of a wider poetic movement that responded to the absurdity of grand-scale war and violence with often cut-up or collaged poems that were composed in direct opposition to the formalistic and aesthetic poetry of the previous era (West 1996). As will be explored in the second half of this article in relation to Sicilia's last poem and his retirement from poetry after the death of his son, it is clear that the writers of the early twentieth century sought to challenge the artistic rules of the past by expressing their outrage and dissent towards an ideological regime that would countenance such a war. In essence, the work contends with and reflects upon the nonsensical nature of war. In the case of El poeta, this deployment of instructive titles coupled with bold typography at the very start of the film emphasizes a keen self-reflexivity on the relationship between language and meaning, the visual and the scriptural, poetry and prose. By opening the film in this manner, the filmmakers foreground the engaged role of poetics in confronting violence.

Beyond this powerful introduction, the documentary follows the evolution of the MPJD starting with the murder of Juan Francisco Sicilia Ortega in March 2011 and terminating with reflections on the final caravan across the USA (12 August to 12 September 2012). The poet figure acts throughout as a linchpin to the development and unfolding of events. After a brief contextualization, in the opening four minutes, of the drug war since the launch of Calderón's militarization strategy, the film's title, *El poeta*, appears onscreen. Soon after, footage from broadcast journalist Carmen Aristegui's news programme announces the death of Juan Francisco, described as the son of beloved journalist and philosopher, the Mexican writer Javier Sicilia. In the interview that follows Rubén Martínez, described in a caption as a 'professor and journalist', explains that every news programme in the Mexican media 'led with Javier's son's murder for days and days and days'. Martínez stresses the importance of the referent 'poeta', which he aligns with the prestige of a degree adding that 'people listen to poets in Latin America'. Martínez's description of the Mexican poet recalls Frances Wilson's idea of 'the poet with a capital P' (1999: 191), a public figure who is rebellious and larger than life.

While the film provides no further support for this assertion, many popular contemporary Latin American poets have and continue to use their art form to engage with socio-political issues and challenge accepted historical or institutional narratives. Gabriela Mistral, Gloria Anzaldúa, Vicente Huidobro, César Vallejo, Pablo Neruda, Juan L. Ortiz, Ernesto Cardenal, Raúl Zurita, among others, have all written poems that seek to contend with the traumatic and appropriated history of Latin America and to restore the memory of those people or events that have been wrongfully excluded from the historical archive (Rowe 2000: 27). As Mike Gonzalez and David Treece (1992: xiv) describe it, 'Latin American poetry has found a voice [...] in an echo of public dissent, of common language.' Gonzalez and Treece suggest that it is through the 'rediscovery of a collective voice and a collective experience' that poetry in Latin America has remained wholly inclusive using a voice that is broadly accessible. Such work testifies to a contemporary tradition in Latin American poetry, in which the poem itself presents a space for revisiting historical trauma, contesting established narratives, and vindicating victims of the past. Poets, then, as the creators of these subversive lyrical spaces, constitute not simply preeminent thinkers but also social activists. Despite his retirement from poetry, Sicilia's language when discussing the movement is still in keeping with Gonzalez and Treece's description of public poetry, specifically his chant 'Estamos hasta la madre' [we are really damn fed up]. As Lizette Jacinto (2011: 59–60) argues, this is one of the most common and colloquial expressions in Mexico and 'una frase que lejos de su academicismo religioso podía ligarse a todas las esferas sociales del mosaico cultural que es México' [a sentence that, far from its religious academicism could bring him closer to all the social spheres of Mexico's cultural mosaic]. Thus, Sicilia still embodies the public Poet persona even in the absence of his poetry.

It is not simply the poem but the performance of the poem that is important when examining the construction of the public poet figure. As Beasley (1994: 33) argues,

> just as performance reclaims a social space for poetry, it reinvents and promotes a poet's public function, perhaps especially as guardian of or challenger to cultural values, and redefines the poet's role to include, for example, community historian, teacher, broadcaster, agitator and entertainer.

What is interesting to note in the context of the MPJD is that it is not Sicilia (the Poet) who performs (his) poetry. As Cornelia Gräbner (2015: 3) notes of the caravans, 'The marchers stopped on public squares where, together with local groups, they spoke of and listened to accounts of violent experiences. The meetings always began with a poetry reading.' The traditional relationship between Poet (to use Wilson and Martínez's word) and audience is thus disrupted. Sicilia has abandoned his role as poet-author and instead wields his title of Poet to create a platform for members of the movement to speak and be heard. Nonetheless performance is still central to Sicilia's role in the movement as evidenced by the documentary. He appears continually in interview-style, as well as in footage of him on stage during the caravans, reinforcing his public role as community historian, teacher and broadcaster, as Beasley states.

Martínez's words regarding the power of the poet are heard over footage of Sicilia at a press conference following the murder of his son on 1 April 2011, when he announces his plan to take to the streets, united with other citizens to seek justice for those affected by the war. The film manages to discuss the significance of the poet's role in creating a sense of collectivity without surrendering the autonomy of the movement. Sicilia is important because his celebrity gave a widespread public presence to the victims of violence that was difficult to ignore. The poet and the poet's son, as evidenced by the titles of both films examined in this chapter, delivered tangible human examples of the personal suffering that has become widespread in Mexico and has resulted directly from the increased violence of war. As the film highlights, before this moment many victims were afraid of the potential consequences of speaking out but with the poet as an agglutinating central example, families were able to come together around Sicilia's loss and to proclaim their loved ones' innocence too. Thus Sicilia plays the role of Poet within the movement and the film without performing any poems.

While the poet in this instance does not actively use poetry as a means of disputing institutional power, the celebrity and leadership of the poet figure adds gravitas to the struggle and his cinematic representation is key to this enhanced value. As acknowledged outright in the documentary, the chief aim of the MPJD is to make the victims of this conflict visible. The movement's 'National pact for peace and justice with dignity' signed by more than 300 civil organizations, lists the principal aims and demands of the protestors commencing by saying, 'Exigimos esclarecer asesinatos y desapariciones y nombrar a las víctimas' [we demand the solving of murders and disappearances and the naming of victims] (Ordaz 2011). Participants in the MPJD argue that the process of identifying each and every victim is crucial to generating trust between the Mexican people and the state (Ordaz 2011). Though the death of Juan Francisco was well covered by the media given the renown of his father, the thousands of other disappeared and murdered victims of the drug war have not received the same level of visibility and public mourning. Instead, official indifference characterized the way Calderón's government dealt with the civilian victims of the drug war (Wolf and Celorio 2011: 693); some of these victims have been baselessly accused of having criminal links, while in some cases families of the disappeared have experienced threats or were instructed by officials to investigate the disappearance themselves (Rodríguez 2010). As an emblem of Mexico's victims, each effort by the filmmakers to contextualize or detail Sicilia's experience further elucidates that of the many families affected by the war, rendering their loss more visible.

True to character, as established at the start of the film, Sicilia quotes Parayam Desai, Gandhi's disciple: 'no importa haber llegado al árbol y tomado el fruto; lo que importa es haber caminado hacia él' [arriving at the tree and picking the fruit doesn't matter, what matters is having walked there]. In keeping with the metaphor, Sicilia suggests that what the movement has achieved through its rallies is to make this 'fruit' visible by marching towards it, an act he believes is beautiful and worthwhile.

El hijo del poeta (2012)

While my discussions on Duane de la Vega and Galloway's documentary focused primarily on the characterization of the poet figure onscreen, Pablo Orta's short experimental film *El hijo del poeta* appropriates another element of Sicilia's personage: the words of his final poem. Alongside the visual depiction of his fatherly grief, the lines of Sicilia's final poem provide the non-diegetic narration of the short. In the form of an internal monologue, the words of the poem offer insight into the personal experience of familial trauma that the unnamed poet protagonist is seen to contend with. The film adopts this story of familial loss for its narrative, focusing on an unnamed protagonist, 'el poeta', played by Carlos Hoeflich, as he searches for a quiet place to lay his son's ashes to rest. Though the film makes no overt reference to the current crisis, its focus on grief, peace and familial relationships as well as its allusion to Sicilia's personal experience all help cement the short film's relevance to the aims and origins of the MPJD.

El hijo del poeta features no dialogue. Instead, the short uses the lines of Sicilia's last poem, 'El mundo ya no es digno de la palabra', delivered as a voice-over by the protagonist of the film. As Sicilia explains, the poem, 'es mi último poema, no puedo escribir más poesía... La poesía ya no existe en mí' (Morelos 2011) [It is my last poem, I cannot write any more poetry... poetry does not exist in me anymore]. Pablo Orta's interest in Sicilia's loss as a filmic subject matter stems, in part, from the idea that, as Orta puts it, 'La vida te saca el arte del cuerpo' [Life

FIG. 10.3. Screen grab from *El hijo del poeta* (2012) by Pablo Orta

pulls art out of your body].[3] In this context of personal loss resulting from war, the ongoing and seemingly endless violence impacting families across Mexico has the potency to quell self-expression in the face of mounting impunity and destruction. Interestingly Gräbner makes a starkly similar comparison when analysing Sicilia's final poem. Gräbner cites Elaine Scarry's *The Body in Pain* (1985: 61) when discussing the internalized pain of violence that victims of the drug war have endured as a result of the socio-political erasure of their suffering. On the subject of such pain Scarry writes, 'the moment it is lifted out of the ironclad privacy of the body into speech, it immediately falls back in. Nothing sustains its image in the world; nothing alerts us to the place it has vacated.' Gräbner (2015: 7) suggests that Sicilia's last poem thematizes this struggle as it 'draws on the difficulty of connecting interiorities, and explicates the impossibility of exteriorizing pain'. Through a close reading of his final poem, Gräbner concludes that the listener is unable to connect with Sicilia's exteriorized pain as it remains trapped within him but that the listener responds instead 'by creating spaces — if not a world — that are worthy of the word' (2015: 7). Orta's film can be understood as one of these spaces created in response to 'El mundo ya no es digno'. What Orta refers to as art can be understood as an articulation of this pain and an attempt to alert the audience to its existence. In this context Sicilia's representation in the short is exemplary of this trapped invisible suffering but through its visualization, Orta attempts to sustain its exteriority.

In the case of Orta's film, the poetry contained within the narrative is literally externalized from the protagonist as it is recited outside of the diegetic world in voice-over. Though the poem occupies most of the voice-over track, supplemented at the end by Sicilia's press statement that the once-poet no longer has poetry in him, the majority of the film features only diegetic sound. Along with this statement, the poem's seven short lines are split across three sections of the five-minute film: the beginning, middle and end. In the first instance Sicilia's lines open the story as the poet drives to collect his son's ashes from the church. The poet is filmed side-on in a medium shot as he drives. The second instance, however, shows the poet's image as reflected in rippling water. The high-angle medium shot provides a visualized representation of the poet's now distorted image, unrecognizable from the movement of the water and by extension the trauma that has put an end to his artistic endeavours. By depicting the character indirectly via his reflection, the shot further emphasizes the way poetry has left his body and is now alien and unrecognizable as a medium of expression for the poet. A Derridian (1994: 12) reading of this representation epitomizes the idea of the spectral or 'the opposition between presence and non-presence, actuality and in actuality, life and non-life'. That is to say, the anaemic undulating reflection of the poet depicts the character as in between presence and non-presence, a metaphorically hollowed out shell only partially there due to the mental weight of his loss that beckons him to the past, despite his being moored physically in the present. The poetry too is caught in a place that cannot be captured in the frame: Orta's framing implies that the words emerge from the thoughts of the implied Sicilia character; yet as a consequence of this externalization of the physical act of speech from the frame the emitter (or speaker) is distanced further from the emitted (or speech), thus creating a representational lacuna. The third and fourth lines of Sicilia's poem accompany the image in voice-over lamenting, 'como te asfixiaron | como te desgarraron a ti los pulmones' [how they suffocated you | how they tore open your lungs]. The violent references to breathing and lungs highlight the extinguishing of life force represented by the endemic drug war that has and continues to destroy lives all over the country. This point is further laboured by the reflection shot which looks down at the distorted former poet from a high angle, suggesting to the viewer that we are looking back at a now warped and faint memory. Much like this shot, Orta's film constitutes an indirect look on the ground-level effects of drug war violence, which have damaged the country's image and misrepresented its victims as complicit with the drug trade and therefore responsible for their own deaths.

This concept of a post-poetic traumatized world was famously captured by Theodor Adorno (1997: 34) in the essay 'Cultural Criticism and Society' (1951) where he wrote, 'To write poetry after Auschwitz is barbaric.' Adorno's much-cited assertion does not signify that symbolic or aesthetic expression is subsequently callous or inhumane after such an atrocity. Instead, Adorno (34) conveys the idea that to continue to represent society using the same means and techniques that were relevant and prevalent prior to an event such as the holocaust is a blithe perpetuation of the societal conditions that created this event and horrific circumstances. Thus it is not that Adorno considers poetry to be unethical after Auschwitz but instead that new methods and tropes are required to express dismay, to challenge the societal structures that led to this traumatic event and, indeed, to cope with the effects of this trauma. This mode of thinking extends not only to the work of Sicilia and the civic movement he started but equally to the representational filmmaking of cineastes whose work attempts to capture the effects of the conflict in distinct and provocative ways. What is important to note in this context is that Sicilia has compared the loss of his son to Auschwitz, additionally aligning the pain of loss felt by all drug war victims as well as the intensity of the conflict to this historic massacre (Bleifuss 2012). This allusion highlights the mass trauma suffered by the Mexican people as a result of the Calderón administration's failed antinarcotics war. Just as was recognized after the Second World War, the deleterious effects of war stretch beyond the realms of combat and have impacted the lives of thousands of civilians. In this sense, and in the context of Mexico's drug conflict, Sicilia's decision to retire from poetry reflects the idea that to continue to create art in the manner he did before the death of his son would be to condone the society in which the poet lives, which he views as a volatile climate that caused the death of his only son. Thus Sicilia's withdrawal from the artistic world, as reflected in the narration of Orta's film, is equally a denunciation of the state of Mexican society. In this sense, it is a lack of poetic output from a beloved popular writer that functions as a rhetorical philippic against the state and its regime of authority. However, Sicilia does not cease to write completely, but simply refrains from writing poetry. The ex-poet has since written extensively for the current affairs magazine *Proceso* as a public means of admonishing the government for its failing and increasingly violent war on drugs.[4] Thus, the importance of discourse in power relations is not entirely undermined but instead greater potency in this instance is placed on prose and the capabilities of public journalism as a tool for reaching a more general audience.

Much in the way home video is used in *El poeta* to establish and visually foreground notions of childhood innocence and unbreakable family unity, in *El hijo del poeta* the words of Sicilia's poem punctuate images of daily life as the poet's son is shown playing with bugs in the garden and the poet is depicted falling asleep in his car on the side of the road. The coupling of Orta's filmic representation of the poet's world and Sicilia's real-life poetic denunciation of this same space, imagined and recreated in the cinematic frame, propels the viewer's mind from the microcosmic example of the onscreen poet and his son to the plight of Sicilia and the MPJD. The drug conflict has infiltrated the quotidian and domestic spaces, rendering its violence and effects all but inescapable. Nevertheless, Sicilia's poem is not exclusive to his own suffering and experience but instead carries with it the pain and struggles of all those affected by the federal state authority's war on drugs. In his role as public poet and founder/leader of the movement for peace, Sicilia has come to represent the thousands of families whose lives are impacted on a daily basis by the rise of drug-related violence in Mexico. The poet's name, image and final poem all function as synecdochic references to the widespread violence sweeping Mexico and affecting individual civilian lives. In Orta's film it is therefore unnecessary to represent the brutality of the conflict directly in order to depict these events, given that the title of the film and the narration alone serve as clear indicators of the subject under scrutiny to a national audience. Orta's short eschews typical representations of the conflict through the absence of visual violence. By challenging concepts of presence

FIG. 10.4. Screen grab from *El hijo del poeta* (2012) by Pablo Orta

and absence, *El hijo del poeta* stands as evidence of Adorno's claim that in order to contend with the trauma of the past and to challenge the systems that caused this trauma, new and innovative representational approaches are required.

Once again the importance of the performance of poetry is foregrounded. Orta's film, through its narration and its depiction of a Sicilia/poet character, effectively performs Sicilia's final poem. Thus, to quote Beasley (1994: 33) once more, the performance of poetry not only reclaims space, 'it reinvents and promotes a poet's public function'. Beasley's words point to the crucial role of the poet in their community, as activist, guardian, and teacher, and Sicilia in this case is no different. Sicilia's search for peace, in a country where people are forced to face the effects of increasing violence on a daily basis, attempts to unite the affected voices of the Mexican people as a means of building a stronger garrison in the creation of a legitimate discursive defence against official narratives. Given that the nature of these victims' trauma is collective, due to the mass violence inflicted as a result of the war on drugs, it is through cooperative organization that these individuals are now attempting to revisit and contend with trauma. Though in Orta's short film this character copes and searches alone, the *Movimiento por la paz* is about collective power, reclaiming public spaces and campaigning together to end violence and re-establish peace.

The collective nature of this trauma and subsequent search for peace is further emphasized in the subtly edited narration of the film. For instance, though the film employs Sicilia's final poem for the narration, the final word, the name of Sicilia's son 'Juanelo', is omitted and replaced with a double repetition of the penultimate word 'silencio'. This building of triadic crescendo as the word is repeated with increasing force and anguish in the voice of the narrator, marginally alters the meaning of the poem, changing the significance of the 'silence' into a command demanding a cessation, most likely to the escalating violence plaguing Mexico. Thus, the film's use of Sicilia's personal experience and poetic response combined with the protagonist's search for a peaceful resting place parallels the real-life poet's pursuit of peace in Mexico, while the removal of the name 'Juanelo' from the dialogue renders the poem's message universal. Sicilia has himself discussed the power of silence in remembering and respecting the dead and disappeared victims of the war: 'Siempre se olvida que el silencio es parte de la palabra. Y hay veces que en un mundo así el silencio dice más que las palabras' [People always forget that silence is a part of language. And there are times when in a world like this silence says more than words] (El Universal 2013). This potency of silence over the spoken word is reflected in an eschewal of dialogue in favour of sparse poetic voiceover and a focus on the search for silence in the plight of the poet. The final sequence of the film, commencing from the narrator's repetition of 'silencio', features neither music nor narration. During a full one minute and thirty seconds (just under a third of the film's duration), the camera follows the poet on the final stages of his journey travelling on foot into the depths of the mountains until he discovers the refuge of an empty cave. The aural track of diegetic sounds such as birdsong and the poet's footsteps lessen as he approaches sanctuary. The near-silence is interrupted only by the final words of narration at the end of the sequence which, instead of Sicilia's son's name, again the actual final word of the poem, finishes with a repetition of the poem's title and first line as well as part of Sicilia's press statement. As depicted in the film, the war has extinguished poetry from within the poet who searches instead for silence and for an end to the suffering that has come to characterize daily life in Mexico. The poet's search is rendered difficult, however, by a society that does not openly recognize his trauma, leaving him removed from the world he inhabits. This immense struggle and isolation is emphasized by the camerawork selected to represent the scene. Within the cave the poet character is framed in a high-angle long shot in the centre of the frame, his son's urn nestled under the stalactites behind him as he lets out an exhausted sigh. This final shot can also be read as emblematic of Sicilia's own role in the anti-war protest movement embodied by the MPJD. The poet stands in the centre of the frame, just as he stands metaphorically in the centre of the struggle; however, the distance of the shot reflects the insignificance of one man alone, isolated from the rest of society in the vast emptiness of the cave. Moreover, unlike the character's solitary journey, Sicilia has succeeded in uniting thousands of families and individuals who are living through endemic violence across the country. Just as the long shot of the poet character in the cave implies, this situation is bigger than any one person or singular experience; however, this particular individual and his relatable familiar journey remain as a fixed emblem at the centre of the anti-war movement. Thus the tenor of the short film's narrative reflects a hopeful journey towards a future of healing and peace.

Conclusion

Sicilia's movement and its rallies across the country have made significant long term changes to the anti-war movement. As Kristin Bricker (2011) comments:

> Before the Movement for Peace with Justice and Dignity emerged, drug war victims were terrified, isolated and silent. On the two caravans, victims learned public speaking skills and how to organize protests and press conferences and hold more effective meetings with public officials.

With Sicilia as its Poet-leader, the MPJD delivered a crucial platform for Mexican citizens to respond to the ongoing and increasing violence impacting their daily lives. Though the movement is not the only civic response to militarization and failed drug war strategy, it is Sicilia's undertaking that has succeeded in uniting civil movements and distraught families across the whole of Mexico. Both films offer distinct insights into the potential significance of the poet figure in the struggle for peace and visibility, both on and off screen. The use of poetic documentary filmmaking in Duane de la Vega and Galloway's *El poeta* highlights the potency of the poet and poetic language as vehicles for collective mobilization. Via the figure of the poet, the film succeeds in highlighting the debilitating effects of Calderón's pervasive drug war and channels the muted struggle of thousands of citizens in their united search for justice and peace. The documentary focuses on Sicilia as a poet character who is able to use his celebrity as a respected public figure to emphasize the growing grief and concerns of a disenfranchised and ignored public. Likewise, as a fictionalized portrait of grief based on Sicilia's public loss of his only son, *El hijo del poeta* too offers a poet character whose pain and poetry transgress the screen to embody more than the individual experience it purports to depict. The fictionalization of the renowned poet, his story and the performance of his final poem transports discussions of the violence to the realms of allegory and poetic reflection. The film thematizes loss and the search for peace, while its use of Sicilia's final poem affords a space for reflection on the role of poetry as both art and a form of expression in the context of deep personal trauma and widespread conflict and loss. The complementary visual texts together deliver a rousing portrait of what it means to be at once (and formerly) a poet and a parent in an increasingly turbulent conflict.

Works Cited

ADORNO, THEODOR. 1997. *Prisms* (Cambridge, MA: MIT Press)

ÁLVAREZ ICAZA L., EMILIO. 2011. 'Caravana de esperanza', *Untitled*, 25 September <https://issuu.com/mxlapazmx/docs/emilioai-caravana-de-esperanza-enfo> [accessed 3 February 2016]

BEASLEY, PAUL. 1994. 'Vive la différance!', *Critical Quarterly*, 38: 28–38

BLEIFUSS, JOEL. 2012. 'Javier Sicilia: Leading his Caravan to Washington', *In These Times*, 17 May <http://inthesetimes.com/article/13175/javier_sicilia_leading_his_caravan_to_washington> [accessed 3 February 2016]

BRICKER, KRISTIN. 2011. 'Inside Mexico's Peace Movement', *Indypendent*, 6 October <http://www.indypendent.org/2011/10/06/mexicos-peace-movement/> [accessed 3 February 2016]

BOULLOSA, CARMEN. 2011. *La patria insomne* (Madrid: Ediciones Hiperión)

CASASÚS, MARIO. 2011. 'La Caravana del Consuelo: origen y recorrido', *La Nación*, April–September, pp. 29–31

CUÉLLAR, MARGARITO. 2017. 'Poesía y balas', *Nexos*, 1 January <https://www.nexos.com.mx/?p=30822> [accessed 3 February 2016]

DERRIDA, JACQUES. 1994. *Specters of Marx: The State of the Debt, the Work of Mourning, and the New International* (New York and London: Routledge)

El Universal. 2013. 'Javier Sicilia se retira de la poesía: "el mundo no es digno de la palabra"', *El Universal*, 12 June <http://www.eluniversal.com/arte-y-entretenimiento/130612/javier-sicilia-se-retira-de-la-poesia-el-mundo-no-es-digno-de-la-palab> [accessed 9 February 2016]

El Universal. 2014. 'Cronología caso Sicilia, el crimen que sensibilizó al país', *El Universal*, 15 January <http://archivo.eluniversal.com.mx/estados/2014/cronologia-sicilia-979830.html> [accessed 3 February 2016]

GOGGIN, GERARD, and CÉSAR TORRES. 2014. 'Political and Mobile Media Landscapes in Mexico: The Case of #yosoy132', *Continuum*, 28: 1–15

GONZALEZ, MIKE, and DAVID TREECE. 1992. *The Gathering of Voices: The Twentieth-century Poetry of Latin America* (London: Verso)

GRÄBNER, CORNELIA. 2015. 'Public Spaces and Global Listening Spaces: Poetic Resonances from the Movement for Peace with Justice and Dignity in Mexico', *Liminalities: A Journal of Performance Studies*, 11: 1–26

JACINTO, LIZETTE. 2011. 'Javier Sicilia: el Movimiento por la Paz con Justicia y Dignidad en México 2011', *iMex. México Interdisciplinario. Interdisciplinary iMex*, 1: 58–73

LOERA, MARTHA EVA. 2012. 'La muerte del hijo', *Gaceta*, 29 October <http://www.gaceta.udg.mx/G_nota1.php?id=12806> [accessed 3 February 2016]

MENDOZA, CARLOS. 2009. 'Periodismo, Documental y Creación', ponencia en el Festival de Cine Contemporáneo de la Ciudad de México (Mexico City: FICCO)

—— 2015. *La invención de la verdad: ensayos sobre cine documental* (Mexico City: UNAM)

MORELOS CRUZ, RUBICELA. 2011. 'La poesía ya no existe en mí', *La Jornada*, 3 April <http://www.jornada.unam.mx/2011/04/03/politica/002n2pol> [accessed 3 February 2016]

MORO HERNÁNDEZ, JAVIER, and CARLOS RAMÍREZ. 2012. *Los salvajes de ciudad Aka* (Mexico City: Deléatur y DOS10)

NAVARRO, LUIS HERNÁNDEZ. 2011. 'La Caravana del Consuelo', *La Jornada*, 14 June <http://www.jornada.unam.mx/2011/06/14/opinion/021a1pol> [accessed 3 February 2016]

NICHOLS, BILL. 2010. *Introduction to Documentary*, ed. by P. D. Dawsonera (Bloomington: Indiana University Press)

ORDAZ, PABLO. 2011. 'Son mexicanos, son valientes', *El País*, 19 June <http://elpais.com/diario/2011/06/19/domingo/1308455553_850215.html> [accessed 8 August 2020]

ORTA, PABLO. 2014. Interview conducted with Orta by the author, 17 May

RIVERA, MARÍA. 2010. 'Los muertos', in *Numéro Cinq*, ed. by Dylan Brennan, August 2017 <http://numerocinqmagazine.com/2017/08/05/numero-cinco-dead-poem-interview-maria-rivera/> [accessed 8 August 2020]

RODRÍGUEZ, ARTURO. 2010. 'Los desaparecidos que a nadie importan', *Proceso*, 10 January, <https://www.proceso.com.mx/110952/los-desaparecidos-que-a-nadie-importan-2 > [accessed 8 August 2020]

ROWE, WILLIAM. 2000. *Poets of Contemporary Latin America: History and the Inner Life* (Oxford: Oxford University Press)

SCARRY, ELAINE. 1985. *The Body in Pain: The Making and Unmaking of the World* (Oxford: Oxford University Press)

SICILIA, JAVIER. 2011. 'Estamos hasta la madre: carta abierta a los políticos y a los criminales', *Proceso*, 3 April, <https://www.proceso.com.mx/266990/javier-sicilia-carta-abierta-a-politicos-y-criminales> [accessed 8 August 2020]

—— 2017. 'Autor: Javier Sicilia', *Proceso*, 29 October <http://www.proceso.com.mx/author/jsicilia> [accessed 8 August 2020]

West, Shearer. 1996. *The Bloomsbury Guide to Art* (London: Bloomsbury)

Wilson, Frances. 1999. *Literary Seductions* (London: Faber and Faber)

Wolf, Sonja, and Gonzalo Celorio Morayta. 2011. 'La guerra de México contra el narcotráfico y la Iniciativa Mérida: piedras angulares en la búsqueda de legitimidad', *Foro Internacional*, 51: 669–714

Notes to Chapter 10

1. Voces is an acclaimed PBS documentary series produced by Latino Public Broadcasting.
2. In his article 'Poesía y balas' (2017) Margarito Cuéllar gives an extensive overview of poetic work in Mexico responding to growing levels of violence. Including for example: María Rivera, 'Los muertos' (2010), Carmen Boullosa, *La patria insomne* (2011), and Javier Moro Hernández and Carlos Ramírez, *Los salvajes de ciudad Aka* (2012).
3. Taken from my own interview conducted with Pablo Orta (2014).
4. The full extent of Sicilia's prose contributions to the magazine *Proceso*, which span until the present day, can be accessed online (2017).

FILMOGRAPHY

❖

Ordered by director and date of production (oldest film first)

ADRIANO, CARLOS, *Remanescências* (Brazil, 1994–97)
——, *Das ruínas a rexistência* (Brazil, 2007)
——, *Santoscópio=Dumontagem* (Brazil, 2007–09)
——, *Sem título #2: la mer larme* (Brazil, 2009–15)
——, *Sem título #1: Dance of Leitfossil* (Brazil, 2013–14)
——, *Festejo muito pessoal* (Brazil, 2016)
——, *Sem título # 3: e para que poetas em tempo de pobreza* (Brazil, 2016)
——, *Sem título #4 Apesar dos pesares, na chuva há de cantares* (Brazil, 2017–18)
——, *Sem título #5: a rotina terá seu enquanto* (Brazil, 2019)
ALONSO, LISANDRO, *La libertad* (Argentina, 2001)
ÁLVAREZ, SANTIAGO, *El tigre saltó y mató, pero morirá...morirá...* (Cuba, 1973)
ANDRADE, JOAQUIM PEDRO DE, *Macunaíma* (Brazil, 1969)
ANTONIONI, MICHAELANGELO, *Il deserto rosso* [*Red Desert*] (Italy, France, 1964)
BADHAM, JOHN, *Saturday Night Fever* (USA, 1977)
BALMACEDA, FERNANDO, *Carbón* (Chile, 1965)
BAUER, TRISTÁN, *Los libros y la noche* (Argentina, 2000)
BEMBERG, MARÍA LUISA, *Camila* (Argentina, Spain, 1984)
——, *Yo, la peor de todas* (Argentina, 1990)
——, *De eso no se habla* (Argentina, Italy, 1993)
BENOÎT, GEORGES, and HÉCTOR QUIROGA, *Juan sin ropa* (Argentina, 1919)
BERGMAN, INGMAR, *Viskningar och rop* [*Cries and Whispers*] (Sweden, 1972)
BERTOLUCCI, BERNARDO, *Prima della rivoluzione* [*Before the Revolution*] (Italy, 1964)
BIRRI, FERNANDO, *La primera fundación de Buenos Aires* (Argentina, 1959)
——, *Tire dié* (Argentina, 1960)
——, *Org* (Italy, 1979)
——, *El Fausto criollo* (Argentina, 2011)
BORCOSQUE, CARLOS, *Santos Vega* (Argentina, 1971)
BRAKHAGE, STAN, *Mothlight* (USA, 1963)
BRAVO, SERGIO, *Mimbre* (Chile, 1957)
——, *Trilla* (Chile, 1958)
——, *Casamiento de Negros* (Chile, 1959)
——, *Día de Organillos* (Chile, 1961)
——, *Amerindia* (Chile, 1962)
——, *Láminas de Almahue* (Chile, 1962)
BUÑUEL, LUIS, *Las Hurdes: Tierra sin pan* (Spain, 1933)
——, *Abismos de pasión* (Mexico, 1954)
——, *El ángel exterminador* (Mexico, 1962)
——, *Le Fantôme de la liberté* [*The Phantom of Liberty*] (France, Italy, 1974)
——, and SALVADOR DALÍ, *Un chien andalou* [*An Andalusian Dog*] (France, 1929)
CAIRO, HUMBERTO, ERNESTO GUNCHE, and EDUARDO MARTÍNEZ DE LA PERA, *Nobleza gaucha* (Argentina, 1915)

CARRERA, CARLOS, *El crimen de Padre Amaro* (Argentina, France, Mexico, Spain, 2002)

CARRI, ALBERTINA, *Los rubios* (Argentina, USA, 2003)

——, *La rabia* (Argentina, Netherlands, 2008)

CASTEDO, LEOPOLDO, *La respuesta* (Chile, 1961)

COCTEAU, JEAN, *Le Sang d'un poète* [*The Blood of a Poet*] (France, 1932)

——, *La Belle et la Bête* [*Beauty and the Beast*] (France, 1946)

——, *Orphée* [*Orpheus*] (France, 1950)

——, *Le Testament d'Orphée: ou ne me demandez pas pourquoi* [*The Testament of Orpheus or Don't Ask Me Why*] (France, 1960)

COHL, ÉMILE, *Le Cauchemar du Fantoche* [*The Puppet's Nightmare*] (France, 1908)

——, *Un drame chez les Fantoches* [*Drama at the Puppets' House*] (France, 1908)

——, *Fantasmagorie* (France, 1908)

——, *Le Petit Soldat qui devient Dieu* [*The Little Soldier Who Became a God*] (France, 1908)

——, *Les Chaussures matrimoniales* [*Matrimonial Shoes*] (France, 1909)

——, *Le Petit chantecler* [*Petit Chantecler*] (France, 1910)

CONNER, BRUCE, *A Movie* (USA, 1958)

CORNELL, JOSEPH, *Rose Hobart* (USA, 1936)

COSIMI, NELO, *Juan Moreira* (Argentina, 1936)

COUTINHO, EDUARDO, *Jogo de cena* (Brazil, 2007)

CUARÓN, ALFONSO, *Sólo con tu pareja* (Mexico, 1991)

DAWI, ENRIQUE, *La vuelta de Martín Fierro* (Argentina, 1974)

DE CHOMÓN, SEGUNDO, *Le Théâtre de Bob* [*Miniature Theatre*] (France, 1906)

——, *La Maison ensorcelée* [*The House of Ghosts*] (France, 1908)

DE PAOLI, CARLOS, *Santos Vega* (Argentina, 1917)

DEBORD, GUY, *La Société du spectacle* [*The Society of the Spectacle*] (France, 1973)

DEL TORO, GUILLERMO, *El espinazo del diablo* (Mexico, Spain, 2001)

——, *The Shape of the Water* (Canada, USA, 2015)

DEUTSCH, GUSTAV, *Film ist* [*Film Is*] (Austria, 1998)

DÍAZ, JESÚS, *Cincuentaicinco hermanos* (Cuba, 1978)

DREYER, CARL TH., *La Passion de Jeanne d'Arc* [*The Passion of Joan of Arc*] (France, 1928)

DUANE DE LA VEGA, KELLY, and KATIE GALLOWAY, *El poeta* (USA, 2012)

DUCHAMP, MARCEL, *Anemic Cinema* (France, 1926)

EIMBCKE, FERNANDO, *Temporada de patos* (Mexico, 2004)

ELIZONDO, SALVADOR, *Apocalypse 1900* (Mexico, 1965)

FAVIO, LEONARDO, *Juan Moreira* (Argentina, 1973)

FERNÁNDEZ, EMILIO, *Salón México* (Mexico, 1949)

FONTÁN, GUSTAVO, *El árbol* (Argentina, 2006)

——, *La orilla que se abisma* (Argentina, 2008)

——, *La casa* (Argentina, 2012)

FRAMPTON, HOLLIS, *Palindrome* (USA, 1969)

——, *Nostalgia (Hapax Legomena I)* (USA, 1971)

——, *Poetic Justice (Hapax Legomena II)* (USA, 1972)

——, *Public Domain* (USA, 1973)

FRANJU, GEORGES, *Le Sang des bêtes* [*Blood of the Beasts*] (France, 1949)

GALLO, MARIO, *Juan Moreira* (Argentina, 1913)

GÁMEZ, RUBÉN, *La fórmula secreta* (Mexico, 1965)

GAVALDÓN, ROBERTO, *El gallo de oro* (Mexico, 1964)

GEHR, ERNIE, *Eureka* (USA, 1974)

GODARD, JEAN-LUC, *Le Mépris* [*Contempt*] (France, Italy, 1963)

——, *Histoire(s) du cinéma* [*History/ies of Cinema*] (France, 1989)

GRECA, ALCIDES, *El último malón* (Argentina, 1917)

GRIFFITH, D.W., *Intolerance* (USA, 1916)

GUERRERO, FELIPE, *Paraíso* (Colombia, 2006)

GUNCHE, ERNESTO, and EDUARDO MARTÍNEZ DE LA PERA, *Hasta después de muerta* (Argentina, 1916)

——, *Fausto, narrado por Anastasio El Pollo* (Argentina, 1922)

——, *La casa de los cuervos* (Argentina, 1923)

GUTIÉRREZ ALEA, TOMÁS, *Memorias del subdesarrollo* (Cuba, 1968)

GUZMÁN, PATRICIO, *Salvador Allende* (Chile, 2004)

HANOUN, MARCEL, *Un film* [*A Film*] (France, 1983)

HITCHCOCK, ALFRED, *Vertigo* (USA, 1958)

HUILLET, DANIELLE, and JEAN-MARIE STRAUB, *Toute révolution est un coup de dés* [*All Revolutions are a Throw of the Dice*] (France, 1977)

——, and JEAN-MARIE STRAUB, *Schwarze Sünde* [*Black Sin*] (West Germany, 1988)

IVENS, JORIS, *Regen* [Rain] (Netherlands, 1929)

——, *A Valparaíso* (Chile, France, 1962)

JACOBS, KEN, *Tom Tom the Piper's Son* (USA, 1969)

——, *Perfect Film* (Ken Jacobs, USA, 1986)

——, *Opening the Nineteenth Century: 1896* (USA, 1990)

JOSKOWICZ, ALFREDO, *Constelaciones* (Mexico, 1980)

KAPADIA, ASIF, *Senna* (France, UK, USA, 2010)

——, *Amy* (UK, 2015)

——, *Diego Maradona* (UK, 2019)

KOHON, DAVID JOSÉ, *El agujero en la pared* (Argentina, 1982)

KUBELKA, PETER, *Unsere Afrikariese* [*Our Trip to Africa*] (Austria, 1966)

LARRAÍN, PABLO, *Tony Manero* (Brazil, Chile, 2008)

——, *Post Mortem* (Chile, Mexico, 2010)

——, *No* (Chile, France, Mexico, USA, 2012)

——, *Jackie* (Chile, China, France, Germany, UK, USA, 2016)

——, *Neruda* (Argentina, Chile, France, Spain, USA, 2016)

LAVERDE, MIGUEL, *Martín Fierro* (Argentina, 1989)

LeGRICE, MALCOLM, *Berlin Horse* (UK, 1970)

LEMAÎTRE, MAURICE, *Erich von Stroheim* (France, 1979)

LEYDA, JAY, *A Bronx Morning* (USA, 1931)

LEZAMA, LUIS, *Tabaré* (Mexico, 1917)

LITTÍN, MIGUEL, *El Chacal de Nahueltoro* (Chile, 1969)

LIUT, MARTÍN, *Inventarios argentinos I: Glosario de la pampa* (Argentina, 2011)

LLINÁS, MARIANO, *La flor* (Argentina, 2018)

LORENTZ, PARE, *The River* (USA, 1938)

LOZA, SANTIAGO, *Rosa patria* (Argentina, 2008)

LYE, LEN, *Rainbow Dance* (UK, 1936)

MARKER, CHRIS, *Lettre de Sibérie* [*Letter from Siberia*] (France, 1958)

McLAREN, NORMAN, *Blinkity Blank* (Canada, 1955)

MELFORD, GEORGE, *East of Borneo* (USA, 1931)

MÉLIÈS, GEORGES, *Escamotage d'une dame chez Robert-Houdin* [*The Vanishing Lady*] (France, 1896)

——, *Le manoir du diable* [The Haunted Castle] (France, 1896)

——, *L'auberge ensorcelée* [The Bewitched Inn] (France, 1897)

——, *Le Voyage dans la lune* [*A Trip to the Moon*] (France, 1909)

MINELLI, VINCENTE, *Lust for Life* (USA, 1956)

MITRE, SANTIAGO, and JUAN ONOFRI, *Los posibles* (Argentina, 2013)

MOGLIA BARTH, LUIS JOSÉ, *Santos Vega* (Argentina, 1932)

——, *Juan Moreira* (Argentina, 1948)

MOLINA, VIRNA, and ERNESTO ARDITO, *Alejandra* (Argentina, 2013)

MURNAU, FRIEDRICH, *Faust* (Germany, 1926)

NEVES, DAVID E., *Paulo Emílio encontra Giuseppe Ungaretti* (Brazil, 1966)

O'FERRALL, GEORGE MORE, *Murder in the Cathedral* (UK, 1947)

ORTA, PABLO, *El hijo del poeta* (Mexico, 2012)

OSPINA, LUIS, and CARLOS MAYOLO, *Agarrando pueblo* (Colombia, 1977)

OZU, YASUJIRÔ, *Sanma no aji* [*An Autumn Afternoon*] (Japan, 1962)

PASOLINI, PIER PAOLO, *Il Decameron* [*The Decameron*] (Italy, France, West Germany, 1971)

——, *I Racconti di Canterbury* [*The Canterbury Tales*] (Italy, France, 1972)

PEIXOTO, MARIO, *Limite* (Brazil, 1931)

PELECHIAN, ARTAVAZD, *Mer dare* [*Our Century*] (USSR, 1982)

PEÓN, RAMÓN, *Sor Juana Inés de la Cruz* (Mexico, 1935)

PEREDA, NICOLÁS, *Perpetuum mobile* (Canada, Mexico, 2009)

——, *Todo, en fin, el silencio lo ocupaba* (Canada, Mexico, 2010)

PERRONE, RAÚL, *Labios de churrasco* (Argentina, 1994)

PIALAT, MAURICE, *Van Gogh* (France, 1991)

PONTECORVO, GILLO, *Kapo* (Italy, France, Yugoslavia, 1960)

QUEIROLO, ENRIQUE, *El último centauro: la epopeya del gaucho Juan Moreira* (Argentina, 1923)

QUESADA, ALFREDO, *Martín Fierro* (Argentina, 1923)

RADFORD, MICHAEL, *Il Postino* [*The Postman*] (Belgium, France, Italy, 1994)

RAY, MAN, *Emak-Bakia* (France, 1926)

REJTMAN, MARTÍN, *Silvia Prieto* (Argentina, 1999)

RESNAIS, ALAIN, *Nuit et Brouillard* [*Night and Fog*] (France, 1956)

REYGADAS, CARLOS, *Japón* (Mexico, 2002)

ROCHA, GLAUBER, *Terra em transe* (Brazil, 1967)

——, *O Dragão da Maldade Contra o Santo Guerreiro* (Brazil, 1969)

ROHMER, ÉRIC, *Stéphane Mallarmé* (France, Canada, 1966)

ROMERO, LILIANA, and NORMAN RUIZ, *Martín Fierro: la película* (Argentina, 2007)

ROSSELLINI, ROBERTO, *Roma, città aperta* [*Rome, Open City*] (Italy, 1945)

SÁNCHEZ, RAFAEL, *Las callampas* (Chile, 1958)

SASLAVSKY, LUIS, *La fuga* (Argentina, 1937)

——, *Vidalita* (Argentina, 1949)

——, *El Fausto criollo* (Argentina, 1979)

SCHUB, ESTHER, *Padenie dinastii Romanovykh* [*The Fall of the Romanov Dynasty*] (USSR, 1926)

SGANZERLA, ROGÉRIO, *O bandido da luz vermelha* (Brazil, 1968)

SKÁRMETA, ANTONIO, *Ardiente paciencia* (West Germany, Portugal, 1983)

SLAVINSKY, YEVGENI, and VLADIMIR MAYAKOVSKY, *Baryshnya i khuligan* [*The Lady and the Hooligan*] (Russia, 1918)

SMITH, GEORGE ALBERT, *Photographing a Ghost* (UK, 1898)

SOLANAS, FERNANDO, *Los hijos de Fierro* (Argentina, 1978)

TARKOVSKY, ANDREI, *Ivanovo detstvo* [*Ivan's Childhood*] (USSR, 1962)

TAYMOR, JULIE, *Frida* (Canada, Mexico, USA, 2002)

——, *The Glorias* (USA 2020)

TORRE NILSSON, LEOPOLDO, *Martín Fierro* (Argentina, 1968)

TORRES RÍOS, LEOPOLDO, *Santos Vega vuelve* (Argentina, 1947)

TSCHERKASSKY, PETER, *Outer Space* (Austria, 1999)

——, *Instructions for a Light and Sound Machine* (Austria, 2004)

VALLEJO, GERARDO, *El camino hacia la muerte del viejo Reales* (Argentina, 1971)

——, *Martín Fierro: el ave solitaria* (Argentina, 2006)

VAN SANT, GUS, *Psycho* (USA, 1999)

VELO, CARLOS, *Pedro Páramo* (Mexico, 1966)

VERTOV, DZIGA, *Chelovek s kino-apparatom* [*Man With a Movie Camera*] (USSR, 1929)

VISCONTI, LUCHINO, *La Terra trema* [*The Earth Trembles*] (Italy, 1948)

WATSON, JAMES SIBLEY, *Lot in Sodom* (USA, 1933)

WEKSLER, LUIS, *Al Martín Fierro* (Argentina, 1962)

WILDER, BILLY, *Sunset Boulevard* (USA, 1950)

INDEX

❖